Financial Globalization, Economic Growth, and the Crisis of 2007–09

William R. Cline

PETERSON INSTITUTE FOR INTERNATIONAL ECONOMICS
WASHINGTON, DC
MAY 2010

William R. Cline has been a senior fellow at the Peterson Institute for International Economics since its inception in 1981 and has held a joint appointment at the Center for Global Development since 2002. During 1996–2001 while on leave from the Institute, he was deputy managing director and chief economist of the Institute of International Finance.

His publications include *Global Warming and Agriculture: Impact Estimates by Country* (2007), *The United States as a Debtor Nation* (2005), *Trade Policy and Global Poverty* (2004), *Trade and Income Distribution* (1997), *International Debt Reexamined* (1995), *International Economic Policy in the 1990s* (1994), *The Economics of Global Warming* (1992), *United States External Adjustment and the World Economy* (1989), and *International Debt: Systemic Risk and Policy Response* (1984).

Previously he was senior fellow, Brookings Institution (1973–81); deputy director of development and trade research, Office of the Assistant Secretary for International Affairs, US Treasury Department (1971–73); Ford Foundation visiting professor in Brazil (1970–71); and lecturer and assistant professor of economics at Princeton University (1967–70). He graduated summa cum laude from Princeton University in 1963 and received his MA (1964) and PhD (1969) in economics from Yale University.

PETER G. PETERSON INSTITUTE FOR INTERNATIONAL ECONOMICS

1750 Massachusetts Avenue, NW
Washington, DC 20036-1903
(202) 328-9000 FAX: (202) 659-3225
www.piie.com

C. Fred Bergsten, *Director*
Edward A. Tureen, *Director of Publications, Marketing, and Web Development*

Typesetting by Susann Luetjen
Printing by Versa Press, Inc.
Cover photos by © Aaron Kohr, Olivier, and Wrangler—Fotolia.com

Printed in the United States of America

12 11 10   5 4 3 2 1

Library of Congress Cataloging-in-Publication Data

Cline, William R.
 Financial globalization, economic growth, and the crisis of 2007-09 /
William R. Cline.
 p. cm.
 ISBN 978-0-88132-499-0
 1. International finance. 2. Economic development. 3. Financial crises.
I. Title.
 HG3881.C5816 2010
 332'.042—dc22

2010008608

The views expressed in this publication are those of the author. This publication is part of the overall program of the Institute, as endorsed by its Board of Directors, but does not necessarily reflect the views of individual members of the Board or the Advisory Committee.

Financial Globalization, Economic Growth, and the Crisis of 2007–09

William R. Cline

PETERSON INSTITUTE FOR INTERNATIONAL ECONOMICS
WASHINGTON, DC
MAY 2010

William R. Cline has been a senior fellow at the Peterson Institute for International Economics since its inception in 1981 and has held a joint appointment at the Center for Global Development since 2002. During 1996–2001 while on leave from the Institute, he was deputy managing director and chief economist of the Institute of International Finance.

His publications include *Global Warming and Agriculture: Impact Estimates by Country* (2007), *The United States as a Debtor Nation* (2005), *Trade Policy and Global Poverty* (2004), *Trade and Income Distribution* (1997), *International Debt Reexamined* (1995), *International Economic Policy in the 1990s* (1994), *The Economics of Global Warming* (1992), *United States External Adjustment and the World Economy* (1989), and *International Debt: Systemic Risk and Policy Response* (1984).

Previously he was senior fellow, Brookings Institution (1973–81); deputy director of development and trade research, Office of the Assistant Secretary for International Affairs, US Treasury Department (1971–73); Ford Foundation visiting professor in Brazil (1970–71); and lecturer and assistant professor of economics at Princeton University (1967–70). He graduated summa cum laude from Princeton University in 1963 and received his MA (1964) and PhD (1969) in economics from Yale University.

PETER G. PETERSON INSTITUTE FOR INTERNATIONAL ECONOMICS

1750 Massachusetts Avenue, NW
Washington, DC 20036-1903
(202) 328-9000 FAX: (202) 659-3225
www.piie.com

C. Fred Bergsten, *Director*
Edward A. Tureen, *Director of Publications, Marketing, and Web Development*

Typesetting by Susann Luetjen
Printing by Versa Press, Inc.
Cover photos by © Aaron Kohr, Olivier, and Wrangler—Fotolia.com

Library of Congress Cataloging-in-Publication Data

Cline, William R.
    Financial globalization, economic growth, and the crisis of 2007-09 /
William R. Cline.
    p. cm.
    ISBN 978-0-88132-499-0
    1. International finance. 2. Economic development. 3. Financial crises.
    I. Title.
    HG3881.C5816 2010
    332'.042—dc22

                                      2010008608

The views expressed in this publication are those of the author. This publication is part of the overall program of the Institute, as endorsed by its Board of Directors, but does not necessarily reflect the views of individual members of the Board or the Advisory Committee.

Contents

Tables

Figures

Preface

In early 2005, the Institute published a comprehensive study of the impact of the trade globalization of the previous six decades on the American economy.[1] That analysis, prepared by an Institute team led by Senior Fellow Gary Hufbauer and employing four separate methodologies, concluded that the US economy was about $1 trillion per year richer—about 10 per cent of GDP at that time—from the country's integration with the world economy via the trade channel. We undertook the project in response to a question posed by our Board member, and former Secretary of the Treasury and future Director of the National Economic Council, Larry Summers; hence we called it "the Summers question" project.

As is usual with major Institute studies, I and the authors briefed top US officials on the results just prior to its release. The most important response came from Alan Greenspan, an Honorary Director of the Institute who was Chairman of the Federal Reserve Board at that time. He indicated keen interest in our findings, and used them extensively thereafter, but suggested that it could be even more important to analyze the impact of financial globalization on the US economy and on the world as a whole. He (and we) doubted that we could come up with a single number to summarize those effects, and noted immediately that such a study would undoubtedly be more difficult and more complex than the one we had completed on trade globalization, but nevertheless urged us to take it on. Hence was born "the Greenspan question" project at the Institute.

---

1. See Scott C. Bradford, Paul L. Grieco, and Gary C. Hufbauer, "The Payoff to America from Global Integration," in *The United States and the World Economy*, ed. C. Fred Bergsten and Institute for International Economics, Washington, January 2005.

This study did in fact turn out to be more complicated, more time-consuming, and more contentious (including among the staff of the Institute itself) than its earlier counterpart. It required an exhaustive review of an extensive literature, new conceptualizations of both the substantive issues involved and the methodologies employed to analyze them, and a focus on the world economy rather than solely the United States (as Greenspan had foreseen). We knew that some of its findings would be hotly debated and therefore subjected it to far more extensive peer review, both within the Institute and especially by outside scholars, than is customary even via our normal rigorous process. We hope that its results will be adopted and used as widely as those of its earlier trade counterpart and that it will make a major contribution to both thinking and policy on the topic.

The study was also delayed, and rendered both more important and even more complicated, by the intervention of the global financial and economic crisis of 2007-09. The breakdown of financial systems around the world raised sharp new questions concerning the merits of financial liberalization in general and its international dimensions in particular. Our project had to incorporate these new developments and the additional analyses and policy initiatives that they spawned, if it was to reach conclusions and make policy recommendations that would be relevant in 2010 and beyond.

The project was conducted by Senior Fellow William R. Cline, whose analytical and practical background made him the ideal author. Dr. Cline is universally regarded as the seminal analyst of the third world debt crisis of the 1980s.[2] He has published the definitive study of *The United States as a Debtor Nation*.[3] He spent six years as the deputy managing director and chief economist of the Institute of International Finance, during the Asian financial crisis of 1997–98 and its aftermath in Russia and Brazil, where he directed and conducted intensive studies of the dramatic swings in capital flows to those hard-hit countries and their economic effects. He has published extensive analyses of trade and trade policy issues and is thus fully conversant with both the similarities and differences in the economics of international capital and trade flows. I congratulate Dr. Cline for the astounding breadth of his research, the pathbreaking methodologies that he has pioneered during the course of the work, and not least his perseverance in producing such a comprehensive analysis of such a difficult and far-reaching topic.

The Peter G. Peterson Institute for International Economics is a private, nonprofit institution for the study and discussion of international economic policy. Its purpose is to analyze important issues in that area

---

2. William R. Cline, *International Debt Reexamined*, Institute for International Economics, Washington, February 1995.

3. William R. Cline, *The United States as a Debtor Nation*, Institute for International Economics, Washington, September 2005.

and to develop and communicate practical new approaches for dealing with them. The Institute is completely nonpartisan.

The Institute is funded by a highly diversified group of philanthropic foundations, private corporations and interested individuals. About 35 percent of the Institute's resources in our latest fiscal year was provided by contributors outside the United States. The Ford Foundation and Goldman Sachs provided partial financial support for this project.

The Institute's Board of Directors bears overall responsibilities for the Institute and gives general guidance and approval to its research program, including the identification of topics that are likely to become important over the medium run (one to three years) and that should be addressed by the Institute. The director, working closely with the staff and outside Advisory Committee, is responsible for the development of particular projects and makes the final decision to publish an individual study.

The Institute hopes that its studies and other activities will contribute to building a stronger foundation for international economic policy around the world. We invite readers of these publications to let us know how they think we can best accomplish this objective.

C. Fred Bergsten
Director
March 2010

Acknowledgments

I thank Thomas Emmons for sustained and gifted research assistance, as well as Melese Tashu for literature summaries in the initial phase of this study. Special thanks go to outside reviewers Jerry Caprio, Jeffrey Frankel, Ross Levine, and Kenneth Rogoff. For suggestions from Institute colleagues I thank without implicating Joseph Gagnon, Morris Goldstein, Adam Posen, Arvind Subramanian, Ted Truman, and John Williamson. I also thank David B. Wilson for comments on my use of meta-analysis.

1

Overview

This study examines the role of financial globalization in economic growth and derives corresponding implications for economic policy. Although economists have debated the importance of openness to international trade, they generally agree that in the market for goods, international openness is more favorable to growth than a largely closed economy.[1] In contrast, whether external financial openness boosts or curbs growth has long been a controversial issue and has become even more so with the outbreak of the global financial crisis of 2007–09.

The East Asian financial crisis of the late 1990s had already raised new doubts on this issue and helped spur a wave of empirical research on it. Supporters of financial globalization—such as Fischer (1998) and Summers (2000)—maintained that, with the right policies, open capital markets continued to be a powerful means for enhancing growth. Critics, including Bhagwati (1998) and Stiglitz (2002), argued that the crisis demonstrated that, unlike free trade in goods, free mobility for capital is counterproductive for growth. In the past decade a large empirical literature has emerged examining this question. Overall it has tended toward "finding positive marginal effects on growth" (Kose et al. 2006, 20).

The US-led financial crisis of 2007–09 swept most of the developed and emerging-market economies into its vortex. The global crisis has set the stage for an intensification of the debate on financial openness. Some analysts and policymakers will be inclined to escalate calls for restrictions on capital flows. In the acute phase of the crisis that began in September 2008, major stock markets around the world plunged along with the US

---

1. For a summary of that debate, see Cline (2004, chapter 5).

equity market, and many currencies fell sharply against the dollar (excluding the yen, which proved, like the dollar, to be a safe-haven currency). If countries had maintained closed capital markets, some may argue, they would not have been vulnerable to these shocks.

This study surveys the extensive literature on this issue to arrive at a broad sense of the state of the evidence for and against the growth benefits of financial openness (chapter 2). The survey is critical in the sense that it seeks to evaluate strengths and weaknesses of the various studies in addition to summarizing their results. Chapter 3 then applies leading quantitative models from the literature to arrive at synthesis estimates of the contribution of financial openness to growth for major industrial and emerging-market economies over the past four decades. Chapter 4 considers the preliminary evidence on whether the 2007–09 financial crisis constitutes grounds for a major change in the policy verdict on financial openness. As part of that reconsideration, the analysis reviews the causes of the global crisis, as well as its principal events and policy interventions.

Research Context

Past work on international capital markets by the present author informs the approach taken in this study. *International Debt: Systemic Risk and Policy Response* (Cline 1984) examined the causes of the 1980s debt crisis centered in Latin America and assessed policies for and prospects of emergence from that crisis. *International Debt Reexamined* (Cline 1995) provided a retrospective analysis of the eventual resolution of the crisis, based on domestic policy reforms and the Brady Plan of debt reduction and collateralization, and examined the early signs of capital-market revival for emerging-market economies. *The United States as a Debtor Nation* (Cline 2005) examined the causes and prospects for resolution of the growing external imbalance of the United States and its resulting swing from being the world's largest creditor to its largest debtor country.

Standard neoclassical economics and prudent macroeconomic policies have been the framework underlying these studies. In the neoclassical formulation, capital flows contribute to growth through "capital deepening" (more capital equipment combined with the same amount of labor) and through technological change. Prudent macroeconomic policies and sound regulatory structures are necessary complements to open capital markets, because, otherwise, distortions are likely to arise that can ultimately provoke a costly crisis.

A proximate spur to the preparation of this study was the need for a summary estimate of gains from financial globalization parallel to the estimates for globalization in goods. In particular, Bradford, Grieco, and Hufbauer (2005) compiled for the Peterson Institute for International Economics (PIIE) a widely noted estimate that US GDP was about $1 trillion higher (about 10 percent) than it would have been without the reduction of trade barriers in the postwar period. Alan Greenspan, then chairman of the Federal Reserve, encouraged the Institute to explore a parallel estimate for financial globalization.

Estimating gains from trade is a difficult task. It involves measurement questions concerning, particularly, how to calibrate the protective effect of nontariff barriers and how to quantify protection in services where impediments such as local regulations are less transparent than tariff schedules for imported goods. Crucially, trade gains depend on quantification of dynamic effects that multiply the traditional static welfare effects, yet there is no generally agreed-upon unique method for capturing dynamic gains.

Arguably, quantifying gains from openness in finance is even more difficult than doing so for trade. For measurement, there is no clear counterpart to the most tangible metric for trade openness (tariffs and, more problematically, nontariff barriers). As discussed below, several alternative measures of financial openness have been applied, divided into de jure and de facto categories, but none is considered uniquely superior. The concept of financial openness is also more ambiguous than trade openness. There are at least four major categories of financial openness: foreign direct investment (FDI), portfolio equity flows, long-term bank flows, and short-term borrowing. The dominant methods also differ between trade and financial openness, with application of calibrated models (including traditional price elasticity partial equilibrium and general equilibrium) characteristic of the trade estimates but cross-country growth regression estimates predominant for financial openness.

Because the central policy issues for financial openness have tended to concern emerging-market economies, especially after the East Asian and other financial crises of the late 1990s, it also seemed essential that estimates of gains from financial openness encompass a substantial number of the major economies, rather than being limited to the United States. At the same time, there is historical interest in attempting to gauge the extent to which the postwar process of financial liberalization in the industrial economies has contributed to their growth.

Because examining gains from financial globalization led to a review of cross-country econometric estimates rather than application of a postulated model with calibrated parameters, there was the further complication of applying the right screen for sorting out the various existing statistical findings. As will be seen, this study has invoked a particular approach more commonly applied in such fields as medicine, education, and psychology than in economics—the synthesis of statistical estimates using "meta-analysis"—to confront this challenge.

Key Analytical Issues

Several dominant issues warrant highlighting at the outset. They include questions of measurement, interpretation of alternative statistical results, differentiation among alternative capital types, statistical versus calibrated theoretical models, and the treatment of crisis effects and policy sequencing.

Measuring Financial Openness

An operational challenge in this literature is that there is no single reliable metric for the degree of financial openness. Empirical studies have developed two types of measures: de jure and de facto. De jure measures are based on classifying legal and administrative practices as either restrictive or nonrestrictive. The International Monetary Fund (IMF) has long maintained an annual survey on capital restrictions, and its binary (before 1996) measure is used in many studies.[2] Quinn (1997) and Quinn and Toyoda (2008) have developed a more nuanced index of financial openness based on the IMF materials and additional country information. Their measure appears to be the best of the de jure type and has been used by a number of other authors.

Recourse to de facto measures has reflected frustration by researchers over the fact that many countries recorded as restrictive on de jure measures seem nonetheless to engage in a large amount of cross-border financial transactions. Typical measures in this category include, relative to GDP: stocks or flows of total capital; direct investment; portfolio equity; or debt capital. Generally it will be better to use gross measures that capture both assets and liabilities. Net measures, such as net inflows, can give misleading representations of openness. For example, with a chronically large current account surplus, Singapore would be judged highly restrictive ("negatively open") if a net capital inflow metric were used to capture financial openness. Yet it is widely recognized that Singapore is highly open financially.

An inherent problem in de facto measures is that they may show wide differences even among economies considered to be identically open in terms of the absence of restrictions. For example, in 1995–2004 gross capital inflows plus outflows averaged 204 percent of GDP for Ireland, 57 percent for the United Kingdom, and 13 percent for the United States.[2] Yet no one could reasonably argue that from the standpoint of policy, Ireland was 16 times as open as the United States, or that the United Kingdom was more than four times as open as the United States. This problem is similar to the greater "openness" of small economies to trade, judged by

---

2. See chapter 3 for a description of the database used in this study.

the ratio of exports and imports to GDP, even when their policy openness (level of tariffs and nontariff barriers) may be identical to that of a much larger economy with more diversification and less reliance on trade. Operationally, the principal risk in the de facto studies is that "outlier" cases will have a disproportionate effect on the slope of the curve estimated for the relationship between growth and openness. Moreover, quantity indicators based on net capital flows suffer from the fact that exogenous forces other than the degree of financial openness can cause the country's domestic saving to be high or low relative to its domestic investment. As a result, one country may rely on capital inflows, whereas another with an identical degree of financial market openness may instead provide capital outflows.

In principle there is a de facto "price" indicator that could be used to complement de facto quantity measures: the difference between domestic and foreign interest rates. Early studies using domestic versus offshore interest rates on assets denominated in the same currency found that this differential tended to disappear among major industrial countries after their financial markets were liberalized (e.g., for France by the late 1980s and Japan by the early 1990s; see Mussa and Goldstein 1993). Frankel (1992) noted four measures of capital mobility related to interest rates that had been used in the literature: the Feldstein-Horioka condition that exogenous changes in saving rates should have no effect on investment rates; real interest parity, in which domestic interest rates were equal to foreign rates after adjusting for inflation; uncovered interest parity (UIP), in which the difference between the domestic and foreign currency interest rate would equal the expected rate of depreciation; and covered interest parity (CIP), in which interest rates would equate across countries when contracted in a common currency. He emphasized that only CIP was an "unalloyed criterion for 'capital mobility' in the sense of the degree of financial market integration across national boundaries" (Frankel 1992, 197). The others required zero exchange risk premium (nominal or real) and, for Feldstein-Horioka, zero correlation of all noninterest determinants of investment with the national saving rate. His tests for 25 industrial countries indeed showed that integration of financial markets had practically eliminated short-term interest differentials and brought CIP, but that exchange rate risk premiums remained (Frankel 1992).[3]

A review of the literature finds that no cross-country econometric

---

3. Using 1985–90 data, Montiel (1994) used the ratio of the monthly mean absolute deviation from UIP to the mean of the foreign interest rate adjusted by (ex post) exchange rate movement as a gauge of financial integration. He was unable to use CIP because "forward markets exist for very few developing-country currencies" (p. 315). However, his findings do not track the Quinn and Toyoda (2008) measures preferred in the present study. Thus, Montiel found greater openness in Chile (ratio of 0.50) and Brazil (0.87), than in Korea (1.0) and Singapore (1.83). For the same period, Quinn and Toyoda's openness index shows just the reverse: Singapore most open at 100; Korea, 50; and Brazil and Chile, 37.5.

growth study has applied either UIP or CIP as the proxy for financial market openness. A likely reason is that for the 50 or so countries typically included in such studies, and for the typical periods (e.g., 1980s through the early 2000s), data series on forward exchange premia have not been available for many of these countries. If tests were to be done, they would have to settle for the weaker variant based on UIP. In turn, perhaps because of the broad perception in the empirical literature that UIP does not hold even for countries known to be financially open, researchers may have been discouraged from applying this alternative as a measure of capital mobility.[4] As shown in appendix 1A, data available for 2004 for about two dozen industrial and emerging-market economies show a relatively close negative relationship between Quinn-Toyoda openness and the size of the absolute deviation from CIP, suggesting that the measure might begin to be used in the cross-country tests at some point in the future.

Robustness and the Weighting of Alternative Model Estimates

The single greatest challenge confronting this study is the divergence in results across (and within) alternative empirical studies and the identification of a methodology for weighting them to arrive at central estimates. In broad terms, one set of authors tends to find statistically significant positive effects of financial openness on growth. Another set tends to find a lack of significant effects. Some studies within this second set conduct an initial set of tests that do find significant positive impacts but then conduct alternative tests that they consider to reveal the initial results are not robust.

In some important cases the analysis in chapter 2 judges that the model-reversals in robustness tests are themselves not convincingly robust. One example is the use of dubious instrumental variables, such as historical political legacies (e.g., British law versus Napoleonic code) that generate results turning the openness variable insignificant. Another is the use of a political-risk metric as an explanatory variable, despite the fact that the political-risk evaluators may be inferring that the political environment must be better because growth performance is better, thereby spuriously removing significance of openness as an explanatory variable.

One approach considered in chapter 2 is thus to focus on statistically significant results, both those in studies treating them as their principal finding, as well as the significant results in other studies whose alternative tests yielding robustness-reversals are not convincing. The preferred method developed in chapter 2, however, is to invoke the "meta-statistical" approach frequently used in medical research and in such social sciences as education and psychology. In this approach, comparison across

---

4. Note, however, that more recent studies have found that for maturities over one year, UIP tends to hold (Chinn and Meredith 2005; Alper, Ardic, and Fendoglu 2007).

studies first converts variables to normalized units and then weights the result of each study by the inverse of the variance of the parameter estimate (the "size effect" in many of the experimental studies). This approach has the virtue that it does not automatically throw out information from studies with parameters that just barely fail the usual statistical significance threshold.[5] Meta-statistical weighting turns out to be important to take account of various model results *within* individual major studies, as well as weighting across studies.[6]

Endogeneity

Many of the statistically significant tests find growth impacts that are not only positive but large. Some authors interpret uncomfortably large estimates as indications that endogeneity problems have not been fully resolved (Henry 2007).[7] Obstfeld (2009) makes the extreme argument that the endogeneity problem constitutes grounds for skepticism about all empirical results showing a growth contribution from financial globalization.

Perhaps the first thing that should be said about the endogeneity critique is that as a methodological principle, the fact that an estimated parameter has the right sign but is larger than might be expected from theory should not constitute grounds for rejecting out of hand the finding that there is a substantial effect and concluding by default that there is none. Otherwise research would take place in an empirical laboratory in which the researcher is always damned if one does (too large an estimate), damned if one doesn't (a small or negative estimate), and blessed only if the outcome is Goldilocks-sized. Instead, surely the principle for interpreting results should be that a too-large estimate serves to support rather than reject the hypothesized effect until demonstrated to be spurious.

Moreover, there are several weaknesses in the proposition that as a general matter the empirical estimates are likely to overstate growth impacts because of endogeneity. Consider first direct endogeneity, in which growth causes financial opening rather than vice versa. At the empirical level, this case is irrelevant if the time period of the growth variable is subsequent to rather than simultaneous with that of the openness variable

---

5. McCloskey and Ziliak (1996) take the economics profession to task for unduly emphasizing significance and ignoring importance based on parameter size.

6. An extreme example is that of Carkovic and Levine (2005), who provide results from 60 different tests on FDI.

7. The endogeneity problem arises when the supposed cause is instead the effect, essentially with the roles of the exogenous and the endogenous variables mistakenly switched; or when there is a third influence that is causing the behavior of both the dependent variable and the supposedly independent variable. The problem broadly reflects the principle that correlation does not necessarily demonstrate causation.

(as is often the case). It is also irrelevant when the openness variable is de jure, if what is observed is a rise in capital flows after growth: Even if good growth performance spurs capital inflows, there will not have been a change in the de jure measure (although de facto measures would show an increase). Many of the studies, moreover, apply GMM (generalized method of moments) techniques to address endogeneity.[8] At the conceptual level, direct endogeneity requires a certain logical inconsistency in policymakers. It assumes that they know that opening is bad for growth, or has minimal effect on growth, but nonetheless embrace opening following a few good growth years, as some sort of luxury good rather than for its own potential contribution to growth. That is implausible.

Indirect endogeneity running from a third variable to both the growth and openness variables is perhaps more problematic. Once again, it is easier to envision indirect endogeneity as a problem when openness is measured de facto rather than de jure. For example, in a period of high global growth and buoyant international capital markets such as that of 2004–06, an export boom could boost growth at the same time that capital flows rise sharply, raising the possibility of spurious attribution of growth to rising de facto openness. Most of the studies do not include a variable for international growth or the state of international capital markets. A potentially important case of indirect endogeneity would be that in which the missing third variable was consistently good economic policies that induced both high growth and high capital flows. Again, however, in this case the endogeneity would show up in the de facto openness measures but not in the de jure ones.

There is a major consideration that works in the direction opposite to overstatement from endogeneity: understatement of growth effects by preemptive attribution to supposedly exogenous investment rates in the control equation. Typically the empirical models test for financial openness effects only in the context of an equation that includes control variables, and the investment rate not only is usually included as a control variable but is also important in size. But if investment is larger than it would be without the benefit of financial openness, which is almost certainly usually the case, denying the financial openness variable some credit for the growth captured by the investment variable will understate the contribution of financial globalization.[9]

In terms of the studies surveyed in chapter 2, perhaps the cleanest test for the size of possible endogeneity bias can be obtained using results reported by Edison et al. (2002). For the study's two most successful financial openness variables, OLS (ordinary least squares) results give a

---

8. For example, Edison et al. (2002) apply lagged differences in explanatory variables as instruments in dynamic panel GMM estimates.

9. Bosworth and Collins (1999) and Mody and Murshid (2005) are among the studies finding a strong influence of foreign capital inflows on domestic investment.

growth-impact coefficient of 0.101 for gross capital flows relative to GDP and 0.183 for capital inflows relative to GDP (p. 33). In contrast, for the same two variables the study's dynamic panel GMM estimates designed to address simultaneity yield coefficients of 0.077 and 0.132, respectively. The comparison suggests that correction for endogeneity reduces the size of the growth-impact parameter by about one-fourth. This amount of shrinkage is more moderate than the two-thirds reduction going from the high-variant to the low-variant estimates in this study. By implication, correction for endogeneity should leave the main estimates well within the range identified here.

On balance, the endogeneity question would seem to constitute a reasonable basis for leaning more toward the lower end of the range of growth impacts identified below, and less toward the upper end. However, it is not a convincing basis for dismissing out of hand the large body of empirical literature on this issue.

Differences by Capital Type

The two largest sets of empirical literature on financial globalization are on the growth effects of overall financial openness, and on growth effects of one particular type of capital: foreign direct investment. A somewhat smaller but still substantial literature provides estimates of growth effects of opening the capital market to portfolio equity flows. In contrast, there is almost no literature focusing primarily on the growth effects of debt capital. This gap is surprising, considering that it is this type of capital that is the *bête noir* of opponents of open capital markets.

One challenge that arises in the literature is a seeming contradiction between the whole and the sum of the parts. Estimates of growth effects of overall capital openness, or at least the significant test results among them, tend to arrive at a given benchmark of annual gains from complete openness (on the order of 1½ to 2 percent). The corresponding estimates for FDI, combined with the typical ranges of FDI flows (or stocks), also tend to generate estimates implying growth contributions of around the same level or higher for high FDI flows that might be interpreted as reflecting complete openness to this type of capital flow. Yet again, the growth impact estimates for opening the market to portfolio equity flows also are in the same range (albeit with effects limited to a number of years rather than permanent increments to growth, in some authors' approaches). Some appear tempted to resolve the seeming adding-up problem by inferring that the other type of capital—debt—must have a large negative impact on growth. However, this diagnosis is a sort of residual econometric inference by default that does not warrant the same credibility as the sets of direct tests.

The proper way to resolve the sum of parts issue is to examine growth effects of debt capital more closely. This chapter presents a few new tests that do so. They do not support the inferential proposition that debt capital must be contributing negatively to growth. That still leaves the summing-up issue.

A tentative resolution of the issue is as follows. First, the best set of tests for openness is that on overall openness. Second, the FDI studies as a class may overstate gains, because they apply only the de facto measure of FDI relative to GDP, and as noted above, de facto measures can give disproportionate impressions of differences in policy openness that instead mainly reflect differences in size of the economy or other structural questions. The high estimates for FDI should mainly be interpreted as supporting the positive overall openness results rather than demonstrating negative contributions from non-FDI capital to achieve consistent results with the total openness measures. As for the portfolio equity tests, these tend to be before-versus-after tests, and the authors recognize that effects may be overstated by policy-regime changes associated with these openings. They too should be read primarily as supportive of the positive overall tests.

Statistical versus Calibrated Theoretical Models

The statistical literature typically conducts cross-country tests by specifying a set of standard control variables (e.g., initial per capita income, investment rate, and human capital) and then adding a variable for financial openness to estimate a parameter for its contribution to growth. In contrast, there is a smaller literature that specifies theoretical growth models incorporating financial globalization and that estimates plausible growth contributions from financial openness by applying calibrated parameters. The gains from consumption smoothing, risk diversification, and factor reallocation have tended to be the subject of such models. The risk diversification results tend to be either large or small, depending on whether the author is applying an equity-portfolio perspective or a consumption-risk perspective (respectively). Models of factor reallocation tend to generate what seem to be small results, but on closer inspection, they do so by focusing on a steady-state that occurs in a distant future that is substantially discounted. So far, it seems fair to say, the calibrated theoretical models have contributed considerably to conceptual understanding of financial openness but relatively less to quantification of actual experience (in part because of large swings between results, sometimes pertaining to the same author a year or two later).

Crisis Effects, Sequencing, and Thresholds

In view of the crisis focus of the opponents of openness, it is somewhat surprising that there has been relatively little econometric testing of the proposition that vulnerability to crises makes financial openness, on balance, counterproductive. Some of the more sophisticated modeling efforts tend to find that greater openness does increase variability but that it increases growth rates by more than enough to compensate. Other work in this area is more in the historical school of economics and seeks to identify patterns from past crises rather than specify any theoretical framework or conduct any econometric tests. This chapter draws on some of this work to consider the extent to which crisis risks may offset growth gains identified in the cross-country openness tests.

A related question is whether there is an appropriate sequence for opening. Typically the stylized fact is that FDI should be opened first, then portfolio equity, and only later, when macrostability is assured (and sound regulatory structures are in place), should debt capital be opened. There is relatively little literature demonstrating this or alternative sequencing, however.

Similarly, some of the literature applies interactive terms to seek thresholds, with countries below the threshold likely to suffer from opening but those above it likely to gain. Perhaps the most convincing study along these lines is by Arteta, Eichengreen, and Wyplosz (2003), who use the Quinn openness variable and find that once a threshold of macroeconomic stability is achieved (proxied by the black-market premium on the exchange rate), increased openness contributes to growth. Most emerging-market economies already meet the degree of macrostability needed for their threshold.

Theoretical Expectations

There is a tendency in the large econometric literature on this issue to specify an estimating equation without setting forth an ex ante model indicating the magnitude of the growth effects that should be anticipated from opening. It is therefore useful to consider the theoretical bases for expecting financial globalization to influence growth and benchmark ranges for the effects that might be expected from them. First, capital inflows into a capital-scarce country should boost the capital stock, rate of investment, and economic growth. Appendix 1B shows that there is a direct analogy between the traditional static welfare gains from international trade and those from reallocation of capital toward economies where it is scarce. Second, financial openness should increase the rate of total factor productivity (TFP) growth in the economy. Direct investment should be expected to improve efficiency through the transfer of technology. Similarly, open capital markets can promote economywide efficiency through the development of domestic financial markets. Third, borrowing from abroad can help to smooth shocks to consumption caused by business cycles. Fourth, investing abroad can achieve portfolio diversification and thus lower risk for a given rate of return. Set against these potential beneficial effects, however, open capital markets may increase vulnerability to financial crises and thus result in negative growth effects.

For capital deepening, neoclassical production theory can be combined with stylized facts about capital-output ratios and capital-income shares to identify plausible ranges for growth effects. This theory states that the share of capital in income is equal to the elasticity of output with respect to capital (percent change in GDP for 1 percent rise in the capital stock). With a capital share of 40 percent, a ratio of economywide capital stock to GDP of 2, and net capital inflows of, say, 5 percent of GDP, a financially open developing economy would be expected to achieve a boost in its growth rate of about 1 percent per year from financial openness.[10]

The second component of growth enhancement from financial globalization comes from the stimulus to TFP growth. Using data for 84 countries for 1960–2000, Bosworth and Collins (2003) estimated that TFP contributed 1 percent per year to growth in each of three major groupings: industrial countries, East Asia less China, and South Asia. The fraction of this total amount that might be attributable to financial globalization and, more specifically, the size of the change in TFP growth that could be expected from moving from complete financial closure to openness, are highly uncertain. Estimates in one recent study suggest a range of about one-half of 1 percent per year.[11] A more plausible estimate would perhaps be one-third of a percent, as it seems likely that at least two-thirds of TFP gains would come from domestic and nonfinancial sources as opposed to financial openness.

Combining the two effects, a developing country might be expected to obtain a boost to its growth rate of about 1.3 percent per year from complete capital-market openness. As indicated in the following section, the statistically significant results in the literature tend to confirm this range for growth impacts.

For industrial countries, it is less straightforward to appeal to neoclassical capital deepening because in principle these economies tend to

---

10. In the Cobb-Douglas production function, $Q = \lambda K^\alpha L^{1-\alpha}$, where Q is output, K is capital stock, L is labor, α is the share of capital in income, and λ is an efficiency parameter reflecting TFP. Differentiating, the marginal product of capital is $\alpha(Q/K)$. The increase in output from foreign capital inflow equals this marginal product times the amount of the inflow. If capital inflows F are the share $\phi = F/Q$ of GDP, and defining the capital-output ratio as $B = K/Q$, the increase in output will be: $[\alpha/B] \times \phi Q$. Dividing by output gives the contribution to the growth rate, $\Delta g = [\alpha\phi]/B$. With stylized parameters $\alpha = 0.4$, $B = 2$, and $\phi = 0.05$, $\Delta g = 0.01$.

11. Kose, Prasad, and Terrones (2008) find that, using de jure measures of openness, the absence of capital restrictions boosts TFP growth by about 0.12 percent per year. Alternatively using a de facto measure, they find that an increase in FDI stock of 10 percent of GDP boosts growth by 0.4 percentage point, but a comparable increase in external debt reduces growth by 0.2 percentage point. As discussed in chapter 3, interpreting a move from the 10th to the 90th percentile of the distribution of the stock of both FDI and debt as the difference between complete closure and complete openness, the result is a boost in the annual growth rate of 1 percent per year. Averaging the two approaches, TFP gains from complete financial openness would be approximately 0.5 percent per year in additional growth (0.12 percent for de jure, 1 percent for de facto).

be suppliers rather than recipients of capital flows. Influences such as the favorable medium-term growth effect of discipline on domestic inflation rates from financial openness (Tytell and Wei 2004) can reasonably be seen as relevant for postwar growth in several industrial economies. Capital inflows to high-growth industrial countries such as the United States, Australia, Spain, and others in recent decades likely facilitated growth (and spurred adoption of new technologies associated with the information revolution) despite the textbook expectation of capital flows in the opposite direction.[12] During 1983 through 2007, the Group of Seven (G-7) industrial economies achieved average growth of about 3 percent (IMF 2009b). As an informal thought experiment, it is not difficult to imagine that growth might have been cut by as much as one-third, or 1 percentage point annually, if these economies had all prohibited cross-border capital flows. Nonetheless, a priori expectations for potential growth effects of openness should generally be smaller for industrial economies than for developing economies.

Empirical Literature

As noted, much of the empirical literature on financial globalization involves the use of cross-country statistical tests that examine whether financial openness boosts growth. This approach typically mounts a standard cross-country growth regression containing generally accepted control variables and then augments the equation with a financial openness variable. The control variables often include initial per capita income, with an expected negative coefficient to capture "convergence," the rate of investment, a measure of macroeconomic stability (such as inflation or the black-market premium on the exchange rate), and/or a measure of trade openness.

General Financial Openness

Table 2.1 in chapter 2 reports the impact of general financial openness as opposed to complete closure on the annual growth rate for nine leading studies in this literature. The measures of openness are de jure for some of the studies and de facto for others. The de jure measures include that of Quinn (1997) as well as a less-nuanced 1 or 0 variable for the presence of capital restrictions as reported by the IMF and other variants of the IMF

---

12. Cline (2005, 29) finds that among 13 industrial countries during 1976–2002, an additional annual reduction of 1.5 percent per year in the ratio of the net international investment position (NIIP) to GDP was associated with 1 percent additional annual growth. Countries with falling NIIPs (and hence net capital inflows) included Australia, New Zealand, Portugal, Spain, Greece, the United States, and the United Kingdom (Cline 2005, 20–21).

measure used in its *Annual Report on Exchange Arrangements and Exchange Restrictions* (AREAER). The table reports the impact of complete openness versus complete closure implied by the parameter estimate in each study. For the de facto measures, the difference between complete closure and complete openness is approximated by applying the difference between the top and bottom deciles in the observed data on the measure in question (for example, total capital flows relative to GDP) or another variation (as indicated in the table).

As noted above, a central question is how to weight alternative estimates, and especially how to treat statistically significant versus insignificant estimates. The summary in chapter 2 considers five concepts: significant results only; intrastudy meta-statistical (inverse-variance) weighting; weighting by *t*-statistic; averaging statistically significant results with insignificant results imputed at zero; and interstudy inverse-variance weighting. The resulting averages across the studies are as follows: 1.99 percent annual growth contribution from complete openness versus complete closedness for the significant-only results; 1.57 percent for the average taking the intrastudy meta-statistical results; 1.84 percent weighting by *t*-statistic; and 1.23 percent imputing nonsignificant results at zero. The fifth concept, the meta-statistical average across the studies, turns out to be 0.56 percent per year growth contribution. In broad terms, then, it can be said that the main empirical studies as a group imply *growth gains on the order of one-half a percent to 1½ percent annually* from complete openness as opposed to complete closure.

A striking feature of the table is that none of the impact entries is negative. If the true picture of the impact of financial globalization were that there is no discernable impact one way or the other, one would expect half the significant results to be positive and half negative. However, three alternative leading models each have potentially both positive and negative effects. They contain interactive variables that create a threshold, below which openness has a negative effect but above which the effect turns positive. These interactive variables include banking depth (Bailliu 2000); income level (Edwards 2001); and macrostability (Arteta, Eichengreen, and Wyplosz 2003). Evaluation of the three models at the 25th percentile of the interactive variable yields positive growth impacts of financial openness in two of the three models (with Edwards 2001 the only exception).

As argued in chapter 2, the 12 studies together generate an overwhelming probabilistic case that the central effect of openness is positive rather than negative. Only one-half of one study turns out to show a negative effect (at a reasonable 25 percent cutoff for the interactive variable). As shown in chapter 3, the chances of this occurring on a purely random basis are 0.3 percent or less.

A second pattern in table 2.1 (and table 2.2 for the interactive models) is the considerable similarity in the range of growth impacts among the estimates. The median estimate is a boost of 1.65 percent in the annual growth rate as a consequence of a move from closed to open capital markets. Across 37 estimates for the different models and concepts, the 25th percentile estimate is 0.7 percent, and the 75th percentile is 2.4 percent. An impact in this range would be enormous if continued indefinitely. Yet these estimates are mostly for multiple decades, not short-term periods, and should thus be interpreted as reflecting persistent effects. Nonetheless, as developed below, considerable attention should be paid to the cross-study meta-statistical estimate, which is substantially lower at about one-half a percent annual growth impact.

Foreign Direct Investment

Numerous statistical studies have examined the growth impact of FDI. A popular view is that this form of capital inflow tends to be the most beneficial to growth. For example, Reisen and Soto (2001) note that foreign capital adds to domestic investment, stimulates efficiency, and smoothes consumption on the favorable side but can magnify existing domestic distortions and cause bankruptcies and output losses because of abrupt reversibility on the unfavorable side. They judge that FDI can make a strong contribution on all three of the favorable influences, is not subject to abrupt reversibility, and is only weakly subject to magnifying distortions now that protection levels are generally much lower than in the early postwar period.

Hermes and Lensink (2003) argue that the growth effects of direct investment spillovers work through the channels of demonstration of improved technologies and management methods, competition that forces domestic firms to upgrade, development of linkages to domestic suppliers, and training. Noting that previous literature had emphasized such domestic preconditions for FDI benefits as human capital, the presence of well-functioning markets, and property rights, they emphasize the corresponding role of the domestic financial sector. Because domestic firms will need to invest to take advantage of new technologies and other spillovers from FDI, a more developed domestic financial system should facilitate this process by mobilizing more savings, monitoring investment, and even funding some investments of the foreign firms themselves.

Table 2.3 in chapter 2 reports the implied growth impacts of FDI in nine leading studies. Several of them apply interactive variables that create a threshold effect, such as the need for a certain minimum level of human capital or domestic financial development. A number of studies apply only to developing economies, and Blonigan and Wang (2005) conducted tests indicating that inappropriate pooling of developing and developed economies can cause statistical tests to fail to capture the positive growth impact for developing countries. The table calibrates the results for the impact of an additional 1 percent of GDP in FDI inflows. An increase of this magnitude is approximately equal to the difference between the 1970–97 average inflows to low-income countries (0.82 percent of GDP) and flows to upper-middle-income countries (1.72 percent; see Lensink and Morrissey 2006). The median estimate is an annual growth increase of 0.5 percent for a sustained increase in FDI by 1 percent of GDP.

Portfolio Equity

A few authors examining the impact of liberalization of portfolio equity markets to capital inflows have found that opening contributes about 1 percent per year additional GDP growth (Bekaert, Harvey, and Lundblad 2000; Henry 2007). One reason they emphasize is that access to foreign equity capital should reduce the cost of capital toward international levels and boost investment. Henry (2003) finds that in the five years after opening compared with the five years before, the growth rate of output per worker increases by 2.3 percentage points. Henry in particular emphasizes that theory would predict the impact on higher growth should be temporary, however, as the capital stock adjusts to a new steady state. In contrast, appendix 3B in chapter 3 uses the same theoretical framework as Henry (2007) and demonstrates that, using parameters similar to his, growth effects on the order of 1 percent should be expected to persist for two decades or so.

Again, nonetheless, a growth impact for some considerable time on the order of 1 percent per year from the opening of portfolio equity alone poses the adding-up problem raised above. Once again, particularly in light of the much smaller size of the portfolio equity empirical literature, this set of results is best seen as lending support to the broader literature results finding positive growth impacts for general openness, rather than constituting evidence that only portfolio equity matters.

Financial Crises

The principal evidence warranting concern about vulnerability to financial crises as a consequence of financial openness pertains to one specific type of capital inflow: short-term debt. In its report on the emerging-market financial crises of the late 1990s, the Institute of International Finance (IIF 1999) emphasized the role that had been played by the buildup of short-term debt to dangerously high levels relative to reserves. It noted that discrimination against long-term capital and in favor of short-term debt—such as the restrictions on bonds in Korea, a special facility for short-term borrowing in Thailand, and the pursuit of fixed exchange rates that induced a large "carry trade"—contributed to this vulnerability. Rodrik and Velasco (1999) provided cross-country tests demonstrating that the probability of a financial crisis, defined as a reversal of capital flows of 5 percent of GDP or more, increased sharply once short-term debt exceeded reserves.

The main policy question is whether disincentives should be applied against short-term external borrowing, such as those used by Chile until recent years. Although it is generally agreed that these disincentives tilted the composition of foreign capital away from short-term and toward long-term debt, they did impose some costs. Edwards (1999) argued that the Chilean policy disproportionately increased the cost of capital to small firms, an outcome documented with firm-level data by Forbes (2003).

Statistical tests on the crisis effects of greater general financial openness have tended either to reject a causal role or to find that any negative growth effects of higher crisis incidence are swamped by positive effects on longer-term growth. Tornell, Westermann, and Martinez (2004) found in statistical tests that after liberalization, the ratio of credit to GDP rises by six percentage points in the subsequent six years and that this credit deepening substantially boosts growth. They tested for negative crisis effects by first showing that financial openness caused greater volatility (measured by "negative skewness") in credit growth and then by including volatility as a variable in their growth equations. Their results were that the extra credit volatility from financial openness reduced economic growth only slightly, whereas the boost to the average growth rate from faster credit growth attributable to openness was much greater.

Edwards (2006) uses data for 163 countries for 1970–2000 to test for crisis effects, defined as a sharp currency depreciation or a severe loss in reserves. He documents that crises do reduce growth. However, when he includes an interaction term between crisis and capital mobility, he concludes that countries that restrict capital mobility have not experienced milder crises than countries that allow freer mobility of capital. Glick, Guo, and Hutchison (2006) have reached similar statistical results. Similarly, the survey by Kose et al. (2006, 21) concludes that "there is little formal empirical evidence to support the oft-cited claims that financial globalization in and of itself is responsible for the spate of financial crises that the world has seen over the last three decades."

Important recent research has focused on identifying historical patterns of crisis events rather than seeking to estimate crisis effects econometrically. Reinhart and Rogoff (2008) find that, historically, industrial countries have been just as likely to experience banking crises as developing countries. They estimate that 40 percent of countries experienced banking crises in the 1930s, but almost none did from the 1940s through the early 1970s. Banking crisis incidence revived to 25 percent in the mid-1980s through the 1990s, declined to zero again at the beginning of the 2000s, but surged to 25 percent again in 2008 in the financial crisis. They suggest that domestic financial repression and capital controls contributed to the interim three-decade absence of crises but state they do "not necessarily" advocate such restrictions.

As shown in chapter 2, the expected output losses from banking crises implied by Reinhart and Rogoff (2008) are modest. They find an average of 1.5 banking crises per country since 1945 and an average cumulative output loss of 3 percent for each crisis. It turns out that over a 63-year period the implied expected cumulative loss from banking crises of 4.5 percent of GDP is equivalent to a cut in the average annual growth rate of only 0.07 percent per year. Indeed, the authors emphasize that it is the fiscal costs rather than the output losses from banking crises that are more severe.

Hutchison and Noy (2005) estimate output losses from banking crises at about twice as high, but the implied expected loss over the long term would still be low. The authors consider both currency crises and banking crises. Chapter 2 shows that when the Hutchison-Noy database on both types of crises is combined with the Quinn-Toyoda (2008) index of financial openness, there is no evidence to support the proposition that openness leads to a greater incidence of crisis. On the contrary, figure 2.1 in chapter 2 shows that for 22 emerging-market economies from 1975 to 1997, those with high financial openness tended to have a somewhat lower frequency of both currency crises and banking crises than those with low financial openness.

In contrast, Reinhart and Reinhart (2008) develop a database on "capital flow bonanzas" from 1980 to 2008 and argue that such bonanzas increase crises. Unfortunately, by their metric even an almost-completely closed economy could have a capital flow bonanza, because the concept is graded on a self-referential curve. By definition, any country has a bonanza in any year that lies in the top quintile of *its* capital flow experiences. For example, the threshold for a bonanza is only 1.8 percent of GDP in more-closed India but 6.6 percent in more-open Malaysia. Subject to this large caveat, their findings indicate that the presence of a capital flow bonanza boosts the probability of a currency crash from about 23 percent to about 32 percent and the probability of a banking crisis from 14 to 21 percent. But their definition means that by construction they cannot examine whether financially open economies have more capital flow bonanzas than more closed economies.

The discussion below returns to the quantification of crisis effects as a caveat to the central findings on general financial openness.

Synthesis Estimates

A central objective of this study is to quantify the extent to which financial openness has in fact contributed to economic growth. This question depends not only on its potential contribution as revealed by parameters in growth-impact equations but also on the extent of openness actually adopted. Chapter 3 applies the parameter estimates examined in the literature survey of chapter 2, in combination with measures of the historical trends in actual financial openness, to calculate synthesis estimates of the contribution of openness to growth in practice.

Trends in Financial Openness

Figure 3.1 in chapter 3 shows the average of Quinn-Toyoda de jure open-ness for four groupings of economies, comprising 20 industrial and 24 developing economies. The index ranges from zero for complete closure to 100 for complete openness. Relatively more-open developed countries averaged near 80 on this index in the early 1970s and were at nearly 100 by the late 1990s. The relatively less-open developed countries began at an index of less than 50, but had reached nearly 90 by the late 1990s.[13] The relatively more-open developing countries began somewhat more-open than the less-open industrial countries, at nearly 60, but ended the 1990s somewhat below them, at less than 80. The relatively less-open develop-ing countries were considerably more closed throughout, with indexes averaging about 20 in the 1970s and about 50 by the late 1990s.[14]

In contrast, the de facto measures of financial openness, tracking ac-tual capital flows or stocks, underscore the fact that some countries with significant restrictions nonetheless experience large flows (e.g., Brazil). Figure 3.3 shows median gross capital flows (inflows plus outflows) as a fraction of GDP for the same four groupings of countries identified in figure 3.1. Once again there is a broad rising trend, this time with a spike in 1999–2000 for the developed countries. Figure 3.4 in chapter 3 shows the corresponding de facto openness to FDI, with median FDI inflows as a fraction of GDP. This measure too shows a general increase over time and a spike in 2000. It also shows developing countries much closer to the heights reached by the industrial countries than is the case for general capital flows.

Calculating Realized Growth Gains from Financial Openness

With the various financial-openness measures in hand for 24 developing and 21 industrial economies for 1970–2004, and after converting the pa-rameter estimates summarized in tables 2.1–2.3 into comparable metrics, chapter 3 calculates past growth impacts of financial globalization for in-dividual countries. For the general financial-openness models, there are eight alternative measures of financial openness and three alternative in-

---

13. The relatively more-open developed countries are Belgium, Canada, Denmark, France, Germany, Ireland, Italy, the Netherlands, Switzerland, the United Kingdom, and the United States. The relatively less-open developed countries are Australia, Austria, Finland, Greece, Japan, New Zealand, Norway, Portugal, Spain, and Sweden.

14. The relatively more-open developing countries are Argentina, Colombia, Egypt, Hong Kong, India, Israel, Korea, Mexico, Malaysia, Peru, Singapore, and Venezuela. The relatively less-open developing countries are Algeria, Brazil, Chile, China, Hungary, Indonesia, Pakistan, the Philippines, Poland, South Africa, Thailand, and Turkey.

teracting variables.[15] In the principal set of estimates (table 3.7 in chapter 3), the intrastudy meta-statistical estimate (inverse-variance weighting) is applied for those studies in which the authors consider their insignificant variants to be the most meaningful.[16] For all other studies, the principal significant-parameter model variant in each study is used.

Table 1.1 reports the results of these calculations applying 11 different models to the individual-country data on financial openness and interacting variables, with the results for each model averaged across countries in three groupings: industrial, Latin American, and Asian developing economies.[17] As indicated in the table's title, this set of estimates is best seen as the "high variant" of the findings in this study. The reason is that it is based on significant results or, for those studies in which authors prefer their insignificant results following robustness tests, the intra-study meta-statistical average. The alternative variant, not shown in table 1.1, would apply meta-statistical weighting both across and within the various studies, and this alternative approach cuts the estimated impact to only about one-third as large.

The overall high-variant averages for industrial countries indicate an annual growth contribution of slightly less than 1 percent from the degree of financial openness actually attained in the 1980s, rising to slightly above 1 percent by the 1990s and 2000–04. For developing countries, the growth contributions are considerably lower, reflecting lesser degrees of openness. Thus, the GDP-weighted Quinn indexes of de jure openness (0 to 100) for 1995–99 stand at 94.4 for industrial countries, but only 53.6 for emerging-market economies in Asia, 63.2 in Latin America, 51.7 in the Middle East and South Africa, and 56.4 in Eastern Europe (for the countries included in table 3.7).[18] The growth impacts are at approximately 0.5 percent per year in the 1990s and 2000–04 in both developing Asia and Latin America. In the 1980s, Latin America shows a considerably lower average impact of

---

15. The openness variables, which vary with the model in question, are the Quinn measure of de jure openness; gross capital flows relative to GDP; net capital flows relative to GDP; gross FDI and portfolio flows relative to GDP; FDI and portfolio inflows relative to GDP; the IMF's capital account restrictions variable (1 or 0); the Tornell, Westermann, and Martinez (2004) variable for financial liberalization (1 or 0); and total capital inflows relative to GDP. The interactive variables are bank assets relative to bank plus central bank assets (financial depth); the logarithm of 1980 real per capita income; and 1 minus the black-market premium.

16. In particular, because they judge that their robustness tests reveal that their initial significant results are not robust.

17. The averages are "trimmed," or calculated after removing the highest and lowest model outcomes for the country and period in question.

18. The additional influence of interactive variables is relatively limited. The principal exception would be for the Edwards (2001) model, but it tends to be screened out of the trimmed averages.

Table 1.1 Average annual increment to GDP growth from general financial openness, 1980–2004, high variant (percent)

Country	1980–89	1990–99	2000–04
Industrial	0.8	1.0	1.1
United States	1.0	1.1	1.1
Japan	0.7	0.8	0.9
Germany	1.0	1.1	1.2
France	0.8	1.0	1.1
United Kingdom	1.1	1.2	1.2
Developing Asia	0.4	0.5	0.4
China	—	0.2	0.4
India	0.2	0.2	—
Korea	0.3	0.5	0.6
Indonesia	0.2	0.3	0.3
Latin America	0.1	0.4	0.5
Argentina	−0.0	0.6	0.5
Brazil	0.0	0.3	0.4
Chile	0.2	0.4	0.6
Mexico	0.1	0.5	0.5
Other			
Poland	—	0.2	0.5
Turkey	0.2	0.4	0.5
South Africa	0.1	0.3	0.3

Sources: Tables 3.7 and 3.8 in chapter 3 (trimmed averages).

0.1 percent, reflecting low capital inflows in that decade of debt difficulties, whereas the growth contribution is about 0.4 percent in Asia.

As summary benchmarks, then, in the high-variant results the average growth contribution from realized financial openness over the past quarter century has been about 1 percent per year for industrial countries, and about 0.5 percent per year for major emerging-market economies. As noted, these estimates apply meta-statistical weighting (when applicable, as discussed above) only *within* studies. If in addition this approach of weighting is applied *across* studies, the estimates are considerably lower.

In particular, from table 2.1 it can be seen that the meta-statistical average across studies shows a growth contribution of 0.56 percent per year for complete financial opening, compared with a corresponding estimate of 1.57 percent per year for the average of study estimates when the meta-statistical approach is applied only within each study. On this basis, a low estimate of growth contributions might reasonably be set at about one-third the levels shown in table 1.1, or 0.36 percent for realized growth benefits in industrial countries in the 1990s through 2004, and about 0.18 percent in major emerging-market economies in this period.

The high-variant growth impact estimates of table 1.1 (and their more detailed source estimates in table 3.7), along with the observation that a low-end estimate might be just one-third as large, provide a basis for calculating the portion of present levels of GDP that can be attributed to the cumulative effects of external financial market openness over 1970–2004 for the economies examined in chapter 3. These 45 economies account for 89 percent of 2008 world GDP at market exchange rates and for 72 percent of world population (IMF 2009b, US Census Bureau 2009b). Country growth rate contributions from financial openness are cumulated, and the component of present-day output attributable to this source is then calculated.[19] Table 1.2 reports the dollar amounts of 2008 GDP attributable to cumulative external financial openness (over 1980–2004) calculated in this way. The "low" variant is based on the ratio of the cross-study meta-statistical estimate to the average of intrastudy meta-statistical averages, as just discussed. The "high" variant is the latter concept, derived from the growth contributions shown in table 3.7 and summarized in table 1.1.[20]

The estimates of table 1.2 suggest that the amount of economic welfare already realized from the extent of financial openness actually undertaken has been large especially for the industrial countries. About 8 percent of their current level of output can be attributed to their almost complete financial openness, in the low estimate, and as much as about 21 percent in the high estimate. For the emerging-market economies the impact is also substantial but considerably smaller, in a range of 2¼ to 6½ percent of current output. The much lower fraction for emerging-market economies represents the combined effect of two influences: lesser financial openness, and higher growth rates than those of industrial economies (i.e., "convergence"). An important implication is that even though other factors are the primary determinants of their higher growth, the emerging-market economies could narrow the gap in realized gains from financial globalization by moving further toward openness more comparable to that typical of the industrial countries. As implied by the regional differences shown in table 1.1, achieving industrial-country openness levels

---

19. For each country, actual annual growth rates from 1980 through 2004 are taken from IMF (2009b). Annual growth contributions underlying table 3.7 (trimmed averages) are subtracted from actual growth rates to obtain hypothetical annual growth in the absence of any financial openness. Cumulative hypothetical growth for 1980 through 2004 is then subtracted from cumulative actual growth to obtain the estimates of table 1.2.

20. There are higher estimates in the "significant only" results reported in chapter 3 (table 3.5), but in light of the discussion of a priori expectations above, prudence and plausibility suggest applying the estimates of table 1.1 (and table 3.7) as the benchmark for the high end of the growth impact range.

Table 1.2 Contribution of 1980–2004 cumulative growth effects of financial openness to 2008 GDP

| Economy | 2008 GDP (billions of dollars) | Contribution from financial opening | | | |
| | | Amount (billions of dollars) | | Percent of GDP | |
		Low	High	Low	High
Algeria[a]	160	−0.2	−0.6	−0.1	−0.4
Argentina	326	9.6	26.4	3.0	8.1
Australia	1,011	73.5	193.3	7.3	19.1
Austria	415	33.4	87.3	8.1	21.0
Belgium	506	44.6	115.7	8.8	22.9
Brazil	1,573	28.0	77.4	1.8	4.9
Canada	1,511	130.6	339.2	8.6	22.5
Chile	170	5.0	13.7	3.0	8.1
China[b]	4,402	68.4	189.3	1.6	4.3
Colombia	241	7.6	20.9	3.2	8.7
Denmark	343	28.9	75.3	8.4	21.9
Egypt	162	4.0	11.0	2.5	6.8
Finland	274	21.3	55.7	7.8	20.3
France	2,866	229.3	599.0	8.0	20.9
Germany	3,668	325.8	844.4	8.9	23.0
Greece	358	20.9	55.6	5.8	15.5
Hong Kong[b]	216	5.0	13.7	2.3	6.3
Hungary	156	3.5	9.8	2.3	6.3
India[a]	1,210	18.6	51.3	1.5	4.2
Indonesia	512	10.4	28.7	2.0	5.6
Ireland	273	21.2	55.5	7.8	20.3
Israel	202	8.9	24.0	4.4	11.9
Italy	2,314	185.0	483.4	8.0	20.9
Japan	4,924	327.3	865.6	6.6	17.6
Korea	947	34.6	93.9	3.7	9.9
Malaysia	222	8.9	24.1	4.0	10.8
Mexico	1,088	34.8	95.0	3.2	8.7
Netherlands	869	79.0	204.5	9.1	23.5
New Zealand	128	9.2	24.2	7.2	18.9
Norway	456	36.3	94.9	8.0	20.8
Pakistan	168	2.4	6.7	1.4	4.0
Peru	128	3.9	10.7	3.1	8.3

a. Growth contribution omitted for 1992–2004 for Algeria and for 2001–04 for India.
b. Growth contribution omitted for 1980–84 for China and for 1980–97 for Hong Kong.

(continued on next page)

Table 1.2 Contribution of 1980–2004 cumulative growth effects of financial openness to 2008 GDP *(continued)*

Economy	2008 GDP (billions of dollars)	Contribution from financial opening Amount (billions of dollars) Low	High	Percent of GDP Low	High
Philippines	169	5.2	14.2	3.1	8.4
Poland[b]	526	5.5	15.4	1.1	2.9
Portugal	244	13.8	36.7	5.6	15.1
Singapore	182	15.1	39.4	8.3	21.7
South Africa	277	5.4	14.9	1.9	5.4
Spain	1,612	105.6	279.7	6.6	17.3
Sweden	485	38.5	100.7	7.9	20.8
Switzerland[b]	493	25.3	68.0	5.1	13.8
Thailand	273	8.1	22.1	3.0	8.1
Turkey	729	21.2	58.0	2.9	8.0
United Kingdom	2,674	251.6	649.2	9.4	24.3
United States	14,265	1,261.7	3,271.4	8.8	22.9
Venezuela	319	4.9	13.6	1.5	4.3
45 economies	54,047	3,581.9	9,373.0	6.6	17.3
Industrial	39,689	3,262.9	8,499.3	8.2	21.4
Developing Asia	8,301	176.7	483.5	2.1	5.8
Latin America	3,845	94.0	257.7	2.4	6.7
Middle East and South Africa	801	18.1	49.2	2.3	6.1
Developing Europe	1,411	30.3	83.2	2.1	5.9
World	60,690	…	…	…	…

b. Growth contribution omitted for 1980–85 for Poland and for 1980–91 for Switzerland.

Source: IMF (2009g); author's calculations.

could boost emerging-market growth rates by about one-half percent per annum, at least in the high-variant results.

For the United States, table 1.2 indicates that over a quarter-century financial openness has cumulatively contributed at least about 9 percent of present-day output, and as much as 23 percent in the high-variant results. Both the theoretical expectations outlined above and the important consideration of possible endogeneity argue for focusing attention toward the lower end of this range. Even so, the resulting benchmark of close to 10 percent of GDP turns out to be approximately the same as the corresponding estimate for the output contribution of trade openness estimated in the Institute study discussed earlier (Bradford, Grieco, and Hufbauer 2005). These results suggest that financial openness has been just as important as trade openness to US growth.

Quantifying Crisis Effects

Because the fear of greater exposure to crises is the main reason some economists and policymakers oppose financial globalization, it is worthwhile considering further whether the gains from openness would be likely to outweigh any additional crisis risks. Four decades ago it could have been said that the more dominant fear was that the "commanding heights of the economy" would be seized by foreigners, but policymakers in most emerging-market economies have progressed beyond that stage. Some of these economies have themselves become important sources of direct investment in other countries.

Chapter 2 develops a simple calibrated model examining this question (equation 2.1 and table 2.4). The exercise first posits a gain in the long-term annual growth rate that could be expected from complete financial openness versus closure. For this concept, a conservative estimate is the 0.5 percent per year identified in the cross-study meta-statistical estimate of table 2.1 for general financial openness. Against this gain must be set the expected crisis loss from financial openness. This loss equals the increase in the crisis probability attributable to financial openness, multiplied by the expected incidence of crisis without openness, multiplied by the output loss associated with a crisis event. This calculation applies to currency crises and banking crises, additively.

For the exercise, parameters are drawn from the Reinhart and Rogoff (2008), Hutchison and Noy (2005), and Reinhart and Reinhart (2008) studies. Adverse and favorable alternatives are set in each of the relevant dimensions. The general incidence of currency crisis is set at between 12 and 8 percent of years, respectively. The general incidence of banking crises is set at between 6.5 and 2.4 percent of years. Cumulative damage from a currency crisis is set between 8 and 5 percent of GDP. Cumulative damage from a banking crisis is set between 10 and 4 percent of GDP. The increase in the probability of crisis from complete opening is set at the extreme at 40 percent for both banking and currency crises (based on the Reinhart-Reinhart study despite its inherent inability to examine this question). At the opposite extreme, this increase in probability of the crisis is set at *minus* 5 percent for currency crises, and minus 15 percent for banking crises. The reduced chances of crisis are based on figure 2.1 and apply a greater crisis-chance reduction for banking on grounds that openness to international banking reduces the risk of a local banking crisis as a consequence of greater presence of major foreign banks (probably still true despite the US and European origins of the 2007–09 banking crisis).

With six variables and two values for each, there are 64 possible outcomes. It turns out that the most adverse combination of all would mean that financial openness causes annual expected crisis losses of 0.64 percent of GDP. The lowest 30 percent of combinations would be within a range of –0.64 to –0.25 percent. The next 45 percent of cases would lie between –0.25 percent and zero. The top 27 percent of cases would instead show expected reduction in crisis losses amounting to annual gains of zero to 0.15 percent of GDP.

Setting the conservative 0.5 percent increase in the annual growth rate from complete financial openness against these expected crisis losses, there would be net gains in all but three of the 64 possible combinations. It is 20 times more likely that openness gains would exceed induced crisis losses than that the reverse would occur.[21] Across the 64 cases, the average expected loss is 0.15 percent per year. Compared against the conservative estimate for openness growth gains, the net annual growth gain would be 0.35 percent per year, or a cumulative 11 percent over three decades. Moreover, net gains could be larger to the extent that the statistical estimates of growth effects have already incorporated induced crisis effects.

Quantifying Debt versus Equity Effects

Similarly, it is worthwhile devoting additional attention to the question of the composition of the capital. In terms of formal tests of growth impact, the existing literature on differential impact of openness across specific types of capital is sparse.[22] Among the few such studies, Reisen and Soto (2001) find that whereas the evidence is strong for a positive growth impact of FDI, the influence of foreign bank debt on growth is negative if domestic bank capitalization is low but turns positive once domestic capitalization exceeds a given threshold. The IMF (2007a) finds a posi-

---

21. As discussed in chapter 2, a sensitivity test with much higher GDP loss from a currency crisis still leaves a strongly favorable net comparison between secular gains from openness and probability-weighted losses from possibly increased chances of experiencing a crisis.

22. Note, however, that there is considerable empirical literature of the "early warning" variety that tends to indicate compositional effects on vulnerability to crisis. Thus, Goldstein, Kaminsky, and Reinhart (2000, 38) find that "the top indicator for banking crises is the share of short-term capital...[which is] more likely to be intermediated through the domestic banking sector than other types of capital flows, such as foreign direct investment and portfolio flow." In contrast, they find that "the composition of capital inflows appears to have relatively little to add to our understanding of what drives a currency crisis" (p. 39), but they suggest that this finding may reflect the fact that currency crises were more frequent (relative to banking crises) in the 1970s when internal and external financial markets were highly regulated and portfolio flows were negligible (p. 40).

tive but insignificant coefficient for growth on the ratio of external debt assets and liabilities to GDP in a series of tests incorporating control variables along with alternative measures of financial openness. In contrast, the same study finds a statistically significant positive growth effect for FDI. Kose, Prasad, and Terrones (2008) find statistically significant positive effects of FDI and portfolio equity but significant negative effects of external debt on TFP growth. In short, the evidence on growth effects of debt capital is far more limited, and ambiguous on direction, than that on growth effects of general financial openness and openness to direct investment (e.g., tables 2.1 and 2.3, respectively). It is fair to say that on a basis of both the limited growth-impact literature and the more extensive crisis-vulnerability literature, the stylized hierarchy for capital composition is that for growth and stability, FDI is better than debt, long term is better than short term, and debt denominated in domestic currency is better than that in foreign currency. The placement of portfolio flows in this hierarchy would be toward the FDI end, in view of the increasing number of studies showing a strong positive growth impact but taking account of its shorter-term nature.

In an effort to shed further light on the impact of debt capital openness, appendix 1C presents two statistical tests on this issue. In the first, it is assumed that along the continuum of openness indicated by the Quinn-Toyoda index, toward the lower end the capital transactions that are open are those for direct investment, whereas toward the upper end, debt capital flows are also treated in an open manner. On this basis, a test of growth gains in a linear versus quadratic formulation of openness provides a test for whether the gains are coming only from equity versus whether they are also coming comparably from debt capital.

In this test, a standard cross-country growth regression with control variables is applied to a panel of five-year periods for the 45 countries examined in this study for 1970–2004. When the linear formulation is used, the test yields approximately the same growth-impact parameter for Quinn openness as found in various other tests in the literature (see table 2.1). In the estimates here, complete openness versus complete closure (index = 0) contributes 2.16 percent additional annual growth, and the parameter estimate is statistically significant. In contrast, when a quadratic formulation is used, the linear term is moderately larger (2.7 percent), albeit less significant, and the sign of the quadratic term is indeed negative; but the quadratic term is statistically insignificant. This test thus fails to confirm the hypothesis that additional openness (most likely associated with debt openness) has a negative impact on growth in contradistinction to the initial range of openness (most likely associated with FDI openness).

A second test in appendix 1C examines the impact of debt openness more directly. This test once again applies the same cross-country panel data and control variables for growth. However, it applies a direct measure of debt openness as the financial-openness variable: the ratio of the stock of external debt liabilities and assets to GDP. In the first variant of this test, the coefficient is positive and statistically significant. An extra 10 percent of GDP on this stock measure contributes an extra 0.03 percentage point to annual growth. However, it turns out that this result is driven by the high-end outlier (Hong Kong), whose debt asset and liability stock is on the order of 700 percent of GDP over the period, in contrast to an average of about 90 percent for other emerging-market economies. When this outlier and two outliers at the opposite extreme (China and India, with debt-asset-and-liability-stock ratios at about 20 percent of GDP) are excluded, the significance of the debt variable disappears. The message is the same as in the quadratic test using the Quinn indicator: A direct test for debt capital does not confirm the hypothesis that it has a negative growth impact.

Implications of the 2007–09 Crisis

The literature surveyed in chapter 2, and the parameters derived from it to carry out the synthesis estimates of realized growth impacts, largely predate the global financial crisis of 2007–09. Chapter 4 examines whether the preliminary evidence from the crisis warrants changing the policy diagnoses reached in the previous chapters.

Causes

On the basis of more extensive analyses in its appendices, chapter 4 first reviews the principal events of the crisis and evaluates its main causes.[23] The most important proximate cause was the bursting of the bubble and severe decline in *housing* prices. Historically, actual reductions in US housing prices had tended to be limited to one geographical region at a time. Adjustment to overvaluation more generally had occurred through extended periods of flat prices rather than outright declines.

Financial innovation acted as an accelerant to the strains from falling housing prices. The innovation of securitized residential mortgage-backed securities (RMBS) and subprime lending helped turn the housing market correction into a financial crisis. Subprime loans were constructed on the premise that housing prices would not come down for the market as a whole. The RMBS proved to be highly opaque. When their triple-A ratings

---

23. In addition to appendices on events and policy interventions (4A) and causes of the crisis (4B), chapter 4 includes an appendix (4C) reproducing several short pieces by the author in the Institute's "RealTime" daily commentary begun during the height of the crisis. These pieces may help capture the contemporary economic policy atmosphere, as well as address certain important specific issues. Similarly, appendix 4D is a more formal analysis of whether the Private-Public Investment Program (PPIP) constitutes an exorbitant public subsidy to private investors, or a reasonable instrument for reviving the distressed market in loans and mortgage-backed securities. (It concludes in favor of the latter interpretation.)

proved to be an illusion, at a key moment in early 2007 when the advent of the ABX index provided data on falling prices, there ensued what Gorton (2008) calls a classic banking panic (including for the shadow banking sector). Essentially, creditors stopped lending to counterparties because they could not determine whether the counterparties were insolvent as a consequence of holding "toxic assets."

Another financial innovation, the credit default swap (CDS), also proved to be a key factor precipitating the crisis. The large insurer AIG had taken one-sided bets on CDSs, and its prospective failure threatened major private financial institutions around the world. One way to look at the crisis is as a negative example of the real business cycle: A technological breakthrough, this time in financial-sector innovation, helped cause a massive downturn (rather than a period of growth as in other historical episodes and sectors).

High leverage and *lax regulation* aggravated the crisis (as illustrated by regulatory capital avoidance through such mechanisms as special-investment vehicles). *Lax monetary policy* contributed by maintaining arguably excessively low policy interest rates in 2003–05. The popular counter-argument that a *global saving glut* caused the crisis does not square with interest rate trends, because the policy rate (short-term federal funds rate) stood at almost exactly the same relationship to the market-based longer-term rate (10-year treasury bond) in mid-2007 (after several years of "glut") as it had in early 2001 (before the glut). In the intervening period, the policy rate had fallen much more sharply, whereas the longer-term market-determined rate should have fallen more sharply than the short-term rate if global finance conditions rather than US Federal Reserve policy had been driving low interest rates. Nonetheless, figure 4B.5 in appendix 4B does suggest that about one-third of the extraordinary buildup in debt of the nonfinancial sectors in the United States during 2003–06 can be said to have been financed by the US current account deficit (net capital inflow). So the global saving glut may be seen as having played a contributing role in causing the crisis, if not a leading role.

Status by Late 2009

By mid-2009 there were encouraging signs that the worst of the crisis was over, at least from the standpoint of financial stability if not from that of employment levels. A key measure of financial-sector risk, the spread between the rate at which banks lend to each other (the London Interbank Offered Rate or LIBOR) and a risk-free rate (overnight index swap or OIS), had surged to 350 basis points in late 2008, but was almost back to precrisis levels by July 2009 and even closer by October (chapter 4, figure 4.1). The JP Morgan Emerging Markets Bond Index (global composite), which had similarly registered a surge in sovereign spreads from about 200 basis points at end-2007 to a peak of about 780 basis points in October 2008, had eased to about 300 basis points by October 2009 (lower than the entire 1997–2003 period).

IMF estimates indicated that by the end of the second quarter of 2009, US banks had written off about 60 percent of their total prospective losses. The IMF figures for total losses amounted to 9 percent of end-2007 assets for US banks, about 5 percent for UK banks, and only about 2 percent for banks in the euro zone. The European banks were thus arguably better off than those in the United States, even though they had written off only about 40 percent of the IMF's total expected loss amount. The US Federal Reserve's April 2009 "stress test" of the largest 19 US banks provided a key boost to confidence. It showed that, after taking account of capital actions taken in the first four months of 2009, as well as first-quarter profits, nine of the banks did not need additional capital, and the amount needed by the other 10 was a manageable amount of only $75 billion, even though the loss rates assumed in the test were worse than in the 1930s. By May the major US banks had already raised about $60 billion in additional capital subsequent to the stress test.

The damage done to the real economy, however, was large. For 34 major economies, weighting by GDP at market exchange rates, real economic growth fell from 4.1 percent in 2007 and 2 percent in 2008 to an estimated –2.2 percent in 2009, but it is expected to recover to 2.9 percent in 2010 (chapter 4, table 4.1). Only the world recession of 1982 came close to such severe damage in the postwar period, and the recession of 2007–09 has been much more synchronized and generalized globally than the 1982 episode. There has been a pattern of extreme collapses in exports, reflecting sharp declines in industrial production in combination with closely linked global production chains. The 2007–09 recession has been worse for industrial countries than the 1982 recession. For the United States, by 2011 per capita output is likely still to be no higher than at the 2007 peak; in contrast, it rose 10.1 percent in the comparable period from 1981 to 1985 (see chapter 4). The current recession has not been worse than that in 1982 for Latin America, however; nor has it been as severe for East Asia as was that region's crisis in 1998. The fiscal legacy of the crisis is also of serious concern. The US budget deficit reached 9.9 percent of GDP in fiscal 2009 and was on track to remain as high as about 4 percent by 2012–15. The corresponding prospective path for federal debt held by the public was an increase from 37 percent of GDP in 2007 to 69 percent by 2011 and 82 percent by 2019. For the main industrial countries, the crisis was projected to increase public debt burdens by about 20 percentage points of GDP.

Capital Flows and Financing Gaps

One important set of estimates indicates that net private capital flows to 30 major emerging-market economies fell from a peak of $1.2 trillion in

2007 to $670 billion in 2008 and $440 billion in 2009, but will revive to $720 billion in 2010 (IIF 2009, 2010). However, because these economies as a group were running large current account surpluses in 2007–08, the large capital inflows were going to finance buildups in reserves and outflows of resident capital, rather than real resources needed for growth, so the consequences of the sharp curtailment in capital flows may be less severe than might have been expected.

Even so, at the April 2009 summit in London, Group of 20 (G-20) leaders pledged a tripling of IMF lending capacity, based on $500 billion in additional lending to the IMF from the United States, European Union, Japan, China, and other G-20 members. The G-20 leaders also called for $250 billion in new Special Drawing Rights (SDRs), as well as $250 billion in trade finance. In June 2009, the World Bank (2009a) issued estimates that there was a financing gap of $350 billion to $635 billion for the developing countries. The gap is calculated as the difference between financing needs (current account deficit plus payments due for the year in short- and long-term private debt) and private capital flows (rollovers on those payments plus equity capital inflows minus resident capital outflows). The World Bank estimates do not explicitly take account of the use of reserves.

Although the World Bank estimate seemed to justify the large additional financing pushed by the G-20, chapter 4 shows that the actual needs to cover financing gaps were likely to be much smaller after considering ample amounts of reserves in the hands of several major emerging-market economies. In one estimate, if the base case assumptions of the World Bank prove correct, and if it is assumed that the emerging-market economies can safely use 25 percent of their accumulated reserves to deal with the extraordinary circumstances of the 2007–09 international crisis, then somewhat less than $100 billion is the right order of magnitude for calibrating the more meaningful net financing gap, after prudential reserve use, for emerging-market economies. If so, then the larger emergency funds pledged by the G-20 may prove to have been useful primarily in terms of boosting global confidence rather than for actual finance.

Indeed, by mid-2009 there were already signs that, partly due to the evidence that the official sector would not allow emerging-market economies to fail, private finance in the emerging bond market was reviving at a relatively brisk pace. In portfolio equities, there was a large swing back to positive net flows in 2009 (chapter 4, figure 4.5). Ironically, by late 2009 the problem for many emerging-market economies had become too much capital inflow, not too little. The zero-interest-rate policy of the US Federal Reserve was having the effect of fostering a large dollar-based carry trade that was bidding up currencies and equity markets across emerging-market economies. In mid-October, to avoid excessive appreciation of its currency and loss of competitiveness, Brazil reinstated the modest tax on foreign purchases of equities and bonds that it had suspended at the height of the crisis a year before.[24] In short, by late 2009 the earlier fears of a new round of emerging-market "sudden stop" crises from a collapse in capital inflows had so far been shown to have been seriously exaggerated.

Evidence on Financial-Openness Effects

For the purposes of this study, the most relevant question raised by the crisis of 2007–09 is whether it has demonstrated that financial openness is more dangerous than had previously been recognized. Chapter 4 presents two tests on this question. Both involve examining whether there is a correlation between the severity of individual emerging-market economies' economic dislocation during the crisis with the degree of financial openness of the economy in question.

In the first test, official and private-sector forecasts are used to estimate average GDP growth over 2008–10, as the crisis period. The amount of the reduction from average growth during 2005–07 to growth during 2008–10 is then used as an indicator of the severity of the damage from the global crisis to the economy in question. With this change in growth on the vertical axis, figure 4.7 in chapter 4 shows the Quinn indicator of financial openness on the horizontal axis. If a single closed outlier, Algeria, is excluded, there is no pattern relating damage to openness. A simple regression including both financial openness and the share of exports in GDP as independent variables, as well as the change in growth as the dependent variable, finds no significant relationship between the severity of GDP loss and the degree of financial openness.

A second test once again uses the Quinn index to measure financial openness. This time the metric for damage is the real percent change in the stock market index from end-2007 to the trough on March 9, 2009. By this measure, too, there is a wide scatter of experience with no evident relationship between damage and financial openness. When emerging-market economies are divided into three groups—more financially open, intermediate, and less financially open—the depth of the average stock market decline from end-2007 to the trough in the first quarter of 2009 turns out to be virtually identical for the more-open and more-closed groups, and somewhat less for the intermediate group. By late 2009 the smallest recovery was for the more-closed group. On the equity market tests as well as tests on growth performance, then, so far the crisis of 2007–

---

24. The previous rate had been 1.5 percent; the renewal placed it at 2 percent. See Paulo Winterstein and Emily Schmall, "Brazilian Stocks, Currency Tumble on Tax on Foreign Purchases," Bloomberg.com, October 20, 2009 (accessed on January 4, 2010). The effect on the exchange rate was small at least initially, however. By the first half of November the average rate against the dollar was less than 1 percent below the level prior to the renewal of the tax.

09 does not provide evidence supporting the notion that more financially open economies will be more severely affected by the spillover from international financial crises.

Even in Eastern Europe, the emerging-market region hit the hardest by the crisis, the extreme growth collapses in the Baltic states are more attributable to risky policy strategies that allowed current account deficits to reach about 15 percent of GDP than to mistaken adoption of financial openness. In the larger economies of the region, fiscal deficits were considerably higher in Hungary than Poland. The more severe recession in Hungary, and the fact that Hungary was forced to seek IMF support whereas Poland was not, are more likely the consequence of differences in macroeconomic policies than in financial openness.[25]

Chapter 4 further suggests that it is helpful to think of the 2007–09 crisis as a 100-year financial storm. In this context, the relevant question is whether the policy approach has stood up well in the face of such a storm. The fact that in general the more financially open emerging-market economies have not fared worse than those that are more closed in the face of this extreme test suggests that more openness may not be as risky as some had warned.

Conclusion

This study first provides an in-depth survey and evaluation of the large economic literature on financial globalization (chapter 2). Several of the previous surveys of this literature tend to conclude that not much can be said about the impact of financial openness on growth because of statistical ambiguities.[26] The main thrust of the present study, in contrast, is that the great preponderance of the empirical evidence is on the side of a positive growth effect of openness. Chapter 2 observes that if the true effect were zero, one should expect an equal number of positive and negative parameter estimates. Instead, they are almost all positive. The analysis

---

25. In the recent study by Ostry et al. (2010), in two out of their three tests it is the growth collapse in the Baltics that is the sole reason for the finding that financial openness was associated with worse growth outcomes in the recent global financial crisis. If a dummy variable for the Baltic states is included in their two cross-country regressions, there is no longer a statistically significant relationship of growth reduction to either external debt relative to GDP or FDI in the financial sector relative to GDP, the two openness measures. The same problem of dominance by tiny, unrepresentative economies plagues their third test, which uses the dichotomous probit technique to distinguish between "growth-crisis" cases comprising just four economies, of which Latvia and Iceland are two, and three dozen "other" emerging-market economies. See William R. Cline, "The IMF's Misleading New Evidence on Capital Controls," RealTime Economic Issues Watch (Washington: Peterson Institute for International Economics, February 24, 2010), available at www.piie.com.

26. For a survey of the surveys, see the penultimate section of chapter 2.

concludes that the odds are greater than 300 to 1 against there being no positive growth impact of financial openness.

Chapter 2 goes further, however, and invokes the methodology of "meta-statistics" used more frequently in some of the other social sciences to arrive at overview parameter estimates that take account of both statistically significant and insignificant model results, at both the intra-study and interstudy levels. The central finding of this approach is that the difference between complete financial openness and complete closure amounts to a sustained contribution to growth rates ranging from one-half a percent per year at the low end to about 1½ percent per year at the high end. For theoretical and statistical reasons, the appropriate summary measure seems likely to lie closer to the lower end of this range than to the upper end.

The synthesis estimates in chapter 3 apply the underlying financial-openness variables to the parameter estimates from chapter 2 to arrive at country-specific calculations of realized growth contributions from financial openness for 1970–2004. Because openness is far from complete, these estimates tend to be somewhat lower. Using the set of estimates corresponding to the upper end of the range just noted, they imply that industrial economies achieved about 0.7 percentage point per year additional growth from financial openness over 1970–90 and about 1 percent additional growth over 1990–2004 (figure 3.5). Emerging-market economies in Asia and Latin America were achieving annual gains on the order of one-half a percent per year by 1990–2004 (after a collapse to zero in the latter half of the 1980s in Latin America with the debt crisis). The conservative lower-end estimate would be about one-third as large.

The summary estimates in this chapter translate these realized gains into differences in present-day GDP levels that can be attributed to the cumulative influence of financial openness. The high estimates amount to about one-fifth of the level of GDP for industrial economies; the low estimates, about 8 percent. The corresponding range for emerging-market economies is about 2.25 to 6.5 percent of present-day output levels. Even if one focuses solely on the conservative estimates, these are large gains from policy choices on financial openness.

These results suggest that many emerging-market economies have further unrealized gains that could be achieved by moving toward more complete financial openness. With respect to the principal fear about doing so—potential losses from additional exposure to crises—this chapter presents a simple model calibrated to historical crisis studies that shows that if there is even a modest sustained annual growth increase from openness, the result will be to swamp any expected losses from greater crisis exposure. As just suggested, the 100-year storm test provided by the crisis of 2007–09 supports the proposition that the increased crisis exposure from financial openness is not severe, because the more-closed economies fared just as badly as those that are more open. The discussion and tests of this chapter also suggest there is little evidence to support the proposition that FDI and portfolio equity openness are good for growth but debt openness is bad for growth. The FDI and portfolio equity impact literature does suggest strong growth effects but should be read as support for overall openness rather that inverse evidence that debt openness has a negative impact.

The estimates of this study tend to refute the more polemical arguments that financial openness is detrimental to growth. They tend to support the position of the advocates of financial openness accompanied by macro-policy prudence, such as Fischer (1998) and Summers (2000), rather than that of opponents who argue that financial openness is dangerous and does not yield gains analogous to those from trade openness, such as Bhagwati (1998) and Stiglitz (2002). At the same time, the diagnosis of substantial net positive growth effects from financial openness seems likely to be more clearly applicable to middle-income emerging-market economies and industrial countries than to lower-income developing economies. Some of the statistical tests have contingent thresholds that tend not to be met by the poorer countries. Moreover, the set of 45 economies for which specific estimates are made in chapter 3 does not include numerous poor countries, particularly those of sub-Saharan Africa. There is an important need for further research on pragmatic guidelines for policymakers on whether there are preconditions that should be in place before opening the economy to various types of capital flows, and if so, what they are and how they can be met.

An aftermath of the global crisis of 2007–09 is that market-oriented policies, and even capitalism itself, are being questioned more intensively than at any time since the 1930s. Financial globalization is and will be one of the prime areas most severely scrutinized in such reassessments. The findings of this study indicate that financial openness can make an important contribution to growth, and has already done so on a substantial scale. It would be a serious mistake to revert toward financial closure, reversing the long-term trend toward financial globalization. Instead, especially once the global economy returns to more normal conditions, it would behoove policymakers in a number of economies to consider making further progress along the path of financial openness. Most of the economies have already been making such progress on trade openness for a long time. The results of this study suggest that financial openness, like that in trade, can make an important contribution to growth.

Appendix 1A
Covered Interest Parity as a Measure of Financial Openness

As discussed in the main text, covered interest parity (CIP) was a relatively early "price" measure of financial openness. However, the large empirical literature on growth effects of financial openness has not applied this measure, perhaps primarily because of the absence of forward exchange markets for many economies in the periods examined. By now, forward markets exist for more economies. However, it may still be some time before sufficient emerging-market economies have historical data series available for forward exchange premia to permit meaningful tests on growth effects of financial openness.

Figure 1A.1 shows the correspondence between Quinn-Toyoda openness and CIP for a relatively recent point in time with available data for

Figure 1A.1 Covered interest parity deviation and Quinn de jure openness, 2004

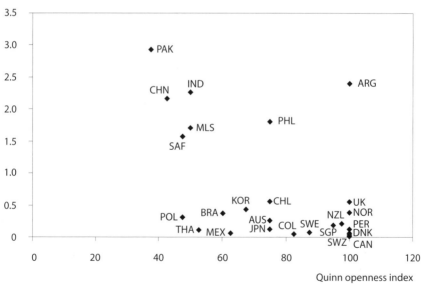

absolute deviation from covered interest parity (percent per annum)

Country abbreviations: ARG = Argentina; AUS = Australia; BRA = Brazil; CAN = Canada; CHL = Chile; CHN = China; COL = Colombia; DNK = Denmark; IND = India; JPN = Japan; KOR = Korea; MEX = Mexico; MLS = Malaysia; NOR = Norway; NZL = New Zealand; PAK = Pakistan; PER = Peru; PHL = Philippines; POL = Poland; SAF = South Africa; SGP = Singapore; SWE = Sweden; SWZ = Switzerland; THA = Thailand; TUR = Turkey; UK = United Kingdom

Source: Author's calculations.

April 2004 for 26 economies. On the vertical axis, the absolute deviation from CIP is shown in percent per annum rates. This deviation is calculated as the money-market rate for the country in question, minus the money-market rate for the United States, minus the annualized three-month forward exchange rate premium over the spot rate. Data are from the IMF (2009a), Datastream, Reuters, and Quinn and Toyoda (2008).

In broad terms, the higher the index of de jure openness, the closer to zero is the absolute deviation from CIP. An outlier, Argentina, may represent greater financial closure of that economy following its 2001–02 crisis than is captured in the extension of the Quinn-Toyoda index through 2004 adopted in the present study (see chapter 3).

Appendix 1B
Analogy to Gains from Trade

Finance from abroad is potentially an important source of finance for development. Openness to finance from abroad should thus provide opportunities for economic gain analogous to those from openness to trade. Figure 1B.1 shows the classic treatment of static gains from trade.

The tariff induces inefficient domestic output and curbs the total volume of cheaper imports; eliminating the tariff generates net welfare gains of areas C + E, after taking account of transfers of revenue from the government to consumers (area D) and transfer of producer surplus to consumers (area B).

It turns out that exactly the same diagram can be drawn to identify the static welfare gains from capital inflows (figure 1B.2). This time total capital stock is on the horizontal axis, rather than importable goods.[27] The rate of return on capital is on the vertical axis, rather than the product price. The demand curve for capital is downward sloping, analogous to the demand curve for importable goods. The world interest rate indicates the horizontal supply curve for capital from abroad, while the upward sloping capital supply curve indicates domestic supply. By making the economy more open to foreign capital and fully eliminating the difference between the domestic and world interest rate, the economy obtains a larger amount of imported capital.

The static welfare gain derives from the difference between the original domestic interest rate and the world interest rate multiplied by the increment in capital inflow. After netting out transfer from domestic suppliers of capital to domestic users, the net welfare gain is once again areas C + E. Moreover, just as in the case of free trade, for free capital entry there should be dynamic gains in addition to the static "little triangles." This is surely the case for direct investment, which is closely linked to improved technology. It should also be the case for the impact of competitive pressure on domestic monopoly in the financial sector.

---

27. It is fair to ask whether the trade diagram can really be applied in this manner considering that in the case of capital the horizontal axis shows a stock, whereas for trade it shows a flow. It turns out that the analogy works because in the case of trade the price on the vertical axis is a pure number, whereas in the capital diagram it is a number per unit of time (percent of capital stock per year). So in both cases the product of vertical and horizontal distances generates a flow (e.g., extra marginal product from capital per year, in the one case, and extra consumption of importables, in the other).

Figure 1B.1 Gains from trade

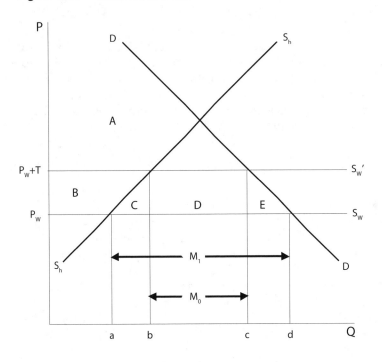

Figure 1B.2 Gains from capital mobility

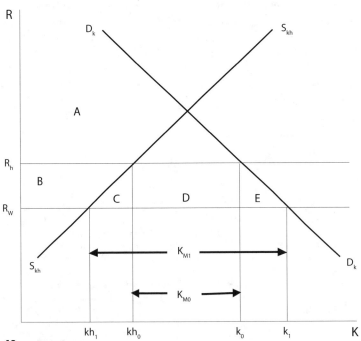

Appendix 1C
Tests for Compositional Differences in Growth Impact of Financial Openness

A recurrent theme in the financial globalization literature is that the composition of capital flows, and hence the degree of openness to each variety, matters for the growth impact. The typical view is that direct investment is the most clearly positive for growth, followed (or equaled) by portfolio equity. The compositional discussion typically casts more doubt on the benefits of debt flows, especially short-term debt.

The dataset developed for the synthesis estimates of chapter 3 can be used to test whether openness of debt markets contributes comparably to openness of direct and portfolio markets. A first test on this issue is to examine whether growth benefits are linear or quadratic in the Quinn-Toyoda measure of financial openness.[28] The argument is that toward the lower part of this financial-openness measure, it is mainly just direct investment that is open. Toward the upper part, credit flows are also open. Figure 1C.1 tends to bear out this interpretation for 24 developing countries over 1995–99. The figure shows the Quinn openness index on the horizontal axis. On the vertical axis it shows the ratio of external debt liabilities and assets to GDP minus the ratio of direct investment assets and liabilities to GDP, as a percent of GDP. The general upward slope in the scatter diagram suggests that the relative openness on debt flows to FDI flows does indeed rise as the overall Quinn openness index rises.

If openness to direct investment is positive for growth but openness to debt has negligible or even negative effects, then one should expect a negative coefficient on the squared term for a quadratic growth equation using the Quinn measure. Initially greater financial openness would be concentrated on direct investment, spurring growth, but subsequent extension of openness to credit would provide little additional growth or would reduce it from levels reached with FDI openness alone.

The tests here apply standard control variables and financial openness to explain annual per capita GDP growth. The control variables include the ratio of investment to GDP (I), the logarithm of per capita GDP (purchasing parity) at the beginning of the period ($\ln y_0$), average years of schooling (E), population growth (n), and dummy variables for Africa and for developing countries. The data are for nonoverlapping five-year panels for 24 developing and 21 industrial countries for 1974–2004, providing a total of 360 observations. The dependent variable, growth, is measured for the five-year period beginning three years subsequent to the period for

---

28. The Quinn-Toyoda (2008) measure is the same as the Quinn (1997) measure but converted from a scale of 0-4 to a scale of 0-100, and including a larger time span and country coverage. The short reference "Quinn" refers to the 2008 Quinn-Toyoda version.

Figure 1C.1 Debt external assets and liabilities minus direct investment assets and liabilities versus Quinn-Toyoda financial openness index, 1995–99

debt minus foreign direct investment (percent of GDP)

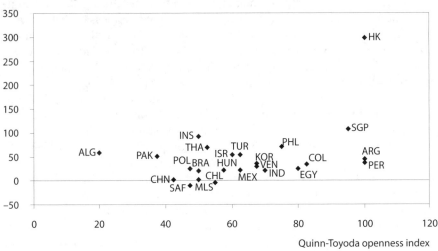

Quinn-Toyoda openness index

Country abbreviations: ALG = Algeria; ARG = Argentina; BRA = Brazil; CHL = Chile; CHN = China; COL = Colombia; EGY = Egypt; HK = Hong Kong; HUN = Hungary; IND = India; INS = Indonesia; ISR = Israel; KOR = Korea; MEX = Mexico; MLS = Malaysia; PAK = Pakistan; PER = Peru; PHL = Philippines; POL = Poland; SAF = South Africa; SGP = Singapore; THA = Thailand; TUR = Turkey; VEN = Venezuela

Source: Author's calculations.

the independent variables, as a means of addressing possible simultaneity problems. A first test applies only the linear term for the Quinn openness index. The results, with t-statistics in parentheses, are as follows:[29]

$$g = 17.18 + 0.146\ I - 2.16 \ln y_0 + 0.128E - 0.370\ n + 0.872\ D_{Af} \quad (1C.1)$$
$$(8.56) \quad (9.00) \quad (-8.49) \quad (1.91) \quad (-2.03) \quad (1.87)$$

$$-0.145\ D_d + 0.0216\ Q;\ R^2\ \text{adj.} = 0.32$$
$$(-0.38) \quad (3.86).$$

This equation places the impact of complete openness versus complete closure at 2.16 percent annual growth impact.[30] The result is highly

---

29. The constant-shift terms for each of the panel periods are omitted.

30. The dependent variable is percentage points of annual growth, and the Quinn variable is on a scale of 0 to 100.

significant. The test thus replicates the Quinn (1997) and Quinn-Toyoda (2008) results, which show comparable growth impacts (see table 2.1).[31]

When a quadratic formulation of the openness variable is applied, the results are as follows:[32]

$$g = 17.08 + 0.146\ I - 2.168\ \ln y_0 + 0.133\ E - 0.372\ n + 0.912\ D_{Af} \qquad (1C.2)$$
$$(8.40)\quad (8.99)\quad (-8.48)\qquad\quad (1.94)\quad (-2.04)\quad (1.89)$$

$$-0.136\ D_d + 0.027\ Q - 0.0050\ Q^2;\ R^2\ \text{adj.} = 0.32$$
$$(-0.35)\qquad (1.55)\qquad (-0.35).$$

In the quadratic specification, the significance of Quinn openness falls below the usual threshold (from the highly significant .01 percent level in equation 1C.1 to a 12.2 percent level in the equation 1C.2). The quadratic term turns out to be highly insignificant (t-statistic of –0.35). The test does not confirm the view that the growth impact of debt openness is significantly negative whereas that of direct investment is positive. Nor does it confirm the view that the growth impact of debt openness is significantly smaller than the growth impact of direct investment.

A more direct test is to examine the influence of debt capital on growth and to focus on developing countries (the economies that are the subject of concern about possible negative effects from debt finance). When the same structure equation as that used in equation 1C.1 is applied to 24 developing economies in five-year panels, but financial openness is measured by the ratio of total external debt liabilities and assets to GDP (percent), the result for 162 observations is as follows:

$$g = 20.04 + 0.181\ I - 2.55\ \ln y_0 + 0.189\ E - 0.314\ n + 1.24\ D_{Af} + 0.00303\ DO$$
$$(7.17)\quad (7.87)\quad (-6.62)\qquad (1.39)\quad (-1.00)\quad (2.03)\qquad (2.08).$$
$$(1C.3)$$

Here, the final term DO is "debt openness" and equals external debt liabilities plus claims as a percent of GDP. The growth coefficient is positive and statistically significant. The size of the coefficient means that if debt liabilities and assets rise by 10 percent of GDP, for example, annual growth increases by 0.03 percent.

It turns out, however, that this positive significant relationship is being driven by the outlier Hong Kong, which has an average ratio of debt

---

31. Quinn (1997) yields 1.6 percent extra annual growth; Quinn-Toyoda (2008) yields 2.9 percent.

32. The quadratic variable is the Quinn variable squared, divided by 100, so it also ranges from 0 to 100.

assets and liabilities to GDP of 734 percent for 1979–2004 (the period with data available), in contrast to the developing-country average of 87 percent (1970–2004 for most). This is a classic case in which the de facto measure conveys a disproportionate sense of the extent of openness of a particular economy in comparison with its peers. When Hong Kong is omitted, and symmetrically the low-end outliers India and China are omitted (with external debt asset plus liability ratios at only 21 and 23 percent of GDP, respectively), the growth coefficient on *DO* turns insignificant.[33]

In short, additional tests using the data developed for this study do not provide statistically significant support to the proposition that debt capital openness is bad for growth. The tests are consistent with the notion that debt capital growth effects may be less powerful than those of direct investment and portfolio equity. The broader empirical literature remains much less developed on this issue, however, than on the effects of overall openness, FDI openness, and portfolio equity openness.

---

33. Coefficient of –0.0041, *t*-statistic of –1.16. Note that the next highest ratio after Hong Kong is 174 percent for Singapore, making it considerably less of an outlier.

2

A Critical Survey of Literature

Over the past several years a large empirical literature has emerged on the impact of financial globalization on economic growth. This survey examines some 80 studies on this issue. Most of them were issued after 1997. This intense research activity almost certainly reflects a reexamination of the advisability of open capital markets after the outbreak of the East Asian financial crisis in 1997–98 and its spread to Russia, Turkey, and some Latin American economies.

Economic first principles suggest that, like open international markets for goods, open capital markets should benefit economic welfare. Static comparative advantage and dynamic gains from open trade have a natural counterpart in open capital markets through the reallocation of capital from where it is abundant to where it is scarce, spillovers of technology and skills, and the bolstering of domestic financial systems. Yet the financial crises of the late 1990s revived the specter of capital mobility as a dangerous influence, a concern sufficiently dominant in past decades that not only was the postwar Bretton Woods system premised on generally closed capital markets but also capital controls in Europe persisted as late as the 1970s. The global financial crisis of 2007–09 has further intensified doubts about the merits of open capital markets.

The IMF was on the verge of adopting amendments to its Articles of Agreement favoring capital mobility just at the most awkward time, as the East Asian crisis erupted. It is thus perhaps no coincidence that a substantial portion of the empirical research on this issue in recent years has taken place within the IMF itself.

The stylized policy wisdom on this issue circa 2007–08 can reasonably be summed up as "yes, but." Yes, financial globalization can be good for the economy; but there are preconditions and caveats. It is better to be open to direct investment and not necessarily a good idea to be open to short-term borrowing; there had better be sound domestic conditions of governance and financial development, or else opening could be risky; and so forth. The stylized fact about empirical evidence seems to be that it is "difficult to detect" a positive impact of financial globalization on growth, albeit easier to do so if the focus is on direct investment in particular.

This survey reevaluates these and other diagnoses of this large body of literature. Wherever possible, it attempts to translate empirical estimates into metrics that are comparable across studies, particularly the amount by which annual growth would rise as a consequence of a shift from complete closedness to complete openness. For this purpose, the study incorporates, in addition to other measures, a metric based on statistical "meta-analysis." The first and most extensive part of the survey concerns cross-country statistical tests. Within this broad grouping, individual sections address the following subcategories: growth effects of general capital-market openness; impact on domestic financial development; impact of direct investment; effects of opening portfolio equity to international investment; the relationship of financial integration to the incidence of financial crises; the role of institutions and the effect of openness in exerting discipline on macroeconomic policies; and the results of tests conducted at the sectoral or even plant level rather than the national level.

The survey then turns to the smaller set of studies that apply calibrated parameters in a theoretical framework to examine the influence of financial integration. The first category in this group involves calculations of the gains from international capital reallocation in a neoclassical framework in which capital flows toward economies where it is scarcer and has a higher return. The second category concerns potential gains from risk sharing and consumption smoothing. Studies with cross-country empirical evidence on consumption volatility are considered in this section as well. The subsequent section offers a brief survey of the surveys, of which by now there are several. The conclusion synthesizes the principal findings of this survey.

Cross-Country Growth Regressions

Much of the empirical literature on financial globalization involves the use of cross-country statistical tests that examine whether financial openness boosts growth. Most of these studies can be seen as decidedly inductive as opposed to deductive, in that they do not necessarily set forth a formal theoretical framework that would clarify just how long the higher growth should persist, and how much if any faster that growth should be, nor correspondingly translate any such acceleration into long-term welfare gains. Instead, the approach is typically to mount a standard cross-country growth regression containing generally accepted control variables and then to augment the equation with some financial-openness variable. The control variables often include initial per capita income, with an expected negative coefficient to capture "convergence," the rate of investment, a measure of macroeconomic stability (such as inflation or the black-market premium on the exchange rate), and/or a measure of trade openness.

The cross-country growth regression school divides into several subcategories. The most general simply examines overall capital-market openness. A separate category focuses on the relationship of growth to, and the influence of financial globalization on, domestic financial development. Another major category of studies is that concerning direct investment, often presumed to be the preferred form of capital inflow for developmental purposes. A parallel category that has been less examined is the impact of equity market liberalization. Still another set of studies examines the role of capital-market openness in exacerbating (or moderating) financial crises.

Most of the estimates either find a positive influence of financial openness on growth or fail to reject the "null hypothesis" that there is no such influence. Few if any studies conclude that financial openness is a recipe for reducing growth. Among the categories, the direct investment studies tend more systematically to find positive growth effects. Another pattern is that regression equations that incorporate terms for interaction between financial openness and some variable for domestic development, such as per capita income, domestic financial development, or availability of skilled labor, tend to identify thresholds. Below these thresholds financial openness tends to reduce growth and above them, increase growth. But the negative effects below the thresholds may be artifacts of the particular specification of the interaction terms. Nonetheless, such thresholds tend to be cited as support for sequencing (e.g., trade openness before financial).

A classic question in econometric tests turns out to be important in interpreting many of the cross-country tests for impact of capital-market openness: What is the meaning of a statistically insignificant result? Authors frequently cite such results as proof that capital-market openness has no influence. However, in econometric tests the absence of a statistically significant result proves nothing. A statistically significant coefficient, in contrast, rejects the "null hypothesis" that the variable in question has zero influence on the dependent variable. It is striking that in a large field of statistical tests, almost none show a statistically significant *negative* effect of capital-market openness on growth, yet such a finding would be required to support the view that financial globalization is counterproductive to growth. Or, as natural scientists sometimes put it, "the absence of evidence is not evidence of absence." Because the theoretical prior is that there should be growth benefits from capital-market openness, it would seem methodologically appropriate to be skeptical about drawing policy implications from econometric tests that fail to find a statistically significant impact of capital-market openness on growth.

As discussed in appendix 2A, there is a formal statistics literature on "meta-analysis" that concludes that the proper way to average alternative econometric estimates is to weight by the inverse of the variance of the parameter estimate. In this procedure estimates are included even if their t-statistic is below the conventional 5 percent threshold for significance. The appendix considers four possible ways of weighting: simple average of significant estimates; weighting by t-statistic; simple average imputing nonsignificant estimates at zero; and inverse-variance (meta-statistical) weighting. The summary results in this chapter take into account these alternative approaches.

Capital-Market Openness

In an early study, Alesina, Grilli, and Milesi-Ferretti (1993) were primarily interested in explaining the presence of capital controls. However, they also included a statistical test for growth impact, and "found no effects of capital controls on growth: we reject rather strongly the hypothesis that capital controls reduce growth" (p. ii).[1] Their tests were for 20 Organization for Economic Cooperation and Development (OECD) (industrial) economies for the period 1950–89. In this period the dominant pattern was one of capital controls, which the authors found were typically maintained to keep domestic interest rates artificially low, permit higher seigniorage and inflation, and facilitate managed exchange rates. As the measure of capital controls, the authors used the binary variable in the IMF's *Annual Report on Exchange Arrangements and Exchange Restrictions* (AREAER).[2] They used pooled time-series and cross-country data (about 550 observations) to apply ordinary least-squares (OLS) regressions. Their independent variables were rather unusual and heavily focused on political conditions.[3] Their equation for the growth of real per capita GDP as a function of 1950 per capita income, a dummy variable for a fixed or managed exchange rate versus a floating rate, three political variables, and the capital controls

---

1. This statement, however, is inconsistent with their failure to find a significant result. They could not reject the null hypothesis of no influence, but that is not the same thing as "rejecting" the alternative hypothesis that the coefficient is nonzero. See appendix 2A.

2. Line E.2 of the AREAER in the years prior to 1997 showed either the presence or absence of "restrictions on payments for capital transactions." Beginning in 1997 the report instead showed the presence or absence of 12 individually distinguished types of controls on capital transactions, with no indication of relative importance.

3. Political variables included a dummy variable for majority-party versus coalition government, a constant for each country indicating the average number of years in power of the executive during 1950–90, and another country-specific constant for the average number of years between "significant" government changes.

dummy variable found a near-zero and statistically insignificant coefficient on capital controls. Nonetheless, the tests were relatively rudimentary compared with most in the subsequent literature.

In a follow-up study, Grilli and Milesi-Ferretti (1995) once again applied the AREAER measure of capital restrictions, this time extending the analysis to include a panel of 61 developed and developing countries using five-year period observations for 1961–89. This study found a statistically significant impact of both capital controls and multiple exchange rate regimes in boosting inflation, confirming an expected adverse impact. However, it found a positive coefficient of capital controls on growth. Nonetheless, the coefficient was not quite significant. In a less aggressive verdict than in the 1994 paper on OECD economies, the authors concluded merely that "we do not find any robust correlation between our measures of controls and the rate of growth...." (p. 1).

One of the earliest studies to find a significant positive effect of general capital-market openness on growth was that by Quinn (1997). Quinn also used the AREAER data but developed his own coding of the intensity of restrictions. His capital payments openness measure was not binary, but instead ascended from 0 (capital payments approval rare and surrender of receipts required) to 0.5 (approval sometimes granted), 1 (approval frequently granted, or approval not required but receipts heavily taxed), 1.5 (approval not required, receipts taxed), and a high score of 2.0 (approval not required, receipts not taxed). He used corresponding measures for capital receipts; and for current account payments for imports, he used payment for invisibles, receipts for exports, and receipts for invisibles. In addition he had a similar scale for presence or absence of country commitment to an international agreement.[4] With a total of seven categories, the maximum overall score for "financial openness" was 14. Surprisingly, the highest regional score in 1960 was for Latin America (11), but this fell substantially by the 1970s (to about 8) and further by the late 1980s (to about 6) before partially recovering (to 9 by 1990).[5] In contrast, for the OECD countries the median overall score was only 7 in 1960 but rose to about 10 by 1975 and 13 by 1990. The score also rose persistently for East Asia (from 5 in 1960 to about 8 in 1975 and 10 in 1990). Broadly similar patterns applied to the capital transactions subcomponents.

Quinn uses the Levine and Renelt (1992) cross-country growth model as his framework and augments the model with his capital openness variable. With per capita real GDP growth from 1960 to 1989 as the dependent

4. For example, the United States scored 1.0 because of its acceptance of obligations of IMF Article VIII commitments; Sweden scored 1.5 because it accepted the same obligations and also belonged to the European Free Trade Association.

5. The Latin American pattern makes sense in view of the region's intensified import substitution in the 1970s and debt crisis in the 1980s, followed by return to the capital markets by the 1990s.

variable, the four control variables in this setup are initial GDP per capita (negative coefficient to account for convergence); share of investment in GDP; population growth rate; and secondary school enrollment rate in 1960. As usual, the strongest statistical significance among the control variables is found for initial per capita income and for investment. It should be noted that direct inclusion of the investment variable will tend to understate the contribution of capital liberalization, because a key mechanism through which this liberalization influences growth is by boosting investment (so the investment variable coefficient may unduly take credit for what is attributable to financial liberalization).

For the panel of about 60 countries, Quinn finds statistically significant positive coefficients ranging from 0.3 to 0.47 for the impact of the change in his capital openness measure on per capita growth. With two components (payments and receipts) ranging from 0 to 2 each, the maximum for the capital openness variable is 4. So a move from complete closure to complete openness would have boosted growth by about 1.6 percent annually (4 x 0.4). For Latin America, the median capital openness measure fell by 0.83, out of a total possible change of ±4. Applying the estimated coefficient of about 0.4, this result means that partial closure of capital markets in Latin America from 1959 to 1988 cut the average annual per capita growth rate by about 0.33 percentage point. This in turn suggests that after three decades, per capita real income levels were about 10 percent lower as a consequence of capital-market closedness than they would have been if there had been no change in capital-market openness. In contrast, the median change in the capital openness measure for industrial countries was +0.83, so the estimates imply that, typically, industrial-country income levels were 10 percent higher at the end of the period than they would have been without capital-market opening. Quinn also examines the relationship of capital opening to corporate taxation (finding no relationship) and income inequality (finding a positive relationship).

A much-cited short essay written by Rodrik (1998) at the height of the East Asian financial crisis in opposition to the contemporary move to make "the International Monetary Fund's next major mission the liberalization of capital account" (p. 56) included some empirical estimates in his case against doing so. He used the AREAER binary measure for capital account restrictions for almost 100 developing and industrial countries for 1975–89. With one observation per country for the entire period, the capital openness variable was the fraction of years in which the capital account was open for the country in question. After controlling for initial per capita GDP, initial secondary-school enrollment, an index of quality of governmental institutions, and regional dummies, he found a small positive but statistically insignificant coefficient for openness in explaining growth of GDP per capita. On this basis, he argued that there was no evidence that capital controls were costly to long-term economic perfor-

mance. However, Rodrik did not report any parameter estimates, so the study cannot be included in a meta-analysis.

Kraay (1998) applied cross-section regression as well as event analysis to examine the impact of financial openness on economic growth, domestic investment, and inflation. He used three alternative measures of openness: the AREAER data, the intensity-tailored version of the AREAER data developed by Quinn (1997), and actual capital inflows and outflows as a percent of GDP.[6] This approach began to address the difference between de jure and de facto measures of financial openness, with the IMF-based regulatory data representing de jure and observed levels of capital flows de facto evidence. Kraay (1998, 11) concludes that there is "very little evidence that growth or investment are higher in more financially open economies," on grounds that only one of his three measures yields a positive and statistically significant coefficient.[7] In the significant result, for the period 1985–97, the coefficient of the growth rate on the actual volume measure of openness is 0.07 for the full sample and 0.11 for non-OECD countries. The average for the top decile of the volume measures is capital flows amounting to 0.2 of GDP, and for the bottom decile, zero. So a move from lowest to highest actual openness on this measure would contribute an increase in average annual growth of 2.2 percent for non-OECD countries and 1.4 percent for all countries on average.[8] Such an impact would be extremely large. Kraay also found some evidence that financially open economies receive relatively more short-term bank credit and nondirect investment flows, but little evidence that volatility of total flows is greater in financially open economies. Further tests incorporating interaction of financial openness with policies and institutions did not lead to findings of greater effects of financial liberalization.

Bosworth and Collins (1999) used instrumental variable techniques for a panel of 58 developing countries for the period 1978 to 1995 to examine the impact of capital inflows on investment and saving. They found that 50 percent of capital inflows goes to increased investment. Including increased consumption, 69 percent goes to resource transfers; the other 31 percent goes to reserve accumulation and the financing of capital out-

---

6. Kraay used data provided by Quinn but noted that the estimates were available only for three benchmark years (1958, 1973, and 1988). His actual flows data were for direct investment, portfolio investment, and other investment items in the financial account of the balance of payments. For the event analysis, he defined opening events as episodes of five years of capital controls followed by five years of no controls.

7. Kraay does not report parameter estimates for the two AREAER-based tests, noting only that they are insignificant. He thus implicitly follows what is questioned in the meta-analysis literature as "vote counting." See appendix 2A.

8. Kraay's dependent variable, GDP growth per capita, is in pure numbers, not percentage points (personal communication, January 29, 2008).

flows. Among capital flow categories, direct investment has the strongest impact on investment, at $1 of increased investment for $1 of inflow. Portfolio investment has the smallest, least significant impact on investment, and loans are intermediate. They noted that the bulk of capital flows in the 1990s had gone to industrial countries and that for developing countries the rebound had merely returned flows to about the same levels relative to GDP that had already been reached in the 1970s. Moreover, flows were concentrated in a few countries, leading emerging-market economies in Latin America and Asia. Because of the particularly strong influence of direct investment on domestic investment, the authors concluded that benefits of open capital markets definitely warranted the risks for direct investment but suggested that for other types of capital flows it could be better to sequence opening later.

Bailliu (2000) obtained statistical results supporting the proposition that private capital flows promote growth, so long as the domestic banking sector is sufficiently developed. The study is an example of a recurrent theme in the literature: that the influence of capital-market openness is contingent, in this case on banking development. She uses tests for 40 developing countries in five-year panels from 1975 to 1990 using generalized method of moments (GMM) estimation. She includes the usual control variables in explaining growth per capita.[9] In this framework she finds the following statistically significant coefficients for the variables of direct interest:

$$-0.27\ F + 0.056\ B + 0.46\ [FB], \tag{2.1}$$

where F is the ratio of net capital flows to GDP; B is the ratio of domestic assets held by commercial banks to total domestic assets held by commercial banks and the central bank (a measure of banking-sector development suggested by King and Levine 1993); and FB is the product of the two measures. Taking the derivative shows that the impact of increased capital inflows (F) on growth is positive if the domestic banking development variable (B) is 0.58 or higher. In practice, most developing countries easily exceed this threshold, so the Bailliu (2000) results imply generally favorable growth effects from capital inflows.[10] More specifically, with B typically in the range of about 0.8, and substantial capital inflows placing

9. Following, for example, Barro, Mankiw, and Sala-i-Martin (1995): initial per capita income, average years of schooling, investment as a share of GDP, government consumption as a share of GDP (to account for resource waste, apparently), and exports plus imports relative to GDP.

10. Using the King and Levine (1993, 721) definition, $B = b/(a + b)$, where a is the sum of lines 12a through 12f in the IMF's *International Financial Statistics*, and b is the sum of lines 22a through 22f. In 2006, for example, this ratio was 0.85 for Brazil, 0.87 for Bangladesh, and 0.75 for Sudan.

F at, say, 0.04 (current account deficit of 4 percent of GDP), boosting capital inflows by 1 percent of GDP would raise the growth rate by 0.1 percent. As noted below, Edison et al. (2002, 30) report the standard deviation of capital flows at 5 percent of GDP, so a rise in capital-market openness by one standard deviation would boost growth by 0.5 percent annually for countries with a typical level of banking development. These examples suggest the coefficient may be on the low side, which in turn may reflect the fact that the control variables already include investment as a share of GDP, whereas a key role of foreign capital is precisely to boost investment. The coefficient on investment may thus be capturing impact that instead should be attributed to capital inflow.

Reisen and Soto (2001) examine differential growth effects across the major alternative forms of capital inflows: FDI, portfolio equity, bonds, long-term bank credits, and short-term bank credits. They use actual data on capital flows rather than regulatory indicators of capital account openness. They summarize the traditional economic cases for and against open capital accounts as follows: foreign capital adds to domestic investment, stimulates efficiency, and smoothes consumption, on the favorable side, but can magnify existing domestic distortions and cause bankruptcies and output losses because of abrupt reversibility, on the unfavorable side. They judge that FDI can make a strong contribution on all three of the favorable influences, is not subject to abrupt reversibility, and is only weakly subject to magnifying distortions now that protection levels are generally much lower than in the early postwar period. At the opposite extreme, short-term bank lending can magnify financial-sector distortions and is highly reversible.

The authors use GMM techniques to address issues of endogeneity. They include national saving, trade openness, government consumption, and terms of trade as control variables. Their estimates for 44 middle-income countries for the period 1986–97 find statistically significant (albeit economically modest) positive effects of FDI and portfolio equity flows on per capita GNP growth. The coefficient on FDI is 0.1, indicating, for example, that it would require a rise of direct investment inflows of 10 percent of GDP to boost the short-term per capita growth rate by 1 percent. The corresponding rise in the level of long-term, steady-state income level would be by 3 percent by their method. They note that this impact is somewhat lower than in earlier studies (reviewed below). The largest coefficient is for portfolio equity inflows (0.5), which they note reduce capital costs for domestic firms and ease allocation from low- to high-growth industries. The strong growth impact of portfolio equity in these capital flow estimates resonates with the findings of studies that examine growth response to the opening of the equity market, as discussed below. Bond flows turn out not to be significant. Both long- and short-term bank credits have a threshold effect, with negative effects unless domestic banks are strongly capitalized.[11] Their broad conclusion is that "equity investment is to be preferred over debt instruments...," especially considering that "FDI flows raise relatively little macroeconomic policy concerns as their reversibility is low" (Reisen and Soto 2001, 12). The broader implication is that the study supports that strand of the empirical literature that finds a significant positive effect of capital flows on growth.

Edwards (2001) uses the Quinn (1997) elaboration of the IMF's capital-market openness data to examine whether openness affects GDP growth and growth TFP. He argues persuasively that the unadjusted, binary IMF (AREAER) data are not meaningful, because they treat countries as totally open or closed and do not capture variation in intensity of restrictions. He cites Brazil, Chile, and Mexico in the early 1990s as examples: The three show identical binary measures but gradations in openness on the Quinn variable. Edwards argues that Mexico was much more open to capital than Chile, which in turn was more open than Brazil. Edwards conducts regressions for about 20 industrial and 40 developing countries, explaining growth (or TFP growth) in the 1980s with a set of control variables and either the level of the Quinn capital openness variable or its change from 1973 to 1987. His control variables have the correct signs. They include the ratio of investment to GDP, which arguably biases the tests toward finding a small capital openness impact considering that openness affects growth by boosting the investment rate (as well as by raising efficiency).

Edwards finds positive and significant coefficients of capital openness on both growth and the increase in TFP. Across alternative formulations, the average coefficient for the level of openness is 0.0055, and for change in openness, 0.0039. Considering that openness varies from 0 to 4, these estimates mean that a completely capital-open economy grew 2.2 percent per annum faster than a completely closed one, and an economy that shifted from complete closedness to complete openness grew 1.6 percent per annum faster than it would otherwise have done. However, Edwards finds that there is a relatively high income threshold for positive effects. After interacting openness with the logarithm of per capita income in 1980, he finds that only five higher-income developing countries out of the total of 40 had a positive rather than negative influence from openness.[12]

Edison et al. (2002) seek to extend tests for growth effects of international financial integration (which they designate IFI) by adding a new measure of openness, adding a new method to deal with endogeneity, and more fully exploring interaction with institutional and other variables. Their broad result is an agnostic one: "We interpret the econometric re-

---

11. The coefficients are such that domestic bank capital needs to exceed 21 percent of assets for long-term claims and 14 percent for short-term claims; both levels are substantially above the traditional 8 percent Basel I requirements.

12. Note, however, that Edwards weights observations by per capita income, which would seem a potential source of bias toward industrial-country patterns.

sults as not strongly rejecting the null hypothesis of no statistical relationship between IFI and economic growth" (p. 21). However, they do find a relatively strong impact of arguably the most relevant measure of IFI in what seem to be the two more reliable of their three methods.

The new measure of openness is the ratio of stock of FDI and portfolio foreign capital to GDP, either just for liabilities (cumulative inflows) or for the sum of both liabilities and assets (two-way openness).[13] These are called "stock of capital inflows" and "stock of capital flows," respectively. The statistical tests are cross-section with one observation for each of 57 countries for 1980–2000, in the case of OLS and instrumental variables tests, and four observations of five-year averages for each of 40 countries in panel GMM estimates. All of the models test for the influence of IFI on growth, while controlling for familiar exogenous variables: initial level of per capita income (convergence), initial level of schooling, government fiscal balance, and inflation. The alternative IFI measures are the AREAER binary variable, stock of capital flows, stock of capital inflows, and flow of capital or inflows of capital for the corresponding ratios of flows to GDP. The IMF restrictions measure and the flow variables are familiar from previous studies (e.g., Kraay 1998).

All of the tests using instrumental variables are insignificant. This should not be particularly surprising. The instruments used are historical legal systems and distance from the equator, which seem likely to introduce far more noise than they remove in the pursuit of controlling for endogeneity. The only significant results are for the flow of capital and inflow of capital in the OLS tests, and the flow of capital in the panel tests. These coefficients turn out to be relatively strong. Significance of the capital flow variables in contrast to insignificance of the AREAER measure is the same finding obtained by Kraay (1998). For the three significant results, an increase in the IFI measure by one standard deviation generates an increase in the annual per capita growth rate by about 0.5 percent.[14] So the statistically significant results of the study imply that this much liberalization would typically have boosted per capita income by about 10 percent over the two decades in question, an impressive amount.

Arteta, Eichengreen, and Wyplosz (2003) elaborate on the tests of Edwards (2001) and find important nuances. Like Edwards, they use both the level and the change in the Quinn measure of openness and find it superior to the IMF's binary restrictions measure. They do not use the Edwards approach of weighting regressions by per capita income and

---

13. The authors take advantage of the new dataset on international financial assets and liabilities developed by Lane and Milesi-Ferretti (2001).

14. The coefficient is about 0.1 for capital flows (OLS and panel) and about 0.2 for capital inflows (OLS). The dependent variable, per capita growth, is in pure numbers (not percent) and averages 0.02. The standard deviation of the capital flows variable is 0.05, and of capital inflows, 0.02.

express concern that to do so will bias results toward a favorable impact of financial openness because of heavy weight on rich countries with well-developed institutions. They apply a pooled test for three subperiods (1973–81, 1982–87, and 1988–92) and find strong evidence of a positive association of capital account liberalization and growth. In contrast, they reject the Edwards finding that openness has a negative effect on growth below a threshold income level but a positive effect at higher incomes. In further tests interacting capital account openness with other variables, they find that the black-market premium component of the Sachs-Warner trade openness variable plays the most important interactive role. The estimates indicate that capital account openness has favorable effects "only when macroeconomic imbalances…have first been eliminated" (Arteta, Eichengreen, and Wyplosz 2003, 25). They interpret the result as evidence that sequencing of reforms influences the effects of capital account liberalization.

In their pooled estimate they find a coefficient of 0.49 for the impact of Quinn openness on growth, significant at the 5 percent level. This is virtually the same coefficient found by Edwards.[15] So again the finding implies that a shift from complete closedness to complete openness (from 0 to 4 on the measure) would boost average annual growth by a remarkable 2 percentage points. This gain is no longer limited to the upper-middle-income countries, because Edwards' income threshold is not confirmed. Specifying the black-market variable as 100 percent minus the percent by which the black-market exchange rate exceeds the official rate (with the variable's minimum constrained to zero), they obtain a linear coefficient of –0.96 on openness and an interacted coefficient of 1.26 (significant at the 5 percent level). A country with no black-market premium will thus have a combined coefficient of 0.30 on Quinn openness. A shift from complete closedness to complete openness will boost annual growth by 1.2 percentage points per year, again a large impact. But the impact of capital account openness turns negative if the black-market premium rises above 24 percent.

Kaminsky and Schmukler (2003) examine the impact of financial openness on the volatility of domestic stock markets. Although their study does not directly examine growth effects, their results are suggestive that long-run growth effects of financial openness are likely to be positive. They find that financial opening boosts stock market volatility moderately in the short run but reduces it substantially in the long run. The authors use detailed country-specific studies and official reports to construct their own dataset on financial liberalization in 28 industrial and emerging-market economies for the period 1973–99. They consider three financial categories: capital account, stock market, and domestic financial sector. They

---

15. The decimal point is moved because of the use of percentages for growth rather than pure fractional rates.

define three degrees of intensity of openness: closed, partially open, and fully open, based on openness in the three categories.[16] Key criteria for full capital-market liberalization include near-automatic authority for banks and corporations to borrow abroad, reserve requirements against foreign borrowing of no more than 10 percent, minimum maturity no longer than two years, no special exchange rates, and no restrictions on capital out-flows. The resulting descriptions can differ sharply from the frequently used IMF binary measure.[17]

Defining fully open as an index of 1 and fully repressed as 3, they find that industrial countries showed a persistent opening (from an average of 2.5 in 1973–80 to 2 in 1981–85, followed by a steady decline in the controls index to a plateau of 1 by 1992 and after). In contrast, the average for emerging-market economies began at 2.9 in 1973, eased to 2.5 by 1982, retreated to 2.75 in 1983–86 before returning to 2.5 in 1987–89, and thereafter eased to 1.5 by 1992 and 1.2 by 1998 (p. 11). Notably, the emerging-market sample excludes China and India, both of which would presumably show far more closedness. Among the sectors, there is a clear pattern of earlier opening of the stock market among the mature economies. In the emerging-market economies, there is joint liberalization of the stock markets and domestic financial sectors in the late 1980s, followed by capital account opening in the 1990s.

Defining the short run as the first four years and the long run thereafter, the authors find that following liberalization the amplitude of stock market booms and crashes amplifies (20 percent higher and 15 percent lower, respectively), but in the long run the amplitude of swings declines to about 60 percent below preliberalization magnitudes. The impact is greater in emerging markets, with the size of booms and crashes increasing about 35 percent in the short run but declining by 30 percent (booms) to 90 percent (crashes) in the long run. This pattern holds even after controlling for international and domestic cyclical conditions. The authors also find that crashes tend to be larger in emerging markets if the capital account opens before the stock market. They find further that an index of law and order tends to show that partial liberalization spurs institutional reform rather than the reverse. Kaminsky and Schmukler (2003, 37) conclude by emphasizing that "stock market booms and busts have not intensified in the long run after financial liberalization [but instead] become less pronounced."

Fratzscher and Bussiere (2004) conduct tests for 45 industrial and emerging-market economies for the period 1980–2002. They note that

---

16. For example, a country is "fully open" if at least two sectors are fully liberalized and the third is partially liberalized.

17. For example, the authors designate Brazil as "fully open" in 1991–93 and again for 1995 and after. In contrast, the AREAER reports Brazil's capital account as closed in these periods.

many of the emerging-market economies opened up their capital accounts between 1985 and 1995, whereas most of the OECD countries liberalized in the 1960s and 1970s. They use both de jure and de facto measures of openness. For the de jure measure, they use the dataset on financial liberalization developed by Kaminsky and Schmukler (2003), augmented by comparable information for Eastern European countries drawn from the European Bank for Reconstruction and Development's annual transition reports. For de facto openness, they use several alternative capital flow and capital stock variables. They use the International Country Risk Guide database for institutional variables such as quality of bureaucracy, corruption, and law and order.

Their tests for explaining real per capita growth use panel data for five subperiods between 1980 and 2002. An openness dummy variable takes the value of 1 if the capital account was open during most of the subperiod and zero if not. Control variables include the logarithm of real per capita income at the beginning of the period, the investment-to-GDP ratio, population growth rate, and government expenditure as a share of GDP. Their method is GMM estimation. Using the de jure measure, they find that when a dummy variable is included for financial crisis (based on the presence of a large currency devaluation), there is a strong and significant positive coefficient for the impact of financial openness on growth. Openness boosts per capita income growth by 1.6 percentage points annually. Presence of a financial crisis reduces per capita growth by 7.5 percentage points (p. 19; or by 6 percent preliberalization versus 8 percent postliberalization; p. 21). The control variables all have the correct sign and are statistically significant. In tests that separate the first five years subsequent to liberalization from later periods, they find an even stronger growth impact in the first period (2.2 percentage point boost) but a weaker and not statistically significant coefficient thereafter (0.8 percentage point). In contrast, their various de facto measures of openness are not statistically significant. Despite the paper's subtitle (which is a reversal of the Kaminsky-Schmukler subtitle), the authors do not find a statistically significant reduction in growth in the long term, and hence the meaningful impact of liberalization is the strongly positive short-term impact. At about 2 percentage points for five years, this result indicates that moving to financial openness boosts per capita income by about 10 percentage points.

Tornell, Westermann, and Martinez (2004) explore the link between financial openness, crises, and growth.[18] They argue that the studies that have not found a positive growth impact have used the wrong indicator of openness (de jure rather than de facto) and have erroneously included many low-income countries that do not meet the conditions for minimal

---

18. A parallel paper, Ranciere, Tornell, and Westermann (2005), appears to have predated this study (being cited in its references but not vice versa) and to have been incorporated into it, even though the dating is later.

financial market functioning. They find that financial liberalization does boost growth. Although it also increases the incidence of crises, the growth gains from financial openness exceed the losses from associated crises.

The authors argue that the tradable sector enjoys finance from FDI. It is the nontradable sector that depends on credit. Because of poor contract enforceability in medium-enforcement countries, nontradable-sector firms are credit constrained. Financial openness makes it possible for them to borrow from abroad, which is risky. The financial opening leads to financial deepening and higher growth. But it also tends to produce crises, as the nontradable-sector firms take on currency mismatches. Credit growth distributions that are left-tail skewed ("bumpy") are good, because they reflect infrequent crises. They argue that those who recommend admitting FDI but restricting bank lending fail to recognize that the tradable sector cannot continue to grow on its own but instead needs inputs from the nontradable sector.

The authors conduct tests for 1980–99 for 52 countries, comprising 17 high-enforcement countries and 35 medium-enforcement countries. The screen for inclusion is stock market turnover of at least 1 percent of GDP. Their measure of financial liberalization is constructed as zero or one, with the opening set at the date when either there is a trend break in cumulative capital inflows or they exceed 10 percent of GDP. This de facto measure means that some African countries with financial markets that are totally open on a de jure basis but that have no access to international capital are not treated as open. Their trade openness variable is also dichotomous, based on a trend break in the ratio of exports plus imports to GDP, a level above 30 percent for this ratio. Their medium-enforcement countries show both measures rising from 25 percent openness in the early 1980s to 84 percent (trade) and 72 percent (financial) openness by 1995 and after, with the upswing larger and earlier (particularly in 1987–89) for trade than for finance (1990), supporting the stylized fact that trade openness preceded financial openness. All high-enforcement countries are open for the full period. They find that their financial liberalization dates broadly track those of Bekaert, Harvey, and Lundblad (2000) and Kaminsky and Schmukler (2003), and their trade opening dates track those of Sachs and Warner (1995). They first find as a stylized fact, and support with Granger causality tests, that trade liberalization has typically been followed by financial liberalization. They argue that open trade typically brings a need for access by exporters and importers to international financial markets.

Their regressions relate the growth rate per capita to the financial and trade liberalization variables, along with controls for initial income level, initial human capital, population growth, and life expectancy. They explicitly recognize it would be a mistake to control for investment, because they expect trade and financial liberalization to affect growth through higher investment. The openness indexes measure the share of years the country was liberalized. They use simple cross-country and panel tests, as well as overlapping time windows of 10-year averages. The number of observations thus ranges from 34 to 300. There is a large positive and strongly significant coefficient on the financial liberalization variable. Financial liberalization boosts average annual per capita growth by 2.5 percentage points per year in both a single cross-section test and the overlapping rolling decades test, and by 1.7 percentage points in the nonoverlapping panel test. When trade liberalization is included, the corresponding coefficient for trade opening is 1.6 percentage points, and the financial liberalization coefficient increases to 2.8 percentage points. They argue that their strong results contrast with "many papers that do not find a significant link [because those] use de jure liberalization indexes or de facto indexes that do not identify liberalization dates" (Tornell, Westermann, and Martinez 2004, 9).

After examining the influence of financial openness on crises (discussed later in this chapter in the section on crisis analyses), Tornell, Westermann, and Martinez (2004) then further examine the "mechanism" of its framework. The tradable sector has access to capital from FDI, but the nontradable sector is credit constrained. The result is a high ratio of tradable to nontradable output before liberalization, a decline with liberalization and rapid nontradable expansion, then a sharp increase when the crisis comes. Statistical tests support this sequence. The authors' central conclusion is that "…although several observers have claimed that financial liberalization is not good for growth because of the crises associated with it, this is the wrong lesson to draw. Our empirical analysis shows that, across countries with functioning financial markets, financial liberalization leads to faster average long-run growth, even though it also leads to occasional crises" (p. 31).

Bonfiglioli and Mendicino (2004) conduct tests using data for 90 countries in the period 1975–99 and apply separate indicators for capital account and equity-market liberalization. They find that "capital account liberalization has a positive effect on growth, once we control for banking crises.… [It] fosters financial development and mitigates the harmful effects of banking crises…[because it] allows firms to raise funds more easily on the international financial markets.… Equity market liberalization instead has a strong direct effect on growth and does not interact with banking crises" (pp. 3-4).

The authors use GMM estimation for a panel of nonoverlapping five-year periods. Their financial-openness measure is the average value over the five-year period of the binary AREAER variable (1 if restrictions are present, 0 if not). They also use the Bekaert et al. (2005) measure of equity-market openness. They include a variable for episodes of banking crises, compiled by Caprio and Klingebiel (2002), ranging from 2 for systemic banking crises to 1 for less severe losses and 0 for no crisis. They include the usual control variables (initial per capita income, secondary school attainment, population growth, government expenditure, and investment as a ratio of GDP). They also add indicators of financial development and institutional quality.

In their central result, the coefficient on the financial-openness dummy variable is 0.087 and the coefficient on banking crises is –0.041, both statistically significant. These results indicate a remarkably high growth impact of 8.7 percent per year for financial openness and about –8 percent per year in the presence of severe banking crises. The equations using the equity market indicator of openness instead have a coefficient of about 0.012 (again significant), indicating a boost of about 1.2 percent in annual per capita growth from equity-market openness. Additional tests show a strong influence of capital account openness on the ratio of private credit to GDP, an important finding in view of the widespread recognition that financial development in turn spurs growth.

Mody and Murshid (2005) examine both whether foreign capital inflows influence domestic investment and whether the extent to which they do so depends on the type of flow and the extent of financial integration (openness). Their data are for 60 developing countries in 1981–98. Half of their countries are in sub-Saharan Africa. They first estimate regressions explaining capital flows and then use these to construct an instrumental variable for capital flows as a determinant of domestic investment. Their measure of financial integration is based on the sum of four of the AREAER categories: the absence of restrictions on the capital account, current account payments, repatriation, and the absence of multiple exchange rates. The first-stage regressions seem to be dominated by lagged capital flows, but in addition there is a strong and significant positive interaction between the financial integration variable and the global aggregate of flows to developing countries for bank loans and portfolio flows. This finding suggests that countries with open financial markets tend to attract a larger share of international flows.

Their main tests then find that there is a strong impact of total long-term capital inflows on investment. One dollar of additional foreign capital boosts domestic investment by 94 cents, with strong statistical significance. When they distinguish among capital types, they find a stronger impact of FDI on domestic investment ($1 of extra FDI boosts domestic investment by 73 cents) than of loans (62 cents but not significant) or portfolio equity (59 cents but not significant). These results are similar to those of Bosworth and Collins (1999). The influence is stronger in sub-Saharan Africa than in East Asia and Latin America. The authors suggest that capital markets are more closed and constrained in sub-Saharan Africa, so additional external finance tends to go into investment, whereas in East Asia and Latin America it has often tended to go to the buildup of reserves or the financing of capital outflows.

Mody and Murshid (2005, 22) also suggest that the marginal impact of financial integration on the efficacy of foreign capital in spurring domestic investment is negative, but most of the coefficients underlying this judgment are insignificant. More fundamentally, it seems questionable to focus on this efficacy taking the inflows for granted rather than on the fact that the inflows are less likely to be present in the first place in the absence of financial integration. The central robust result of the study thus would seem to be a confirmation that capital inflows tend to boost domestic investment, and that FDI tends to do so more than loans and portfolio equity. A positive impact on investment implies a positive impact on growth. But the study's reliance on de jure financial openness, and treatment of capital inflows as somehow exogenous rather than themselves being a de facto index of financial openness (the approach often adopted in other studies), would seem to limit the implications of the results for the influence of financial openness.

Chanda (2005) examines the relationship between growth effects of capital controls and the degree of ethnic homogeneity in a country. His theoretical premise is that controls on capital outflows contribute to growth by boosting the amount of capital forced to remain in the country and hence available for infrastructure investment. This approach would seem to ignore the more important potential role of financial integration in attracting foreign capital. He argues that whereas homogeneous societies can effectively obtain growth gains from capital controls, heterogeneous ones cannot because disparate groups compete to appropriate government revenue and thereby siphon it off from productive investments. He applies two measures of capital controls, one the familiar AREAER variable and the other an internationally reported variable on ease of holding foreign bank accounts. His direct tests (with control variables) for about 100 countries in 1975–95 find no statistically significant influence on growth of either measure of capital controls. However, when he interacts the capital control variable with a variable for ethnic homogeneity, he obtains a significant negative effect on the linear term for capital controls but a significant positive coefficient on the capital controls variable multiplied by ethnic homogeneity. The coefficients are such that a complete move from openness to closedness under circumstances of complete ethnic homogeneity would boost the growth rate by 0.78 percent per year. However, actual heterogeneity is such that, instead, about two-thirds to three-fourths of non-OECD countries had negative effects of capital controls on growth. The study's premise of potentially favorable effects from trapping domestic capital seems sufficiently doubtful, however, that skepticism about the results would seem warranted.[19]

Prasad, Rajan, and Subramanian (2007a) present statistical tests showing paradoxically that larger current account deficits in developing coun-

---

19. Moreover, the interaction term may be suspect. With two variables varying from 0 to 1, if distribution is centered around 0.5 for each, the center of the distribution for their product will be 0.25, and the extreme value of 1 will represent a small tail of the distribution but will have a large influence on the coefficient estimated.

tries have been associated with slower rather than faster growth. They interpret their results as indicating that foreign capital has not contributed to growth. Whatever the merits of this diagnosis, it is by no means synonymous with a finding that financial openness reduces growth. As discussed in appendix 2E, their findings do not bear directly on the financial-openness literature and are potentially misleading even with respect to the narrow question of current account deficits and growth. It is shown in the appendix that the current account deficit as a percent of GDP is a poor proxy for financial openness. The most dramatic examples are those of Singapore and Hong Kong. Both are unambiguously highly open financially, but both have large and persistent current account surpluses, which place them at the extreme maximum of closedness using the Prasad-Rajan-Subramanian measure. The divergence between financial openness and the current account deficit should not be surprising from a mechanical sense, because several measures of financial openness are quite different from net capital inflows (all de jure measures and all gross as opposed to net de facto measures). More importantly, the divergence should not be surprising in economic terms. If some developing countries adopt mercantilist growth strategies, they will be using macroeconomic and exchange-intervention policies to achieve current account surpluses even if their financial markets are completely open. It is also shown in the appendix that if attention is restricted to the middle-income economies, thereby avoiding distortions associated with aid inflows to poor countries, on the one hand, and the somewhat unrepresentative cases of China and India, on the other, the conventional negative relationship between the current account balance and the growth rate reappears.

In a major set of statistical tests, IMF staff researchers have examined the impact of financial openness on growth using eight alternative de facto measures of openness and one de jure measure (IMF 2007a). Using panel regressions for 87 developing and industrial countries for the period 1975–2004, with a single full-period observation per country, they find a positive growth coefficient for all eight of the de facto variables, of which three are statistically significant at the 5 percent level or better and one is significant at the 10 percent level. In contrast, the de jure measure (based on the AREAER information) showed a negative but statistically insignificant influence. The authors concluded that "the results appear to be fragile" (p. 29). This important study serves as the basis for a close examination of the alternative approach of meta-analytical weighting of results by the inverse of the variance of the estimate, as discussed below and developed in appendix 2A. For the purposes of the present summary, however, it is useful to note that for the four tests with significant results, the findings implied that a shift from financial closedness to openness (defined at the 90th percentile of the de facto measure in question) contributed an increase of two-thirds of one percentage point to annual growth over the three decades considered.

Kose, Prasad, and Terrones (2008) examine the relationship between financial openness and TFP growth. As discussed in chapter 3, a synthesis of their de jure and de facto estimates can be interpreted as placing the contribution of complete financial openness at about a one-third of 1 percent increment to annual TFP growth.[20] However, as this measure refers to only one component of the financial openness influence and omits the traditional influence of gains from capital deepening, it is not directly comparable to the other studies considered in this section.

Finally, Quinn and Toyoda (2008) present updated estimates using the de jure capital account openness variable originally developed in Quinn (1997). They update their measure of openness to cover a 50-year period (1950–99) for 94 countries. Once again they find a strong positive impact of de jure openness on growth, with the difference between complete closedness and complete openness contributing 2.2 percentage points to annual growth for the period from 1955–2004 in strongly significant estimates. They also discuss why other researchers using this openness variable have come to varying conclusions. In particular, they report that they do not find the interaction-term results of prior studies, in which de jure openness only yields positive growth effects if the interacting variable exceeds some threshold, to be robust.

Summarizing Estimates

Arriving at a central range for the statistical results in the cross-country growth regression studies of financial globalization requires key decisions on interpretation. A first task is to translate the parameters estimated with the particular variables used to represent financial openness into comparable measures that normalize for differences in units across studies. A second and perhaps more profound task is to decide what weight, if any, to give to nonsignificant results.

A tendency in this literature is to conclude that there is "no effect" or "fragile evidence" if the number of insignificant tests exceeds the number of significant tests. This approach implicitly reaches a binary judgment and also implicitly attributes zero as the proper estimate if the insignificant results are the more numerous. As discussed in appendix 2A, this approach suffers from at least four problems. The first is that the particular threshold set for significance is inherently arbitrary, and an effect that is of great importance in economic terms could be unadvisedly rejected if its significance level were just slightly below a critical threshold. McCloskey and Ziliak (1996), in particular, argue that the economics profession has

---

20. The de jure measures translate to a gain of about 0.12 percent annually for the difference between complete closedness and complete openness. The de facto measures imply large gains from FDI but partially offsetting losses from debt flows, with a net of about 1 percent per year. The one-third percent estimate is toward the conservative end of this range.

tended to exaggerate the importance of meeting the 5 percent significance level and to pay inadequate attention to the economic size of estimates.

A second problem is the conceptual one of the meaning of an insignificant estimate. Because hypothesis tests are set up in terms of *rejecting* the null hypothesis, which is usually that the parameter in question is zero, an insignificant result should be seen as *no* result because it merely means that the zero value cannot be rejected, not that zero has been demonstrated to be the true parameter value (see appendix 2A for various statistical textbook references to this effect).

A third problem is that significance depends heavily on sample size, and it will often be the case that a sample that is too small is driving the result rather than a lack of underlying economic influence. In particular, cross-country panel results using, say, 50 or 60 countries will be subject to the small sample problem. Hedges and Olkin (1985, 50) demonstrate that unless the "effect size" (parameter size) is large, samples on the order of 50 observations will tend heavily toward finding more insignificant than significant results.[21]

A fourth problem is the possible misinterpretation of robustness testing. Several studies first find significant results but then run additional tests with insignificant results and conclude that the initial findings are not robust. But unless there is a careful specification of the robustness test, simply finding an alternative that turns the openness variable insignificant may be misleading. In particular, some of the studies adopt frameworks for their robustness tests that require unconvincing instrumental variables. It is doubtful that the disappearance of significance in these tests should be considered as persuasive demonstration of lack of robustness. More generally, Sala-i-Martin (1997, 179), in particular, has warned against excessive rejection of results in cross-country growth econometrics on grounds of nonrobustness and notes that "one is bound to find one regression for which the estimated coefficient changes signs if enough regressions are run."

One particular dimension of the robustness issue is paradoxical. It is a popular view of this literature that endogeneity, from growth to financial opening, gives rise to spurious estimated gains from financial openness (e.g., Obstfeld 2009, discussed below). But from a policy standpoint this concern would not logically point to advocating closedness. On the contrary, if countries achieve strong growth using the strategy of financial closedness, their leaders would have to have a curious preference for financial openness as a "luxury good" to be willing to curb future growth by adopting it. So the implicit assumption that growth stimulates financial

21. More specifically, based on sampling theory the *t*-statistic should be expected to rise proportionally with the square root of the number of degrees of freedom (or, approximately, the square root of the sample size). See Card and Krueger (1995, 239) and Stanley (2001, 142).

opening rather than the other way around is inconsistent with a policy diagnosis that financial opening is bad for growth. At most, endogeneity would exaggerate positive estimates of the growth impact of financial openness; it would not make sense for endogeneity to create a positive coefficient where the true causal relationship from opening to growth is negative.

The approach adopted in this study to address this set of issues is to appeal to the literature on statistical meta-analysis. This literature has arrived at the *weighting of alternative results by the inverse of the variance* of the estimates (see appendix 2A). This literature formally demonstrates that there will be a tendency to bias downward estimates of the size of an effect if a simple "vote-counting" approach is used in which the influence is judged to be verified if the number of significant results exceeds the number of insignificant ones and rejected if the reverse is true (Hedges and Olkin 1985, 3, chapter 4). Weighting by the inverse of the variance of estimates gives some weight to estimates that fall short of the standard statistical significance threshold, using their actual parameter estimates rather than imputing them at zero.

Because of the principle that an insignificant result can be seen as no result, the analysis here first considers just those results that are significant. Of course, both positive and negative significant results should be included in principle, but it turns out there are no significant negative estimates. Secondly, a strong alternative approach is included: meta-statistical weighting by inverse variance. For purposes of comparison, simple vote counting and imputing nonsignificant results at zero are also reported even though both are likely to bias the average downward.

Table 2.1 reports the results of this summary analysis. The standardized measure for the summary is the impact on the average annual growth rate for complete financial openness as compared with complete closedness. For de jure models, this difference corresponds to moving from zero to the maximum openness index value.[22] For de facto models applying such measures as gross capital flows (or stocks) relative to GDP, the difference between complete closedness and openness is evaluated using movement from zero to the 90th percentile value of the measure in question.[23]

The average for significant estimates shows a remarkably high 1.99 percent per year annual growth increase from the consequence of maintaining a completely open financial market as compared with a completely closed one. If instead the simple average of the within-study meta-analysis (inverse variance) is considered, this total openness impact is additional

---

22. The maximum is 4 for Quinn (1997) and 100 for Quinn and Toyoda (2008). Edwards (2001) and Arteta, Eichengreen, and Wyplosz (2003) also use indexes based on Quinn (1997).

23. The 90th percentile value is taken from the underlying study for Kraay (1998), Edison et al. (2002), and IMF (2007a). For Fratzscher and Bussiere (2004) it is estimated from the database developed in chapter 3 for 45 industrial and emerging-market economies.

Table 2.1 Impact of complete financial openness versus complete closedness on annual growth (percent)

Study	Years	Number of countries	Type[a]	Number of tests	A Significant	B Meta	C t-weighted	D 0-imp.	E Percent significant
							Averages of estimates		
Quinn (1997)	1960–89	58	J	3	1.61	1.58	1.65	1.61	100
Kraay (1998)	1985–97	117	F	3	1.4	n.a.	1.4	0.47	33.3
Edwards (2001)	1973–87	60	J	2	3.18	1.82	2.47	1.59	50
Edison et al. (2002)	1980–2000	57	J,F	14	1.17	0.7	0.89	0.25	21.4
Arteta, Eichengreen, and Wyplosz (2003)	1973–92	58	J	4	3.37	3.37	3.61	1.69	50
Fratzscher and Bussiere (2004)	1980–02	45	F	6	1.61	0.15	0.99	0.27	16.7
Tornell, Westermann, and Martinez (2004)	1980–99	52	J	2	2.03	2.07	2.1	2.03	100
IMF (2007a)	1975–2004	87	J,F	9	0.68	0.43	0.67	0.3	44.4
Quinn and Toyoda (2008)	1955–2004	85	J	2	2.9	2.45	2.8	2.9	100
Average		69	—	5	1.99	1.57	1.84	1.23	57.3
Meta-average[b]				42	—	0.56	—	—	42.2

a. J = de jure   F = de facto.

b. Weighting by inverse variance across 42 individual tests.

n.a. = not available

Notes: A = significant results only; B = meta-statistical weighting by inverse variance (see appendix 2A); C = weighted by t-statistics; D = average including insignificant imputed at zero; E = percent of tests with significant openness coefficient.

growth of 1.57 percent per year. For its part, the average weighting by *t*-statistics (1.84 percent) is close to that for significant results only, as might be expected. Despite a downward bias, even the averages for imputing impact at zero for nonsignificant results and for vote counting also show a strong contribution, at 1.23 percent additional annual growth and a 57 percent majority of significant tests when each study is weighted equally.

It is also useful to examine the meta-statistical average allowing each individual test considered for the nine studies to count, rather than taking the corresponding average at the level of counting each study equally. The result is to give considerably more weight to the studies with more tests (Edison et al. 2002; IMF 2007a) and/or containing tests in which the standard error is especially low (Fratzscher and Bussiere 2004). This "meta-meta" average turns out to be a still substantial growth impact of 0.56 percentage point per year additional growth from complete openness versus complete closedness. At this level the vote count turns to a minority of 42 percent, illustrating the point that in meta-analysis, vote counting is likely to understate the effect being measured. The overall result in table 2.1 is that the growth impact of complete financial openness versus complete closedness ranges from a conservative 0.5 percent (meta-meta) to 2 percent (significant only) additional annual growth for the main studies of general financial openness.

It is important to note that in this meta-meta calculation, the overall result is dominated by just a few cases. Out of 42 individual tests assembled across eight studies, just two tests (from Fratzscher and Bussiere) account for 22.1 percent of the total weight and another five tests (all from IMF) account for 43.4 percent.[24] Two-thirds of the weight thus stems from only one-sixth of the individual tests, suggesting substantial sensitivity in application of this procedure.

It is also informative to consider further those studies that have a contingent outcome, depending on the level of an interactive variable. Table 2.2 reports the result of evaluating the three such contingent studies at the 25th and 75th percentile levels of their interactive variables.[25] For this purpose, the distributions of the interactive variables in question are taken from the data developed in chapter 3 for 45 industrial and developing economies.[26] It should be noted further that two of the three interactive

---

24. Insufficient detail is available to include the three tests in Kraay (1998) in the meta-meta exercise.

25. For this purpose, the measure for growth contribution at zero openness for the study by Bailliu (2000) cannot be set at zero because the lower bound of the openness measure is not zero (the study uses net capital inflows instead of gross flow or stock). The zero openness base is instead set at the 10th percentile of the openness variable.

26. This application may give some upward bias in contrast to the results that would be obtained including all developing countries, because the emerging-market economies considered in chapter 3 do not include numerous low-income countries.

Table 2.2   Growth impact of complete versus zero financial openness in interactive models (percent per year)

Study	Interactive variable	Openness impact at percentile of interactive variable	
		25th	75th
Bailliu (2000)	Banking system depth	1.02	1.76
Edwards (2001)	Log of per capita income	−5.92	4.19
Arteta, Eichengreen, and Wyplosz (2003)	1−black market premium	0.55	1.17

models are from studies that also report results for noninteractive tests and are thus included in table 2.1 (Edwards 2001; Arteta, Eichengreen, and Wyplosz 2003).

It is evident that the most sensitive interactive model of the three is that by Edwards (2001), which indicates a remarkable –6 percent growth impact of openness at the 25th percentile of per capita incomes but a +4 percent contribution at the 75th percentile. The other two interactive models yield a much narrower range that is broadly consistent with the noninteractive model results reported in table 2.1.

Taking account of both tables 2.1 and 2.2, two important patterns emerge. First, the various estimates broadly lie within the same range. Of the 42 separate estimates in the two tables, the range from the 20th to the 80th percentile is from a growth impact of 0.56 percent (complete openness versus closedness) to 2.9 percent. The corresponding range from the 25th to 75th percentile is 0.68 to 2.07 percent. These ranges indicate sizable positive growth impact.

Second, it is striking that only one of the model results shows a negative impact of openness (Edwards 2001, for the lower-income case). For the nine studies in table 2.1 and the three in table 2.2, or a set of 12 studies, one would expect six to show negative results and six positive results if the true influence of financial openness were zero. Instead, only half of one of the studies turns out negative. The chances of this outcome occurring on a random basis are between 0.3 percent and 0.024 percent, or vanishingly small.[27] These results thus seem to contradict the stylized fact in much of the literature that not much can be said about whether financial openness spurs growth because the empirical estimates are "fragile."

---

27. With a probability of 0.5 for either a positive or negative outcome if the influence is truly zero and the estimate is random, the chances that of n trials, m or more will turn out positive is $(1 + C_{n,\,n-1} + C_{n,\,n-2} + \ldots C_{n,m})/2^n$, where $C_{n,\,r}$ is the number of possible combinations of n things taken r at a time, or $C_{n,\,r} = n!/[(n-r)!\,r!]$. For $n = 12$, the probability that all will be positive is $1/2^{12} = 1/4{,}096$. The probability that 11 or more will be positive is $12/4{,}096$. So the probability that between 11 and 12 will be positive (the case here) is in between these limits (between 0.29 and 0.024 percent).

Finally, it is useful to consider a "reviewer's preferred" approach to arriving at a summary parameter estimate. In this approach the reviewer would select those studies that seem qualitatively the best, and omit all others in arriving at a summary estimate. An important tenet of the meta-analysis view is that this approach runs a severe risk of reviewer bias; it should be added that it similarly runs the risk of opening the reviewer to the critique of bias. Thus, Stanley (2001, 132) observes that "...some economists are reluctant to trust a meta-analysis, which mixes what they might consider to be 'good' and 'bad' studies, as much as they trust the individual study that they prefer." Quite apart from the question of superior statistical merit of the meta-analysis alternative (for which Stanley cites the imprimatur of the American Statistical Association), there is the problem that the reviewer's preferred summary might be conducted in "...a subjective and selective manner...disqualifying findings which run contrary to the beliefs of the author" (p. 131).

Subject to this caveat, and largely in response to the urging of two reviewers of an earlier draft, this study will hazard a reviewer's preferred summary estimate based on the author's perception of the relative quality of the various studies. As a first screen to arrive at a preferred subset, for the reasons discussed above it is appropriate to eliminate those studies that reject their own significant estimates on "vote-counting" grounds that they find more insignificant than significant results. These studies are labeled as category "B" in table 3.8 in chapter 3. Among the others, the Edwards (2001) study seems appropriate to omit because of certain idiosyncrasies (extreme dichotomization into large positive or negative growth effects depending on per capita income; weighting regressions by GDP, criticized by Arteta, Eichengreen, and Wyplosz 2003). The Bailliu (2000) study is hindered by the use of net capital flows as the proxy for financial openness, a problem as seen in the case of such open economies as that of Singapore (as discussed above). Finally, as between the two Quinn studies, for the purposes here the more appropriate is probably Quinn (1997). The later study (Quinn and Toyoda 2008) has perhaps too many countries (85 instead of 58) to be representative of the main set of industrial and emerging-market economies that are the primary focus of this study.[28]

Three of the studies in tables 2.1 and 2.2 survive this screening. The first, Quinn (1997), places the growth impact parameter at $\Delta g = 1.61$ percent additional growth per year as the impact of a shift from complete closure to complete financial openness. The second, Tornell, Westermann, and Martinez (2004), places the estimate at 2.03 percent. The third study, Arteta, Eichengreen, and Wyplosz (2003), has an estimate that is contingent on the interactive macroeconomic-stability variable. When the average is

---

28. Moreover, the central estimate of 1.6 for the annual percent growth impact of openness in the earlier study is much closer to the theoretical prior discussed in chapter 1 than the estimate of 2.9 percent in the later study.

taken of two bracketing impact values at the 25th and 75th percentiles for that variable (table 2.2), the result is $\Delta g = 0.86$ percent per year. The average across the three studies then yields a reviewer's preferred estimate of $\Delta g = 1.5$ percent additional growth per year for complete financial openness versus closedness. Considering the caveats about a reviewer's preferred estimate, the best interpretation of this exercise is to treat it as further support for 1.5 percent annual growth gain as the upper end of the estimate range, or "high-variant" finding. The alternative estimate of about 0.5 percent per year obtained applying meta-statistical weighting at both the intra- and inter-study levels (table 2.1) then serves as the conservative "low-variant" finding. It is this range that provides the basis for the overview estimates of chapter 1. Moreover, as argued there, on grounds of both theoretical expectations (especially for industrial economies not reliant on capital inflow for investment) and possible endogeneity, the low end of this range warrants greater weight than the upper end.

Financial Development

One of the most important specific categories of growth effects from financial globalization concerns the role of the domestic financial sector in spurring growth, combined with the importance of openness to foreign capital in strengthening the domestic financial sector. Schumpeter (1911) stated the classic case for the contribution of the financial sector to growth by mobilizing saving and channeling resources to sectors where returns are high. Goldsmith (1969) documented the association of a rising ratio of financial assets to wealth with rising per capita income levels but was cautious not to attribute causation. McKinnon (1973) emphasized the importance in developing countries of domestic "financial liberalization"—removal of official controls on interest rates—to mobilize saving and channel resources to productive investment.

More recently, the vast improvement in available cross-country data and the advent of more powerful econometric techniques has enabled some to argue not only that finance stimulates development but that the direction of causality is robust. Thus, in tests for 77 countries for 1960–89, King and Levine (1993) found a strong statistical influence of financial "depth" on growth, with financial depth measured by the ratio of liquid liabilities of the financial system to GDP. Their results indicated that if countries with the mean financial depth ratio of the slowest-growing quartile of countries (at 0.2) were to boost this ratio to the mean of the fastest-growing quartile (0.6), the size of the coefficient meant that there would be an increase in the annual growth rate by 1 percentage point, an enormous influence.[29]

---

29. Note that Aghion, Howitt, and Mayer-Foulkes (2005) arrive at a parallel finding on the importance of domestic financial development for growth. They find that the usual finding

If it is accepted that financial development spurs growth, the question for financial globalization becomes whether openness to international capital flows contributes to domestic financial development. Several empirical studies address this issue.

Klein and Olivei (1999) argue that capital account liberalization boosts growth through strengthening a country's domestic financial system, by introducing international standards and adding subsidiaries or branches of foreign banks to the national banking system. They first test for an impact of capital account liberalization on financial depth and then for the impact of financial depth on growth. They use three measures of financial depth suggested by King and Levine (1993): overall liquidity relative to GDP, corresponding private liquidity, and the same bank development measure (B) discussed above for the Bailliu (2000) results. Again following the literature, they adopt a binary indicator of capital-market openness using the AREAER, and construct a variable for the share of years between 1986 and 1995 that this measure indicated openness. Using data for 21 OECD countries and 50 non-OECD countries during this period, their data show a strong dichotomy between mainly closed capital accounts for developing countries and mainly open capital accounts for industrial countries. They regress the change in financial depth on its initial level, the share of years with capital account openness (both OLS and instrumental variable versions), and a set of control variables. The results show a strongly significant impact of capital account openness on domestic financial depth. A rise of the openness "share" variable from zero to the sample mean (0.22) boosts the three predicted financial depth measures by a range of 4 to 11 percent.

When the authors conduct the tests for two subsamples, they find the significant results hold up for the OECD countries, but that for a Latin American subsample, only one of the three financial depth measures continues to show a significant response to openness: the bank development measure (B). The Latin American estimate shows a significant coefficient of 0.25 for the influence of the capital account openness "share" on the change in the logarithm of this measure of financial development. However, the authors suggest caution about the latter result because they are concerned that it may reflect fiscal consolidation and a reduction in seignorage rather than banking-sector development.[30] Their summary then

---

of growth convergence, namely a negative coefficient of growth on initial per capita income, turns out to be contingent on domestic financial development. In tests interacting initial per capita income with domestic financial development as measured by the ratio of private credit to GDP, they find that if the latter does not exceed a threshold of 25 percent, growth is divergent rather than convergent (p. 195).

30. That is, with central bank claims in the denominator, the bank development measure B will tend to be low where there are large central bank claims on the government resulting from printing money.

leaps questionably to stating that there is an "observed failure of capital account liberalization to promote financial deepness among developing countries" as opposed to industrial countries (p. ii). But this conclusion contradicts their significant finding for the Latin American subsample for the usual banking development measure.

The authors then revisit the earlier King and Levine (1993) results and use data for 71 countries for 1986–95 to test for the influence of financial deepening on growth. Their later dataset confirms a strong influence for all three measures of financial development. The combined result is that a move of the capital account openness measure from 0 to 0.65 (the median for nonzero observations) would boost per capita income by 3.8 percent over this period, a large increment compared with the sample mean increase of 12 percent. Although the authors emphasize their interpretation that this type of favorable impact applies "only in the subsample of highly industrialized economies" (p. 20), their own results suggest otherwise. The elasticity of per capita income with respect to the banking development indicator B is estimated at 0.25. For developing countries, the average for this ratio for 1986 and 1995 was about 0.6 (Klein and Olivei 1999, figure 1). Applying the Latin American coefficient for the impact of openness noted above, the combined effect for the Latin American subsample would imply that a move from 0 to 0.5 on the openness variable would have raised per capita income by 4 percent over this period, or by the same amount as the illustrative summary example given by the authors.[31]

Vanassche (2004) repeats the Klein-Olivei test for the influence of financial openness on domestic financial development using essentially the same set of countries but extending the data period backward to 1980 (with the ending year again 1995). She confirms the positive significant effect for the full sample. However, she reverses the Klein-Olivei finding that the effect does not hold up well for developing countries. Instead, for 43 developing countries she finds the same openness "share" variable has a statistically significant positive effect on two alternative measures of domestic financial development (growth of private credit and growth of liquid liabilities).[32]

Levine (2001) emphasizes the role of international financial liberalization in spurring TFP growth. He cites two channels: the impact of opening to foreign inflows into portfolio equity on stock market liquidity and the impact of the presence of foreign banks on domestic banking-sector efficiency. Based on data from Levine and Zervos (1998b), he obtains statisti-

---

31. That is, $\partial B/\partial K = 0.25$, where B is the ratio of bank to bank plus central bank claims and K is the share of years with the capital account open. An increase of K by 0.5 would raise B by 0.125, or by about 20 percent of the average B for developing countries in this period. With an elasticity of 0.25, the resulting impact on per capita income would have been a rise by 4 percent.

32. The main focus of the study is on industry-level tests, as discussed below.

cally significant positive effects of capital-market opening on the ratio of total shares traded on the stock market divided by GDP for 14 of 15 emerging-market economies that opened during 1980–93.[33] Combining this finding with results in Levine and Zervos (1998a,) finding that countries with greater stock market liquidity grow faster over future decades, Levine (2001) concludes that the evidence supports a positive growth effect of the opening of capital markets to portfolio equity inflows.

Levine then turns to banking-sector efficiency. He argues that superior skills, management techniques, technology, and products of foreign banks stimulate domestic competition in the banking sector, placing downward pressure on profits and overhead expenses. He cites the experiences of Australia, Korea, and Turkey as examples. He reproduces summary regression results from Demirgüç-Kunt and Detragiache (1998) indicating a significant negative impact of foreign bank entry on the ratios of both before-tax profits and overhead costs to total assets, using data on about 8,000 banks in 80 countries. Arguing that reductions in these ratios represent increased competitive pressure, Levine concludes that capital account openness to foreign bank entry spurs TFP growth by increasing the efficiency of the financial sector. Considering that there is already substantial evidence that financial development spurs economic growth (King and Levine 1993), the link from foreign bank presence to financial-sector development in Levine (2001) serves as major support for a positive growth effect of openness of the capital account, or at least openness to direct investment in financial services.

The study by Bonfiglio and Mendicino (2004) cited above also contains analysis of the influence of openness on domestic financial development. Their alternative tests (p. 26) find that there is an elasticity of about 0.5 relating financial-sector development (as measured by the ratio of private credit to GDP) to the AREAER measure of capital account openness (this time with 0 for closed and 1 for open). This means that a move from completely closed to completely open induces a 50 percent rise in the ratio of private credit to GDP. The authors use data from Bekaert, Harvey, and Lundblad (2000) for this variable, and the data reported in that study place the average ratio of private credit to GDP at 0.39 for 30 developing countries over 1980–97. A shift from closed to open capital markets would raise this ratio by half, or from 0.39 to 0.58. King and Levine (1993, 727) found a highly significant coefficient of 0.032 for the growth impact of the ratio of private credit to GDP, after controlling for standard international growth variables. The combination of this coefficient with the Bonfiglio-Mendicino estimate implies that a move from financial closedness to

---

33. Argentina, Brazil, Chile, Colombia, India, Jordan, Korea, Mexico, Pakistan, the Philippines, Portugal, Thailand, Turkey, and Venezuela. Malaysia was the exception, with opening but no rise in the value-traded ratio.

openness raises the annual growth rate by 0.6 percentage point.[34] Considering this estimate in turn against the range of broader gains in table 2.1, induced financial development could account for at least one-third of the total growth gains from financial globalization.

Baltagi, Demitriades, and Law (2007) also examine the influence of openness on domestic financial development. They follow Rajan and Zingales (1998), who argue that because financial development increases competition to incumbent interest groups, opposition from such groups will be weaker (and financial development greater) when an economy allows cross-border trade and capital flows. Whereas Rajan and Zingales used data spanning the 20th century for 24 industrial and developing countries, Baltagi, Demitriades, and Law consider data for 42 developing countries from 1980 to 2003. They relate various measures of financial development to per capita income, institutional quality, trade openness, and financial globalization or liberalization. Their financial globalization measure is the ratio of external assets plus liabilities to GDP; their financial liberalization measure is the Abiad-Mody (2005) indicator, which includes both domestic and external liberalization. In their preferred specifications the authors find that both the trade and financial-openness indicators positively affect financial development, but that the interaction term between them has a negative sign. They find that when the partial derivative of financial globalization (liberalization) is evaluated holding trade openness constant, the result is a positive impact when the trade openness variable is at its minimum, a mixed impact (negative for the first financial-openness measure but positive for the second) at the trade openness mean, and negative for both at the trade-openness maximum. Because there is little theoretical basis to expect financial opening to have a negative effect on domestic financial development when trade is highly open, the implications of the results may be limited. Nonetheless, the findings do suggest that both trade and financial openness contribute to domestic financial development when the starting point is relative closedness in either dimension.

On balance, the weight of the evidence amounts to substantial support for the view that financial openness contributes to domestic financial-sector development. This finding is clear in Vanassche (2004), Levine (2001), and Bonfiglio and Mendicino (2004), and clear for industrial countries as well as in one test for Latin America in Klein and Olivei (1999).

Direct Investment

The greatest concentration of research in the category-specific literature on financial globalization has been in the area of the impact of foreign direct investment. It seems likely that the focus on FDI has reflected a

---

34. That is, 3.4 percent (from King-Levine) x 0.19 (the increase derived from Bonfiglio and Mendicino).

general perception that this type of international capital flow is the most likely to promote development, because it is less susceptible to "sudden stops" than other forms and because it is likely to have spillovers from technological transfer and export market linkages.

In an early study Balasubramanyam, Salisu, and Sapsford (1996) found a significant positive growth impact of FDI, but only if the economy was open in trade policy terms. The authors invoked the hypothesis of Bhagwati (1978) that inflows of direct investment would be both relatively larger and more efficient in promoting growth in economies oriented toward an export-promoting strategy than in those pursuing a strategy of import substitution. Bhagwati had defined an import-substitution orientation as placing a higher effective exchange rate on imports than on exports. In contrast, a trade-neutral effective exchange rate was defined as an export-promoting strategy, in which the size of inflows would not be limited to the dimensions of the domestic market, and investments would not flow into low-return sectors as a consequence of distortions.

The authors conducted cross-section regressions for 46 developing countries for the period 1970–85. They regressed the growth rate on the rate of growth in employment, ratio of investment to GDP, ratio of FDI to GDP, and rate of growth of exports. For all countries pooled they estimated a strongly significant coefficient of 1.84 relating growth to the FDI/GDP ratio. When they divided the countries by trade orientation (with high import-to-GDP ratios indicating open trade and low ratios indicating import-substituting strategies), they found the coefficients almost unchanged, still statistically significant for the open economies but no longer significant for the import-substituting economies. When a World Bank classification of trade regimes was used, the sign and size of the coefficient remained about the same, and significant, for the trade-open economies, but the sign reversed and the coefficient became insignificant for the import-substituting economies. The authors thus concluded that FDI boosted growth, but only for open-trade regimes.

Despite deficiencies that warrant caution,[35] the study's parameter estimates imply a substantial positive impact of FDI on growth. For example, if FDI inflows rise from zero to 1 percent of GDP, the annual growth rate

---

35. Notably, the authors mistakenly call the coefficient on FDI/GDP an "elasticity of output with respect to foreign capital" (p. 101), whereas this would be false by definition unless the stock of existing direct investment just happened to be identical in size to GDP (i.e., only in that case would the FDI/GDP ratio represent the percent change in the stock of direct investment). Similarly, the authors include the growth of exports directly on the right-hand side of the growth equation, raising questions about the appropriateness of treating exports as a specific factor of production as well as issues of simultaneity given that exports are a component of GDP in the national income accounts. Finally, they take at face value their finding that the investment/GDP ratio has a negligible and statistically insignificant impact on growth, which flatly contradicts the great bulk of the international growth comparison literature.

rises by 0.2 percentage point.[36] Such an impact seems broadly in line with the range of estimates discussed above for the growth impact of overall capital account openness versus closedness, albeit on the low side.

Borensztein, De Gregorio, and Lee (1998) provided another early benchmark study on the growth impact of direct investment. They invoke new varieties of capital and foreign firms as providers of qualitatively different capital. They arrive at an estimating equation specifying growth as a function of FDI relative to GDP; average years of male secondary schooling; interaction between these two terms (i.e., their product); initial per capita income; and a set of commonly used control variables. Their data are for two-decade-long panels (1970s and 1980s) for 69 developing countries. The direct investment data are for inflows from OECD countries. Their central result obtains an insignificant coefficient of –0.85 on the linear term for FDI alone but a significant positive coefficient on the FDI-human capital interaction term (1.62). The threshold at which the impact of FDI turns positive is 0.5 of a year for average male secondary schooling at the start of the period; 46 of the 69 countries exceeded this threshold. At the sample average for human capital (0.9 of a year), an increase of one standard deviation in the FDI/GDP ratio, or by 0.005 (half of 1 percent of GDP), boosts the annual growth rate by 0.3 percentage point (Borensztein, De Gregorio, and Lee 1998, 125). Separate inclusion of additional variables tends to raise the human capital threshold. Additional tests suggest that direct investment tends to crowd in rather than crowd out domestic investment (the coefficient of investment on FDI is greater than unity). Overall, the authors interpret their findings as indicating that FDI contributes to growth by stimulating technological progress, and needs the cooperation of domestic human capital for this process to take place. Correspondingly, they see the growth effects of FDI as coming mainly from increased efficiency rather than from increased availability of capital stock.

De Mello (1999) uses panel estimation methods to examine the impact of FDI, using data for 32 countries for 1970–90. His main results, which regress output growth on the stock of FDI and growth lagged one year, find "a positive impact of FDI on output growth in all panels" (p. 145) but more variable results for the corresponding impacts on domestic capital growth and growth in TFP. However, various aspects of the study suggest that its parameter estimates may not be among the most reliable.[37]

---

36. That is, 1.84 x 0.01.

37. Perhaps most importantly, the author creates his stock of direct investment variables by cumulating net FDI flows, but unfortunately this generates bizarre results. For example, the stock of direct investment swings from 300 percent of GDP in 1986 to –1,300 percent in 1988 in Zimbabwe and from 450 percent of GDP in 1989 to 150 percent in 1990 in New Zealand. Such idiosyncrasies probably explain why the results reporting unweighted means of country-specific FDI impacts on growth show a negative coefficient for non-OECD countries, in contrast to the positive estimate in the panel results.

Haveman, Lei, and Netz (2001) apply panel techniques to data for 74 countries for 1970–89 to examine the influence of direct investment, trade openness, and preferential trade on growth. With five-year subperiods, they have approximately 230 observations. They first regress per capita growth on the control variables—ratio of investment to GDP, initial per capita income, adult male schooling, population growth, and government spending share—and find coefficients that are typical of the literature in sign and size. They then sequentially add alternative measures of international interaction: direct investment, trade openness, trade block participation, and trade preferences. Then when they include all of the international interaction variables at the same time, the international variables' coefficient sizes tend to diminish, suggesting that when tested individually, any one of these influences tends to pick up the influence of others correlated with it. Thus, the coefficient on FDI is 0.035 when it is the only international variable added to the control variables but drops to 0.025 (statistically significant in both cases) when all of the international variables are included. Even so, the implied growth impact of FDI remains extremely large. For example, increasing direct investment from 2 to 3 percent of GDP would raise the annual growth rate by 1 percentage point.[38]

Carkovic and Levine (2005) conduct 62 cross-country statistical tests to examine whether earlier positive estimates of the impact of FDI on growth are robust after taking account of other variables and simultaneity between growth and direct investment. Their broad answer is in the negative. Their tests are for 67 countries in the period 1960–95. All of their equations have two control variables: initial per capita income and average years of schooling. Their FDI variable is the ratio of direct investment inflows to GDP. They consider five competing variables: inflation, government size, openness to trade, black-market premium, and private credit relative to GDP. Starting with the basic equation relating growth to the two control variables and FDI, they sequentially enter one of the competing variables to the equation, and include an equation with all of the competing variables, to determine whether the FDI coefficient remains significant. They then repeat the process but with both an FDI term and an interaction term of FDI multiplied by, respectively, schooling, income per capita, private credit, and trade openness. For each test they have two variants: OLS and panel GMM. The panel uses five-year periods and hence multiplies the number of observations about fourfold. The GMM tests are meant to address simultaneity.

Of the 31 OLS tests, six show a significant FDI coefficient. Of the 31 GMM tests, 11 find FDI significant. So the authors' preferred GMM approach shows stronger support for an FDI impact than the OLS results.

---

38. That is, $0.025 \times (\ln 0.03 - \ln 0.02) = 0.01$. In comparison, with the coefficient for log share of investment in GDP estimated at 0.1, raising investment from 20 to 30 percent of GDP would raise the annual growth rate by 4 percent: $0.1 \times (\ln 0.3 - \ln 0.2) = 0.04$.

The authors conclude that "the exogenous component of FDI does not exert a robust, positive influence on economic growth" (p. 197) but recognize the ambiguity of their results in acknowledging that "many growth regression specifications yield a positive coefficient on FDI" (p. 203).

The strongest results for FDI are the OLS tests in which an interaction term with private credit is included and the GMM tests in which interaction with education is included.[39] The authors question the GMM-education results because higher education reduces the impact of FDI. However, although this result is the opposite of the Borenzstein, De Gregorio, and Lee (1998) result for developing countries, the Carkovic-Levine tests are pooled for developing and industrial countries. In the richer countries, it is plausible that the spillover training effects of FDI would be less important than in developing countries. In any event, the interaction term does not turn the overall FDI impact negative until well beyond the range of observed schooling levels (16 years).

With its five dozen tests, the Carkovic-Levine study seems especially appropriate for application of within-study meta-analysis, or weighting by inverse variance. There are 10 types of tests.[40] Weighting by the average inverse variance within each type provides an overall estimate of the "size effect" of FDI.[41] As reported in table 2.2, whereas the average of the significant parameter results for the growth impact of FDI is relatively large (about 1.75 percentage points of additional annual growth for 1 percent of GDP of additional FDI), the inverse-variance-weighted average is smaller but still substantial (0.44 percentage point).

Choe (2003) applies Granger causality tests to determine whether the close correlation between FDI and growth typically found in statistical studies represents causation from FDI to growth or vice versa. He uses panel data on 80 countries in five-year periods from 1971 to 1995. He regresses growth on both successively more distant lagged values of growth in previous periods as well as on corresponding lagged values of FDI as a fraction of GDP. In his full dataset he finds that FDI Granger-causes growth with a two-period lag, but growth also Granger-causes FDI with a

---

39. Evaluated at the sample means, with FDI at 1.1 percent of GDP and credit to the private sector at 40 percent of GDP, an additional 1 percent of GDP in FDI boosts the annual growth rate by 1.86 percent per year (OLS). At the sample mean of 5.01 years schooling, an additional 1 percent of GDP in FDI boosts annual growth by 1.7 percent per year (GMM).

40. Five types each for OLS and GMM: simple, and interacting with each of four variables.

41. The coefficient estimate is the sum of the FDI coefficient plus the increment from the FDI-interactive coefficient evaluated at the sample mean for the interactive variable. The associated standard error is obtained by dividing the resulting parameter by the average of the t-statistics for the FDI coefficient and the interactive coefficient. One extreme outlier observation is omitted, because its parameter estimate is near zero, and hence its inverse variance is extremely small. As discussed in appendix 2A, the inverse-variance weight turns out to be proportional to the square of the t-statistic and inversely proportional to the square of the parameter estimate.

one-period lag. However, when he eliminates nine countries or 11 percent of the sample on grounds that they are extreme outliers (for example, high FDI in Singapore and low FDI in Cameroon), the significance of FDI disappears, while that of growth-causing FDI with a one-period lag remains. His conclusion is that although there is causation in both directions, the causation is weaker from FDI to growth.

It is unclear what to make of this finding. Whereas discarding, say, 1 percent of data as outliers might be warranted in some circumstances, eliminating outliers surely becomes more questionable rapidly as the percentage of the sample discarded rises, because doing so robs the dataset of cases that can show the influence of major variations in the variable in question. More fundamentally, whether it is meaningful to dismiss a developmental impact of a key variable just because it is Granger-caused by, rather than the Granger-cause-of, growth is doubtful. Surely most economic theory would say increased capital stock and hence investment is essential for growth, yet there are studies finding that it is Granger-caused by rather than the Granger-cause-of growth. If it does not make sense to dismiss a role of investment as a source of growth for domestic investment because of the Granger direction found, neither would it seem to make sense to do so when considering whether FDI plays a role in growth.

Hermes and Lensink (2003) examine the role of the domestic financial sector in determining whether FDI benefits growth. They argue that the growth effects of direct investment spillovers work through the channels of demonstration of improved technologies and management methods, competition that forces domestic firms to upgrade, development of linkages to domestic suppliers, and training. Noting that previous literature had emphasized such domestic preconditions for FDI benefits as human capital, presence of well-functioning markets, and property rights, they suggest that the corresponding role of the domestic financial sector had been neglected. Because domestic firms will need to invest to take advantage of new technologies and other spillovers from FDI, a more developed domestic financial system should facilitate this process by mobilizing more saving, monitoring investment, and even funding some investments of the foreign firms themselves.

The authors use data on 67 developing countries for 1970–95 to apply a standard cross-country growth analysis that includes a core set of control variables as well as the FDI variables. The core variables are initial level of secondary school enrollment, initial GDP per capita, credit to the private sector as a percentage of GDP, and investment as a share of GDP (all in log form). They add as the variables for direct investment the logarithm of the ratio of FDI to GDP and the product of that variable with the log-credit-to-private-sector variable as an interaction term. In their regressions, tests including the core variables and the FDI variable alone do not show a significantly positive effect of direct investment. The authors then add the interaction term for domestic financial development (log FDI times log private credit). The interaction term is positive and significant, and the FDI term turns negative and significant. The threshold at which additional FDI has a positive impact on growth is a ratio of credit to the private sector of 12 percent of GDP. Of their 67 countries, 55 percent meet this criterion. Most sub-Saharan African countries fail to reach this threshold, whereas most of Latin American and Asian economies reach it.

If the parameters estimated in Hermes and Lensink (2003) are applied at the average ratio of private credit to GDP, which (as noted earlier) Bekaert, Harvey, and Lundblad (2000) place at 39 percent for 30 developing countries over 1980–97, it turns out that boosting FDI from 1.1 to 2.1 percent of GDP would raise the per capita growth rate by 0.45 percentage point annually.[42] So the authors find what amounts to a significant and relatively large impact of FDI on growth, but at low levels of domestic financial development this impact turns negative.

Alfaro et al. (2004) also examine the influence of FDI with threshold effects for domestic financial development. They use data for 20 industrial and 51 developing countries for 1975–95 in tests using four alternative banking-sector measures to capture financial development. When they use two alternative stock market measures for this purpose, the sample is reduced to 20 industrial and 29 developing countries. They too argue that FDI spillover effects will be furthered if there is domestic finance available for local firms to make new investments. In their first set of growth regressions including the standard controls but omitting the financial development variable, they do not find a significant coefficient for the FDI term (ratio of FDI to GDP) in the full set of countries, but for the 49 countries with information available on stock markets they obtain a positive and statistically significant coefficient.

The authors find a positive coefficient on FDI and on the FDI-financial development interaction term. However, because the financial-development term is in logarithmic terms for the ratio of the financial variable to GDP (e.g., credit to the private sector), this term is negative except when the financial variable exceeds GDP. As a consequence, frequently the product of the FDI variable and the (log) financial variable, multiplied by a positive estimated coefficient, has a negative sign and deducts from growth.[43] The threshold exceeds domestic financial-development levels in two-thirds of the sample when the four banking variables are used, and

---

42. The parameters used in this calculation are −1.587 for the coefficient of log of FDI as a percent of GDP and 0.621 as the coefficient for the interaction term (Hermes and Lensink 2003, table 3).

43. For example, for the private credit (PRC) case, the growth equation (pure number, not percent) contains additively the terms 0.588 FDI/Y + 0.777 (FDI/Y)(ln (PRC/Y)). At the sample mean of 0.01 for FDI/Y and 0.44 for PRC/Y, the contribution from the terms involving FDI amounts to: 0.00588 + 0.777 x 0.01 x (−0.82) = −0.00049. Boosting FDI to 2 percent of GDP makes matters worse, shifting the contribution to −0.00098.

in four-fifths on the sample when the stock market variables are used. The authors conclude that "FDI plays an important role in contributing to economic growth. However, the level of development of local financial markets is crucial for these positive effects to be realized" (Alfaro et al. 2004, 108).

This interpretation implies that the authors are skeptical that more FDI actually reduces growth in countries with poorly developed financial markets below their thresholds. That is a reasonable interpretation, because there is nothing in their theory of the interrelationship that would call for a negative impact, merely a less-strong positive impact of FDI in the absence of a developed financial market. More generally, the results flag a possible problem that may characterize many studies: spurious attribution of negative effects of FDI below some conditional threshold that result solely from specification problems. Such a misspecification seems to be present in Alfaro et al. (2004). With the interaction term multiplying the FDI variable by the logarithm of a variable that is usually less than unity but sometimes more than unity, the specification inherently constrains the outcome to forcing an initial negative influence of the interaction. Surely there would be no economic difference if the financial variable had been specified as a percentage (or even the logarithm of a percentage) rather than the logarithm of a ratio, yet in that case the term would have been always positive, and the interaction term would always have been either positive or negative, depending on the coefficient.

In an important study, Blonigen and Wang (2005) shed light on the divergence between the findings of Balasubramanyam, Salisu, and Sapsford (1996) and Borensztein, De Gregorio, and Lee (1998)—who find a positive impact of FDI on growth—and those of Carkovic and Levine (2005) and Choe (2003), who do not. The authors point out that the first two studies were for developing countries, while the latter two also included industrial countries. When Blonigen and Wang rerun the Borensztein, De Gregorio, and Lee tests using the original data of that study augmented by comparable data for industrial countries, the positive impact of FDI on growth disappears. When dummy variables are incorporated for developing countries, however, the positive impact is reaffirmed for developing countries. The authors thus conclude that the reason for disappearance of a growth benefit from FDI in the Carkovic-Levine and Choe studies was that they inappropriately pooled developing and industrial countries, rather than testing the two groups separately or incorporating developing-country dummy variables. They argue that the main theoretical arguments for a special role of FDI do indeed apply primarily to developing countries, where the need to catch up technologically through spillover benefits from foreign investors is much greater.

The authors then extend their analysis to investigate whether FDI crowds out domestic investment (e.g., by preempting the attractive investment opportunities) or crowds it in (e.g., by creating new investment opportunities in sectors supplying inputs, i.e., backward linkage). Their results again find that the original Borensztein, De Gregorio, and Lee (1998) result of crowding in turns out to be valid for the developing countries, whereas for industrial countries the coefficient shifts to crowding out.

In estimates for a panel of two decades (1970–79 and 1980–89), using data for 69 developing and 19 industrial countries, Blonigan and Wang (2005, 238) obtain a coefficient of –2.152 for FDI relative to GDP and 2.836 for the FDI variable times schooling variable interaction term, for developing countries.[44] Borensztein, De Gregorio, and Lee (1998) reported initial average male secondary schooling of 0.78 years for the median country, and 0.89 years at the 58th percentile and 1.13 years at the 68th percentile.[45] Applying these alternatives, boosting FDI by 1 percent of GDP would raise the average annual growth rate of per capita income by a negligible 0.06 percentage point for the median education country, but by a large 1.05 percentage points at the 68th percentile country and 0.37 percentage point per year at the 58th percentile.[46] So not only do Blonigan and Wang (2005) resurrect the positive significant impact of FDI on growth found in Borensztein, De Gregorio, and Lee (1998) after distinguishing between developing and industrial countries (in contrast to the pooling in Carkovic-Levine and Choe); they also obtain specific estimates that show relatively large growth impacts for at least about the upper 40 percent of developing countries.

Lensink and Morrissey (2006) examine the growth impact of FDI with special attention to FDI's volatility. They frame the problem in terms of evidence that volatility is bad for investment. There seems to be a logical nonsequitur in their framework, however. If the concern is that (a) lower investment caused by volatility is bad for growth and (b) FDI is volatile, surely it does not follow that FDI is bad for growth. Quite the contrary, unless the crowding out factor for FDI exceeds unity, so that $1 million of FDI reduces domestic investment by more than an offsetting $1 million, then more FDI will boost investment, not reduce it. Yet the studies of crowding out noted above (Borensztein, De Gregorio, and Lee 1998; Blonigan and Wang 2005) find either minimal crowding out or actual crowding in. The authors argue that by conveying new technology, FDI increases the domestic rate of return; but at the same time, an increase in volatility of FDI reduces the rate of return in certainty-equivalent terms given risk aversion. On these grounds they justify statistical tests including both FDI and its volatility in explaining growth.

The authors first report evidence on FDI volatility. For 1970–97 as a

---

44. With probability values of 0.12 and 0.04, respectively.

45. Borensztein, De Gregorio, and Lee (1998, 124); interpolated for the median.

46. For example, at the 58th percentile the change in annual growth rate (pure number) is –2.152 x .01 + 2.836 x .01 x 0.89 = 0.0037.

whole they place average FDI at 0.82 percent of GDP for lower-income countries, 1.38 percent for lower-middle-income countries, and 1.72 percent for upper-middle-income countries. The corresponding standard deviations around an autoregressive forecast of FDI are 45 percent, 30 percent, and 39 percent, respectively. This volatility is substantial, as it would mean that an upper-middle-income country, for example, might expect to receive 2.4 percent of GDP in FDI one year but then encounter a decline to only 1.33 percent the next year. The authors do not examine whether the volatility is driven mainly by fluctuating international capital markets or by domestic business cycles. Nor do they address the fact that in the financial crises of the late 1990s, it was direct investment that persisted in its steady upward climb even as bank credits swung to large net outflows for many of the emerging-market economies.

Their tests use data for 87 countries (of which 20 are industrial) for 1975–97. They regress per capita growth on standard variables (initial per capita income, secondary school enrollment, black-market premium, trade volume index), together with FDI as a percent of GDP (called GFDI) and the standard deviation of errors from an autoregressive equation for FDI as a percent of GDP (called UGFDI). For the subsample of developing countries only, their estimated coefficients are 1.48 for GFDI and −2.52 for UGFDI, both highly significant.[47] When the authors convert their results to normalized beta coefficients, which take account of the means and standard deviations of the variables, the positive coefficient on GFDI is found to be about twice as large as the negative coefficient on UGFDI, so the positive contribution of FDI strongly dominates any negative effect from its volatility. This is consistent with the suggestion above that because FDI contributes to investment, volatility of FDI might attenuate its potential benefits but would not be expected to turn them negative. The authors' bottom line is that there is "quite a consistent finding that FDI has a positive effect on growth....Volatility of FDI is an important negative influence on growth, but is not as important...as the level of FDI" (Lensink and Morrissey 2006, 490).[48]

The coefficients estimated by Lensink and Morrissey imply high contributions of FDI to growth in middle-income countries but not in low-income countries. Applying the coefficients, FDI levels, and FDI volatilities just described, FDI can be estimated to have contributed 1.57 percentage points to annual growth in the upper-middle-income countries and 1.29 percentage points in the lower-middle-income countries but a negligible 0.09 percentage point to growth in the lower-income countries. For given volatility, an extra 1 percent of GDP boosts the per capita growth rate by

---

47. For the equation without an interaction term with education.

48. Curiously, the main text thus contradicts the abstract's summary that "the evidence for a positive effect of FDI levels on growth is not robust ...." (p. 478).

about 1.5 percentage points. Moreover, additional FDI seems to be associated with lower rather than higher volatility of FDI (the volatility measure is highest for the low-income countries), so there is no offset from a rise in volatility. Overall, these results stand toward the upper end of the spectrum of estimates of positive impact of FDI on growth.

Alfaro and Charlton (2007) examine data at the level of 19 economic sectors for 22 OECD countries in three five-year periods during 1985–2000. FDI flows in this period are the lowest in agriculture (averaging less than 1 percent of value added) and the highest in finance, business services, and real estate (15 percent of value added). The authors regress sectoral growth rates on the logarithm of the volume of FDI in the sector, the logarithm of sectoral value added, the share of the sector in initial economy-wide value added, and dummy variables for country, sector, and time period. They find a positive and significant impact of FDI on growth. The principal result shows an elasticity of 0.45 for the growth rate with respect to the volume of FDI, although this is difficult to interpret.[49] An increase in flows comparable to moving from the 25th to the 75th percentile in the distribution is associated with a 13 percent rise in the growth rate above the different industries' sample means. The impact is even stronger when tests are limited to sectors that have higher skill requirements and for sectors relatively more dependent on financing external to the firm. The size and significance of the results increases when tests are restricted to just those sectors that the countries themselves state they are promoting for FDI. Among these, a move from the 25th to the 75th percentile of FDI is associated with a 73 percent rise in the growth rate. This impact remains large at 34 percent in corresponding tests using countries' target lists of sectors as an instrumental variable.

Although intriguing, these results may be of limited relevance to macroeconomic growth in developing countries. First, the estimates are just for OECD countries, and although these increasingly include some developing countries (Mexico, Korea), the findings of Blonigan and Wang (2005) would suggest that findings for industrial countries are likely to be different from those for developing countries. Second, it is unclear what to make of the sectoral differences. One could imagine that investment of all types, including FDI, will be greater in the more dynamic sectors, and that, among the industrial countries, relative expansion of the dynamic sectors will be greatest in the faster-growing economies. It is not clear that the instrumental variables used in the endogeneity tests successfully resolve this question. For various reasons, then, the study does not lend itself to the extraction of summary parameters relating FDI to growth. Even so, it provides at least qualitative support to the view that there is a positive growth impact from FDI.

Finally, an IMF study (2007a, 31) includes a statistical estimate for the

---

49. In particular, no normalization of the volume of FDI for sectoral or country size is reported, raising questions about the specification.

growth impact of FDI and portfolio equity investment. For a panel of six five-year periods for 87 countries from 1975–2004, the study estimates average growth in GDP per capita as a function of the ratio of the stock of FDI and portfolio equity liabilities to GDP and a set of control variables.[50] The estimated coefficient of 3.0 is significant at the 10 percent level. Given the mean value of 0.20 for the stock of FDI and portfolio equity relative to GDP, the implied average growth contribution is 0.6 percent per year.[51]

Table 2.3 summarizes the implied estimates from the studies reviewed in this section for the impact of a rise in FDI by one percentage point of GDP.[52] As noted in the discussion above of Lensink and Morrissey (2006), an increase of this magnitude is approximately equal to the difference between the 1970–97 average inflows to low-income countries (0.82 percent of GDP) and flows to upper-middle-income countries (1.72 percent).

The estimates in table 2.3 are broadly consistent with the estimates in table 2.1, which indicate a range of about a 0.5 to 2 percent increase in annual growth for the impact of a move from complete closedness to complete openness in capital markets.

Portfolio Equity

There is a smaller literature, by a considerably more limited number of researchers, that focuses on the impact of liberalization of portfolio equity markets. In an early paper, Bekaert, Harvey, and Lundblad (2000) examined this impact for 30 emerging-market economies for the period 1980–97. Their reported official liberalization dates for foreign purchase of domestic equities show a heavy concentration in 1989–92, broadly the phase marking the end of the Latin American debt crisis and transition to the upswing in emerging capital markets. About half of their sample liberalized in these four years.[53] Four countries had already liberalized in 1986–88, and another six liberalized in 1993–97.[54] Six remained closed as of 1997.[55]

---

50. The control variables include initial income level, years of schooling, population growth, investment as a share of GDP, inflation, trade openness, and private credit as a share of GDP.

51. The mean value of the variable is by communication from the IMF authors.

52. The table includes the results of Reisen and Soto (2001), discussed in the initial section on general growth impact studies. For the IMF study, the table entry assumes that the stock ratio of 0.2 (20 percent of GDP) corresponds to an annual inflow of 1.2 percent of GDP. If nominal dollar GDP grew steadily at 6 percent of GDP, this inflow would eventually lead to a steady-state stock ratio of 20 percent of GDP.

53. Argentina, Brazil, Chile, Colombia, India, Indonesia, Korea, Mexico, Pakistan, the Philippines, South Africa, Sri Lanka, Turkey, and Venezuela.

54. Portugal, Greece, Malaysia, and Thailand, in the early group; and Egypt, Israel, Jordan, Morocco, Nigeria, and Zimbabwe, in the later group.

55. Bangladesh, Côte d'Ivoire, Kenya, Jamaica, Trinidad and Tobago, and Tunisia.

Table 2.3   Impact of foreign direct investment on growth (percentage points for increase by 1 percent of GDP)

Study	Number of countries; period	Impact	Comments
Balasubramanyam, Salisu, and Sapsford (1996)	46; 1970–85	0.20	For open-trade economies. Not significant for import-substituting economies
Borensztein, De Gregorio, and Lee (1998)	69; 1970–90	0.60	At sample mean schooling; at low education, turns negative
Haveman, Lei, and Netz (2001)	74; 1970–89	1.00	Evaluated at increase of FDI from 2 to 3 percent of GDP (see text)
Reisen and Soto (2001)	44; 1986–97	0.10	Middle-income countries
Carkovic and Levine (2005)	67; 1960–95	1.74	Average, significant coefficients
		1.02	t-weighted average
		0.47	Average imputing nonsignificant at zero
		0.44	Meta-average (inverse variance weighting)
Hermes and Lensink (2003)	67; 1970–95	0.45	At mean ratio of private credit to GDP. Turns negative at low levels of financial development
Blonigan and Wang (2005)	88; 1970–89	0.06	Developing countries, median education
		0.37	Developing countries, 58th percentile education
		1.05	Developing countries, 68th percentile education
Lensink and Morrissey (2006)	87; 1975–97	1.50	For given volatility of FDI
IMF (2007a)	87; 1975–2004	0.50	For stock liability estimate translated to flow concept

FDI = foreign direct investment

The authors use GMM techniques, including Monte Carlo testing of alternative weighting schemes, to test for the difference in the per capita growth rate subsequent to equity market liberalization. Their tests include control variables (initial per capita income, government spending relative to GDP, trade relative to GDP, inflation, secondary school enrollment, banking development, and domestic stock market development). With these controls included, they find strongly significant positive coefficients for equity market liberalization on growth. Their summary conclusion is that "financial market liberalizations are associated with higher real growth, in the range of one percent per annum" (p. 19).

The authors do not explicitly address how long this higher growth persists, but a reading of their estimates would seem to imply that this boost to growth lasts for about four years before expiring. Thus, if the results for their three alternative weighting schemes are averaged, the annual average growth rate increase in relationship to the horizon is 1.33 percent for one year, 1.24 percent for two years, 1.11 percent for three years, 0.97 percent for four years, and then 0.75 percent for five years. But this means that by year five there is no further increment to growth.[56] So their study would appear to indicate that equity market liberalization raises GDP per capita by about a cumulative 4 percent over four years, but thereafter growth returns to its pace characteristic of the preliberalization period.

In a subsequent study, Bekaert and Harvey (2005) find that their earlier estimate is robust to extensive experiments, such as the addition of more countries (including five developed countries—Iceland, Japan, Malta, New Zealand, and Spain). They examine differing versions of the equity liberalization variable (including a continuous rather than binary variable, showing the ratio of stocks eligible for foreign ownership to the total domestic market). As a parallel test, they confirm earlier results that for the broader question of overall capital-market openness, the standard IMF variable does not find a significant boost to growth but the more nuanced Quinn (1997) and Edwards (2001) measures succeed in doing so. They find in addition, however, that the equity liberalization variable remains important even when including the influence of broader capital-market opening.

Once again the authors find "a 1 percent increase in annual real economic growth" (p. 3) as a consequence of equity market liberalization, which they call "surprisingly large" (p. 15). Once again they do not focus on the question of whether this impact is constrained to the five-year period they examine, and this time they do not report the coefficients estimated for each time horizon, so it cannot be determined whether the effect tails off at the end of five years. However, their initial summary statistics lend some support to the notion of greater permanence of the growth effect than just five years, considering that the increment between post and preliberalization is virtually the same comparing three-, five-, and seven-year periods before and after liberalization for 95 countries.[57]

---

56. That is, comparing the cumulative growth increment for five years versus four years gives $(1.0075)^5/(1.0097)^4 < 1$.

57. The comparisons for 95 countries are 1.6 percent/2.65 percent; 1.59 percent/2.76 percent; and 1.53 percent/2.64 percent, respectively. All three of the differences are significant at the 1 percent level.

In their test including both the Quinn capital account openness indicator and their own equity market liberalization variable, they find an increment to the growth rate of 0.77 percent annually from equity liberalization and 1.79 percent annually from a shift from closedness to openness on the Quinn measure (p. 22, table 5). The latter coefficient is almost the same as that found in Quinn (1997; see also table 2.1). The additive contribution just from equity liberalization would bring the total boost from financial openness to a remarkable 2.6 percentage points per year in annual growth.

Henry (2000) examines the response of private investment to the liberalization of stock markets to purchases by foreign investors. He argues that such liberalization should reduce the cost of equity capital by setting it closer to international levels rather than the autarkic level, and by increasing risk sharing and liquidity. The reduction in the cost of equity should cause a rise in the stock market price index. It should also spur an increase in investment in plant and equipment, because of the lower hurdle rate and the transformation of some investment projects from negative to positive net present value. He investigates 11 emerging-market economies: Argentina, Brazil, Chile, Colombia, India, Korea, Malaysia, Mexico, the Philippines, Thailand, and Venezuela. He identifies the date of liberalization on a basis of official policy decree, first country fund, or jump in the International Finance Corporation's (IFC) investability index (ratio of market capitalization of stocks open to foreign investment to total market capitalization) by at least 10 percent.[58] Importantly, he notes that every country examined still had restrictions on outflows of capital at the time its stock market was liberalized. So together with openness to direct investment, openness to stock market investment can be seen as typically the first phase of eventual wider capital-market opening.

The author regresses the logarithm of investment on dummy variables for each of the first three years after liberalization, as well as dummy variables for each calendar year to take into account worldwide shocks. He finds that the mean growth rate of investment in this period exceeds the sample mean by 22 percentage points. (He also finds that FDI tends to rise after stock market liberalization rather than fall, so that portfolio equity inflows are not simply substituting for prior FDI inflows.) In comparison with Bekaert, Harvey, and Lundblad (2000), Henry's approach suggests a more explicit focus on the temporary nature of the acceleration of growth, however. Indeed, in a summary event analysis diagram, he plots average investment growth for the 11 economies and shows averages of about zero

---

58. The resulting liberalization years are the same as those in Bekaert, Harvey, and Lundblad (2000) for four countries and within one year for two more. However, for five countries, there is a major difference showing earlier liberalization. The average liberalization year for Brazil, Chile, India, Korea, and the Philippines is set at 1987 in Henry (2000, 316) but at 1992 in Bekaert, Harvey, and Lundblad (2000, 21).

in the five years prior to stock market liberalization, 22 percent in the three years after liberalization, and then only about 2 percent in the fourth and fifth years after liberalization. Henry argues that the temporary nature of the acceleration in investment is consistent with a neoclassical model in which the capital/labor ratio must rise from one plateau to a higher plateau if the marginal product of capital falls to match the falling cost of capital but that the capital stock will then resume its previous pace of growth after this adjustment.[59]

In a short, heuristic study, Henry (2003) extends his analysis to cover 18 economies to examine the impact on growth in output per worker. In simple comparisons of five-year periods before and after stock market liberalization, he reports three findings. First, dividend rates fall by 240 basis points, from an average of 5 percent to 2.6 percent. This pattern is consistent with the proposition that opening reduces the cost of equity capital. Second, the growth of investment accelerates by an average of 1.1 percentage points per year, from an average of 5.4 percent to 6.5 percent per year. He does not clarify why the boost is so much smaller than in his earlier study, although the concept this time is total investment (rather than private), and the country coverage is larger. Third, the annual growth rate of output per worker rises by 2.3 percentage points: from an average of 1.4 percent in the five years before liberalization to 3.7 percent in the five years after. This increase is far greater than could be explained by acceleration in investment (which he gauges at only about 0.36 percentage point, using a capital share of one-third), and he suggests that the cause is a rise in TFP growth stemming from general economic reforms. Although this follow-up essay tends to support the findings of temporary stimulus to investment and growth as a consequence of equity-market liberalization, Henry settles for the modest conclusion that "these facts cast doubt on the view that capital account liberalization brings no real benefits" (p. 12), and suggests that analysis at the firm level is needed to more rigorously sort out the causality questions that linger from aggregative analysis. In a subsequent study, Chari and Henry (2004) use firm-level data in 11 emerging-market economies to estimate that the opening of equity markets to international investment boosts stock prices by an average of 15.1 percent. They find that in the three years subsequent to liberalization the growth rate of capital stock at the firm level rises by 5.4 percentage points above its preliberalization rate.

---

59. Henry (2000) distinguishes his analysis from that of Levine and Zervos (1998b) in three ways. First, he tests for, and finds, a temporary increase in investment after stock market liberalization, whereas they test for (and do not find) a permanent increase. Second, his tests are for developing countries only, where the capital costs of autarky should be higher, rather than including both industrial and developing countries. This difference anticipates the findings by Blonigan and Wang (2005) for direct investment (positive growth effect for developing countries but not for industrial countries), as reviewed above. Third, he allows for different stock market liberalization dates, whereas Levine and Zervos enforce the same date (1985) on all countries.

Two additional studies of the impact of equity-market openness on growth—Gupta and Yuan (2006) and Mitton (2006)—are reviewed below in the section considering studies that use data at the sectoral and firm levels. Both studies find evidence of a positive impact of equity market liberalization on growth in manufacturing industries. Overall, the literature on cross-country tests for the impact of equity market liberalization on growth seems less well developed than that for general openness or for openness to FDI. The studies available do imply large gains for investment rates but tend to be ambiguous with regard to how long the increase persists and the magnitude of the growth effect resulting from the investment effect.

Crisis Impact

The principal concerns about negative effects of capital-market opening have to do with the resulting exposure of the economy to financial crises. Following the East Asian financial crises, these concerns were prominently raised at the heuristic level by such authors as Bhagwati (1998) and Stiglitz (2002).

Rodrik and Velasco (1999) conduct cross-country tests for 32 emerging-market economies for 1988–98 on the relationship of financial crises to the stock of short-term external debt, under the hypothesis that large short-term debt increases vulnerability to a confidence crisis. They define a financial crisis as a reversal in net private capital flows amounting to 5 percent of GDP or more from flows the previous year. When they conduct a probit test relating the event of a financial crisis to a dummy variable for high short-term debt (set to unity if short-term external debt exceeds reserves), they find that such exposure triples the probability of a crisis. Greater short-term exposure is also associated with more severe crises, measured by the reduction in the growth rate, when crises do occur. The increased severity reflects the more extreme currency depreciations associated with higher short-term debt relative to reserves. Essentially, higher short-term debt relative to reserves means a larger potential forced reduction in the external current account deficit, which will likely involve a reduction in growth and currency depreciation. The authors find no relationship of short-term debt to trade and infer that trade credit is not the driver of short-term debt. The authors recommend the lengthening of public debt as well as introduction of disincentives to short-term borrowing as policies to avoid financial crises.

Tornell, Westermann, and Martinez (2004) specifically examine the relationship between openness and financial fragility, and hence the role of financial liberalization in contributing to crises. After first examining the overall impact of financial openness on growth (as discussed above), they turn to specific tests on the costs of crisis vulnerability. For this purpose, they use "negative skewness" of credit growth (long left tail in the distribution) as a measure of financial fragility.[60] They show that in the medium-enforcement countries, negative skewness is much greater in financially liberalized country years (averaging −1.1) than in nonliberalized country years (+0.16). For example, there was high average credit growth over 1988–99 but also negative skewness in Thailand (14.3 percent and −1.95, respectively) and Mexico (9.1 percent and −0.54), in contrast to slow credit growth and slightly positive skewness in India (1.4 percent and +0.16). They find that for their medium-enforcement countries as a group, credit growth accelerates from 3.8 percent annually in years before financial liberalization to 7.8 percent in years after, and skewness shifts from about zero before to −1.08 after. In contrast, absence of credit-market distortions in high-enforcement countries means skewness is moderate and positive even though all country-years are financially liberalized.

Using event analysis, Tornell, Westermann, and Martinez find that "over the six years following the liberalization date, the credit-to-GDP ratio increases on average by 6 percentage points" and "the average negative skewness increases from about zero to −2.5" (p. 13).[61] They surmise another stylized fact: "Over the last two decades countries with bumpy credit paths have grown faster than those with smooth credit paths, when the standard variables are controlled for" (p. 14). The authors then present regressions for growth per capita including as explanatory variables the mean, standard deviation, and negative skewness of credit growth, as well as the control variables and the financial and trade liberalization variables. The coefficients are significant, with values of about 0.15 on mean credit growth, −0.03 on standard deviation, and +0.17 on negative skewness. For example, Thailand has higher growth than India because it is a credit risk-taker. If the financial liberalization variable is included, the negative skewness coefficient swings to negative, because given openness, extra skewness has an adverse (greater crisis) effect. The authors infer that "clearly, liberalization without fragility is best, but the data suggest that this combination is not available to medium-enforcement countries" (p. 18).

Despite their emphasis on the partial negative offset to gains from financial liberalization caused by increased financial crises, the actual coefficient estimates in Tornell, Westermann, and Martinez (2004) seem to indicate that there is much gain with little pain. Applying their coefficients to the sample means for liberalizing medium-enforcement countries to nonliberalizing medium-enforcement countries, it turns out that gain

---

60. Skewness is the third standardized moment of a distribution and equals the ratio of the third moment about the mean to the cube of the standard deviation.

61. Although they do not explicitly say so, this finding provides strong support for the argument that financial openness spurs financial deepening, which in turn the literature strongly suggests translates into faster growth. Importantly, this time the first link does not depend on foreign bank presence, which means it is not limited to FDI in the financial sector.

from financial liberalization (1.89 percentage points per year) greatly exceeds the loss from increased negative skewness of credit (0.09 percentage point).[62] Viewed from another standpoint, the tests incorporating credit growth skewness only moderately reduce the growth coefficient on financial openness in the simple cross-country tests (with control variables): from a 2.8 percentage point per year boost to growth to 1.89 percentage points. From this perspective, incorporation of financial crises might be said to cut the large positive growth impact of financial openness by about one-third. The strong results in the simpler tests also suggest that it is the use of de facto openness, together with the screening out of countries that do not meet minimal financial market tests, that drive the strong results for openness in the study, rather than its special attention to financial crises and skewness of credit growth.

Edwards (2006) addresses the same question: whether financial openness is counterproductive for growth because it makes countries more susceptible to costly financial crises. He uses a specially constructed index of capital mobility, based on the measures of Quinn (1997) and Mody and Murshid (2005), and refined with additional country information. As such, his measure is for de jure capital mobility, not de facto. Using data for 163 countries for 1970–2000, he divides country-years into three equal-sized groups of high, intermediate, and low mobility. He notes a trend of opening over time—the low category includes 44 percent of the observations for 1970, but only 24 percent by 2000.

He uses the Eichengreen, Rose, and Wyplosz (1996) definition of crisis, which captures a sharp currency depreciation and/or a severe loss in reserves. By this definition, the incidence of crises is nearly as high for industrial countries (13.5 percent of country-years) as for Latin America (14.1 percent), but notably higher for Asia (17.5) and especially Eastern Europe (31.3 percent). He divides the sample into three equal groupings by degree of capital mobility. Surprisingly, he finds statistically significantly greater incidence of crises in countries with low capital mobility (17.1 percent) than with high (12.8 percent). When he conducts this same comparison regionally, this pattern holds up for industrial countries, Latin America, Asia, and the Middle East, but not for Africa and Eastern Europe (where high mobility economies experience greater incidence of crises). The implication is that higher capital mobility does not increase the chance of financial crisis.

Edwards then conducts growth regressions examining the effect of crises, which, as expected, significantly reduce growth. He then extends the tests to examine whether an interaction term between crisis and capital mobility intensifies the growth loss. He finds that the coefficient of the interacted variable is not significant in any of the various regressions. He concludes that "countries that restrict capital mobility have not experi-

---

62. Calculated from tables 2 and 3 in Tornell, Westermann, and Martinez (2004).

enced milder crisis than countries that allow for a freer mobility of capital" (p. 13).[63]

Glick, Guo, and Hutchison (2006) examine whether capital account liberalization increases or reduces the incidence of currency crises. They cite previous work (Glick and Hutchison 2005) that found a significant positive correlation between capital controls and the occurrence of currency crises. This subsequent study seeks to determine whether this result holds up after taking account of self-selection bias: namely, countries that are under less pressure on their currencies and hence less likely to experience crises may be precisely the countries that are more inclined to liberalize capital accounts. They use three approaches to "matching" liberalization cases with comparable nonliberalization cases and then examine whether lower crisis incidence holds up after using the matching method to screen out selection bias.

The authors use the AREAER de jure measure of capital account openness. For 69 developing countries in 1975–97, there were currency crises in 11.7 percent of the country-year observations. For the full period, liberalized country-years accounted for 16.2 percent of the observations, starting higher at 20.6 percent in 1975–79 but falling to a trough of 11 percent in 1985–89 before rising to 23.8 percent in 1995–97. An initial simple test shows that capital account liberalization was in place in a smaller, rather than larger, percent of the crisis cases (6.8 percent versus 12.7 percent), with the difference highly significant. This finding parallels the results in Edwards (2006), as just discussed. The authors then estimate a probitliberalization propensity equation that includes current account position, level of international interest rates, government spending relative to GDP, and trade openness as explanatory variables. With this propensity equation in hand, they use three alternative matching techniques to compare incidence of currency crises in the liberalized group against that in the matched nonliberalized group.[64] They find that the liberalized group has a statistically lower incidence of currency crises, by 5 to 7 percentage points, than the nonliberalized control group, across the three matching methods. They thus conclude that their own, and other, previous studies showing lesser incidence of currency crises for countries

---

63. Although he does not specify why, Edwards apparently judges that this new finding supersedes his result in Edwards (2005) to the effect that although capital mobility does not increase the incidence of crises, "once a crisis occurs, countries with higher capital mobility may face a higher cost, in terms of growth decline" (Edwards 2006, 30). The two studies use the same new index of capital mobility.

64. The first matching technique is "nearest neighbor": a country-year of crisis with liberalization propensity "x" is matched with another country-year with the propensity score closest to "x" but without a crisis. The second is "radius": a crisis case is matched with the average of all country-year cases with liberalization propensity scores within a given distance (radius) from the score for the country-year in question. The third is a "stratification" approach, dividing the sample into several strata of propensity scores.

with liberalized capital accounts are confirmed even after taking account of possible selection bias.

In late 2008, at a time of acute global financial crisis, Reinhart and Rogoff (2008) released a new historical study finding, surprisingly, that industrial countries are just as likely as developing countries to experience banking crises. Their data show that weighting by share of world income, about 40 percent of countries encountered banking crises in the 1930s. From the early 1940s to the early 1970s the incidence dropped to almost zero, but then surged to an average of about 25 percent in the mid-1980s through 2001. After another brief decline to zero, banking crises again swept 25 percent of countries in the 2008 financial crisis. Reinhart and Rogoff suggest that the three-decade calm was associated with repression of domestic financial markets and capital controls but caution that they are "not necessarily" advocating such repression and controls as the way to deal with risk of financial crises (p. 7).

In the early 1980s, banking and sovereign debt crises afflicted Latin America and then Africa. In the United States the savings and loan crisis began in 1984. In the late 1980s and early 1990s, large capital inflows and surging real estate prices provoked severe banking crises in the Nordic countries. The bursting of the asset bubble brought a decade of banking crisis in Japan beginning in 1992, and collapse of the Soviet bloc prompted crises in Eastern Europe. A renewed series of banking crises then ensued in emerging-market economies, including Mexico and Argentina in 1994–95; East Asia and Russia in 1997–98; Argentina in 2001; and Uruguay in 2002. Then the US subprime crisis in mid-2007 triggered the global financial crisis of 2007–09.

The authors examine the number of years spent in sovereign debt crisis and in banking crisis. They find that whereas advanced countries have graduated from sovereign defaults, they have not been able to do so in the realm of banking crises. From 1945 (or year of independence) through 2008, there were an average of 1.7 banking crises per country in emerging-market economies and 1.4 in advanced economies (p. 17). They present a provocative graph showing a seeming correlation between capital mobility and incidence of banking crises from 1800 to 2008. However, it seems questionable to seek to learn much about capital markets and growth in the postwar period from experiences from 1800 through the 1930s. The correlation breaks down in the decade 1995–2005 as banking crises subside but capital mobility rises further. Nonetheless, the authors judge that "one common characteristic of the run-up to banking crises is a sustained surge in capital inflows," and cite the cases of the United States, United Kingdom, Spain, Iceland, and Ireland (pp. 25–26). They also cite the role of housing market bubbles, however, raising the possibility of too many culprits.

Reinhart and Rogoff present summary estimates on the loss of output associated with banking crises. Their graph implies a typical cumulative loss of about 3 percent of GDP from baseline growth (although this may be overstated because growth before the crisis was unsustainable). Combining this loss estimate with the incidence estimate of about 1.5 banking crises per country since 1945, one can infer that typical total output loss attributable to banking crises amounts to a once-for-all value of 4.5 percent of GDP. If GDP is 4.5 percent lower after 63 years than it would have been with no banking crises, the implication is that these crises on average cut the annual growth rate by 0.07 percent per year, or less than one-tenth of 1 percent.[65] This finding is almost diametrically opposed to the authors' tone of great concern about the risks of banking crises. It means that growth losses are almost negligible compared with ongoing growth, which is typically in the range of about 2 percent per capita annually in purchasing power terms for non-African countries, with higher rates for those countries beginning at lower incomes and lower rates for richer countries (Cline 2004, 56).

The authors indeed pass quickly over growth costs and instead emphasize fiscal costs. They find that the real stock of public debt typically rises 86 percent by three years after the crisis and that the principal source of the increase in debt is the collapse of revenue from recession rather than direct bailout costs (Reinhart and Rogoff 2008, 45).[66] For purposes of the present study, it is important to recognize that the authors do not conduct formal tests of the role of financial liberalization in causing banking crises. It is perhaps even more striking that their numbers, if not their rhetoric, suggest that it would not matter very much to long-term growth even if financial liberalization were completely responsible for banking crises, because those crises are not very important in suppressing long-term growth.

Hutchison and Noy (2005) examine the economic cost of currency crises and banking crises, and in particular, whether the costs of simultaneous "twin" crises are more than additive because of adverse feedback effects between the two. They use instrumental variable and GMM techniques applied to 24 emerging-market economies for 1975–97 for their tests.[67] They use the Kaminsky-Reinhart (1999) index of currency crises, which weights two alternative indicators (reserve loss and severe currency depreciation). For banking crises, they use episodes identified by previous researchers.[68] Their estimating equations for economic growth as a func-

---

65. That is, $1.0007^{63} = 1.045$.

66. In contrast, for nine episodes of banking crises the authors report average estimated bailout costs of 12.8 percent of GDP and median costs of 8 percent, albeit with wide spreads in the estimate range for several of the cases (p. 36).

67. Their definition sets $2,000 per capita income in 1992 as the threshold for emerging-market economies and as a result excludes both China and India from the set considered.

68. Caprio and Klingebiel (1996) and Demirgüç-Kunt and Detragiache (1998).

tion of control variables and the crisis dummies use a rather unusual set of economic environment and policy proxies for the controls. The proxies include trade-weighted growth of G-3 industrial countries and a lagged index of exchange rate overvaluation (both significant), as well as lagged changes in government budgets and credit growth (neither significant).

For their set of 24 emerging-market economies over 22 years, the authors identify 51 currency crises, lasting an average of 1.3 years, and 33 banking crises, lasting an average of 3.2 years. Of these, there are 20 "twin"crises (in which a currency crisis occurs within two years of a banking crisis). Their central estimates indicate that a currency crisis imposes a cumulative output loss of 5 to 8 percent of GDP, and a banking crisis imposes a cumulative loss of 8 to 10 percent of GDP (p. 725). However, there is no additional loss associated with twin incidence of the two types of crises (beyond their additive effect). Even so, the authors' loss estimates for a banking crisis are about twice as high as those implied by Reinhart and Rogoff (2008), as noted above.[69]

The authors do not examine (or mention) the influence of financial globalization in increasing the probability of either a currency crisis or a banking crisis. However, it is useful to think about their results in terms of incidence frequency combined with event severity. The average incidence of currency crises is 2.1 per country over 22 years, or 0.097 per country-year. This frequency is sobering, as it suggests that in any given year an emerging-market economy faces a 10 percent probability of a currency crisis. Applying the midpoint of the cumulative output loss, the expected output loss would be 0.65 percent per year from currency crises.[70] There are fewer banking crises: 1.375 per country, or 6.25 percent per year over the 22-year period. Nonetheless, this incidence is almost three times as high as that estimated by Reinhart and Rogoff (2008).[71] Although the Hutchison-Noy banking crises are less frequent than their currency crises, greater severity of banking crises means that their results imply approximately equal expected annual output losses (0.56 percent per year for banking crises).[72]

The episodes of currency crisis and banking crisis compiled by Hutchison and Noy (2005) can be combined with the financial-openness

---

69. The cumulative loss per banking crisis is 4.5 percent of GDP in the Reinhart-Rogoff results. With a typical incidence of 1.5 banking crises per country over the 63 years since 1945, the corresponding incidence rate is 2.4 percent per year, in contrast to 6.25 percent in the Hutchison-Noy results.

70. Annual probability of 9.7 percent multiplied by 6.5 percent of GDP loss.

71. As discussed above, their rate is 1.5 crises per country over a 63-year period, for an incidence rate of 1.5/63 = 2.38 percent per year.

72. Annual probability of 6.25 percent multiplied by an average 9 percent of GDP cumulative loss.

index compiled by Quinn and Toyoda (2008) to examine whether financial globalization is associated with greater incidence of crisis. For 22 emerging-market economies, in each of two periods, three groups can be separated: low, medium, and high financial openness.[73] As shown in figure 2.1, in both the earlier and later periods, the frequency of both currency and banking crises is modestly lower for the high-openness group than for the low-openness group.[74] This pattern supports the finding of Edwards (2006) in challenging the usual assumption that greater financial openness leads to greater crisis incidence.

In contrast to this pattern of surprising insensitivity of crises to financial openness or closedness, Reinhart and Reinhart (2008) present evidence suggesting indirectly that such openness is a substantial factor in crises. They work with data for 181 countries for the period 1980–2008. They define a "capital flow bonanza" as being present for any country when for the year in question, the amount of capital flow (measured as the negative of the current account deficit) relative to GDP is in the top quintile *for that country*. This definition is problematic because it implicitly assumes that—if bonanzas are a problem—all countries have equal frequency of such "problems." They report that because of their metric, for example, the threshold current account deficit for a "bonanza" is only 1.8 percent of GDP in India, but it is 6.6 percent in Malaysia (p. 10). They also adopt a curious approach of attributing crises (or more specifically, estimating the "conditional probability of a crisis") to the presence of a capital flow bonanza within three years before or three years *after* the crisis. Just how a posterior event is supposed to be causal is never clarified.

The Reinhart and Reinhart results would thus seem to warrant considerable skepticism. Subject to this caveat, their results suggest that for middle- and low-income countries, the presence of a capital flow bonanza increases the probability of a currency crash from 22.7 to 31.5 percent (or by the proportion 0.39), and increases the probability of a banking crisis from 14.3 to 20.7 percent (a proportional increase of 0.45). There would be an additional step needed, however, to translate such estimates into a corresponding calculation of the increase in crisis probability as a consequence of external financial openness. It would be necessary to assume that only financially open economies can experience a capital flow bonanza. This inference would be mistaken, because their set of developing countries includes many low-income aid recipients, whose current account deficits

---

73. With seven, eight, and seven countries, respectively, the average Quinn-Toyoda openness scores were 27, 45, and 81 for 1975–84 and 45, 67, and 88 for 1985–97. Note that some countries migrated from one grouping to another from the first to second period.

74. Note that the proportion of years in crisis is higher than the frequency incidence of crises as defined by Hutchison and Noy, especially for banking crises that persist longer, because the second year of a crisis is defined as constituting continuation of an earlier crisis rather than a new one.

Figure 2.1 Proportion of years in crisis and degree of financial openness (22 emerging-market economies)

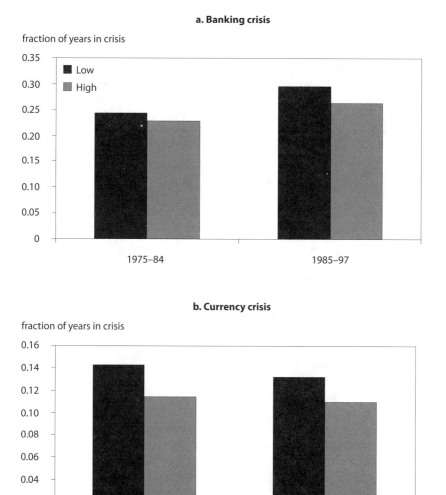

a. Banking crisis

fraction of years in crisis

■ Low
▨ High

1975–84   1985–97

b. Currency crisis

fraction of years in crisis

1975–84   1985–97

Source: Calculated from databases of Toyoda and Quinn (2008) and Hutchison and Noy (2005).

could be large even in the face of rigorous controls on capital. In short, the study seems useful mainly as providing an upper bound on the plausible impact of financial openness on the frequency of crises. That is, by automatically imputing bonanzas one-fifth of the time, by assuming inverse chronological causation and by pooling poor with emerging-market economies, the study seems likely to overstate the incidence of crises associated with financial openness.

Finally, it is useful to combine alternative benchmark parameters for crisis incidence and impact with the earlier range of general growth impact to trace out an implied range of net effects of financial globalization. Suppose that the cumulative damage of a currency crisis, as a fraction of GDP, is d_c. Similarly, let d_b be the cumulative damage of a banking crisis, as a fraction of GDP. Define ϕ_c as the expected annual incidence rate for currency crisis in a given country and ϕ_b as the corresponding incidence rate for banking crisis. Suppose that the effect of complete financial openness versus closedness is to multiply the probability of a currency crisis by $(1 + \pi_c)$, and multiply the probability of a banking crisis by $(1 + \pi_b)$. (For example, if the probability of currency crisis is 8 percent under closed external financial markets and 12 percent with complete financial openness, $\pi_c = 0.5$.) Suppose that the annual growth impact of general financial liberalization (as opposed to specific crisis effects) is estimated at Δ_g. Then the expected annual net output gain from financial globalization is:

$$W = \Delta_g - \pi_c d_c \phi_c - \pi_b d_b \phi_b . \tag{2.1}$$

Table 2.4 sets forth stylized ranges for the crisis impact parameters of equation 2.1 based on the crisis studies considered here. With such ranges in hand, it is possible to calculate a range of alternative estimates of the influence of financial openness on economic losses from crises.

The incidence estimates in table 2.4 are set as follows. The Hutchison and Noy estimate of 10 percent frequency for currency crises is translated to 12 percent for the adverse case and 8 percent for the favorable case. The Hutchison and Noy study also provides the basis for the adverse estimate of banking crisis incidence (6.5 percent). Reinhart and Rogoff (2008) provide the basis for the favorable estimate (2.38 percent). The Hutchison and Noy study gives the range of 5 to 8 percent of GDP as the output loss associated with a currency crisis. The same study provides the basis for the unfavorable estimate of output loss from a banking crisis (10 percent of GDP). The Reinhart and Reinhart study is the basis for the favorable estimate of banking crisis loss (4 percent of GDP). For the fractional increment of crisis incidence resulting from financial openness, Reinhart and Reinhart provide the adverse cases for both currency and banking crises (0.4 each, as discussed above). In contrast, on the basis of figure 2.1, in the favorable cases financial openness is assumed to *reduce* the frequency of crises. For currency crises the reduction is set at 5 percent. For banking crises, the reduction is set greater at 15 percent, on grounds that financial openness makes it possible to strengthen the domestic banking system through the presence of stronger international institutions and greater competition.

Table 2.4   Illustrative parameters for expected annual crisis impact of financial openness

Concept	Symbol	Value Adverse	Value Favorable
General incidence of currency crisis	ϕ_c	0.12	0.08
General incidence of banking crisis	ϕ_b	0.065	0.024
Damage from currency crisis (fraction of GDP)	d_c	0.08	0.05
Damage from banking crisis (fraction of GDP)	d_b	0.10	0.04
Proportional increase in probability of currency crisis from financial openness	π_c	0.40	−.05
Proportional increase in probability of banking crisis from financial openness	π_b	0.40	−.15

Although these stylized-fact parameters are mainly illustrative, they do serve to trace out the boundaries of likely output impact of financial openness. With six parameters and two alternative values of each, there are 64 cases (= 2^6). When these are enumerated, the final two components of equation 2.1 yield the following range of the expected annual impact of financial openness versus closedness. At the adverse extreme, in any given year the expected output loss from currency and banking crises would be 0.64 percent of GDP under complete openness rather than under closedness. At the favorable extreme, output would instead be 0.15 percent *higher* under openness than closedness as a consequence of reducing crisis frequency.[75] Across the 64 possible combinations, the lowest 30 percent range from −0.64 percent to −0.25 percent impact; the next 45 percent, from −0.25 percent to zero; and the remaining 27 percent, from zero to +0.15 percent impact on full-period output from financial openness with respect to crisis effects.

Now consider the trade-off of crisis risk against general growth gains from financial openness shown in equation 2.1. The first term in the equation would conservatively set Δ_g at 0.5 percent, based on the meta-statistical estimate in table 2.1. If the worst-case expected crisis loss is used, it would indeed be a poor bargain to open financially, because the secular growth boost of 0.5 percent of GDP would be more than offset by the annual expected loss from crisis risk (0.64 percent of GDP). However, it turns out that expected annual crisis loss is greater than 0.5 percent of GDP in only three of the 64 cases resulting from table 2.3. So one can say that *the odds are 20 to 1 that secular output gains from financial openness exceed expected losses from increased crisis vulnerability* even if the most conservative estimate is

---

75. Calculated respectively as: −0.4 x 0.08 x 0.12 − 0.4 x 0.1 x 0.065 = −0.00644; and − (−0.05) x 0.08 x 0.12 − (−.15) x 0.1 x 0.065 = 0.00146. (These are the last two components of equation 2.1.)

used for the gain in secular growth from financial openness. If instead the average of statistically significant estimates for growth gains were used (2 percent per annum; see table 2.1), there would be unambiguous net gains from financial openness because the expected crisis losses would be much smaller in comparison. Moreover, the median expected crisis loss from the 64 cases turns out to be 0.14 percent of GDP, and the average expected loss, 0.15 percent. So using the conservative 0.5 percent per year secular growth gain as offset by about 0.15 percent expected crisis loss, there is a clear and relatively large net gain from financial openness. The net growth gain of 0.35 percent per year would translate into a GDP that was 3.6 percent higher after a decade and 15 percent higher after four decades. Furthermore, it may be more appropriate to view the secular growth gain as already having been estimated on a net basis deducting expected crisis losses, because the econometric studies are capturing observed behavior rather than hypothetical outcomes in the absence of any crises.

In short, a calibrated simulation of plausible crisis impacts suggests that for emerging-market economies, the long-term gains from financial openness are likely to exceed cumulative losses from occasional crisis (if any) induced by greater openness.[76] At the same time, the cross-country statistical studies focusing on the relationship of crises to financial openness may also be seen as pointing to a need for a more nuanced diagnosis. First, the evidence does suggest that countries that ran up high short-term debt relative to reserves (and relative to GDP) tended to get into trouble (Rodrik and Velasco 1999). Second, however, financially open countries seem to have lower rather than higher incidence of crises (Edwards 2006; Glick, Guo, and Hutchison 2006). In any event, financially more-open economies achieve faster growth even after taking account of their more "bumpy" credit expansion experience (Tornell, Westermann, and Marti-

---

76. This result appears to be robust to even sharply increased damage estimates. Thus, in an unpublished paper my colleague John Williamson (2008) places the average cost of a currency crisis at 35 percent of one year's GDP. The estimate is based on 34 episodes in industrial and emerging-market economies during 1991 through 2003. Although his damage estimate is far higher than the range of 5 to 8 percent used here, this difference derives importantly from his concentration on the worst crises. Thus, his incidence of 34 cases out of 391 country-years considered is only 3.7 percent, well below the range of 8 to 12 percent used here. (The high average damage estimate also reflects an arguably exaggerated estimate of 76 percent of a year's GDP in the case of Argentina, for which he departs from his general methodology.)

If the currency crisis damage parameter is set at Williamson's d_c =0.35, the incidence parameter at his ϕ_c =0.037, and all other parameters of the exercise here are left unchanged, then there are 16 possible outcomes. Of these, only four cases result in expected annual crisis losses in excess of the secular gain from financial openness of 0.5 percent extra growth, with the annual crisis losses at 1.0, 0.7, 0.62, or 0.55 percent. So the odds are still 3 to 1 in favor of growth gains in excess of crisis losses (i.e., 12 out of 16 cases). Moreover, there are five favorable cases in which the contribution of crisis effects is positive rather than negative, because of the possibility that openness reduces rather than increases crisis incidence (as implied by figure 2.1).

nez 2004). The need for nuance arises because the smoking gun of vulnerability seems to be associated with one very specific form of financial openness: unencumbered short-term debt. In contrast, the salutary effects of financial openness seem to be associated with the much broader gauges based on overall de jure (AREAER, including Quinn and Edwards derivatives) or de facto (Tornell, Westermann, and Martinez) measures. It is tempting to harmonize these results by concluding that for purposes of achieving higher growth while limiting vulnerability to crises, it makes sense to pursue overall capital-market openness but in a fashion that avoids excessive buildups in short-term debt. This differentiation is also consistent with the hierarchy of contribution to growth from alternative capital account components found by Reisen and Soto (2001), as discussed above (with FDI as most positive and short-term debt as negative).

The main caveat to this conclusion is evidence that inhibitions on short-term debt may impose costs of their own. If so, the question becomes one of a trade-off between increased probability of a crisis with high short-term debt, on the one hand, and persistent costs from disincentives to short-term debt, on the other. The classic market-friendly disincentive to short-term capital inflows is Chile's *encaje*, a tax imposed on inflows of short-term capital during 1991–98. Most analyses do conclude that the *encaje* tilted the composition of capital inflows from short- to longer-term forms (e.g., Cline 1999). However, Forbes (2003) uses microeconomic data to show that the policy disproportionately increased the cost of capital to small firms and reports findings of other studies reaching the same conclusion. Edwards (1999) similarly reports that the Chilean arrangements increased the cost of capital substantially for small and medium-sized firms, noting that borrowing costs to small firms in 1996–97 were on the order of 20 percent. Because short-term structure is in effect a means of obtaining greater security for the creditor in lieu of better collateral or an ideal legal environment, it is plausible that restricting short-term borrowing abroad would adversely affect the smaller firms more than large firms. At the same time, in recent years many emerging-market economies have addressed the question of risk from a high ratio of short-term debt to reserves by building up reserves dramatically, and although there is an opportunity cost of the low return on these reserves, it is by no means obvious that this cost exceeds the cost that would be incurred by curbing access to short-term credit.

In early 2010, the International Monetary Fund (IMF) issued a Staff Position Note examining the conditions under which capital controls might be a useful policy tool (Ostry et al. 2010). The paper identified four conditions as necessary to warrant controls: the economy is operating near potential and overheating is a concern; there is an adequate level of reserves; the exchange rate is not undervalued; and the excessive flows are likely to be transitory. The study acknowledged that "widespread adoption of controls could have a chilling longer-term impact on financial integration and globalization, with significant output and welfare losses" (p. 5). It further acknowledged that "widespread use of controls, especially by systemi-cally important countries, could also impede necessary steps to address global imbalances…where currencies are undervalued and where appre-ciation is needed to support global demand rebalancing" (p. 10).

The first test for policy is whether the exchange rate is overvalued. Unfortunately, the authors do not give a clear criterion for answering this question, such as a threshold current account surplus that should be a pre-sumptive indicator of undervaluation. If many emerging-market econo-mies sought to pursue mercantilist growth in a period of weak growth and low interest rates in industrial countries, the consequence could be a prolif-eration of capital controls designed to prevent exchange rates from appre-ciating in an effort to maintain current account surpluses (a severe problem in recent years in the case of China and some other East Asian economies). It is difficult to envision an operational effect of the authors' injunction to take "due account" of "multilateral impact," as finance ministers would typically and understandably place higher priority on their own econo-mies than on international considerations. The authors' sequence of hur-dles includes "scope for fiscal tightening." If such scope exists, then their advice is to tighten fiscal policy. If not, their hurdle is cleared to impose controls. Tighter fiscal policy, along with currency appreciation, is the tra-ditional macroeconomic response to excessive inflows, working through a reduction in domestic interest rates and hence in the incentive to capital inflows. The authors do not clarify under what conditions there would be no "scope" for fiscal policy tightening, however. Their initial condition is a construct in which the economy is overheating, and typically tighter fiscal policy would be precisely what is appropriate under these conditions. Yet determining that there was nonetheless no scope for tightening could too easily be an excuse for avoiding the political difficulties of tightening.

The authors summarize that "there are two main reasons why govern-ments might want to impose capital controls—to limit the appreciation of the exchange rate and to limit crisis vulnerability due to excessive or particularly risky forms of foreign borrowing" (p. 11). Yet the general in-terpretation of Chile's experience with the *encaje* is that it failed in the for-mer objective (by stretching out maturities rather than reducing volume of capital inflows). As for the latter concern, the analysis and discussion of this section suggest that concerns about crisis vulnerability may have been exaggerated relative to potential gains from financial openness.

Institutions and Policy Discipline

Another category of statistical studies examines the relationship of capi-tal mobility to institutions and policies. One of the standard arguments in support of financial openness is that it can act as a form of discipline on country policies. Tytell and Wei (2004) conduct cross-country tests of this hypothesis using data for 22 industrial and 40 developing countries for five-year periods from 1975 to 1999. Their measure of openness is the ratio of the sum of external assets and liabilities to GDP. Their initial summary information shows a remarkable rise in this indicator, especially for industrial countries, which reached an average level of 165 percent of GDP in the late 1990s, about four times the average for developing countries. They find a negative simple correlation of both inflation and the budget deficit as a percent of GDP with financial globalization. In three-stage least-squares regressions that include other variables such as the frequency of change of central bank governors, trade openness, and an industrial country dummy variable, they find a significant negative impact of financial openness on inflation but not on the budget deficit. The strength of the negative impact on inflation increases, but the impact on budget deficits remains insignificant, when the authors use the average financial-openness measures of neighboring countries as an instrument for financial openness.

The authors then pursue a Markov-chain approach to examine the probability of transition across low (less than 10 percent), medium (10 to 40 percent), and high rates of inflation (above 40 percent) from one five-year period to the next. Although inflation performance is relatively persistent (the diagonals are 84 percent probability for low to low, 52 percent for medium to medium, and 66 percent for high to high), the long-run probabilities are clustered at low inflation (70 percent incidence), with only 4 percent long-run incidence of high inflation. They then estimate the influence of financial openness on the transition probabilities. They find that financial openness has a negative and statistically significant effect on the probability of transition from low to medium inflation and (when the instrumented variant is used) a significant positive effect on the probability of transition from high to medium and from medium to low. Three of the four possible combinations thus show a statistically significant beneficial effect of financial globalization on inflation, and the fourth (medium to high) has a beneficial sign but is not statistically significant. When the authors conduct a similar test for transition across alternative budget deficit thresholds, however, they find no influence of financial globalization. They conclude: "There is some modest evidence that financial globalization may have induced countries to pursue low-inflation monetary policies...[but] no evidence that it has encouraged low budget deficits" (Tytell and Wei 2004, 34).

It is not clear why the authors consider the evidence for discipline on inflation only "modest," considering the systematic significant negative impact of financial globalization on this variable. Moreover, the coefficients appear to be of substantial economic size. For example, in the three-stage least-squares results, the estimated coefficient implies that moving from 40 to 80 percent in the ratio of external assets plus liabilities to GDP would reduce inflation from, say, 60 to 40 percent annually for a high-inflation country and from 25 to 17 percent for a medium-inflation country.[77]

Klein (2005) examines the influence of institutional quality on the impact of financial globalization on growth. He begins with a reminder that even the critics of financial openness (e.g., Rodrik 1998) do "not suggest that open capital accounts cannot have a salutary effect; rather, they argue that the environment in which capital account liberalization occurs is a potentially important determinant of its consequences" (Klein 2005, 2). He first constructs a theoretical model that is consistent with an inverted-U shape for the influence of financial openness on growth. Namely, opening should have stronger positive growth effects on countries with relatively high, but not the highest, institutional quality. The framework is a neoclassical growth model with standard capital, noncollateralizable capital including human, raw labor, and labor efficiency units. The dynamic growth rate in such a model turns out to be a constant multiplied by the difference between the logarithm of per capita income and the logarithm of steady-state per capita income.[78] Klein introduces the role of institutional quality as representing assurance against expropriation of capital. The risk premium is lower, capital accumulation is higher, and the eventual steady-state level of per capita income is higher for higher institutional quality because of lower expropriation risk. Crucially, autarky steady-state per capita income is closer to the full potential attainable under financial openness if the country has high institutional quality. This is the reason why the greatest contribution of capital openness to growth is at an intermediate rather than the highest level of institutional quality.

Having motivated the inverse-U response, Klein uses data on 71 countries for 1976–95 to make empirical estimates. The estimation equation includes the usual control variables. He uses the AREAER de jure measure for the share of years the capital account is open. His indicator of institutional quality is an average of five series from the International Country Risk Group. His preferred specification includes interactions between the share of years open and the first, second, and third powers of the institutional quality index, with an expected positive coefficient for the square and negative coefficient for the cube. The estimates indicate that capital account openness is a significant determinant of growth for countries with

---

77. The dependent variable is the logarithm of the percentage rate of inflation. Financial openness is measured as a percent of GDP. So the estimated coefficient of –0.01 means, in the first example, that log inflation would start at $\ln(60) = 4.094$; the rise in financial globalization would reduce it by $0.01 \times 40 = 0.4$, leaving log inflation at 3.694, which corresponds to an inflation rate of 40 percent.

78. The constant is: $-(1 - \alpha - \beta)(n + g + \delta)$, where α is the elasticity of output with respect to normal capital, β is the elasticity with respect to capital that cannot be collateralized, the output elasticity of efficiency labor units is $(1 - \alpha - \beta)$, n is the growth rate of labor, g is the growth rate of labor efficiency, and δ is the rate of depreciation.

above-median levels of institutional quality. At the peak of the inverse U, about the institutional quality level of Korea, average growth for a financially open economy is an enormous 3.35 percentage points per year greater than that for a closed economy. Even at lower institutional-quality levels, such as the 55th percentile as represented by Mexico, the boost to annual growth from financial openness is 1.79 percentage points (p. 24).

Klein interprets his results as indicating that 24 percent of the countries, those from the 55th to 79th percentile of institutional quality, have a significant positive impact of capital account openness on growth (the large impacts just noted). However, his coefficients are all highly significant for openness and the three interaction terms of openness with level of institutional quality. So it would seem at least equally arguable that the impact is significant over any range to which this equation is applied. It turns out that applying the equation gives an even higher growth impact at some of the lowest institutional qualities.[79] In this sense, then, Klein does not at all find that financial openness has a deleterious impact on growth at low levels of institutional quality. Instead, his results indicate that over almost the entire range of institutional quality (except the very highest), the impact on growth is positive but that this impact is statistically significant only for countries in the third quartile of the institutional quality distribution.[80] In any event, as noted below in the discussion of Edison et al. (2004), as well as in appendix 2D, tests depending on the institutional risk measure applied by Klein warrant skepticism because this measure is likely to be endogenous rather than exogenous to growth.

Wei (2006) examines the role of corruption in affecting the composition of capital inflows. He first notes that the past literature can be grouped into a "composition" school, which tends to argue that there is good foreign capital (e.g., FDI) and bad foreign capital (e.g., short-term bank loans), and a "thresholds" school, which tends to argue that foreign capital is positive for growth if a minimum threshold for some cooperating catalyst (e.g., financial development) is met, but may be bad for growth if not. He then suggests that the two schools might better be seen as interlinked rather than as competitors. In particular, he cites some of his earlier studies as showing that higher corruption (which may be seen as failure to meet an

---

79. From Klein (2005, figures 2 and 3), although the Mexico institutional quality level (4.65 composite indicator) has a higher growth impact than at a somewhat lower level (3.7), at an even lower institutional quality level (e.g., 2.45) the growth impact of openness is considerably higher than at the Mexico level. This follows directly from the large positive coefficient on the openness variable by itself, meaning that there would be a positive impact of financial openness on growth even with the institutional quality index at zero and hence the interaction terms contributing nothing.

80. The basic phenomenon behind this result is that with a given width of the confidence interval around a growth contribution curve that is rising as institutional quality (on the horizontal axis) rises, a zero contribution will be within the range of random variation toward the lower end of the institutional quality range.

institutional threshold) is associated with a lower share of FDI in capital inflows (the bad composition pattern). Wei does not spell out why creditors would be willing to lend to firms and governments in countries with high levels of corruption even though corporations would shy away from placing direct investment in them. Nonetheless, the 2006 study provides estimates with more recent data that tend to confirm this diagnosis.

Wei uses surveys of the World Bank's *World Development Report* and the World Economic Forum's *Global Competitiveness Report* for measures of corruption in 1996. His cross-section OLS regression on 65 countries for the ratio of FDI to total foreign liabilities in 2003 shows significant negative coefficients on corruption (as hypothesized) and on financial development and significant positive coefficients on resources and trade openness.[81] Nonetheless, the coefficient on corruption is relatively small. Its value of 0.04 means that if the corruption index rises by one standard deviation (0.99) above its median (0.18), the ratio of FDI to total external liabilities would rise by only 0.04, against its median of 0.25. The coefficient is much larger in the instrumental variable regressions, but these unfortunately use 19th century settler mortality as well as legal origins, a popular practice that may be useful for some purposes but seems highly dubious in explaining the evolution of virtually anything in recent decades. As Wei himself points out, these instruments condemn a country to a once-and-forever structure and make it impossible to use time series, because by definition they never change.[82] Overall, it would seem that the study sheds only limited light on whether more corrupt countries do indeed borrow more and receive less direct investment.

Sectoral- and Firm-Level Analyses

A number of the more recent statistical studies apply data at the level of manufacturing sectors (and in one case, a sample of individual firms) to examine the influence of international financial openness on growth. An important feature of this approach is that it inherently multiplies by about 30-fold the number of observations possible, given that there are about this many sectors at the level typically used. A benefit of this greater richness of observations is the often greater degree of statistical significance of results. At the same time, the implications for the overall economy are

---

81. As for the negative coefficient on domestic financial development, Wei argues that low domestic financial development would mean residents send capital abroad while FDI provides the capital for development.

82. "Since both legal origin and settler mortality are part of a country's economic history, they are essentially fixed in modern times. This dictates the focus on cross-country comparisons" (Wei 2006, 14). In any event it seems unnecessary to use instrumental variables to explain a dependent variable of 2003 using an independent variable of 1996, because the former cannot cause the latter, and so endogeneity should not be a problem.

less direct than in the aggregative studies because the estimates refer only to the manufacturing sector. Moreover, several of the studies focus on the question raised by Rajan and Zingales (1998) with regard to financial depth: Do sectors more dependent on finance external to the firm grow faster in countries with greater financial depth? Although the parallel question for financial openness is of great relevance, it is a separable issue from the question of whether financial openness boosts growth. It could easily be true that there is no difference at all across sectors but that all of them benefit (or, for that matter, do not benefit) from financial openness.

Vlachos and Waldenström (2002) were the first to invoke the approach of Rajan and Zingales (1998) as a basis for examining the influence of financial openness on growth at the sectoral level. Rajan and Zingales found that sectors more heavily reliant on financing external to the firm (based on US patterns) tend to grow more rapidly in countries with more developed financial markets. It was natural to pose the follow-up question of whether such sectors also grew faster in countries more open to foreign capital, an alternative source of finance. Vlachos and Waldenström use the Rajan-Zingales measures of sectoral external dependence (D) at the level of 36 manufacturing industries and examine 42 countries over 1980–90.[83] They authors regress growth in industry i and country j on two interaction terms, DxL and DxF, where L is a measure of financial liberalization or integration and F is a measure of financial development, as well as the share of the industry in 1980 and country as well as industry dummy variables. It should be emphasized that by focusing solely on the interaction with sectoral dependence, they risk missing a possible general influence of financial openness on growth that applies to all sectors equally.

For financial openness, the authors use alternatively the AREAER data, the Quinn measure, the Bekaert, Harvey, and Lundblad (2000) equity market liberalization data, and data on the total stocks and flows of external assets and liabilities relative to GDP. For financial development, their preferred variable is the sum of domestic credit and stock market capitalization relative to GDP. They examine growth impact separately for value-added and gross output. For value-added, they find little influence of financial openness, but a strong influence of financial development.[84] For gross output they similarly find little influence of financial openness for the full sample. However, when dividing the sample into countries with lower and higher development of domestic financial markets, they

---

83. Rajan and Zingales (1998, 564) define the external dependence ratio as capital expenditures minus cash flow, divided by capital expenditures. Although Vlachos and Waldenström do not report the number of sectors they consider, they state that their sectoral data are the same as those used by Rajan and Zingales (36 sectors; pp. 566–67).

84. Only one of the several openness measures (that of Bekaert, Harvey, and Lundblad 2000) has a positive, significant coefficient.

find that growth is increased by financial openness in the latter.[85] The overall thrust of the results is to provide modest support for a positive growth impact of financial openness contingent on "a relatively well developed financial market" (Vlachos and Waldenström 2002, 1).

For output growth in the high-financial-development countries, the authors estimate a coefficient of 0.033 on the interaction of the IMF financial-openness variable for 1980 and the degree of sectoral external dependence (p. 39). Going from 0 to 1 on the IMF openness variable would thus boost annual growth by 3.3 percentage points for a sector with external dependence of 1.0 (e.g., office machinery and computing), but not at all for a sector with dependence of zero (e.g., footwear; see Rajan and Zingales 1998, 566–67). With the median sector dependence ratio at 0.23 (ibid.), the implication is that on average, going from full financial closedness to openness would boost industrial growth by 0.76 percentage point per year, but only in countries with above-average levels of domestic financial development. Again, however, the authors conduct no direct tests for the potentially more important influence of financial openness on overall average growth, but instead focus solely on the interaction between openness and sectoral dependence on financing external to the firm.

Vanassche (2004) uses data for 27 manufacturing sectors in 45 countries for 1980–97 to test for the influence of international financial integration on growth. She applies the share of total years for which the AREAER measure shows openness for the capital account as the measure of financial openness. She first examines an economy-wide test regressing growth in each sector on a set of control variables (the sector's initial share of value added, financial depth, initial per capita GDP, government share in GDP, human capital, and trade) as well as the financial-openness variable.[86] The result is a large and statistically significant positive coefficient on financial openness. She reports that moving from the first to the third quartile for financial openness boosts cumulative growth for 1980 to 1997 by 11 percentage points, which is large relative to the mean cumulative sectoral growth of 38 percent for the period. Similarly, using her sample average of 0.33 for the share of years open, her estimated coefficient implies that moving from average to complete openness (1.0) would boost

---

85. Although the authors seek to explain the contradictory results for value-added versus gross output growth (and growth in the number of firms) by invoking increased competition and lower profit margins, it remains puzzling that the results would not be more similar for gross output and value added. Because the authors use the Rajan-Zingales data for value added but supplement it with United Nations data on gross output, it is possible that the price indexes they use for deflating the latter are not fully comparable to those used by Rajan and Zingales, despite the authors' efforts at comparability.

86. She uses an instrumental variable for the share of years with financial openness, estimated on dummy variables for no restrictions in 1985, for Latin America, Asia, and Africa.

cumulative growth over the period by 16.4 percentage points, or by 0.88 percent per year.[87]

When Vanassche adds the differential growth impact for the interaction of financial openness with sectoral dependence on external finance, once again using the Rajan-Zingales measure, she finds a significant positive impact for the interaction term. Focusing in on this interaction in additional tests, she concludes that, for example, a high-dependence sector such as machinery (external-finance dependence of 22 percent) would obtain an additional 6 percentage points of cumulative growth over the period (beyond the economy-wide financial-openness effect) in comparison with a low-dependence sector such as glass (3 percent dependence). When she adds a corresponding interaction term between domestic financial depth and external dependence, the interaction term between financial openness and sectoral dependence turns insignificant for the full sample but retains its significance for established firms of 10 years or more. She argues that it is these firms that pass information hurdles that allow them to benefit more from international capital flows. She further examines the influence of financial openness on domestic financial-sector depth and finds a statistically and economically significant effect. The significant impact is found for industrial countries as well as developing countries (whereas Klein and Olivei [1999] found a significant effect only for developing countries).

Gupta and Yuan (2006) investigate sectoral data at the level of 27 three-digit International Standard Industrial Classification (ISIC) manufacturing sectors for 31 developing countries to identify the characteristics of sectors that benefit the most from stock market liberalization. For the period 1981–98, their initial summary statistics indicate that sectoral real value added grows about one percentage point faster after liberalization than before (4.8 versus 3.7 percent), as does investment (10.4 versus 9.3 percent). In panel-regression estimates they find support for the hypothesis that sectors that depend more heavily on finance external to the firm (based on the Rajan-Zingales measure) benefit relatively more from opening, confirming at the sectoral level the notion that foreign investment in portfolio equity boosts growth by reducing capital costs. Thus, for textiles at the 75th percentile of external-finance dependence, opening boosts value-added growth by 1.8 percentage point per year more than for the petroleum-refining industry, which is at the 25th percentile of external-finance dependence. However, certain questionable characteristics of the estimates suggest caution in relying on the results.[88] Their tests do not confirm a parallel hypothesis that the impact of opening is greater for in-

---

87. The estimated coefficient is 0.245; 0.67 x 0.245 = 0.164.

88. The coefficient on stock market liberalization appears too high, at a boost of 16 percent in annual real value-added growth. The standard control variables for per capita income and private credit have the wrong signs but are statistically significant.

dustries ranked higher by international growth opportunity (as measured by international price-earnings ratios).

Mitton (2006) carries disaggregation in the analysis of financial openness one step further, examining data at the firm level for a sample of about 1,140 firms in 28 developing countries for the period 1980–2000. The data are for firms that are not only included in the IFC's emerging-markets database but also have data available in the Worldscope financial information system. The IFC reports whether a firm is "investable" by foreign investors. Mitton argues that because identifying a particular year as the date a country becomes open to foreign equity investment is problematic, as opening is typically gradual, the firm-level detail on investability by foreigners should give a superior measure of openness. In panel regressions on approximately 9,000 firm-year observations, he finds that real sales growth is 2.3 percentage points higher per year for investable firms; investment relative to assets is about 2.2 percent higher, and earnings before interest, taxes, depreciation, and amortization relative to assets is 2.3 percent higher, all with a high degree of statistical significance. Investable firms have about 10 percent higher output per worker and 3 percent lower leverage (debt to assets), again with strong significance. He argues that access to foreign equity investment makes equity capital cheaper and more attractive relative to debt than before opening to foreign investment.

Comparing his growth impact estimate of about 2 percent annually to the estimate of about 1 percent in Bekaert and Harvey (2005), Mitton suggests that the more accurate timing of opening using firm-level data, and the focus on firms directly benefiting rather than on economy-wide effects, account for the difference.[89] His event tests, comparing growth in the five years before and the five years after investability (opening) at the firm level, indirectly provide evidence that his estimates are not simply capturing generally superior performance by the better firms, which consequently are also the ones that achieve foreign investability. Instead, even though these firms do indeed have above-average performance prior to opening, the extent of their superior performance after opening rises by an estimated 1.9 percentage point in annual growth, approximately the same as the estimate from the panel data.

In another firm-level study, Desai, Foley, and Hines (2006) use US Department of Commerce survey data on foreign activities of about 20,000 US multinational firms for 1982, 1989, and 1994 to examine the influence of capital controls. Their datasets are thus far richer than in the usual summary tests at the country level. They supplement the usual AREAER binary measure of capital controls with a measure developed by Schatz (2000)

---

89. The author also suggests that his use of output unadjusted for population growth contributes to the difference, but this would seem incorrect given that his noninvestable firms in the same country confront the same population growth and the coefficient for investability conveys the difference from them.

that focuses on restrictions on capital repatriation and profits remittances. The Schatz measure frequently shows absence of controls for countries classified in the IMF measure as controlled, but the reverse never occurs, suggesting that the usual measure exaggerates the incidence of controls.[90] Regressions of interest rates paid by US multinational affiliates indicate that, after controlling for other relevant variables, interest rates are 5.25 percent higher in countries with controls using the Schatz measure and 0.8 percent higher using the IMF measure.[91] Using the annual survey data (with far fewer observations than in the benchmark years), the authors estimate that in countries with capital controls (Schatz measure), reported profit rates are 5.2 percent lower, confirming expected efforts to relocate profits to uncontrolled countries through transfer pricing and other means. They calculate that this difference is equivalent to the profit-relocation impact of an increase of 27 percent in the tax rate. The tests also show that after controls are removed, reported profits rise 6 percent. Similar tests find that affiliate investment in plant and equipment rises by about 10 percent after liberalization of capital controls. Overall the study provides support, using detailed survey data, for the view that the removal of capital controls spurs foreign investment.

Levchenko, Ranciere, and Thoenig (2007) use data at the level of 28 manufacturing sectors for 56 countries during the period 1963–2003 to examine the influence of financial liberalization on growth and volatility.[92] They compile a panel of three nonoverlapping 10-year periods with at least 10 sectors for any country-year included. They use both de facto measures of financial integration (ratio of gross capital inflows and outflows relative to GDP; ratio of gross external assets and liabilities to GDP) and de jure measures (a 0–1 version of the Kaminsky-Schmukler measures based on IMF data on domestic, capital account, and stock market liberalization).

The de facto measures all show highly significant coefficients of about 0.24 for the impact of financial liberalization on the growth rate of output, with the high significance reflecting the use of almost 4,000 observations (the consequence of three periods, 56 countries, and 28 sectors within each country). Edison et al. (2002, 30) report that the ratio of capital flows to GDP had a mean of 0.05 and standard deviation of 0.05 percent for 57 countries in 1980–2000. Applying the coefficient estimated by Levchenko, Ranciere, and Thoenig (2007), the implication is that an increase in de facto financial openness by one standard deviation increases the country's

---

90. For example, for 1982–87 the IMF reports Austria, Denmark, Finland, France, Ireland, Italy, Spain, Sweden, and Turkey all as having capital controls, whereas the Schatz measure shows no controls for these countries in these years.

91. The control variables include country tax rate, private credit relative to GDP, quality of institutions, inflation rate, and trade openness.

92. The sectors are 3-digit ISIC Revision 2 classifications. Data are from the 2006 United Nations Industrial Development Organization's (UNIDO) Industrial Statistics Database.

growth rate by 1.2 percentage points per year over the 10-year period of the observation (i.e., 0.24 x 5 percent). The authors find that the impact works through the number of firms, employees, and capital stock, rather than through increased TFP. Comparable tests show a significant impact of de facto liberalization on volatility, measured as the standard deviation of growth. The tests also indicate a greater impact of liberalization on sectors characterized by greater dependence on financing external to the firm.

The tests using the de jure measure examine the difference in growth between the 10 years before and after the financial liberalization event, based on comparison with selected control countries. Highly significant coefficients are estimated at 0.03 for number of firms, 0.024 for employment, and 0.04 for capital accumulation in the preferred specifications. Using the employment result as indicative of output, these results indicate a boost of 2.4 percent annually for growth rates in the 10 years after liberalization. There is a comparable significant increase in volatility.

The authors conclude by examining the timing of these effects. They find that the bulk of the impact is within the first six years of the liberalization; that capital accumulation effects are more persistent than effects on growth in number of firms and employees; and that the most lasting effect is an increase in competition as reflected by a decline in the price markup over cost.

Table 2.5 summarizes implied growth-impact results of the sector-based studies.[93] Once again the most striking feature is that none of the estimates is negative, an outcome that is inconsistent with zero impact (because in that case there would be a random distribution between positive and negative statistically significant estimates). Moreover, the estimates tend to be large in economic terms, like the aggregate estimates in table 2.1, once again broadly on the order of 1 to 2 percentage point increases in growth (although this time at the level of manufacturing sectors) as a consequence of openness (variously defined).

---

93. As this study went to press, a new unpublished study of sectoral effects by Eichengreen, Gullapalli, and Panizza (2009) came to the author's attention. Their analysis is similarly structured along the lines of differential growth performance by external-finance-dependent (in the Rajan-Zingales sense) sectors in the presence of financial openness. They use UNIDO industrial value-added data for 36 sectors in 49 countries, with panel data for decades of the 1980s, 1990, and early 2000s. They apply either the stock of external assets and liabilities relative to GDP de facto or the IMF binary de jure measure of financial openness. They obtain generally statistically positive estimates for the interaction term involving external-finance dependence and financial openness. For example, for open economies (above the median), a one-standard-deviation difference in external-finance dependence is associated with additional value-added growth of about 1 percent per annum. However, the coefficient on a crisis interaction term indicates that this positive effect is eliminated in periods of crisis.

Table 2.5   Sector-based studies: Implied impact of financial openness on growth in manufacturing (percent per year)

Study	Years	Number of countries	Number of sectors	Impact	Comment
Vlachos and Waldenström (2002)	1980–90	42	36	0.8	For move from complete closedness to complete openness, impact on gross output in high financial development economies at median sectoral dependence on external finance (see text)
Vanassche (2004)	1980–97	45	27	0.88	Overall, move from average to complete openness
				0.34	Additive impact for high versus low dependence sectors
Gupta and Yuan (2006)	1981–98	31 D	27	1.1	Overall, subsequent to stock market liberalization
				1.8	Additional, for sector at 75th percentile of dependence versus 25th percentile
Mitton (2006)	1980–2000	28 D	1,140 F	2.3	Firm-level increase in real annual sales after openness (IFC investability index)
Levchenko, Ranciere, and Thoenig (2007)	1963–2003	56	28	1.2	For increase in capital inflows/GDP by one standard deviation
				2.4	Move from complete closure to complete openness on Kaminsky-Schmukler de jure measure
Desai, Foley, and Hines (2006)	1982, 1989, 1994	54	20,000 F	...	US multinational affiliates abroad pay higher interest rates, earn lower profits in capital-controlled countries; investment rises 10 percent after liberalization

D = developing; F = firms; IFC = International Finance Corporation

Theoretical and Calibrated Studies

In contrast to the literature on cross-country regression tests for the impact of financial openness on growth, the corresponding theoretical and calibrated-model literature is considerably smaller. In a heuristic paper written in the early 1990s at the outset of the emerging-markets boom, Krugman (1993) appealed to basic production-function theory to cast doubt on the likely magnitudes of gains from capital mobility. He first noted that, implicitly, the great attention given to the need for foreign exchange following the debt crisis was a throwback to the "two-gap" models of the 1970s that had broadly been discredited and forgotten but may have contained a kernel of truth for special circumstances. He then emphasized that Solow-type residuals in the neoclassical growth literature ascribe most of growth to unexplained residual productivity increases (usually attributed to technological change) rather than to accumulation of capital and labor. He read the existing empirical evidence as indicating that developing countries did not so much lack capital as that they suffered from lower productivity of capital than industrial countries.

Illustrating limits of growth gains from capital inflows under the standard neoclassical production function, Krugman noted that with a capital-output ratio of 3 and a capital share in income (and output elasticity of capital) at one-third, a huge capital inflow of 5 percent of GDP would boost the capital stock by 1.67 percent and raise the short-term growth rate by only 0.56 percentage point. He then acknowledged that the new endogenous growth theory, in which there are externalities that essentially make economy-wide returns to capital constant rather than diminishing, might boost the impact but would in turn raise the paradox that capital should flow from small developing economies to large developed ones (an uphill flow of capital not unlike that of the early 2000s). His acknowledgedly "pessimistic" conclusion about limited potential for spreading global growth through capital flows was further based on his view that, historically, capital flows from rich to poor countries had never been very large in any event.

Despite Krugman's pessimism, such basic production-function considerations do help set a minimum floor to what one should expect from capital inflows. With no boost to productivity but solely capital deepening, the expectation would be that a persistent inflow of foreign capital of 1 percent of GDP would increase the annual growth rate on an ongoing basis by $\alpha\,(1/B)$ percentage point, where α is the share of capital in GDP (typically about 0.4 in developing economies) and B is the capital/output ratio (typically 2 to 3). On this basis, capital inflows of 1 percent of GDP would be expected to boost the growth rate by at least 0.13 to 0.2 percentage point per year. The increment could be considerably greater if the inflows boosted productivity (e.g., through technological spillovers from FDI or by enhancing the domestic financial system).[94]

Barro, Mankiw, and Sala-i-Martin (1995) examine the scope for capital flows to accelerate convergence in per capita incomes in the context of a neoclassical model with human capital as a factor of production separate from physical capital and raw labor. Their framework is that of steady-state growth, in which saving and capital accumulation occur at a decelerating rate until capital, production, and consumption per unit of effective labor all reach constant (steady-state) levels. The corresponding absolute levels relative to raw labor (and hence per capita levels, with labor equal to population for simplicity) grow at a constant rate equal to the rate of labor-augmenting technical change.[95] The authors postulate plausible values for their model parameters as a suite of twos: 2 percent each for annual growth from technical change, annual pure time preference, and elasticity of marginal utility, together with 1 percent population growth, 5 percent for depreciation, and factor shares of 0.3 for physical capital and 0.5 for human capital (with 0.2 left for raw labor). They calculate that these values imply a rate of convergence to the steady state of 1.4 percent per year.

They then open the model to international capital flows. They note that if all physical and human capital could be collateralized, the convergence rate would jump to infinity because steady-state capitalization could be achieved by borrowing rather than only through saving over time. With credit constrained to the value of physical capital that can be collateralized, the effect is still to speed up convergence, but by far less. With their parameters, convergence rises from 1.4 percent per year in the closed economy to 2.2 percent with capital mobility (p. 112). They conclude that "[although] capital mobility tends to raise the rate at which poor and rich economies converge...the quantitative impact of this effect is likely to be small" (Barro, Mankiw, and Sala-i-Martin 1995, 114). However, while a boost of 0.8 percent per year is small relative to international income gaps on the order of several hundred percent, it is by no means small compared with actual per capita growth rates typically on the order of 2 to 3 percent.

---

94. See chapter 3 for a more thorough discussion of growth impacts of foreign capital inflows in the neoclassical framework.

95. Specifically, the present value of utility is maximized and the steady state is reached where the marginal product of capital per efficiency-unit of labor equals the rate of depreciation plus the rate of (pure) time preference (impatience) plus the elasticity of marginal utility multiplied by the rate of labor-augmenting technical change; see Barro and Sala-i-Martin (1992, 225). In terms of net rather than gross marginal product, this is the familiar Ramsey (1928) result that the rate of return on capital equals the rate of pure time preference plus the elasticity of marginal utility times the growth rate of per capita consumption. In Barro and Sala-i-Martin (1992), the model is extended to treat human capital separately from physical capital.

This much acceleration of convergence would imply, for example, that after 20 years a financially open economy would stand at a per capita income level 17 percent higher than a financially closed economy that started out at the same per capita level. Nonetheless, the highly abstract framework, and postulated instead of estimated parameters, suggest that the specific numerical results should be seen mainly as illustrative.

Gourinchas and Jeanne (2006) present an analysis of prospective gains from financial internationalization formulated within this same steady-state growth framework. They apply a Cobb-Douglas production function in which national output depends on capital and effective labor (in their basic model). Effective labor equals raw labor multiplied by an efficiency parameter that rises over time at a steady rate for labor-augmenting technical change. Utility equals the sum over all future years of utility in the year in question discounted back to the present. Utility in a given year equals the utility function applied to per capita consumption, multiplied by the size of the population. In their reported case, utility is the natural logarithm of consumption.[96] In the optimal growth framework, such a set-up generates convergence to a steady-state path in which output grows at the rate of population growth plus the rate of labor-augmenting technical change. Capital also grows at this rate, to keep the ratios of capital to effective labor and to output constant. Saving is at a steady-state rate equal to the depreciation rate plus the growth rate of effective labor. Consumption is the difference between output and saving.

The authors calibrate the model at 0.74 percent population growth, 4 percent pure time preference (discount rate for impatience), labor-augmenting technical change at an international benchmark of 1.2 percent annually, and with the share of capital at 0.3. Under these conditions the steady-state capital-output ratio converges to 2.6 to 1. Then the authors conduct experiments starting an economy at lower capital-output ratios. In autarky, the economy must accumulate capital until it converges to its steady state. With open international capital flows, the economy instead leaps immediately to the capital intensity of its steady state. The basic finding is that financial integration merely advances the eventual steady state, rather than enabling a country to escape the limits of that steady state. In their calibration, it turns out that the value of this earlier arrival at steady state is relatively small. For an economy starting out at their estimated international population-weighted average capital output ratio of 1.4, the value of the jump-start from immediate capitalization to international levels turns out to be only 1.74 percent of all future consumption ("equivalent variation"). By implication, financial openness will not make a poor country rich, or at least not much richer than it eventually would have been on its own.

The authors emphasize that this approach omits any gain in overall

---

96. The general utility function is the constant relative risk-aversion form. When the coefficient for relative risk aversion equals unity, this form becomes the logarithm of consumption.

productivity growth from the act of opening the economy to international capital. They suggest that if financial internationalization is to have major welfare gains for developing countries, it seems likely that these will have to be through dynamic effects that supplement the static effects, and they draw an analogy to a similar argument that is popular in the trade liberalization literature. Essentially their result turns on the same relative impotence of capital at a factor share of only 0.3 (with resulting rapidly diminishing marginal product and hence returns to capital deepening) that was identified in the earlier heuristic remarks of Krugman (1993), which in turn was cited by Levine (2001) in support of his emphasis of the productivity-enhancing role of foreign capital on the domestic financial system.

At the same time, a permanent gain of 1.7 percent in attainable consumption levels should not necessarily be seen as small in terms of the payoff to a government policy. Moreover, as developed in appendix 2B, their estimate may be understated for more policy-relevant horizons of a few decades rather than infinity. As shown there, using the same framework and parameters, cumulative discounted consumption would be almost 8 percent higher under integration than under autarky for the first decade and about 4 percent higher by year 25. By year 500 the cumulative discounted gain would be closer to the Gourinchas-Jeanne estimate, at a gain of 2.47 percent versus their estimated 1.74 percent. So the small welfare gain in their construct is to some extent an artifact of the use of infinite horizon. Under more meaningful policy horizons there would be significantly larger potential gains from financial integration even in the strict neoclassical framework with no induced changes in TFP, simply from the benefits of earlier capital deepening.

Diversification Gains and Consumption Smoothing

Another branch of the calibrated-model literature considers possible welfare gains from risk diversification through financial globalization. A classic formulation of the motive for borrowing abroad is to smooth consumption in the face of domestic output cycles. Although the literature contains calibrated models examining this effect, it also features models that focus on the gains from diversification of investment portfolios to include foreign as well as domestic assets. Sometimes the ellipsis from the one to the other does not seem to be fully recognized. In part because of an intermixture of consumption-investment and portfolio-investment approaches, the literature shows a wide range of estimates. Thus, writing a decade ago on estimates of the potential permanent increase in expected consumption from international risk sharing, Van Wincoop (1999, 110) recounted "at least fourteen papers in recent years…[whose] reported results vary enormously, ranging from less than 0.1 percent to over 100 percent."

To set the stage for consideration of such ranges, consider first a bare-bones model of welfare gains from consumption smoothing in a highly simplified world. Appendix 2C develops a "Gemini" model in which the world economy has two countries that are identical except that when one is in the trough of its business cycle, the other is always at its peak. Under autarky the level of consumption fluctuates for each (around a constant mean, for simplicity). Under financial integration consumption is fully smoothed for each, as the country in its boom production phase always lends to the country in its recession phase.

The Gemini model implies that welfare gains from consumption risk sharing are likely to be on the order of 1 percent of GDP or less. The magnitude of the gain will depend on the size of the annual positive or negative shock to output in the cycle, and on the degree of risk aversion. With calibration at relatively large assumptions for each (10 percent annual output swing around the average, and elasticity of marginal utility of 2), the welfare gain from risk sharing to smooth consumption turns out to be 1 percent of consumption. This magnitude is sizable if not huge, but it also reflects shocks that are larger than likely to characterize the real world, as well as an elasticity of marginal utility that is arguably too high. With the annual shock set at 2.7 percent of GDP (the estimate by Cole and Obstfeld 1991, for the United States), and with the elasticity of marginal utility at a preferred level of 1.5, the compensating variation from consumption smoothing in the Gemini model falls to 0.1 percent of GDP. On first principles, then, one might expect gains from risk sharing in consumption smoothing to be modest.

But now consider a different optic: gains from placing a higher fraction of investment portfolios abroad, where returns are higher. Thus, in her formulation (examined below), Lewis (2000) calibrates stock returns in the United States at an expected 4.6 percent annually, far below her 7.8 percent annual return on "foreign" stocks. With her correlation of 2/3 between the two, it turns out that depending on risk aversion, placing anywhere from about half to 100 percent of the portfolio into the foreign stocks boosts the risk-adjusted value of wealth on the order of 10 to 50 percent, with a median of 18 percent across alternative parameter values (p. 10).[97]

There are fundamental questions about the use of stock market returns to reach conclusions about economic welfare, however. The risk-sharing literature shows a dichotomy reflecting this issue. As discussed below, this conflict is present even in the work of the same author (Cole and Obstfeld 1991 versus Obstfeld 1994a); and Lewis (2000) recognizes explicitly the dangers of conflating one with the other. Basically, rates of return on stock markets tend substantially to exceed growth rates of GDP and consumption, in part reflecting the equity premium puzzle. So when

---

97. Lewis (2000) follows Obstfeld (1994a) in distinguishing between the rate of risk aversion and the inverse of the elasticity of intertemporal substitution. She reports estimates for a range of 2 to 5 for each.

calibrated studies using stock returns are treated as if their implications applied directly to consumption, they can exaggerate.

Even within the framework solely of investment portfolios, a substantial inconsistency arises between the results for a single country, such as the United States in investor decisions on allocation between home and "foreign" stocks, and all countries. The home country may improve returns by investing more abroad, where the expected rate of return is higher (higher market "alpha"), and also reduce risk by diversifying into assets not closely correlated with the home asset (reducing volatility from "beta"). But then by definition at most the foreign country can obtain welfare gains through integration by virtue of reducing volatility (its beta) but not by piggybacking on the home country's expected return, because foreign alpha exceeds home country alpha. In addition, to the extent that international equity markets have become more highly correlated, diversification estimates from earlier periods could overstate potential for risk abatement at present.

In short, the literature on calibrated gains from international risk sharing warrants a cautious approach. This section examines some of the leading studies that convey the wide range of results as well as the varying emphasis on consumption models versus equity portfolio models.

In an important early study, Cole and Obstfeld (1991) argue that there are three contradictory stylized facts. First, returns on comparable assets are well arbitraged across borders. Second, foreign portfolio diversification is below what would be predicted by models of financially integrated economies. Third, intertemporal trade is low, as measured by current account balances. They suggest that these seeming contradictions can be explained by the fact that the potential gains from diversification are sufficiently small that even "minor impediments" to foreign asset trade are sufficient to limit foreign portfolio diversification. The authors use simple general equilibrium models to examine the scope for gains from international risk sharing. Based on data for Japan and the United States, they estimate that the cost of a ban on international portfolio diversification would be on the order of only 0.2 percent of GDP. An important element in their framework is the inclusion of terms-of-trade effects. When a negative output shock occurs in a given country, the contraction in its supply boosts its terms of trade, and for certain parameter assumptions this effect alone provides "perfect insurance against output shocks" (Cole and Obstfeld 1991, 5).

Using data for 1968–87, they calibrate both Japanese and US growth features as the US outcomes for mean growth (1.8 percent per year), standard deviation of growth (2.7 percent), and first lagged autocorrelation of growth (0.102). They place the correlation coefficient between the two countries' growth rates at the level observed for this period (0.375). These assumptions generate a set of four possible growth-performance combinations (high and low, United States and Japan) and a 4 x 4 Markov matrix of transition probabilities of moving from one state to another. Using Monte Carlo methods with 10,000 runs, they calculate welfare losses from portfolio autarky (inability to borrow consumption from the other country) as a function of the degree of substitutability between the production of the two countries and the degree of risk aversion, or elasticity of marginal utility.[98] If the two goods are Cobb-Douglas substitutes, there is no gain from diversification, because a country's loss in volume from a production fall is exactly offset by the rise in the relative price of its good. If they are perfect substitutes there is no terms-of-trade effect and diversification gains are at their maximum. With perfect substitution the simulated gains range from 0.17 to 0.49 percent of GDP, as the risk-aversion coefficient (elasticity of marginal utility) rises from 2 to 30. The authors prefer risk aversion at R = 4 and product substitutability at ρ = 0.25 to 0.75; under these conditions the simulated gains from diversification are around 0.2 percent of GDP. These results are similar to those obtained in the highly simplified Gemini model of appendix 2C.

In sharp contrast, Obstfeld (1994b, 1310) concludes that "most countries reap large steady-state welfare gains from global financial integration." This reversal in his view reflects in part a shift from an essentially static-trade formulation in Cole and Obstfeld (1991) to a dynamic efficiency framework. Obstfeld (1994b) argues that the availability of global diversification to reduce risk enables holders of capital to shift toward riskier high-return technologies, generating higher growth. However, his framework for this analysis involves shifting to an "endowment economy" with no labor and only capital, and income is hence solely return on capital. As such, it may be seen as belonging to a subcategory of models focusing on investment portfolio returns rather than directly on consumption smoothing. The large gains he identifies for wealth would seem misleading, as potential indicators of gains in consumption in real economies in which capital has only a minority share in contribution to production. Even so, the intuition that higher growth could result from a general shift toward higher return but more risky technologies seems important, if somewhat ambiguous in translation into consumption growth effects in economies requiring labor.

The heart of Obstfeld's model comprises two equations. The first states that the share of the risky asset is a positive function of its excess return over the risk-free rate and an inverse function of the product of the relative risk-aversion parameter and the variance of return on the risky asset.[99] The second states that the growth rate of consumption varies positively with the rate of excess return on the risky asset, positively with the elas-

---

98. The substitution parameter is ρ in a composite consumption good $(x^\rho + y^\rho)^{1/\rho}$, where ρ = 1 is perfect substitution and ρ = 0 is Cobb-Douglas with equal weights (or, $x^{0.5}y^{0.5}$). The risk-aversion parameter is R in the utility function $u = [c^{1-R}]/[1 - R]$.

99. Or $\omega = (\alpha - i)/(R\sigma^2)$.

ticity of intertemporal substitution, negatively with the rate of pure time preference (discount rate for impatience), negatively with the risk-aversion parameter, and negatively with the variance of the return on the risky asset.[100] Obstfeld illustrates the growth dynamics from risk sharing with a two-country world. In both countries the risky asset yields α = 5 percent, the risk-free asset yields i = 2 percent, and the standard deviation of return on the risky asset is σ = 10 percent. Risk aversion is at R = 4, pure time preference is at δ = 2 percent, and the intertemporal elasticity of substitution is at ε = 0.5. For each country in isolation the optimal portfolio is ω = 0.75, or a 75 percent share for the risky asset and 25 percent for the risk-free asset. Mean consumption growth based for each, with these parameters, is 1.69 percent annually. But when the two countries can trade assets, the optimal world portfolio is simply half each of the two respective countries' risky asset. Return variance for the world portfolio is $(0.1)^2/2 = 0.005$. The world risk-free rate of return rises from 2 percent to α = 3 percent, which is consistent with the portfolio share of the world portfolio of the risky assets rising to ω = 1.0.

In this setup, an "endowment economy" that is a kind of world of retirees living solely on capital income, it turns out that the discounted sum of future utility is a function of wealth, risk aversion, intertemporal substitutability, the growth rate of consumption, pure time preference, and the risk-free rate of return. Obstfeld finds that the compensating variation that holds the present value of utility constant under financial integration amounts to 37 percent of initial wealth in the example just described, a "very large welfare gain" (p. 1319). Of this total gain, 21.5 percent, or about two-thirds, comes from the exogenous source of lower risk, and the rest comes from the endogenously induced rise in consumption growth from the reallocation toward riskier, higher-return assets. But this result is already a hint to the fact that the setup in Obstfeld (1994b) differs from that in Cole and Obstfeld (1991), because the exogenous change that solely considers equivalent variation from lower risk and no induced change in portfolio composition is far higher, at 22 percent, than the minimal gain of 0.2 percent of GDP in Cole and Obstfeld (1991). The difference would appear to be driven by defining consumption in a world of retirees living on capital with no labor in the system, raising questions about the meaning of the much larger welfare gains.

Obstfeld (1994b) then concludes with corresponding calibrated exercises using estimates of risk-free and risky rates of return in eight world regions, along with estimates of covariance. He finds that gains from financial integration then amount to extraordinarily large amounts: 125 percent

---

100. Or $g = \varepsilon(1 - \delta) + (1 + \varepsilon)(\alpha - i)^2/(2R\sigma^2)$, where ε is the intertemporal elasticity of substitution and δ the rate of pure time preference. In the frequently assumed case in which $\varepsilon = 1/R$, the formula developed by Merton (1971) for the ratio of consumption to wealth obtains: $\mu = C/W = (1/R) \times \{\delta - (1-R)[i + (\alpha - i)^2/(2R\sigma^2)]\}$.

of wealth for North America, 240 percent for South America, 480 percent for North Asia, 460 percent for Africa, 99 percent for Southern Europe, 60 percent for Northern Europe, and 23 percent for East Asia (p. 1324). This time the bulk of the gains are the induced shift toward higher-risk assets, rather than risk reduction on existing portfolios. Obstfeld concludes that "this paper has demonstrated that international risk sharing can yield substantial welfare gains through its positive effect on expected consumption growth. The mechanism linking global diversification to growth is the attendant world portfolio shift from safe, but low-yield, capital into riskier, high-yield capital" (p. 1327). But once again the question of meaning given the labor-free economy arises.

Van Wincoop (1999) also finds relatively large welfare gains from international risk sharing, even though their magnitudes are less breathtaking than the potential wealth effects estimated by Obstfeld (1994b). Van Wincoop sticks more closely to a consumption-smoothing as opposed to investment-return-enhancing framework. He concludes that "gains from risk sharing are quite sizable," amounting to "a permanent increase in tradables consumption in the range of 1.1 to 3.5 percent for a 50 year horizon" for OECD countries (p. 109).

Van Wincoop identifies a stylized industrial country growth rate for consumption of tradable goods at 2.35 percent per annum, with a standard deviation of 3.23 percent. With relative risk aversion set at 3, this translates into risk-adjusted growth of 2.19 percent.[101] He sets the correlation coefficient between any two countries' consumption growth at 0.21. Then if N countries pool their consumption (where N is set at 20 for the OECD countries), the risk-shared standard deviation falls to 1.61 percent.[102] His key equation for welfare gain depends positively on the amount of variance reduction from risk pooling, the rate of risk aversion, the length of the horizon, and the risk-free interest rate.[103] The equation involves division by the difference between the risk-free interest rate and the risk-adjusted rate of consumption growth, and as the two become closer the gains can balloon to very large numbers. Van Wincoop's central estimates place the risk-free interest rate at 0.85 percent, the average short-term government rate for OECD countries in 1970–89. His overall gains from risk sharing for a 50-year horizon are 3.3 percent of tradables consumption (or, using an

---

101. That is, $\bar{\mu} = \mu - 0.5\gamma\sigma^2$, 0.5 where μ is the growth rate of consumption, the overbar indicates the risk-adjusted rate, γ is the rate of relative risk aversion (or elasticity of marginal utility), and σ^2 is the variance of consumption growth.

102. That is, $\sigma_s^2 = \sigma^2(1/N - [1-1/N]\rho)$, where subscript s refers to shared and ρ is the correlation between consumption growth rates of pairs of countries.

103. Let $k = r - \bar{\mu}$, where r is the risk-free rate of interest. Let H = horizon, in years. Let $d\sigma^2 = \sigma_s^2 - \sigma^2$. Then Van Wincoop's equation for welfare gain over the horizon is $G = -\{1 - [Hke^{-Hk}]/(1 - e^{-Hk})\}(0.5\gamma d\sigma^2)/k$. Note also that $r = \beta + \gamma\bar{\mu}$, where β is the rate of pure time preference, or the discount rate for impatience.

alternative grouping of tradable consumption goods and modestly higher cross-country correlation, a gain of 1.18 percent).

In view of the enormous potential wealth gains from international portfolio diversification in such studies as Obstfeld (1994b), in contrast to the much smaller consumption-based, risk-sharing gains in such studies as Cole and Obstfeld (1991) and (albeit somewhat larger) Van Wincoop (1999), Lewis (2000) directly examines why the results should diverge so much between the two vantage points. She begins with the investment portfolio approach. The gain from shifting from an autarkic portfolio to one with optimal weight on foreign stocks depends on the difference between the domestic rate of return and the foreign rate of return and between the domestic variance of return compared with the variance in the optimal portfolio.[104] She measures US mean return for 1969–93 at 4.64 percent and other G-7 mean return at 7.78 percent, and she places the corresponding standard deviations at 16.9 and 21.75 percent. The correlation coefficient between US and other G-7 return is 0.673. The optimal portfolio turns out to be 100 percent in foreign stock for her lowest risk-aversion coefficient ($\gamma = 2$) and in a range of 74, 54, and 44 percent as risk aversion rises to 3, 4, and 5. Given these optimal portfolios, she calculates the gains from foreign diversification (for the US investor) in a range of 29 to 52 percent for $\theta = 2$; 18 to 26 percent for $\theta = 3$; 13 to 22 percent for $\theta = 4$; and 10 to 19 percent for $\theta = 5$. These gains are large, as is typical when risk sharing is measured for stock portfolio diversification.

Lewis then repeats her exercise but with a focus on consumption. The world is divided into the seven industrial countries and the rest-of-world. Consumption of the representative agent is treated as being paid out of a stock that has a claim to output of the country divided by the population, in autarky. With financial integration, these "stocks" can be purchased across countries. Growth correlations are taken into account (for example, at 0.62 between Canada and the United States but only 0.11 between Japan and Italy). The upshot is that Japan, with its high-growth potential, gets an initial boost in consumption by selling off rights to its future high growth, whereas the picture is reversed for the United States. With both the inverse of the intertemporal elasticity of marginal utility (θ) and the rate of relative risk aversion (γ) set at 2, and pure time preference at 2 percent, the resulting gains amount to 0.85 percent of consumption for the United States, 4.9 percent for Japan, 3.9 percent for Italy, about 1.5 percent for Canada and the United Kingdom, and about 0.4 percent for

---

104. In her setup, θ is the inverse of the intertemporal elasticity of substitution, γ is the rate of relative risk aversion, μ is expected return, and σ is standard deviation. The optimal share (ϕ) of foreign stocks is where $\partial \bar{\mu} / \partial \phi = 0.5 \gamma (\partial \bar{\sigma} / \partial \phi)$, where the overbar refers to the portfolio including foreign stocks. With β = unity less the rate of pure time preference, and defining for convenience: a = $1 - \theta$; b = $\mu - 0.5\gamma\sigma^2$; then her measure of the gain from diversification is (Num/Denom) – 1, where Num = $(1 - \beta e^{ab})^{1/a}$ and Denom = the same but using $\bar{\mu}$ and $\bar{\sigma}$.

Germany and France. In a variant in which all countries are forced to have the same mean growth, the gains are all much smaller (e.g., 0.1 percent for the United States, 0.4 percent for Japan). So Lewis has confirmed that the use of consumption growth rates and correlations within the same portfolio framework generates much lower estimates of risk-sharing gains than does the use of equity value growth rates.

She then recalculates the consumption gains using a counterfactual in which stock return rates rather than consumption growth rates are applied to the same set of seven countries and the rest-of-world. This time gains are far higher, on the order of 90 percent for Japan and 60 percent for France, Germany, and the United Kingdom, and 12 percent for the United States (with $\theta = \gamma = 2$). She concludes that the reason for the large differences in the literature for gains from risk sharing is primarily that some studies use equity-based calculations while others use consumption-based approaches. The high return variance of equity generates greater gains from risk-pooling. However, she also concludes that when the risk-aversion parameter chosen is high, gains using consumption can be comparable with those based on equity.

Mercereau (2006) applies the model developed by Lewis (2000) to estimate potential gains from financial integration in Asia. His analysis is strictly in the category of risk sharing for equity portfolios. For 1988–2003, he finds that mean equity returns were 7 percent in Australia, about 10 percent in Japan, and about 11 percent in Singapore and Hong Kong. Standard deviations were about 25 percent for Australia and 33 percent for the three Asian economies. The correlation coefficient between Australian equity returns and those for the three Asian economies was 0.49 (or, 0.47 just with Japan). For a coefficient of relative risk aversion of $\gamma = 2$, the optimal portfolio share for an Australian investor would be 43 percent in equities in the three Asian economies and 57 percent in the home market. The corresponding welfare gains calculated using the Lewis model would range from 14 to 27 percent (for the inverse of intertemporal substitutability ranging from $\theta = 5$ to 2, respectively). So once again a risk-sharing quantification based on equity returns shows remarkably high potential for welfare gains. Once again the result depends on a mixture of being able to take advantage of higher mean returns abroad and pooling imperfectly correlated risk.

In the risk-sharing literature, then, one dominant strand is the use of calibrated models to examine potential welfare gains. The five studies just reviewed are in this category. There is another prevalent category, however, that instead of asking what is the potential, merely asks the question of whether nations behave in a risk-sharing fashion. This set of studies tends to involve cross-country statistical tests on the correlation of international consumption and the extent of home bias.

Kose, Prasad, and Terrones (2003) provide evidence in this second category of studies. Using the same criteria as in Prasad et al. (2003), they divide 55 developing countries into 22 more financially integrated economies (MFIE) and 33 less financially integrated economies (LFIE), with the two groups broadly corresponding to emerging markets versus other developing countries. They examine median volatility for each group for each of four decades beginning with the 1960s. Their preferred measure is growth of consumption (private and government) in comparison with growth in income (output plus terms of trade change). They find a sizable increase in income volatility in the 1970s and 1980s compared with the 1960s, and a decline again by the 1990s, for both groups.[105] This pattern is consistent with the commodity price shocks of the 1970s and the debt crises of the 1980s. For the MFIEs, consumption volatility is relatively constant over the four decades at a standard deviation of about 4.5 percent. In contrast, for the LFIEs consumption volatility rises sharply from 5.4 percent in the 1960s to about 7.1 percent in the 1970s and 1980s, before easing again to 5.7 percent in the 1990s. The authors emphasize that "median relative volatility of total consumption to that of income has risen from the 1980s to the 1990s for the MFIEs, precisely in the period when financial integration should have paid off in terms of better consumption-smoothing opportunities and, therefore, lower relative volatility of consumption for these economies" (p. 9–10). The implication is that their data contradict consumption smoothing. But the data can be read in exactly the opposite way. The excess of output volatility over consumption volatility was consistently greater (and hence consumption smoothing greater) for the MFIEs than for the LFIEs in both the 1980s and 1990s.[106]

The authors then conduct statistical tests explaining volatility with a set of explanatory variables that includes income level, trade openness, monetary and fiscal variables, and three measures of financial openness (presence of restrictions on current account transactions, restrictions on capital account transactions, and ratio of gross capital flows to GDP). None of the financial-integration variables is significant in explaining volatility of consumption. When the gauge of consumption smoothing is changed to the ratio of consumption volatility to income volatility, however, financial integration turns out to aggravate relative consumption volatility over the range relevant to most developing countries (but reduces it once gross capital flows exceed 100 percent of GDP). However, it is not obvious that the ratio of consumption volatility to income volatility is more germane to considering the role of financial openness than is the volatility of con-

---

105. In the MFIEs, the median standard deviation of income rose from 3.6 percent in the 1960s to 5.4 percent in the 1970s and 1980s and then moderated to 4.8 percent in the 1990s. The surge and retreat was much higher for the LFIEs: from 4.4 percent to an average of 8.6 percent and then back to 4.6 percent.

106. This excess volatility avoided, as it were, amounted to 136 basis points in the 1980s and 12 basis points in the 1990s for the MFIEs but stood at 31 basis points in the 1980s and a negative smoothing of –113 basis points in the 1990s for the LFIEs.

sumption itself, considering that numerous other control variables have been included (arguably more relevant than "controlling" consumption volatility by dividing it by income volatility). Nonetheless, the statistical results surely do not support consumption smoothing through financial integration even if they are read not to reject it. Even the estimates for consumption volatility have the wrong sign (positive impact of integration on volatility) despite a lack of statistical significance.

Another vantage point for analyzing risk sharing is to ask whether a country's consumption is more highly correlated with domestic production or with international consumption. The rationale is that with complete international risk sharing, for any individual country the path of consumption would be highly correlated with international consumption instead of domestic production.[107] Typically, just the reverse is found, with the results often presented as amounting to evidence against the presence of major cross-border risk sharing.

Imbs (2006, 2) begins by noting that the empirical rejection of "perfectly correlated consumption plans" internationally "was famously labeled a 'quantity puzzle' by Backus, Kehoe, and Kydland (1994)." He finds that not only is consumption more closely correlated with domestic production than with international consumption but also that fluctuations in GDP are more synchronized internationally than fluctuations in consumption. Using measures based on bilateral holdings of assets in and liabilities to partner countries, as well as the usual IMF (AREAER) financial restrictions data, Imbs finds that correlations in GDP growth between pairs of 41 countries are positively related to financial integration. Thus, contrary to international business-cycle theory, financially integrated countries have more rather than less synchronized business cycles.[108] This result is even stronger in a test of correlations between a group of 12 industrial (center) countries and 31 developing (periphery) countries. Disaggregation of the financial integration data indicates that it is debt, especially short-term debt, that dominates the positive business-cycle correlation between center and periphery.

The author then turns to consumption. He first finds it is highly correlated with domestic output but also notes that simply the fact that consumption is a component of GDP could explain this correlation. He finds a significant coefficient for financial integration, indicating that economies with restrictions on capital flows have less synchronized consumption (although the relationship is weaker using asset data). The main results hold up after addressing endogeneity through instrumental variables.

---

107. This would be exactly the case in the Gemini model of appendix 2C.

108. The theoretical case for the opposite is that if positive innovation shocks affect one country, spurring a boom, capital will flow into it from another country, where activity will slow as a result.

Imbs next shows that the influence of the financial integration variables is stronger on production correlation than on consumption correlation. He concludes that the bulk of the quantity puzzle stems from the tendency of GDP correlations to rise with financial links, not from low risk sharing. He considers the positive influence on GDP correlation to be a puzzle, given the opposite expectation in theory. The bottom line for risk sharing, however, is by implication that it can be a mistake to diagnose an absence of risk sharing from the presence of higher correlation of consumption with output than with international consumption.

Kose, Prasad, and Terrones (2007) similarly revisit their earlier analysis of the risk-sharing question by examining whether consumption is more closely correlated with domestic output or with international consumption. In findings representative of this literature, the authors find high correlations of domestic consumption with domestic output for 69 economies divided about evenly among industrial, emerging-market, and other developing countries, for the period 1960–2004. This correlation stands at about 70 to 75 percent regardless of the period: Bretton Woods (1960–72), common shocks (1973–86), and globalization (1987–2004). Emerging markets actually show an increase in the correlation of domestic consumption for the globalization period (to 86 percent). By contrast, the only substantial evidence for correlation of domestic with international consumption is for the industrial countries (at about 50 percent in both the common-shock and globalization periods). Domestic consumption is virtually uncorrelated with global consumption for emerging-market economies and other developing countries (with correlations ranging from –11 percent to +4 percent in the two later periods). Regressions of the deviation of consumption growth from average world consumption growth on the corresponding deviation of output growth then confirm that there has been an increase in international risk sharing (by this metric) for industrial countries but not for emerging-market and other developing countries.

It is important to ask, however, where the benchmark for risk sharing should be set. A parallel in the trade theory literature is the factor price equalization theorem: Free trade should wind up making wages identical in Bangladesh and California. If that were the benchmark, one might conclude that international trade has had no influence whatsoever on relative wages of the unskilled, because this factor price equalization has not occurred. But a more accurate diagnosis is that international trade has some effect in this direction but is only one of many influences, and the conditions for full factor price equalization are far from being met. By analogy, it would be a mistake to conclude in the financial integration sphere that there is no contribution to international risk sharing just because consumption is more highly correlated with domestic production than international consumption. The more relevant question is: would domestic consumption be even more volatile (and even more correlated with domestic production) in the absence of financial integration?

The authors then conduct panel regressions that directly incorporate financial integration, as measured by the ratio of gross external assets and liabilities relative to GDP. Domestic consumption growth minus international consumption growth is the dependent variable, adhering to the international consumption correlation framework. Two variables are on the right-hand side: domestic output growth minus international output growth; and this same variable multiplied by the financial integration ratio. The degree of risk sharing by a country is then measured as 1 minus the coefficient on domestic versus international output growth, minus the financial integration variable times the coefficient on the final interaction term.[109] The panel estimates find a significant coefficient with the right sign only for the later (globalization) period, and only for industrial countries. Moreover, the authors interpret the size of the coefficient as small.[110] They then conclude by disaggregating types of foreign capital. Their additional regressions suggest that the risk-sharing benefits in industrial countries stem from direct investment and portfolio equity, whereas for developing countries debt stocks reduce rather than increase risk sharing. They suggest that the heavy reliance of developing countries on debt could explain their lack of risk-sharing benefits.

To recapitulate, the literature on risk sharing and consumption smoothing exhibits a considerably wider dispersion of estimates of gains from financial integration than those in the other major approaches to this question. Some of the largest divergences are between successive studies by the same author. In general, calibrated models applying risk-aversion utility functions to plausible consumption smoothing tend to find small gains (Cole and Obstfeld 1991; and the Gemini model in appendix 2C). Calibrated models based on international equity returns in so-called endowment economies in which consumption is solely out of capital stock (and there is no labor or production function) tend to find gains that are in the tens of percentage points of GDP (Van Wincoop 1994; Lewis 2000; Mercereau 2006) or even hundreds of percentage points of wealth (Obstfeld 1994b) if dynamic effects of shifting to higher-return and riskier capital projects are incorporated. Lewis (2000) usefully shows that consumption-smoothing setups tend to show high gains as well if they are allowed to apply equity-type rates of return as the consumption growth rates rather than lower observed levels. In all of the calibrated studies, gains are higher with greater risk aversion. Then there is another strand of literature that argues that the whole consumption-smoothing case is weak

---

109. Thus, $\Delta \ln c - \Delta \ln C = \alpha + \mu(\Delta \ln y - \Delta \ln Y) + \gamma F (\Delta \ln y - \Delta \ln Y)$, where C is consumption, Y is output, lower case is the country in question, upper case is the international average, and F is the financial integration ratio. The degree of risk sharing is then $1 - \mu - \gamma F$.

110. Average financial openness is 266 percent for industrial countries. The coefficient on the interaction term is –0.02, so 10 percentage points increase in the financial integration ratio boosts the risk-sharing measure by only 0.002, against a total potential of 1.0.

because in contrast to international business-cycle theory, consumption correlates more closely with domestic output rather than with international consumption, and for that matter domestic output correlates positively rather than negatively with international output (Kose, Prasad, and Terrones 2003 and 2007; Imbs 2006).

On balance, the estimates toward the lower end of these wide ranges seem more plausible. The ellipsis from realistic economies to endowment economies facing high foreign equity returns seems less than convincing. So do some of the constructs required for some of the higher estimates, such as the ability to purchase a warrant against the future consumption growth of, say, Japan. At the same time, dismissal of risk-sharing gains by the discovery of correlation of consumption with domestic output hardly seems warranted either. The appropriate question to such findings is: compared to what?

Summary Surveys

In recent years there have been several surveys of the empirical literature on the impact of financial globalization on growth.[111] Some authors have written several surveys. One of the most useful surveys, which seems to have become a basis for some of the overviews in subsequent ones, is that by Edison et al. (2004). The principal contribution of this study is to rerun the tests of half a dozen prominent earlier studies to see if their results can be replicated and then to modify the models to examine whether those results remain robust in the face of inclusion of an institutional variable ("government reputation"). When this is done, the authors find that the previous findings of positive growth effects become dependent on threshold levels for the government reputation variable. They conclude that "recent results do offer a consistent effect of capital account openness and stock market liberalization on economic growth for middle-income countries, though not for poorer or richer countries" (p. 251). They also argue that concerns about differences among the various alternative measurements of capital account openness may have been exaggerated, because they tend to show "a common cross-country picture" (p. 254).[112]

The authors first replicate the results of Quinn (1997), Arteta, Eichengreen, and Wyplosz (2001), Grilli and Milesi-Ferretti (1995), Bekaert, Har-

---

111. For an early survey that predates the large majority of the studies examined in this chapter, see Eichengreen (2001).

112. This proposition does not square, however, with visual inspection of their restrictions-based and cumulative-capital-flow measure openness. Although the two moved together for advanced economies, for developing countries after about 1980 there was little increase in financial integration based on the restrictions measure but a large increase based on the cumulative-capital-flow measure.

vey, and Lundblad (2000), and Rodrik (1998). Three of these studies show a significant positive impact of capital account liberalization on growth (Quinn; Arteta, Eichengreen and Wyplosz; and Bekaert, Harvey, and Lundblad). The other two do not. All of the studies use data for approximately the same period: the early 1970s through the early 1990s. The authors then rerun the models including the Knack and Keefer (1995) measure of "government reputation," which had not been included in any of the tests except that by Rodrik. In the expanded tests, this variable always turns out to be strongly significant, and the significance of the capital liberalization variable disappears.

But the authors do not stop there. They then conduct cross-country growth regressions for about 50 to 70 countries for 1976–95 in which they interact the government reputation variable with the logarithm of per capita income in 1976 and the square of the logarithm of per capita income, drawing on the work of Klein (2005). They use alternatively the capital liberalization variables of Quinn (1997), Bekaert, Harvey, and Lundblad (2000), and the standard AREAER "share" of years showing restrictions. All three tests reveal a negative coefficient on the capital liberalization variable by itself, a positive coefficient (strongly significant for two of the three) on the interaction of capital liberalization and per capita income, and a negative (significant) coefficient on the square of per capita income. The result is that the positive contribution of capital account openness to growth is restored for middle-income countries. The three tests show a positive significant impact for either a relatively narrow range of middle-income countries (48th to 56th percentile of 1976 per capita income, Quinn indicator), a somewhat wider range (42nd to 64th percentile, "share" measure), or a range covering two-fifths of countries (38th to 76th percentiles, Bekaert, Harvey, and Lundblad stock market measure).

There is a serious question, however, about the validity of growth equations employing the Knack-Keefer government reputation variable. Appendix 2D sets forth evidence that this variable is not independent but instead responds to changes in past growth, not unlike the tendency of most rating agencies' ratings to follow rather than predict performance. Including such a variable in a statistical test is akin to placing the dependent variable (growth) on both the left-hand and the right-hand sides of the equation. Doing so will surely tend to rob the independent variables of their statistical significance. For this reason, neither the Edison et al. (2004) nor the Rodrik (1998) findings, both of which rely heavily on the Knack-Keefer government reputation variable, should be seen as definitive bases for reversing results of prior studies.

Four researchers associated with the IMF have provided some of the most influential surveys of the literature on financial integration and growth (Prasad et al. 2003; Kose et al. 2006). In their first survey, the authors use the AREAER restrictions index as well as the estimated stock of foreign assets and liabilities relative to GDP to divide 55 developing countries into 22 more financially integrated (MFI) and 33 less financially integrated (LFI) countries. They include both China and India in the MFI group, which is noteworthy considering that the two countries are sometimes considered to be major examples of high growth performance without financial integration with the rest of the world.[113] They note that on the surface there is a positive association between financial globalization and development; from 1970–99 per capita output rose almost six times as much in the MFI economies as in the LFI economies (Prasad et al. 2003, 26). But they note that the causation could run from success to integration rather than the other way around. They also cite China, India, Mauritius, and Botswana as high-growth countries in their MFI group that were open to, and received high amounts of, FDI but were relatively closed to financial flows. They cite Jordan and Peru as examples of economic decline despite opening to foreign capital. They present a scatter diagram of per capita growth against the increase in financial integration over 1982–97, showing no relationship. A second scatter diagram of the residual of per capita growth after taking account of the usual set of growth variables again shows no relationship to the increase in financial openness. They then classify 14 recent studies on this issue (many of them reviewed above). They indicate that only three found a positive effect of financial integration on growth, writing that "the majority of the papers tend to find no effect or a mixed effect for developing counties. This suggests that, if financial integration has a positive effect on growth, it is probably not strong or robust" (p. 31).

It is this diagnosis that dominates the survey literature, including subsequent surveys by the same authors. But as suggested above, this summary view may be misleading. The term "mixed" in particular would imply that there are numerous studies that show a negative influence of financial integration on growth, counterbalancing those that find positive influences. As indicated above, that is not the case. The authors then draw on the results of Kose, Prasad, and Terrones (2003) to examine volatility. They judge that although "international financial integration should, in principle, help countries to reduce macroeconomic volatility…developing countries, in particular, have not attained this potential benefit" (Prasad et al. 2003, 37). This diagnosis would seem to diametrically contradict their finding that "MFI economies on average have lower output volatility than LFI" (p. 38). It is based on the finding that volatility of total consumption relative to income rose to 0.92 in the 1990s from 0.76 in the 1980s. But as noted above in the discussion of Kose, Prasad, and Terrones (2003), just the opposite verdict can be reached on financial openness if the contest is between MFIs and LFIs in the degree of moderating consumption volatility. Presumably that should be the more basic test, rather than comparing the MFIs against themselves over decades, especially considering that the

---

113. As in Prasad, Rajan, and Subramanian (2007a), discussed above.

rise in the ratio in question was driven by a decline in output volatility rather than a rise in consumption volatility.

The authors then argue that better governance can increase the likelihood that financial integration has a positive effect on growth. They cite tests by Wei (1997) indicating a strong negative effect of corruption on FDI. They present data indicating that higher corruption is associated with a greater share of loans and smaller share of FDI in capital inflows and invoke results of Frankel and Rose (1996) and others to the effect that reliance on loans rather than FDI increases the likelihood of currency crises.

The authors conclude that "the empirical evidence has not established a definitive proof that financial integration has enhanced growth for developing countries" (Prasad et al. 2003, 58). Of course, in econometrics "definitive proof" is extremely rare and always tentative pending the next round of robustness tests using yet other variables and techniques. The more relevant question is whether the bulk of the evidence points to a positive, zero, or negative influence of financial openness on growth. Based on the results shown in tables 2.1 through 2.3, the answer is not negative. (The only qualification concerns the somewhat more open question of whether output losses provoked by financial crises exceed general gains associated with openness and gains from FDI in particular.) The operational question then becomes whether the body of evidence suggests a negligible or sizable positive growth impact.[114] As indicated in table 2.1, an economically important positive contribution remains in the body of estimates even if nonsignificant results are imputed at zero or if the inverse-variance weighting of meta-statistics is applied.

The authors also judge that financial integration "may be associated with higher consumption volatility" (p. 58). That diagnosis is questionable, however, as suggested in the above discussion of the method used in the underlying Kose, Prasad, and Terrones (2003) study. The authors conclude with the advice that developing countries "experiment with different paces and strategies in pursuing financial integration." They add that "empirical evidence does suggest that improving governance, in addition to sound macroeconomic frameworks and the development of domestic financial markets, should be an important element of such strategies." (p. 58).

The same authors return to a more comprehensive literature survey in Kose et al. (2006). Their principal new theme in this assessment is that financial globalization conveys collateral benefits in the areas of domestic financial development, governance and institutional development, and macroeconomic discipline. Over time these improvements yield gains in TFP, which is more important than traditional capital accumulation in contributing to growth. They suggest that econometric estimates will tend

---

114. Again it is worth recalling the emphasis on this perspective proposed by McCloskey and Ziliak (1996).

to understate the benefits of financial-globalization benefits when they apply controls for these factors, thereby missing the point that they are enhanced by capital openness rather than exogenous to it. The authors also suggest that empirical studies have tended to missestimate because of the general use of de jure measures of capital openness, which can be much less relevant than de facto openness. The authors conclude that:

> ...[T]he weight of the evidence seems to be gradually shifting towards finding positive marginal effects on growth, especially when financial integration is measured using de facto or finer de jure measures, when data over longer time periods are used, and when interaction terms accounting for supportive conditions (such as good policies and institutions) are properly included in cross-country regression frameworks....[T]here is little empirical evidence to support the view that capital account liberalization by itself increases vulnerability to crises....[H]owever...there is no evidence that financial globalization has delivered on the promised benefit of improved international risk sharing and reduced volatility of consumption. (Kose et al. 2006, 20)[115]

In emphasizing the collateral benefits of financial integration, the authors usefully raise a red flag about empirical studies that discard statistically significant growth effects after including institutional variables. Thus:

> There is considerable evidence...that financial integration serves as an important catalyst for a number of...'collateral benefits' [that] could include development of the domestic financial sector, improvements in institutions (defined broadly to include governance, the rule of law, etc.), better macroeconomic policies, etc. These collateral benefits then result in higher growth, usually through gains in allocative efficiency...[I]n a regression framework, it may be difficult to disentangle the effects of financial integration if one includes measures of institutional quality, financial sector development, quality of macroeconomic policies etc....This problem cannot be resolved simply by using a technique such as instrumental variables estimation: that would entirely miss the logic of the scheme above since our interest is in how financial integration affects growth through all channels, direct and indirect.... (Kose et al. 2006, 33–34)

Indeed, this could explain why simple correlations tend to show that financially integrated economies have higher growth rates, on average, than less-integrated economies, yet it has proven more difficult to find a causal effect of financial integration on growth once the other factors mentioned previously are controlled for (pp. 8–9).

The authors' overall conclusion from the literature is that "for developing countries, financial globalization appears to have the potential to play a catalytic role in generating an array of collateral benefits that may help boost long-run growth and welfare. At the same time, premature opening of the capital account in the absence of some basic supporting conditions

---

115. On the latter, the authors repeat, erroneously in my view, the diagnosis that volatility of consumption growth relative to income growth is positively associated with financial integration (see the discussion of Kose, Prasad, and Terrones 2003, above).

can delay the realization of these benefits, while making a country more vulnerable to sudden stops of capital flows" (p. 52).

In their critique of the Kose et al. (2006) study, Rodrik and Subramanian (2009) counter that if the problem is that introducing institutional conditions that are actually collateral benefits spuriously removes correlation of growth with financial globalization, then "evidence of an *unconditional* kind" should reveal such a correlation. They present scatter diagrams that do not do so and are thus "not kind to this view" (p. 122). But this critique is not convincing. Surely the standard control variables should be included (initial per capita income, investment share in GDP, educational level, population growth) and the scatter then presented as a residual from the control-equation prediction of growth. The "conditional" influence that should not be incorporated in the regressions is a vague "institutional quality" metric that, as shown in appendix 2D, is more likely to be consequence than cause—precisely as suggested by Kose et al. (2006). As shown in chapter 3, when instead the deviation of per capita growth from the level predicted by the core set of control variables is placed on a scatter diagram against the Quinn measure of financial openness (Quinn and Toyoda 2008), there is indeed a pattern of faster growth of countries with greater openness.

A subsequent survey by the IMF staff (IMF 2007a) further examined the influence of financial globalization on risk sharing, volatility, and growth. The study finds that the standard deviation of worldwide output is 0.8 percentage point, much lower than the median standard deviation of consumption of 4.4 percentage points for individual countries, and also lower than the lowest country-specific consumption volatility (1.4 percentage points). Citing empirical analysis by Imbs and Mauro (2007), the IMF authors judge that the bulk of risk-sharing benefits can be obtained "in a small pool consisting of a handful of well-chosen partners" (p. 21). At the same time, benefits are greater from choosing partners from a worldwide sample rather than within a region.[116] Nevertheless, this type of analysis remains highly abstract in that it does not address realistic mechanisms for consumption pooling. The IMF authors do note evidence of declining home bias among industrial countries and cite evidence from Sørensen et al. (2007) that this trend has reflected increased international risk sharing. They note, however, that home bias has not changed much for developing economies, citing Kose, Prasad, and Terrones (2007).

On volatility, the IMF authors regress consumption volatility on financial integration (measured by the ratio of external assets plus liabilities to GDP) and other variables for about 80 economies for 1965–2004. They

---

116. For example, the median volatility of consumption growth in Latin American emerging-market economies of 6.2 percentage points could be lowered to 1.9 percentage points by pooling with the five optimally chosen Latin American economies, but to 1.3 percentage points by pooling with the five optimal economies worldwide.

find a significant positive (destabilizing) coefficient on financial integration, but only for countries with low perceived institutional quality and domestic financial development. For an economy at the 25th percentile in the distribution of both domestic financial development and financial integration, an increase in financial integration to the 75th percentile in the distribution would reduce consumption volatility from 6 to 4.6 percent. They find that by 2000–04, virtually all advanced economies and about one-third of emerging-market economies (but no "developing" countries) met the thresholds beyond which the influence of financial integration on consumption volatility turned insignificant. Moreover, they note that a majority of existing studies find that, in contrast to consumption volatility, crises are "if anything, less frequent in financially open countries" (p. 27). Institutional and policy thresholds are again relevant. A test examining only countries with above-median financial integration finds that among them, countries below the median on three of four economic environment criteria (financial-sector development, institutional quality, sound macroeconomic policy, and trade integration) have statistically significantly higher incidence of sudden stops, debt crises, and currency crises.[117]

Turning to growth impact, the IMF authors (IMF 2007a, 29) state:

> A survey of more than 40 empirical studies based on macroeconomic data and cross-country regressions concludes that the evidence of a link between financial integration and economic growth is not robust: while a few studies, mostly focusing on equity market liberalizations, find positive and significant effects, the majority of studies find insignificant effects, or results that do not hold up to changes in specification and country sample (Kose and others, 2006). This is corroborated by cross-country and panel regressions" [estimated in the present study].

The reported confirmation of lack of robustness, however, is questionable from reading the study's own estimates (IMF 2007a, table 8). The cross-country regressions for 1975–2004, including the usual control variables (initial per capita income, investment relative to GDP, years of schooling, population growth, and a dummy variable for Africa) do indeed show statistically positive coefficients for four measures of financial integration (gross external assets and liabilities relative to GDP, total inflows relative to GDP, gross flows relative to GDP, and external assets relative to GDP). The coefficients are positive but not significant for four other measures (outflows relative to GDP, external liabilities relative to GDP, liabilities of FDI and portfolio relative to GDP, and debt liabilities relative to GDP). Only one of the nine measures has a negative (and insignificant) coefficient: de jure openness. If half of the tests show statistically positive growth effects and the other half show insignificant effects, it is by no means clear that the correct conclusion is that results "do not hold

---

117. But not banking crises—an equal opportunity area as exemplified by the United States in 2007.

up." A more appropriate conclusion may be that some measures of openness are better than others. More formally, appendix 2A demonstrates that when meta-statistical weighting by inverse variance is applied to the IMF (2007a) estimates, the result is a substantial positive coefficient for the growth impact of financial openness, albeit of a smaller magnitude than indicated by the average for significant estimates only.[118]

The IMF authors then conduct tests focusing on direct investment, essentially arguing that FDI is a preferred type of external capital for growth benefits. This time the regression including the usual controls finds a statistically significant positive coefficient on FDI and equity liabilities as a share of GDP. "Concretely, keeping constant the stock of foreign liabilities, an increase in FDI by 10 percentage points of GDP (about the average of FDI in the sample) is associated with an increase in average growth of 0.3 percentage point" (p. 29). As shown in table 2.2, translation of this stock estimate to a corresponding flow coefficient implies a growth impact of 0.5 percent per year for 1 percent of GDP additional FDI inflow.

The study then turns to indirect benefits. A test using 10-year non-overlapping growth in TFP for 1965–2005 for 68 countries finds a highly significant positive coefficient on de jure financial openness, controlling for initial TFP, trade openness, and population growth. The coefficient is 0.08, indicating that a rise in de jure openness from zero to 1 is associated with an increase in annual TFP growth by 0.08 percentage point, so the impact is small albeit significant in statistical terms. In another test for indirect benefits, the authors regress change in the logarithm of private credit relative to GDP on control variables and de jure financial openness. This impact also is positive and statistically significant. The coefficient implies that, for example, an economy at 50 percent private credit relative to GDP with complete closure would rise to 61 percent after shifting to complete financial integration.[119]

Rather than emphasizing the positive growth effects identified for FDI, let alone the significant positive results among several of the broader tests, the IMF authors conclude by calling attention to the risk of greater volatility for countries that integrate financially without meeting preconditions. They invoke "the IMF's integrated approach, which envisages a gradual and orderly sequencing of external financial liberalization and emphasizes the desirability of complementary reforms in the macroeconomic policy framework and the domestic financial system as essential components of a successful liberalization strategy" (p. 3). Despite this cau-

---

118. There is also a major potential problem with the estimates: Like most of the literature, the study includes investment relative to GDP as an explanatory variable, and it is always strongly significant. But if the whole point of financial integration is to increase investment, then its positive impact seems likely to be masked if a high investment-to-GDP ratio is somehow considered to be exogenous to the extent of financial globalization.

119. The coefficient is 0.21. In the example: $ln\ 50 + 1 \times 0.21 = 4.11$; $e^{4.11} = 60.9$.

tious conclusion with its emphasis warning about preconditions, several of the specific econometric estimates in the study would seem to suggest potential for gains from financial integration.

The survey by Henry (2007, 887) argues that "studies that actually test the theory show that liberalization has significant effects on the costs of capital, investment, and economic growth." His main point is that neo-classical theory would not predict a permanent increase in the growth rate as a consequence of an opening of the capital market. Instead, there would be a temporary increase, as the economy made a transition to a higher cap-ital-labor ratio in response to the reduction in the cost of capital. However, thereafter growth would slow down again "because capital accumulation, which is subject to diminishing returns, is the only channel through which liberalization affects growth in the neoclassical model" (p. 889). He also argues that inappropriate pooling of developing countries together with industrial countries has distorted empirical estimates and that the inad-equacy of the various measures of openness has also plagued analysis.

Henry emphasizes instead that several studies (including his own work, considered above) have found large temporary boosts to growth in shorter periods such as five years following the opening of capital markets to portfolio equity flows. He suggests plausible transition mechanics that would be consistent with this phenomenon (in contrast to an instanta-neous surge in capital and output in the extreme neoclassical formula-tion). At the same time, he acknowledges that these empirical studies tend to find growth impacts that are larger than can be explained by the corre-sponding increases in the growth rate of country capital stocks associated with opening (growth increases of about 1 percent per year for both out-put and the country's capital stock, whereas with a capital share of one-third the boost to output growth would be expected to be only one-third as high as that for capital growth). He acknowledges that the studies have not been able to fully dispel possible endogeneity (capital inflow growth in response to, rather than as a cause of, faster output growth).

Henry's approach would seem to give too little attention to influences that should indeed raise the permanent growth rate by focusing solely on a neoclassical model that does not incorporate any response of technical change to foreign capital. Certainly the literature on FDI as well as that on the influence of foreign investment on the domestic financial system would suggest that financial openness does more than simply boost the quantity of constant-quality capital. Moreover, his summary of the cross-country literature on financial openness and growth accepts too readily the frequent view that the "bulk of the evidence" supports the no-impact school (which he typifies citing Rodrik 1998 and Levine and Zervos 1998b) rather than the positive-impact school (citing Quinn 1997). As suggested above, in contrast, if in fact there were no impact, one would expect an equal distribution of negative and positive statistically significant estimates, rather than a strictly positive set. Moreover, when weighting all estimates by inverse variance, a sizable positive impact remains.

In their most recent survey, Prasad and Rajan (2008, 3) suggest as a stylized fact that "the correlation between growth and the use of foreign capital is strongly positive for industrial countries but not for low-income countries." This suggests that "the lack of domestic savings is not the primary constraint" in low-income countries (p. 2). As noted above in the discussion of Prasad, Rajan, and Subramanian (2007a), this stylized fact is questionable for at least middle-income economies. In any event, their bottom line is that open capital markets are desirable for growth because of the collateral benefits they bring. These include exposing a country's financial sector to competition, spurring improvement in domestic corporate governance, and imposing discipline on macroeconomic policies. But there is a tension in the timing of opening, because precisely the types of institutional development that make it safer to open are ones that could be expedited by capital opening itself. Moreover, the authors judge that "countries don't have much of a choice but to plan for capital account liberalization, because capital accounts are de facto becoming more open irrespective of government attempts to control them" (p. 25).

After providing a rapid *tour d'horizon* of almost 80 studies, the authors offer a "modest proposal for controlled outflows" (p. 23). The country would authorize a number of closed-end mutual funds to issue shares denominated in local currency for use in investment abroad, with the central bank controlling timing and amounts of foreign exchange made available for this purpose. The approach "essentially securitizes reserves" and is in part tailored to an era of massive buildup of reserves by governments still nervous about the risk of capital flight in bad times. However, to adopt it would require the new imposition of controls on outflows for the large number of emerging-market economies that currently do not have them. Yet doing so would contradict the stylized policy diagnosis that outward capital controls are more detrimental than market-friendly disincentives to inflows (such as Chile's former *encaje*).

Obstfeld (2009) provides the lead survey in a recent IMF compendium of studies on financial globalization and covers much of the same territory as that reviewed here in terms of the specific empirical studies. In a helpful initial framework, he argues that financial openness may be less beneficial than trade openness because of "the intertemporal nature of financial trades and…the potential for asymmetric information to eliminate trade gains" (p. 73). Payment is contingent for financial instruments, and they involve moral hazard and adverse selection. Comparable "lemon" problems in goods trade are less severe. He suggests that second-best principles imply that eliminating restrictions on foreign asset trade may cause welfare losses rather than gains if the domestic financial system has distortions. Problems arise in the areas of sovereignty, regulatory end-run, undue prudential laxity for purposes of maintaining competitiveness with foreign institutions, currency mismatches, and contagion. He judges that "many crises have been provoked by the opening of unsound systems to capital flows" (p. 75).

On the econometric studies, Obstfeld judges that the "endogeneity critique is perhaps *the* major reason for being skeptical of *all* the econometric work suggesting that financial opening, in and of itself, spurs more rapid economic growth (or reduces macroeconomic volatility)" (p. 84). He considers that severe econometric difficulties have meant there is "strikingly little convincing documentation of direct positive impacts of financial opening on the economic welfare levels or growth rates of developing countries," whereas "opening the financial account does appear to raise the frequency and severity of economic crises." Yet he recognizes that countries are moving toward openness if only because "a growing financial sector in an economy open to trade cannot long be insulated from cross-border financial flows" (p. 63). For countries not yet open financially he thus recommends a "gradual and cautious" (p. 104) approach, starting with FDI ("the available evidence suggests that FDI flows have the biggest positive effect on domestic investment and growth"), then portfolio equity flows, and only later long-term debt, with short-term debt coming last (p. 91).

Obstfeld's summary of the econometric findings is conventional in its flavor that the positive impact is difficult to document. As argued above, that approach fails to recognize that if the effect were truly zero or negative, the overwhelming preponderance of positive results for significant estimates would not be encountered. Nor does it take a meta-statistical approach of weighting all results rather than dismissing previous statistically significant results as soon as another test is found that can eliminate significance. On the key question of whether financial openness increases the incidence and severity of financial crises, Obstfeld's summary is somewhat at odds with his text discussion. He cites Edwards (2005) as finding no greater incidence of crises in countries with higher capital mobility and Tornell and Westermann (2005) as finding higher growth despite more credit growth volatility in these countries.[120] He does cite Hutchison and Noy (2005) as finding that currency crises cost 5 to 8 percent of GDP and banking crises 10 to 13 percent, with the effect additive for "twin crises," but he does not report evidence attributing greater incidence of such crises to financial openness.

---

120. In a footnote, Obstfeld cites Edwards as finding that "crises tend to reduce economic growth more in countries that are more open financially" (p. 76). However, he fails to report that in a subsequent study using the same index of openness, Edwards finds instead that countries restricting capital mobility have not experienced milder crises (see the discussion above of Edwards 2006).

Conclusion

The broad pattern that emerges from this survey is that there is considerable empirical support for sizable economic benefits from financial globalization. As shown in table 2.1, among the general impact studies, those that obtain statistically significant estimates tend to show that a shift from complete closure to complete financial integration translates into an increase in growth rates on the order of 1 to 2 percent annually over time horizons of two decades or so. The corresponding meta-statistical average weighting by inverse variance is about one-half a percent per year, still a relatively large impact. The only estimates that show statistically significant negative effects are those in contingent models that show a positive effect once the threshold of an interacting variable (e.g., per capita income) has been passed. As discussed above, the probability of this set of empirical findings falsely portraying positive impacts is vanishingly small. Similarly, table 2.3 shows sizable positive effects of direct investment. Once again the inverse-variance weighting of results in one key study retains a sizable positive impact despite its smaller size than for the significant coefficients only. The review of growth impacts of the opening of portfolio equity markets systematically shows surprisingly large benefits, but over shorter horizons of five to 10 years. Overall, then, the tendency in the present literature to treat gains as being "difficult to detect" is distorted. This diagnosis is reinforced if one judges that several of the studies that claim to discard positive results as nonrobust do so only with the use of highly questionable instrumental variables, on the one hand, or potentially circular exogenous variables such as government reputation, on the other.

Potentially large gains are also implied by evidence on the influence of financial globalization on domestic financial development in combination with ample evidence of growth benefits from such development. There is also a more theoretical literature about gains from risk sharing, but the calibrated estimates in this literature tend to show a wide range from small to enormous potential gains. The large gain estimates may conflate opportunities from portfolio investment diversification with realistic gains in consumption smoothing in real-world (as opposed to theoretical "endowment") economies. Simple exercises applying plausible welfare functions and risk-aversion parameters with plausible magnitudes of reduction of consumption volatility through financial globalization (appendix 2C) suggest that the estimates toward the smaller end of the scale may be the more germane among this literature. At the same time, a prominent study by IMF researchers (Kose, Prasad, and Terrones 2003) claiming that emerging markets experienced greater rather than lesser volatility from financial integration in the 1990s would appear to misinterpret its own results, considering that the more financially integrated economies systematically fared better than the less-integrated ones, and it was only the fact that their consumption volatility did not decrease as much as their output volatility in the 1990s that led to the study's conclusion.

Traditionally, the principal downside of open capital markets in the theoretical literature was the risk that direct investment would go into hothouse industries protected by high tariffs. That was a risk and in some cases happened, but by now it is largely an artifact of the past, as most economies have sharply reduced protection and those that have not done so are not in the forefront of receiving direct investment in an era of global sourcing of production by multinational corporations. By far the greater question of relevance to the costs of financial integration in recent years has been whether open capital markets, especially for short-term debt, are on balance negative for growth because they are likely to lead to financial crises. One of the better empirical studies on this issue (Tornell, Westermann, and Martinez 2004) suggests that there is indeed some potential increase in volatility but that nonetheless the gains from more openness exceed crisis losses. Moreover, there is evidence that controls on short-term capital may be disadvantageous to investment in small firms in particular. A calibrated exercise using implied parameters from recent crisis-impact studies suggests that the expected output losses from any crises induced by financial openness are likely to be considerably smaller than the long-term gains from openness, on the order of 0.15 percent of GDP annual crisis losses compared with at least 0.5 percent secular growth gains. Even so, the most plausible case for restrictions remains the need for prudence on opening economies fully to short-term capital flows before minimum thresholds have been met in such areas as financial-sector development.

Appendix 2A
Weighting Cross-Country Regression Results in Meta-Analysis

Cross-country growth regressions have been used to test a variety of hypotheses about sources of growth and merits of alternative policy regimes designed to spur growth. Frequently the tests are conducted by relating growth performance as the dependent variable to a core set of control independent variables and then augmenting the regression with a variable representing the policy in question. An issue arises for policy inference, however, when some of the tests find the policy variable to be statistically significant (typically at the 5 percent level) and other tests do not. The question is how to arrive at a central estimate. This appendix considers four conceptual approaches to this question.

Dichotomous Vote Counting, the Null Hypothesis, and Critical Range

One approach is to count all statistically significant results on one side of the ledger and all insignificant results on the other side. The policy in question is then judged to contribute to growth if the number of significant results exceeds the number of insignificant ones but is interpreted as having no effect if the converse occurs. This approach can be called "dichotomous vote counting."

A key problem with this approach is that by giving equal weight to significant and insignificant results, it violates the econometric principle that the "null hypothesis" cannot be accepted by a statistical test; it can only be rejected in favor of the "alternative hypothesis."[121] The null hypothesis is typically that the coefficient of growth on the policy variable is zero. The alternative hypothesis is that it is significantly different from zero. A probability distribution of the estimate is assumed to lie around the true parameter value. If the coefficient estimate lies toward the positive extreme (or, for "two-tailed tests," either the positive or negative extreme), then it is considered to have cleared the "critical range" hurdle and to represent

---

121. Thus, Lane (2010, B33945) states: "A null hypothesis is not accepted just because it is not rejected. Data not sufficient to show convincingly that a difference between means is not zero do not prove that the difference is zero." Similarly, Motulsky (1995, 114) states: "If the P value is greater than a preset value of alpha, the difference is said to be not significant. This means that the data are not strong enough to persuade you to reject the null hypothesis. People often mistakenly interpret a high P value as proof that the null hypothesis is true. That is incorrect. A high P value does not prove the null hypothesis. ...[C]oncluding that a difference is not statistically significant when the null hypothesis is, in fact, false is called a Type II error." (Note that the P value is the probability that the coefficient estimate would be arrived at by random chance. A typical critical P value, or alpha, is 0.05.)

an outcome that is too unlikely to have occurred solely by random chance. The null hypothesis of zero influence is statistically rejected in favor of the coefficient estimate (typically obtained by least-squares regression).

Suppose, however, that among several different studies, more studies find an insignificant coefficient than find significant coefficients. Is the proper conclusion that there is no influence of the policy variable? An important reason for not adopting this approach is that because the null hypothesis cannot be "accepted," insignificant findings should not be construed as demonstrating zero influence. Indeed, insofar as insignificant results are given any credence at all, it turns out that their information should be registered as the parameter coefficient they estimate, not at zero (see meta-analysis below). The question then becomes how to weight them in comparison with the weights attached to statistically significant results.

An implicit extension of the problem with dichotomous vote counting is that there is nothing sacrosanct about the selection of the conventional 0.05 as the critical threshold. McCloskey and Ziliak (1996) argue that economic applications have often conflated statistical significance with economic significance, and that the critical threshold for significance should take into account a loss function for type I versus type II errors. They note that this issue was classically debated on one side by Ronald Fisher (1925), who was influential in setting the conventional 5 percent threshold, and on the other by Neyman and Pearson (1933) and Wald (1939), who argued for setting the significance level in light of the importance of the two types of errors. Dichotomous vote counting in a fashion that imputes zero influence to a statistically insignificant finding commits not only the error of accepting a null hypothesis but also the error of confusing significance with importance. One implication of the McCloskey-Ziliak critique is that under some circumstances it may be appropriate to set the critical threshold at a much higher P level than 5 percent. Another implication is that researchers should consider both the economic size and the statistical significance of their estimates.

Measured Averages Imputing Insignificant Estimates at Zero

Although few if any studies take the step of calculating the average estimated coefficient using the average of the significant results and zero for all of the insignificant results, doing so would be the logical conclusion of dichotomous vote counting. It would make explicit the error of attributing zero to the "result" for the nonsignificant estimates.

Measured Averages Excluding Insignificant Estimates

A more defensible method for arriving at an average of estimates would be to consider only those results that are statistically significant. This approach would be the logical consequence of treating insignificant results as "nonresults" rather than "zero" coefficients on grounds of the proscription of "accepting" the null hypothesis. It would be broadly consistent with the Fisher approach insisting on a standard level of significance (typically $P = 0.05$).

Meta-Analysis Weighting Averages by the Inverse of Variance

An alternative approach that has gained considerable following in such diverse fields as agricultural research, education, and psychology is to weight estimates by the inverse of the variance of the estimate. In this approach, an estimate is not excluded just because it does not meet a particular level of statistical significance. However, its low significance will reflect a larger than typical variance, and so it will receive lower weight than a significant estimate. Pioneer studies in this approach include Pearson (1904), on effectiveness of inoculation against enteric fever, and Glass (1976), on the effectiveness of psychotherapy. Pearson surveyed just six studies; Glass, about 400.

Hedges and Olkin (1985) note that statistical procedures for combining results of research in agriculture date from the 1930s. Such approaches were unusual in the social studies, however, in considerable part because unlike agricultural yields, such variables as educational results are frequently measured using divergent variables and scales. They credit Glass (1976) with proposing the solution of estimating an "effect magnitude that did not depend on the arbitrary scaling of the dependent variable" (Hedges and Olkin 1985, 6). They also note that the common alternative of "vote-counting procedures" based solely on statistical significance "can be strongly biased toward the conclusion that the treatment has no effect" (p. 3).

The framework that has developed in meta-analysis is first to estimate an "effect size" (*ES*), second to estimate its standard error (*SE*), and then to obtain weights based on the inverse of the standard error (Lipsey and Wilson 2001, 36, 47). For example, in a meta-analysis of differences between two groups (such as male versus female), the effect size is simply the mean difference between the groups ($ES = \overline{X}_{G1} - \overline{X}_{G2}$). The standard error of the effect size is the standard deviation of the sampling distribution (in this case $SE = s_p[1/n_{G1} + 1/n_{G2}]^{0.5}$, where s_p is the standard deviation of the pooled sample). The weight for the i-th estimate is then proportional to the inverse of the square of the standard error ($w_i = [1/SE_i]^2/\Sigma [1/SE_i]^2$).

The inverse-variance weighting following this sequence is well developed for several types of size effect: proportion of a population with a particular characteristic; mean gain between pre-treatments and post-treatments; mean difference between two groups; and association between two variables (Lipsey and Wilson 2001, chapter 3). Analysis of multivariate relationships is less fully developed and faces such challenges as the fact that studies being surveyed typically do not report correlation matrices.

Because meta-analysis has typically been applied in such contexts as comparing medical trials across differing sample sizes, a reasonable question is whether the approach is applicable to cross-country statistical tests in which sample size is relatively similar. In practice there is considerable dispersion in what may be thought of as effective sample size. As shown in table 2.1, country inclusion ranges from about 50 to about 100. Time spans range from about 20 to about 50 years. Moreover, whereas meta-analysis in medical or agricultural tests will typically test a single variable (e.g., application of the medicine does or does not reduce incidence of the disease), the cross-country tests for financial-openness effects typically are multivariate. Each time a different variable is used as a control or interacting variable, the "sample" might be thought of as being different; and each time an additional variable is included, the effective sample size might be thought of as having shrunk.

An Approach for Multivariate Meta-Analysis of a Key Policy Variable

The principles of identifying size effect and standard error, and then weighting by inverse variance, should be applicable in a meta-analysis of the influence of a key policy variable used in a multivariate analysis in the following manner. Consider cross-country studies of the influence of financial openness on economic growth. Suppose that there is a set of j control variables X_j and the policy variable of interest, Z. Suppose that Z is normalized so that it ranges from a minimum of 0 to a maximum of 1. Suppose the growth rate is the dependent variable. Then the statistical studies typically follow the form:

$$g = \alpha + \sum_j \beta_j X_j + \gamma Z. \tag{2A.1}$$

The coefficient γ is the increment in growth attributable to the presence of the policy variable at its maximum level, or in this case, with $Z = 1$ indicating complete financial openness. This means that in the framework of meta-analysis, *the coefficient on the normalized key variable should be the "effect size."*

The standard error of the effect size is simply the standard error of the coefficient estimate for γ. Typically, cross-country regression analyses will report either the standard error of the coefficient using the scale of the variable applied in the study (which will rarely be the normalized scale applicable across studies), or the t-statistic for the coefficient estimate. The relationship between the t-statistic and the standard error can be exploited to arrive at the standard error of the normalized variable as follows. By definition, the t-statistic is the ratio of the estimated coefficient to the standard error. Given the coefficient estimate and the t-statistic in the un-normalized (original-study) results, then:

$$SE_u = \frac{\gamma_u}{t},$$

(2A.2)

where subscript u indicates "un-normalized," SE is the standard error, and t is the t-statistic.

Before obtaining the meta-analysis weighted average of the "effect size" of the policy, it is necessary to normalize the variable Z across the various studies. The scale of this normalization will affect the scale of the coefficient estimate. In the most trivial example, suppose one study varies financial openness from 0 to 100 and another uses simply 0 to 1. Then if the 0 to 1 scale is set as the benchmark, normalizing the other study will require dividing its policy variable by 100. The consequence of doing so will be to multiply its estimated coefficient by 100, so that the product of the normalized coefficient and the normalized variable remains unchanged. For the k-th study surveyed, then, the normalized standard error will be:

$$SE_{nk} = \frac{v_k \gamma_k}{t_k} = \frac{\tilde{\gamma}_k}{t_k},$$

(2A.3)

where subscript n refers to normalized, subscript k refers to the k-th study, the parameter v is the scalar used to convert the policy variable specification in that study to the normalizing benchmark form, and $\tilde{\gamma}_k$ is the normalized value of the coefficient estimate.

For the case of financial openness, the normalized variable should be scaled from zero (for complete closedness) to unity (for complete openness).[122] In the tests using de jure measures this scale is typically already applied (or 0 to 100, easily converted to 0 to 1). However, in tests using de facto measures, the variables are typically open-ended. The approach adopted here is to designate the value of the variable at the 90th percentile of its distribution as the effective level that corresponds to "complete" openness, and thus corresponds to a normalized value of unity. For the de facto measures, the lowest value is typically zero. Normalization thus involves

---

122. The author is indebted to Thomas Emmons for key suggestions regarding normalization.

dividing the variable in question by the 90th percentile value, and setting a ceiling of 1 for the transformed variable. Thus:

$$\tilde{Z}_k = Min\{Z_k / Z_{k90}; \ 1\}, \tag{2A.4}$$

where Z_{k90} is the value of the unadjusted financial variable at its 90th percentile and ~ indicates normalized value.

As an example, for 87 countries during 1975–2004, the ratio of gross capital flows (inward and outward) to GDP had a mean of 0.13 and a 90th percentile level of 0.48 (IMF 2007a).[123] The normalized version of this variable will then be Z/0.48, with a ceiling of 1.0 and a floor of 0.

The estimated coefficient of growth on financial openness needs to be adjusted correspondingly to be consistent with the normalized version of the de facto openness variable. In equation 2A.3, the value of the normalization scalar that will convert the measured coefficient to a value compatible with the normalized independent variable will simply be the 90th percentile level of the underlying variable (Z_{k90}). The normalized coefficient is thus obtained as:

$$\tilde{\gamma}_k = v_k \gamma_k = Z_{k90} \gamma_k; \ v_k = Z_{k90}. \tag{2A.5}$$

The pieces are now in place to arrive at the meta-analysis weights. For study k, the weight that should be applied is in proportion to the inverse of the square of its normalized standard deviation. Thus:

$$
\begin{aligned}
w_k &= \frac{1/(SE_{nk})^2}{\sum_k 1/(SE_{nk})^2} \\
&= \frac{t_k^2 / (v_k \gamma_k)^2}{\sum_k t_k^2 / (v_k \gamma_k)^2} = \frac{t_k^2 / \tilde{\gamma}_k^2}{\sum_k t_k^2 / (\tilde{\gamma}_k)^2}.
\end{aligned} \tag{2A.6}
$$

It thus turns out that the weight of a particular study's coefficient in arriving at the overall meta-analysis varies directly with the square of the t-statistic in the study and inversely with the square of the normalized coefficient estimate of the study. This result is intuitively appealing, because it not only gives greater weight to estimates with a higher degree of statistical significance, but it also incorporates a counterweight against the tendency for the t-statistic to be larger when the coefficient estimate is larger. This tendency arises from the fact that the statistical test is (typi-

---

123. See footnote 125 below.

cally) for difference from zero. The larger the coefficient, the more likely it is that a significant difference will be detected.[124]

An Example: Meta-Weighting Individual Results of an IMF Study

Normalized inverse-variance weighting can be applied at the level of a single study with multiple tests, just as it can be applied across studies. As an important example, consider the survey of financial openness conducted by the IMF staff (IMF 2007a). Table 2A.1 reports the regression coefficients and t-statistics obtained for nine alternative measures of financial openness. The dependent variable was average economic growth in 87 countries during 1975–2004. The control independent variables were log of initial per capita income, average ratio of investment to GDP, years of schooling, population growth, and a dummy variable for Africa. The 90th percentile value of each variable is imputed on the basis of observed mean and standard deviation.[125]

The only surprise in the coefficient estimates is the result for openness using the de jure measure of openness compiled by the AREAER. This variable has the wrong sign. Openness is reported as 1 and closedness as 0. A likely reason for the negative coefficient is the strong positive correlation between per capita income and openness, combined with the negative relationship between growth and per capita income (convergence). The coefficient is not significant but is almost so at the 10 percent level.[126]

Normalization across the nine alternative models yields the result that the difference between complete openness and complete closure can range from –0.84 percent per year additional growth (de jure openness) to as much as 2.7 percent per year additional growth (total outflows; see column E). The meta-analysis method of weighting by the inverse of the square of the normalized standard error yields a weighted average estimate of 0.428 percentage point additional growth per year for complete openness versus complete closure.

---

124. For example, Hedges and Olkin (1985, 5–7) indicate that in a sample of 100 observations, if the true effect size, or standardized mean difference, between two groups is small (at 0.20), the expected outturn of significant results at the 5 percent level will only be about 15 percent; if the effect size is large (at 0.80), the expected proportion of significant results reaches nearly 100 percent. If the effect size is intermediate (at 0.50), the expected proportion of significant results reaches 50 percent only when the sample size exceeds 70 observations.

125. The variable means and standard deviations are not reported in the study but were kindly made available by the IMF (by communication, April 25, 2009). The imputed 90th percentile value assumes normal distribution, in which case the value in question equals the mean plus 1.645 times the standard deviation.

126. With 87 observations and six variables, the t-statistic needs to be 1.66 to achieve significance at the 10 percent level. The t-statistic for the de jure openness variable is 1.65.

Table 2A.1   Meta-analysis normalized inverse weighting of regression results in IMF (2007a) study of financial openness and growth

Variable	Mean	Standard deviation	Coefficient	Z_{90}	$\tilde{\gamma}$	t	SE_n	Weight
	A	B	C	D	E	F	G	H
Gross foreign assets and liabilities/GDP	1.573	2.768	0.06	6.13	0.368	2	0.184	0.309
Total inflows/GDP	0.05	0.04	8.62	0.12	0.998	2.13	0.468	0.048
Gross flows/GDP	0.131	0.214	1.56	0.48	0.754	3.71	0.203	0.254
Total outflows/GDP	0.081	0.194	6.75	0.4	2.701	1.27	2.125	0.002
External assets/GDP	0.613	1.509	0.19	3.1	0.588	2.11	0.279	0.135
External liabilities/GDP	0.96	1.326	0.02	3.14	0.063	0.18	0.346	0.087
FDI, portfolio equity liabilities/GDP	0.207	0.161	0.93	0.47	0.439	0.83	0.528	0.037
Debt liabilities/GDP	0.756	1.289	0.01	2.88	0.029	0.08	0.345	0.088
De jure openness	0.296	0.317	−0.84	1	−.840	−1.65	0.51	0.04
Nine variables, weighted			—	—	0.428	—	—	1

FDI = foreign direct investment

Note: Z_{90} = value of variable at 90th percentile, or 1.0 for de jure; D = A + 1.645 x B; E = CD; G = E/F; H is proportional to $1/G^2$.

Table 2A.2 summarizes five alternative ways to arrive at weighted average results for the same example. The averages again use the normalized coefficient estimates.

Overall, the alternative approaches suggest an economically meaningful contribution of financial openness to growth: the addition of about one-third to two-thirds of a percentage point to annual growth as the potential gain as against financial closedness. In terms of the various possible sources of growth, this range represents an important role. This interpretation is considerably at odds with the conclusion reported in the IMF (2007a, 29) in the study itself: "…[T]he results appear to be fragile…[with an] apparent lack of robust evidence of a link between financial globalization and economic growth." This interpretation seems to be driven by simple vote counting: Three results are significant at the 5 percent level or better; one is significant at the 10 percent level; and five are not significant at even the 10 percent level. Yet even imputing zero to the insignificant results and then averaging with the significant results would give an estimate of about 0.3 percentage point annual growth contribution potential from financial openness.

A comparison of the results counting only significant findings, or weighting by t-statistic, with the meta-analysis results does suggest that solely considering significant results will tend to overstate the "size effect." At the same time, it is difficult not to be given pause by the seemingly extreme variability of the weights that are generated by the inverse-variance method: about 30 percent for the first variable but only about 5 percent for the second variable even though its t-statistic is higher (and both are significant at the 5 percent level).

Conclusion

Meta-analysis techniques developed primarily in such disciplines as agricultural science, education, and psychology provide an approach for arriving at a weighted average of research findings that goes beyond simple "vote counting" of significant versus insignificant results. For comparison, results must first be normalized. This appendix has presented a way to normalize and identify the standard error of the normalized estimate in order to arrive at the elements needed for weighting by inverse variance. When this approach is applied to an example of a recent IMF (2007a) study on the impact of financial openness on growth, the results are suggestive that such studies may be biased against finding meaningful results. However, the results also indicate that the alternative of solely including statistically significant estimates may bias the size estimate upwards. Moreover, actual application of the inverse-variance approach generates an extreme range of weights for the individual estimates. Finally, it should be reiterated that the approach suggested here remains heuristic. Although

Table 2A.2   Alternative weighted-average estimates for annual growth impact of complete financial openness versus closedness (percent): IMF (2007a) study example

Approach	Result
Dichotomous vote counting	4 significant/5 nonsignificant
Imputing zero to nonsignificant	0.301
Significant results only	0.677
Weighting by t-statistic	0.668
Meta-analysis (inverse-variance weighting)	0.428

it follows the principles of identifying the "effect size," the standard error of the effect size, and then weighting by the inverse of the square of the standard error, as developed in the literature on meta-analysis, the implementation here applies these principles to the case of a parameter from multivariate analysis, and the statistical theory for the multivariate case is not yet well developed.

Appendix 2B
Gourinchas-Jeanne Model of Gains from Financial Integration

Gourinchas and Jeanne (2006) use a steady-state growth model to examine the gains from a shift from financial autarky to openness to international capital flows. Production is Cobb-Douglas. Raw labor grows at the population growth rate n. Labor-augmenting technical change increases the ratio of effective labor to raw labor at a rate of g. The rate of pure time preference is ρ. The discount factor is thus $1 + \rho = \beta$. The rate of capital depreciation is δ. Utility in year t is:

$$U_t = \sum_{s=0}^{\infty} \beta^s N_{t+s} u(c_{t+s}),$$ (2B.1)

where N is population (and raw labor), c is per capita consumption, and utility is constant rate of risk aversion in principle and logarithmic in their reported analysis:

$$u(c) = \frac{c^{1-\gamma}}{1-\gamma} \; ; \gamma > 0, \text{ and } u(c) = \ln(c) \text{ for } \gamma = 1.$$ (2B.2)

In this setup, steady-state growth is eventually reached at the rate $g + n$. Capital, effective labor, and output all grow at this rate. Labor and population grow at n, so per capita income grows at g.

Instead of using optimization software to evaluate this setup over an infinite horizon (as in Gourinchas and Jeanne), it is informative to explore its implications for a more policy-relevant horizon. In order to adhere to steady-state properties, however, it is also useful to frame such an examination within the context of a long horizon. This appendix uses 500 years.

Using the Gourinchas-Jeanne production structure, production in year t equals:

$$Y_t = BK_t^{\alpha} (\tilde{L})_t^{1-\alpha},$$ (2B.3)

where B is a constant, K is capital, $\tilde{L}$ is effective labor, and α is the factor share of capital. Effective labor is:

$$(\tilde{L})_t = N_0 (1+n)^t (1+g)^t.$$ (2B.4)

With the saving rate at ϕ, capital in year t is:

$$K_t = K_{t-1} + \phi_t Y_t - \delta K_{t-1}. \tag{2B.5}$$

That is, capital equals the previous year's stock of capital plus the saving rate in the year in question applied to that year's output, minus the rate of depreciation applied to the previous year's capital stock. At the steady state, the saving rate will be:

$$\phi^* = \Gamma^* \; (\delta + n + g), \tag{2B.6}$$

where the steady-state capital-output ratio is $(K/Y)^* = \Gamma^*$. Saving needs to be high enough not only to offset depreciation but also to enable the capital stock to keep pace with the the growth of raw labor and the pace of labor-augmenting technical change. If the capital-output ratio were one to one, the final expression in parentheses would suffice for these three effects, respectively. Because capital substantially exceeds output, this expression must be multiplied by the capital-output ratio to obtain the steady-state saving ratio.

So far the model is for autarky. The economy starts out with capital-output ratio Γ_{A0}, and through saving eventually approaches the steady-state level Γ^*. Now open the economy and allow it to borrow enough capital from abroad at the outset to catapult its capital-output ratio to the international steady-state level, $\Gamma_W = \Gamma^*$. The amount of borrowing and hence initial external debt needed for this purpose is:

$$D_0 = \Gamma_W Y_1^I - \Gamma_{A0} Y_1^A = \Gamma_W Y_1^I - K_1^A, \tag{2B.7}$$

where subscript 1 denotes the first year of the horizon, superscript I on income denotes the level obtained through immediate full integration, and superscript and subscript A denotes autarky. If external debt is amortized in equal payments over T years, then annual amortization will be D_0/T, and the corresponding amount of debt outstanding at the end of year t will be $D_t = D_0(1-t/T)$, for $t \leq T$ and zero thereafter. In addition to principal, the country must pay interest on the amount of its external debt outstanding, in the amount rD, where r is the international interest rate.

Under financial integration, the capital-output ratio must rise to the steady-state level and stay there. This means that capital is no longer an unknown that is residual from a given saving rate. With effective labor known and the capital-output ratio known, capital can be calculated as follows. First, from equation 2B.3 and given the required capital output ratio Γ_W:

$$\frac{K_t}{BK_t^\alpha \widetilde{L}_t^{1-\alpha}} = \Gamma_W;$$

$$K_t^{1-\alpha} = \Gamma_W B \widetilde{L}_t^{1-\alpha};$$ (2B.8)

$$K_t = \widetilde{L}_t \Omega$$

where $\Omega \equiv (\Gamma_W B)^{1/(1-\alpha)}$

It must also be true, however, that capital rises to keep pace with rising effective labor and that the rise in capital must be net of depreciation. At the same time, there is a predetermined amount of debt service to take care of, equal to the principal plus the interest on the outstanding external debt. Consumption can then be determined as the residual left after output is allocated to take care of debt service, depreciation, and the increment in capital needed to keep pace with effective labor. Thus:

$$\Delta K_t = \Delta \widetilde{L}_t \Omega = Y_t - \delta K_{t-1} - DS_t - C_t,$$ (2B.9)

where debt service is $DS_t = D_0/T + r D_0(1-t/T)$ for $t \le T$ and zero thereafter.

Consumption for the year is thus determined residually, as:

$$C_t = Y_t - \Delta \widetilde{L}_t \Omega - \delta K_{t-1} - DS_t.$$ (2B.10)

In the main Gourinchas-Jeanne experiment, the parameter values are as follows. Capital's share is $\alpha = 0.3$. The international and autarkic capital-output ratios are $\Gamma_w = 2.63$ and $\Gamma_a = 1.4$. Labor and population grow at $n = 0.0074$, the depreciation rate is $\delta = 0.06$, labor-augmenting technical change is at a constant rate of $g = 0.012$, and the rate of pure time preference is $\rho = 0.04$. Utility is logarithmic ($\gamma = 1$). Given the Gourinchas-Jeanne parameters, their international interest rate is 5.4 percent per annum.

A simple implementation of this system with initial population specified at 1,000 and initial capital for the internationalized economy specified so as to yield per capita income of $25,000 results in a required initial capital stock of $65 million. The constant term B that yields the desired output of $25 million is $B = 900$. With this same production function and an initial capital output ratio at the autarkic level (1.4), production equals $19.2 million, and per capita income, $19,200. Under autarky, capital is only $26.9 million, so the initial amount borrowed from international capital markets is the capital difference of $38 million (or 150 percent of integrated GDP).

The dynamics differ between autarky and integration. In autarky, the fixed saving rate that eventually raises the steady-state capital-output ratio

Figure 2B.1   Illustrative paths of per capita consumption under financial autarky and financial integration

per capita consumption

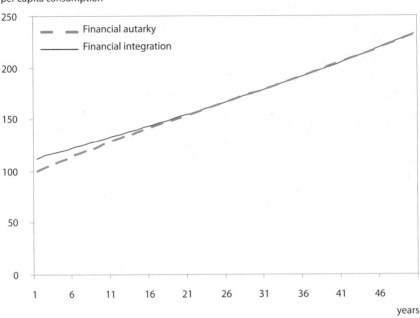

Source: Author's calculations.

to the same as the international level is: $\phi^* = 0.2088$ (applying parameter values to equation 2B.6). In contrast, the rate of saving out of disposable income, defining the latter as output minus debt service, is a residual in the integration scenario. It starts out at 0.23 and by year 51 stabilizes at 0.2051, practically the same over the long term as the autarkic rate.

Figure 2B.1 shows per capita consumption under autarky (ca) and financial openness (cw) for the first 50 years (and indexed to $ca_1 = 100$). The financially integrated consumption level starts out 11.7 percent higher than the autarkic level. By year 10, it is down to 3.9 percent above the autarkic path. By year 50 the integration path is down to 0.2 percent above the autarkic path. By then external debt is fully paid off, so there is no balance due to be paid by future generations.

With per capita consumption growth in the steady state at $g = 1.2$ percent, and with pure time preference at $\rho = 4$ percent, and the elasticity of marginal utility at unity given logarithmic utility, the social rate of time preference is $g + \rho = 5.2$ percent annually. When the total consumption amounts are discounted at this rate, by year 10 the cumulative discounted aggregate consumption is 7.74 percent higher under integration than under autarky; by year 25, the corresponding difference is 4.4 percent. At the end of 500 years, cumulative discounted consumption is 2.47 percent higher under integration.

An increase in the present value of consumption by almost 8 percent over a decade is large. So is an increase by 4 percent over a quarter-century. It is difficult to think of any policies that, in simply passing a law making international financial transactions free, could generate welfare gains on this scale. In contrast, Gourinchas and Jeanne emphasize that they interpret the gains from financial integration as small. Their central estimate (p. 720) is 1.74 percent of consumption for equivalent variation (change in consumption to generate equivalent change in utility). The exercise here suggests, however, that their result stems in considerable part from their use of an infinite horizon. Thus, by 500 years the cumulative proportionate gain in the estimates here is relatively close to that in Gourinchas and Jeanne. In contrast, a more policy-relevant horizon of 25 years yields gains from integration that are more than twice as high at about 4 percent.[127] Although the analysis here overstates what is feasible in the real world through financial integration in some important respects (a safe level of external debt would be on the order of 40 percent of GDP, not 150 percent; and speed limits or absorptive capacity would preclude a sudden surge in capital and income levels from the autarkic to the fully integrated level), the implication is that the Gourinchas-Jeanne analysis understates potential gains from financial integration over a relevant policy horizon of several decades rather than infinity.

---

127. Their use of an optimal saving path rather than obtaining saving residually given a set profile for debt repayment also means that under integration the home country surges to initially higher consumption and lower saving than in the formulation here, which also means that there is a larger initial consumption gain but smaller eventual gain. Finally, their formulation never repays principal on external debt and thus at some point in the path makes future generations worse off than under autarky because of ongoing debt payments combined with convergence to the long-term autarkic output path.

Appendix 2C
Gemini: A Simple Model of International Risk Sharing

Different authors using alternative calibrated models have come to sharply divergent conclusions about the size of potential welfare gains from consumption smoothing across countries through global financial integration. For example, Cole and Obstfeld (1991) find small potential gains while Van Wincoop (1994) finds large ones. This appendix seeks to identify benchmark ranges for such gains from an extremely simple model.

Consider a world economy with two nations of the same size, both producing completely interchangeable goods that are fully tradable. The two economies are twins except for one thing: their cycles are reversed. Whenever annual production is above average in one country, it is below average by the same amount in the other country. Normalize so that population is unity in each country and average output is constant over time (e.g., at 100 units) in each country. Consider a two-year horizon. In country A, output is always higher than average by the proportion σ in year 1, and lower than average by this same proportion in year 2. Country B always has output that is lower than average by proportion σ in year 1 and higher than average by the same proportion in year 2. There is no depreciation, saving, or investment, so consumption equals output. In autarky, each country's consumption experiences a downswing (country A) or upswing (country B) amounting to 2σ times average output from year 1 to year 2. Under financial integration, country A lends to B in year 1 and B returns the favor in year 2, so that consumption is smoothed to a steady level of 100 annually in both countries.

How large would the welfare gains from integration be in this "Gemini" world economy? The answer will depend on the size of the annual output swing (i.e., the typical shock) and the degree of nonlinearity in the utility function. The more rapidly marginal utility drops off as consumption rises (the more concave the utility function), the greater will be the welfare gains from avoiding the downswing in consumption by giving up some of the upswing.

Applying the constant relative risk-aversion utility function, utility for either country in either year 1 or year 2 is:

$$U_{it} = C_{it}^{1-\eta}/(1-\eta), \tag{2C.1}$$

where η is the absolute value of the elasticity of marginal utility. Cline (1992) suggests $\eta = 1.5$ as the value for this parameter, and more recently the author has argued that this magnitude is consistent with observed progressivity in income tax structures, whereas a value as low as 1 (the logarithmic utility function) would imply a relatively regressive flat percentage tax (such as a tithe). But a value of 2 or higher would imply essentially confiscatory average taxes at higher income levels.[128]

With average annual output constant at Q^* in both countries, output over the two-year horizon is:

$$Q_{a1} = Q^* \times (1+\sigma); \; Q_{b1} = Q^* \times (1-\sigma);$$
$$Q_{a2} = Q^* \times (1-\sigma); \; Q_{b2} = Q^* \times (1+\sigma),$$
(2C.2)

where subscripts a and b refer to the respective countries and the second subscripts refer to the year.

Under autarky, consumption must equal domestic production. Under integration, lending from country 1 to country 2 in the first period and repayment in the second period permits complete consumption smoothing. Thus, with superscript A for autarky and I for integration:

$$C_{it}^A = Q_{it}; C^I = Q^*.$$
(2C.3)

There is no time discounting in this system, either because the cycle is sufficiently short that it can be ignored or because there is zero pure time preference. For either country, then, under autarky average annual utility will be:

$$\overline{U}^A = 0.5[\{Q^* \times (1+\sigma)\}^{1-\eta} + \{Q^* \times (1-\sigma)\}^{1-\eta}] / (1-\eta).$$
(2C.4)

In contrast, under integration average annual utility will be:

$$\overline{U}^I = Q^{*(1-\eta)} / (1-\eta).$$
(2C.5)

Because of the concave utility function it will necessarily be true that $\overline{U}^I > \overline{U}^A$. The annual level of completely smoothed consumption under integration that will generate the same average utility as the cyclical path under autarky will thus be smaller than the full potential constant smoothed consumption attainable with integration. From equation 1, and taking the $(1 - \eta)^{th}$ root of both sides after rearranging, this equivalent level of constant consumption will be:

$$\hat{C} = [(1-\eta)\overline{U}^A]^{1/(1-\eta)}.$$
(2C.6)

---

128. William R. Cline, "Comments on the Stern Review," remarks at the Roundtable Discussion on the Stern Review, American Economic Association, Annual Meeting, New Orleans, January 5, 2008, available at www.piie.com (accessed on February 2, 2010).

Table 2C.1   Welfare gain from international consumption smoothing under alternative assumptions (compensating variation as a percent of consumption)

Run	Eta	Sigma	CV
1	1.5	0.2	3.1
2	1.01	0.2	2.1
3	2	0.2	4.2
4	5	0.2	10.0
5	1.5	0.027	0.1
6	1.01	0.027	0
7	2	0.027	0.1
8	5	0.027	0.2
9	1.5	0.1	0.8
10	1.01	0.1	0.5
11	2	0.1	1
12	5	0.1	2.5

Note: Eta = elasticity of marginal utility; Sigma = proportionate shock to output annually; CV = compensating variation.

The compensating variation welfare gain from integration, or the proportionate increase in consumption equivalent to the increase in welfare achieved by smoothing the otherwise cyclical path of consumption, will thus be:

$$\Delta W_{cv} = [(C^I/\hat{C}) - 1].$$
(2C.7)

Table 2C.1 reports the model estimate of compensating variation welfare gain from integration under alternative assumptions about the elasticity of marginal utility (eta) and the size or the proportionate shock to output (sigma). The first four runs depict a system with huge swings in output, by 20 percent annually above or below the average. Under these conditions, with the preferred value for the elasticity of marginal utility (1.5), the ability to smooth annual consumption completely through international financial (and trading) integration would convey a welfare gain equal to about 3 percent of the average level of consumption. This is an order of magnitude larger than the 0.2 percent identified in Cole and Obstfeld (1991). However, the next set of runs makes it clear why their estimate is much lower: They apply as their standard deviation of annual growth the 2.7 percent observed for the United States in 1968–87. Here, when the annual shock to output is set at 2.7 percent, compensating variation from international consumption smoothing shrinks to one-tenth of 1 percent of consumption under the preferred elasticity of marginal utility.

When the size of the shock is cut by half (from 0.2 to 0.1), the size of the welfare gain shrinks to about one-fourth as large (run 9 versus run 1, using the preferred value for eta), reflecting concave utility. When the size of the elasticity of marginal utility is varied, it turns out that the welfare gain from integration varies approximately linearly. For example, with eta a bit more than three times as high as the preferred value (at 5 instead of 1.5), welfare gain is also about three times as large as in the preferred case (run 4 versus run 1).

If one were to posit that the maximum size of the annual shock to output would be somewhere in the range of 10 percent, and that the maximum plausible elasticity of marginal utility would be about 2, then run number 11 would indicate that the welfare gain from financial integration (strictly from the standpoint of consumption smoothing) would be on the order of 1 percent of GDP. Even though this is considerably larger than the central estimate in Cole and Obstfeld (1991), in qualitative terms it remains modest, especially considering that it represents a once-for-all boost in the level of the time path of consumption equivalence, rather than an increment in the annual growth rate of consumption.

Appendix 2D
Potential Circularity in the Knack-Keefer Government Reputation Variable

An important challenge to several statistical studies showing positive effects of financial globalization on growth is raised by Edison et al. (2004). They find that when a variable for government reputation is included, the statistical significance of the financial-integration variable disappears. They then qualify their finding by showing that even after including government reputation, a significant positive impact of financial integration on growth reappears if the integration variable is interacted with per capita in quadratic form, but only for middle-income countries.

However, the first step in this diagnosis warrants a closer look. The Knack-Keefer (1995) government reputation variable they use (*GovRep*) is constructed from measures by a country-risk rating agency. It would thus seem subject to the general tendency of rating agencies to follow performance rather than predict it. The International Country Risk Guide compiles the five ratings used in the *GovRep*. They are expropriation risk, rule of law, repudiation of contracts by government, corruption in government, and quality of bureaucracy. Especially the last two would seem susceptible to circular reasoning. If a rating agency observes stellar growth in, say, China, it seems likely to rate the bureaucracy as being of high quality. So there is considerable risk that *GovRep* is merely a proxy for past growth performance, rather than an independent variable. If so, including it in a regression will be like putting growth not only on the left-hand side but also on the right-hand side. Doing that will surely tend to rob other right-side variables of their significance.

It turns out that there is considerable evidence that this is happening. Edison et al. (2004) apply cross-country data on about 50 countries in periods that lie within 1970–95 in replicating the results of five previous leading studies. The *GovRep* variable is for 1982 (or for industrial countries, 1984) and is hence at the middle rather than beginning of the period. If *GovRep* is an independent causal variable, it would be expected to cause growth subsequent to the date it is measured. If it is instead a reflection of growth performance, then growth in the years prior to the measurement would predict *GovRep* rather than vice versa.

It turns out that this is the case. Thus, a regression of *GovRep* or GR in 1982 (or 1984) on growth (G) from 1970 to 1982 for 43 developing countries yields the following results, with *t*-statistics in parentheses:

$$GR = 11.6 + 112.5\ G_{70-82}; \text{adj. } R^2 = 0.17 \tag{2D.1}$$
$$(9.8)\quad (3.2).$$

This means there is a strong possibility that when the International Country Risk Guide identified its ratings in 1982, their differences across countries reflected growth performance in the previous dozen years.

An additional test for endogeneity of the *GovRep* variable can be made by comparing its change for a given country against the preceding change in growth for the same country. Pooling data for 62 countries with a total of 706 observations for income over 1977–96 and *GovRep* over 1982–97, such a regression yields:

$$\Delta GR_4 = 3.0 + 21.4\ \Delta g_4 + \Sigma_i D_i\ ;\ \text{Adj. } R^2 = 0.21 \qquad\qquad (2D.2)$$
$$(2.5)\ \ (5.7),$$

where ΔGR_4 is the change in the government reputation variable from its level four years earlier, Δg_4 is the change in average per capita growth from the period $t–9$ to $t–5$, as the earlier four-year base, to $t–5$ to $t–1$, as the most recent four-year period, and with t-statistics in parentheses.[129] Once again the coefficient of change in government reputation on prior change in growth is positive and highly significant.[130] The scale of the growth impact is relatively small. Thus, with the growth variable in pure number (rather than percentage) form, a boost in the growth rate from 3 to 5 percent annually would cause an increase in the *GovRep* variable from, say, 30 to 30 + 21 x .02 = 30.42. Nonetheless, despite the small scale of the impact, the strong statistical correlation of the change in *GovRep* with the change in growth will tend to mean that a proxy for growth is being put on the right-hand side of a growth regression when *GovRep* is used as an independent variable. This will likely cause a spurious reduction in the significance of the other right-hand-side variables.

The problem is not necessarily (or even likely) a standard one of simultaneous equations based on economic behavior, moreover. Instead it is a sort of reverse-Heisenberg problem: The observation is affected by what is being observed. There may be no change at all in rule of law and so forth, but the observers judge that it must have improved because the country is doing better. Correspondingly, finding an economic variable to use as an instrumental variable may miss the point.

---

129. The first observation thus refers to the change in *GovRep* from 1982 to 1986; the last observation, the change from 1993 to 1997.

130. The variable has a maximum value of 50, scaled to a perfect score of 10 on each of five components. The average value of the variable for all observations is 32.9.

Appendix 2E
Current Account Deficits and Growth

Prasad, Rajan, and Subramanian (2007a, 1) conduct statistical tests that they argue demonstrate that "non-industrial countries that have relied more on foreign finance have not grown faster in the long run." They use data on 51 developing countries from 1970–2004 to regress growth and current account balances as a percent of GDP and find that "surprisingly …the correlation is positive…[so] developing countries that have relied *less* on foreign finance have grown faster in the long run" (Prasad, Rajan, and Subramanian 2007b, 18).

For the subject of the present study, it might be tempting to equate larger current account deficits with greater financial openness. If this approach were followed, the implication would be that greater financial openness reduces growth rather than enhances it. The study would then become the single exception (the one that proves the rule?) to the nearly uniform pattern of a positive impact of general financial openness on growth in the statistically significant results surveyed in this chapter. It would be mistaken, however, to identify larger current account deficits with greater financial openness. The size of the current account deficit certainly does not test de jure openness. It does not test de facto openness either, even for capital inflows (as opposed to the preferable sum of inflows and outflows). Consider the case of an economy that experiences a collapse in the price of its main export commodity. Suppose it has capital controls and weathers the crisis by drawing heavily on its external reserves. There will be a large measured current account deficit and a collapse in growth but no capital inflow. More generally, a completely financially open country such as Singapore may choose to follow a high-savings and competitive exchange rate policy that leads it to have persistent current account surpluses despite being financially open.

In practical terms, the current account deficit turns out to be a poor proxy for the broad set of alternative measures of financial openness used in the empirical literature. Chapter 3 sets forth eight measures of general financial openness and three additional measures for FDI openness, all of them measures used in the empirical estimates surveyed in this chapter. Figure 2E.1 examines this relationship for the 24 developing countries considered in chapter 3. The horizontal axis shows the average ranking across the 11 financial-openness measures in the period 1995–2004. The vertical axis shows the average current account balance as a percent of GDP in this period. It is evident that there is little if any relationship. Indeed, the highest current account surplus of all is for nearly the most financially open economy (Singapore) rather than the least open.

Even as a test of current account impact it is by no means clear that the Prasad, Rajan, and Subramanian results should be considered as representative for at least the main emerging-market economies. In their diagram

Figure 2E.1   Average financial openness ranking (11 measures) and current account/GDP for 24 developing countries, 1995–2004

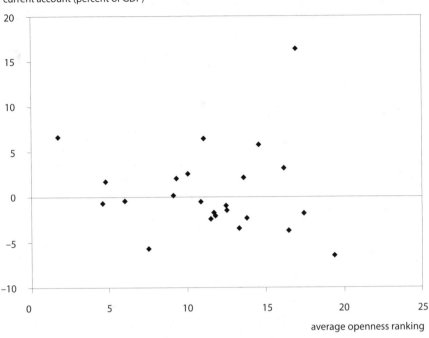

current account (percent of GDP)

average openness ranking

Sources: Calculated from IMF (2009g) and Quinn and Toyoda (2008).

it appears that their result is being driven by Singapore and China at one extreme (high current account surplus, high growth) and Côte d'Ivoire and Madagascar at the other extreme (large current account deficit, low growth). But Singapore for some considerable time has been considered an advanced economy, and most African countries have institutional problems as well as aid inflows that make their outcomes unrepresentative of those for emerging-market economies closely tied to international private capital flows. Indeed, poor countries with sluggish growth that attract humanitarian aid are likely to have large current account deficits and low growth, without providing much relevant evidence on the potential contribution of private foreign investment to growth in more typical emerging-market economies. For its part, China certainly has achieved high growth without large current account deficits (although the outsized surpluses of recent years are new even for China). But it is highly questionable whether China, with its by now massive saving by state enterprises, should be lumped together with most developing countries in such

Figure 2E.2   Average growth and current account balance in middle-income, nonoil economies, 1991–97 and 1998–2008

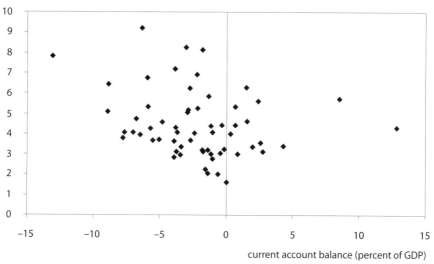

average growth (percent)

current account balance (percent of GDP)

Source: IMF (2009g).

analysis, because most developing countries do not have the option of adopting such state-corporate saving.

An alternative is to look only at middle-income countries (which do not include China, India, and most African countries). Figure 2E.2 shows the relationship between average economic growth and current account balance as a percent of GDP from 1991–2008 (IMF forecast) for 37 non-oil, middle-income countries.[131] (Oil-exporting economies are excluded because of their unrepresentative swings in growth associated with boom and bust in the international oil market.) For 23 countries in Asia, Latin America, and the Middle East, and South Africa, the figure includes two observations each: for 1991–97 and for 1998–2008. The other 14 countries are all Eastern European and transition economies, and only data for 1998–2008 are included for them because of lack of data for part of the earlier period and, more importantly, because of the unrepresentative up-heavals of the early transition period.

The figure supports the textbook negative slope relating growth to the current account (i.e., a positive relationship between growth and the cur-

---

131. The countries are all those defined as middle-income in the mid-1990s by the World Bank (1997, 214–15), excluding oil-exporting countries and countries with populations smaller than 3 million. Two outlier small countries are also excluded (Papua New Guinea and Lebanon). The data are from IMF (2007b).

rent account deficit and hence capital inflow), rather than the revisionist positive slope suggested by Prasad, Rajan and Subramanian (2007a, b). The negative slope is statistically significant.[132] It is also apparent, however, that there are outliers, namely Uzbekistan and Malaysia (1998–2008) to the far right. Malaysia was in the opposite camp from 1991–97, when its growth was rapid (averaging 9.2 percent) and its current account deficit was enormous (averaging 6.3 percent of GDP).

In short, the Prasad, Rajan, and Subramanian diagnosis that larger current account deficits are associated with slower growth is reversed when the focus is on middle-income economies. This group of economies excludes the set of poor countries with high aid inflows, as well as the unrepresentative cases of China and Singapore.

---

132. For the 60 observations comprising two periods for 23 nontransition economies and one period for 14 transition economies, a simple regression yields $g = 4.2$ (16.5) $- 0.095$ CAY (-1.87), where CAY is current account as percent of GDP.

3

The Impact of Financial Globalization on Growth: Country-Specific Estimates

Chapter 2 presented an analytical survey of the economic literature on the impact of financial globalization on economic growth. Much of this literature comprises econometric estimates of this impact based on statistical tests across countries for recent decades. Such estimates generate equations that explain growth, as the dependent variable, as a function of a set of control variables (such as initial per capita income, level of education, and the rate of investment), and financial openness as measured by a chosen variable. Different studies adopt different measures of openness (as well as different sets of control variables). The purpose of this chapter is to arrive at synthesis estimates of the contribution of financial globalization to growth for industrial and emerging-market economies through the application of parameters found in this literature.

The estimates of this chapter are for 45 countries divided about evenly between industrial and emerging-market economies over a 35-year period from 1970–2004. The objective is to detect whether, where, and by how much financial openness has contributed to (or possibly detracted from) growth. Two classes of growth-impact models are applied for this purpose: those for general financial openness and those for foreign direct investment. The principal statistically significant model estimate from each underlying study is applied. For those studies in which the authors find mixed results, meta-statistical weighting is applied to the full set of estimates in each study in question. The discussion then places the estimates in perspective by considering the magnitudes of growth effects that might reasonably be expected on the basis of growth theory. The final section arrives at an overview of the country-specific and regional estimates.

Appendix 3A presents the details on the conversion of underlying model estimates into the standardized coefficients for application to the openness variables used for the various models. Appendix 3B addresses the question of whether theory predicts only a relatively brief escalation of the growth rate from financial opening or a much more persistent increase in the growth rate. Appendix 3C examines the degree of convergence and divergence among the alternative measures used for financial openness.

The Synthesis Approach

The general form for calculation of the growth impact of financial globalization is:

$$g = \alpha + \beta X + \sum_i \gamma_i Z_i, \tag{3.1}$$

where g is the annual growth rate (either total or, depending on the model, per capita), X is the measure of financial openness, and Z_i is one of i control variables.[1] In models in which openness interacts with another variable V (such as domestic banking depth or educational level), the form becomes:

$$g = \alpha + \beta X + \delta(XV) + \sum_i \gamma_i Z_i. \tag{3.1a}$$

For purposes of a synthesis of country estimates on the model parameters from a number of separate studies, both the constant α and the control variables (final term in the equation) drop out as exogenous to the impact of the financial-openness influence, leaving only the terms βX and $\delta(XV)$. Several models from the literature are assembled to calculate these terms and arrive at the implied contribution of financial openness to growth. The particular variable for openness, X, will vary across the models. So will the interaction variable V. For different time periods, the set of openness measures will show variation in the level of openness, hopefully in a uniform direction across the alternative measures for any given country. The full set of models will tend to show a change in the growth impact that reflects the changing degree of openness. The overall patterns from the analysis are obtained by taking, for each of the 45 countries, the average over the various models of the calculated growth impact of the observed degree of openness in a particular period. Similarly, it is useful to examine the pattern of results for subgroups of countries (industrial, Latin American emerging-market, Asian emerging-market) by model, to examine whether some models systematically tend in one direction and others in another direction.

---

1. With population growth exogenous to financial openness, the coefficient on openness from a particular model can be applied in the analysis regardless of whether total or per capita growth has been used as the dependent variable in a particular study.

The driving force in the analysis is the level and trend in financial openness. The next section thus first considers trends in openness for some of the more important measures used.

Trends in Financial Openness

The analysis of this chapter applies eight alternative measures of general financial openness and three alternative measures of openness to FDI. At the outset it is useful to obtain a sense of the trends in openness by considering some of the main measures. For this purpose, it is helpful to identify groupings of more-open and less-open economies, and then to examine the trends for each group.

The Quinn version of financial openness, a de jure measure based on the IMF annual reports on capital account restrictions, provides a useful criterion for identifying subgroups (Quinn 1987; Quinn and Toyoda 2008; IMF, AREAER, various years). The Quinn "CAPITAL" openness measure is based on a score of 0 for completely closed to 4 for completely open. It is converted to a scale of 0 to 100, and averaged over five-year periods. Table 3.1 reports the level of this measure for an early period (1975–79) and a recent period (1995–99) for four groups. Two include developed countries, divided into more open and less open. The other two groups are the corresponding categories for developing countries.[2]

There are few surprises in the resulting groupings. For example, Japan shows up as in the relatively less-open group of developed countries; the United States, in the more-open group. Among developing countries, Brazil and Chile wind up in the relatively less-open group, reflecting the de jure nature of the Quinn measure (and despite sizable actual capital flows). As expected, China is in the less-open group. Somewhat surprisingly, India is in the more-open group. Similarly, as would be expected, the developed countries tended to have higher degrees of openness than the developing countries in both the early and late periods.

Figure 3.1 shows the time paths of the average Quinn openness measure for the four country groupings.[3] There is a substantial rise for all four groups for the period as a whole. The principal exception to the consistently rising trend is for the more-open developing countries, which began at a level even higher than the less-open industrial-country group in

---

2. Countries in the more-open groups included all those above the median for their comparators (developed or developing) in both the earlier and later periods (high-high), as well as those with 1970–99 averages above the midpoint between these countries and their opposites (low-low). All other countries were in the less-open group (i.e., low-low and full-period averages below the dividing point).

3. The final period shown is for 1995–99, even though the variable is applied for the meta-analysis tests through 2004. See footnote 13 for a discussion of the updating here of the Quinn and Toyoda (2008) estimates, which extend only through 1999.

Table 3.1   Degree of financial openness: Quinn IMF-based measure, 1975–79 and 1995–99

Category	Countries	1975–79			1995–99		
		Minimum	Median	Maximum	Minimum	Median	Maximum
Developed, more open	Belgium, Canada, Denmark, France, Germany, Ireland, Netherlands, Switzerland, United Kingdom, United States	65	75	100	92.5	100	100
Developed, less open	Australia, Austria, Finland, Greece, Japan, New Zealand, Norway, Portugal, Spain, Sweden	37.5	50	70	75	87.5	100
Developing, more open	Argentina, Colombia, Egypt, Hong Kong, India, Israel, Korea, Mexico, Malaysia, Peru, Singapore, Venezuela	22.5	57.5	100	50	75	100
Developing, less open	Algeria, Brazil, Chile, China, Hungary, Indonesia, Pakistan, Philippines, Poland, South Africa, Thailand, Turkey	0	25	37.5	20	49	75

Source: Calculated from Quinn and Toyoda (2008) database.

Figure 3.1 Quinn measure of financial openness: Five-year averages, 1970–99

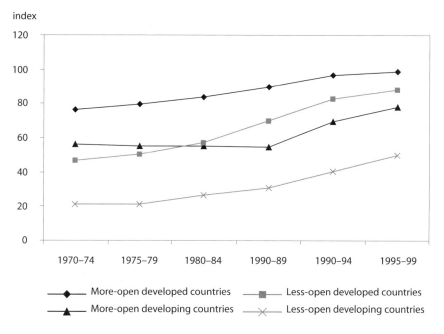

index

	More-open developed countries		Less-open developed countries
	More-open developing countries		Less-open developing countries

Source: Calculated from Quinn and Toyoda (2008) database.

the early 1970s but then essentially did not open further until the early 1990s.[4]

It is useful to examine the relationship between growth and financial openness in a summary, heuristic fashion using the Quinn-Toyoda measure of de jure openness. For this purpose, it is necessary first to apply standard cross-country growth control variables to predict real growth per capita and then to investigate whether the departure from predicted growth is related to financial openness. The models of Levine and Renelt (1992) and the IMF (2007a) are used here to calculate expected growth. Both studies use initial per capita income, the share of investment in GDP, population growth, and educational level as control variables.[5] Expected average growth of real per capita GDP was predicted for 1975–2004 for each of the 45 countries examined here, based on the average of the two models. Figure 3.2 then shows the deviation of actual per capita growth

---

4. In this grouping there was a decline in financial openness from the late 1970s to the early 1980s for Israel, Mexico, Malaysia, and Venezuela, approximately offset by a rise in openness for Argentina, Korea (where the measure rose from 25 to 47.5), Peru, and Singapore.

5. The IMF (2007a) also includes a dummy variable for Africa.

Figure 3.2 Deviation of per capita growth from cross-country regressions and Quinn-Toyoda measure of financial openness, 1975–2004

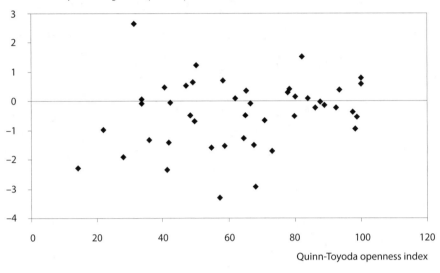

actual minus predicted growth (percent per annum)

Quinn-Toyoda openness index

Source: Author's calculations.

from the predicted rate, on the vertical axis, and the Quinn measure of financial openness (Quinn and Toyoda 2008), on the horizontal axis.

Except for a few outliers, the observations in the scatter diagram show a broadly positive relationship between unexplained growth performance and financial openness. Not surprisingly, China is one of the outliers, with average per capita growth of about 2.7 percent higher than predicted by the control variables despite a relatively low average financial-openness index (31). On the other side, it is also perhaps not surprising that Venezuela is an outlier, with average growth 2.9 percent below that predicted despite a relatively high openness index of 68. Although there is no statistically significant relationship between growth deviation and openness in the scatter for the full set of 45 countries, if China, Venezuela, and one other outlier (Peru) are excluded there is a statistically significant coefficient of 0.015 relating growth deviation to the openness index.[6] This relationship means that going from complete closedness to complete openness (0 to 100 on the index) causes growth per capita to rise by 1.5 percent per year above what would be expected from the standard control variables,

---

6. For Peru, growth deviation averages −3.3 percent per year, and financial openness, 57. For the relationship excluding the three outliers, the *t*-statistic is 2.6.

Figure 3.3   Gross capital flows as a fraction of GDP: Median, 1970–2004

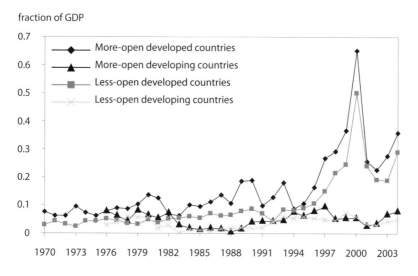

fraction of GDP

Source: IMF (2009a).

a result consistent with the "significant" set of estimates in table 2.1 of chapter 2.

The alternative de facto approach measures financial openness by actual flows or stocks of foreign capital. One such measure is the ratio of total capital inflows plus outflows ("gross flows") to GDP. Figure 3.2 shows the path of this ratio for the same four groupings of countries.[7]

For this measure, whereas the developed countries show a broadly persistent rise in de facto openness, the developing countries show a substantial reduction in openness from the late 1970s to the mid-1980s before a return to approximately the original level of openness by the late 1990s and early 2000s.[8] The groupings are the same four sets of countries classified by the Quinn measure of figure 3.1. An even more dramatic pattern in the figure is the surge of gross capital flows relative to GDP in the industrial countries in the final decade or so of the series, with an extreme peak in 2000. That spike appears to reflect the equity-market bubble, and the rebound by 2003–04 is consistent with the path of equity markets.

The difference between the gradual upward trend in figure 3.1 and the sharp spike after 1997 in figure 3.3 is suggestive that the de facto measures

---

7. For this measure, which can reach extreme levels for some countries (over 100 percent of GDP in some country-years), the figure reports the median rather than the average to convey a level more representative than the average.

8. For the developing-country groups, many countries are missing data for the first few years, so the series begin in 1976.

may be misleading toward the end of the period. It is much more plausible that the relatively more-open group of developed economies were almost identically financially open in the early 1990s and late 1990s (figure 3.1) than that they were threefold or so more open in the latter period. Problems with the de facto approach also become apparent when one considers sharp divergences between countries that are more specialized as financial centers, or have much smaller economies, against large economies that are nonetheless equally open in terms of financial market rules. For example, for the period from 1995–2004, the average ratio of gross capital inflows and outflows to GDP was 13 percent for the United States. In contrast, this ratio was 54 percent for Switzerland, 57 percent for the United Kingdom, and 59 percent for the Netherlands. For the small economy of Ireland in a phase of major direct investment inflow, the average ratio of gross capital flows to GDP stood at a remarkable 204 percent.

It makes no sense whatsoever to judge Ireland as being 16 times as open as the United States (or Switzerland, the United Kingdom, and the Netherlands as being four times as open as the United States) if the measure is to meaningfully represent the liberality or repressiveness of rules governing capital transactions. There is of course an analogy to the question of "openness" in the sphere of trade. Few would argue that large economies have lower "revealed protection" than small economies just because they have lower ratios of imports and exports to GDP; trade ratios are widely understood to be a function of the size of the domestic economy as well as protection. The principal motivation in the financial globalization literature for introducing de facto openness has been the observation that some emerging-market economies, such as Brazil and China, have experienced periods of relatively large capital flows despite the presence of formal impediments. A major caveat of the de facto measures, then, is that they seem likely to introduce spurious differences in financial openness among industrial economies that are otherwise known to have approximately comparable and highly open financial markets.

Figure 3.4 shows time trends for the same country groupings for FDI inflows relative to GDP. For this category, the trend is broadly a persistent increase. Notably, there is no distinctive reduction for the developing countries during the 1980s, indicating that the fall-off shown in figure 3.3 was driven by debt capital rather than direct investment (in particular, the influence of reduced inflows and increased repayments of external debt during the Latin American debt crisis of the 1980s).

For both figures 3.3 and 3.4, there are smaller differences between the relatively more-open and the relatively less-open groups (both within the developed and developing countries) than seen as measured by the de jure Quinn measure (figure 3.1). This difference in part simply reflects the fact that the divergence would be expected to be greatest when the classification is based on the measure being reported (because random swings

Figure 3.4 Foreign direct investment inflows as a fraction of GDP: Median, 1970–2004

fraction of GDP

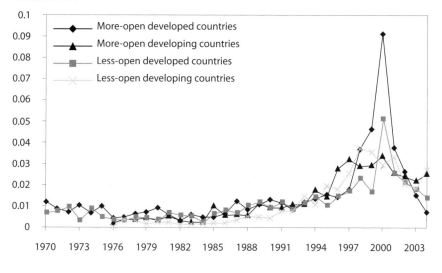

Source: IMF (2009a).

might place a country in one group or the other only under this measure). However, it also likely reflects the generally recognized phenomenon that some countries that are relatively closed based on de jure practices are de facto relatively open because capital flows manage to respond to opportunities despite administrative impediments.

Furthermore, there is a key difference between the direct investment measure of figure 3.4 and gross capital flows in figure 3.3. For FDI, with the exception of the unique year of 2000, in the period from 1991–2004 median inflows were actually higher for developing countries (about 1.8 percent of GDP in 1991–99 and 2.5 percent in 2000–04) than for developed countries (about 1.4 percent and 2 percent, respectively). The 2000 spike for FDI in industrial countries was, again, apparently driven by the equity-market bubble (see OECD 2002).

Finally, the simple scale difference between figures 3.3 and 3.4 is notable. Gross capital flows have been in the vicinity of 20 to 50 percent of GDP in recent years for developed countries, although only about 5 to 10 percent of GDP for developing countries. For the developed countries, this scale is much greater than that for FDI inflows, which have typically been in the range of 2 to 4 percent of GDP in recent years (in this case, for both developed and developing countries). For gross capital flows, the difference of as much as an order of magnitude between industrial and developing countries suggests enormous cross-hauling of portfolio and bank credit flows among these economies, in contrast to much lesser flows of this nature for developing countries.[9]

Calibration

The leading statistical studies of financial globalization discussed in chapter 2 provide the basis for the synthesis estimates of this chapter. To apply such an analysis it is necessary to standardize the units used for the same variables across different models. The simplest example concerns the growth-impact dependent variable. Some models express growth as a pure number (such as 0.05 for 5 percent growth), and others refer to percentage rates. The analysis of this chapter refers to percentage rates. Appendix 3B clarifies the definitions of the variables used for each model included in the analysis, and reports the translation of the estimated coefficients in each underlying study into corresponding coefficients normalized for comparison across the studies.

Table 3.2 reports the definitions for the variables applied across the models considered in the synthesis analysis, along with descriptive statistics for the 45 countries considered (for 1970–2004). Eleven models enter into the analysis for the effect of general financial globalization on growth; another seven models are included in the corresponding analysis for FDI.

The dependent variable is annual real GDP growth (or real per capita GDP growth, as discussed above), expressed as a percent. The first measure of financial openness is the Quinn (1997) variable based on in-depth interpretation of the AREAER. The version used here is the variable "Capital" used in Quinn and Toyoda (2008), which is on a scale of 0 for complete closedness to 100 for completely open.

The second openness measure is the ratio of gross inward and outward capital flows as a fraction of GDP. It is the sum of the values of financial flows in either direction for direct investment, portfolio, and "other investment" (bank and other claims), relative to GDP.[10] As the entry for the minimum value indicates, this measure can be negative.[11] For example, the repatriation of direct investment constitutes a negative gross flow of direct

---

9. The differences between figures 3.3 and 3.4 are too large to be driven by the fact that figure 3.4 refers to only one category of capital and only inflows rather than inflows plus outflows.

10. IMF (2009a, lines 78bdd, 78bed, 78bfd, 78bgd, 78bhd, and 78bid).

11. The minimum is for Hong Kong in 1998, with negative gross flows of 161 percent of GDP, reflecting large debt repayments during the East Asian financial crisis. Otherwise the largest negative gross flows are 19 percent of GDP for Chile in 1986, reflecting external debt repayments in the 1980s debt crisis.

Table 3.2 Variables and descriptive statistics for 45 countries, 1970–2004

Variable	Definition	Mean	Median	Standard deviation	Maximum	Minimum	90th percentile
g	Per capita GDP growth (annual percent)	2.4	2.5	3.4	21.2	–15.4	6.2
X_1	Quinn measure of de jure openness	63.4	62.5	27.2	100	0	100
X_2	Gross capital flows relative to GDP (ratio)	0.134	0.065	0.287	3.14	–1.61	0.301
X_3	Net capital flows relative to GDP (ratio)	0.0114	0.0115	0.0469	0.173	–0.216	0.0631
X_4	Gross FDI and portfolio flows/GDP (ratio)	0.077	0.032	0.197	2.91	–0.042	0.165
X_5	Total FDI and portfolio inflows/GDP (ratio)	0.042	0.02	0.097	1.49	–0.047	0.085
X_6	1 – AREAER restriction measure	0.38	0	0.49	1	0	1
X_7	Tornell, Westermann, and Martinez financial liberalization	0.43	0	0.46	1	0	1
X_8	Total capital inflows relative to GDP (ratio)	0.073	0.043	0.143	1.56	–0.84	0.16
V_1	Bank /(bank + central bank assets) (ratio)	0.89	0.94	0.131	1	0.16	0.993
V_2	Log of per capita income (1980 dollars)	8.43	8.55	1.6	10.3	5.11	9.76
V_3	1 – Black-market premium (≥ 0)	0.889	0.983	0.234	1	0	0.998
FX_1	FDI inflow relative to GDP	0.02	0.01	0.043	0.923	–0.06	0.047
FX_2	Log (FDI inflow as percent of GDP)	–0.112	0.086	1.53	4.52	–7.52	1.6
FX_3	Stock of FDI liabilities/GDP (ratio)	0.177	0.09	0.272	2.75	0.0002	0.383
FV_1	Average years male secondary schooling	2.27	1.93	1.31	6.02	0.26	4.49
FV_2	Private credit relative to GDP (ratio)	0.605	0.527	0.398	2	0	1.17
FV_3	Log of private credit as percent of GDP	3.72	3.96	1.72	5.3	–11.14	4.76

FDI = foreign direct investment; AREAER = IMF, *Annual Report on: Exchange Arrangements and Exchange Restrictions*.

Source: Author's calculations. See text.

investment liabilities.[12] The third measure is the corresponding value for net total flows, using the same concepts but subtracting outflows from inflows. The fourth measure is once again gross flows as a ratio of GDP, but this time including only direct investment and portfolio flows and excluding "other investment" flows. This measure captures bond debt but not debt to banks. The fifth measure is the same FDI plus portfolio concept but for inflows only.

The sixth measure of openness is unity minus the IMF's indicator of capital controls (1 for presence, 0 for absence, in the underlying IMF measure). This binary variable was reported through 1995. Beginning in 1996, the IMF replaced the single indicator with a set of 10 subcategory indicators. For 1996 and after, a proxy for the AREAER binary restriction variable is estimated using a logit function that most closely explains the 1995 single-indicator observations using the 1996 multiple-indicator observations, under the implicit assumption that there were no meaningful changes in practices from 1995 to 1996.[13]

The Tornell, Westermann, and Martinez (2004) financial liberalization measure is also binary, with unity for open and zero for closed. The variable is always unity beginning in and after the year of liberalization. The study bases the year of liberalization on the date when cumulative capital inflows after 1980 reach 10 percent of GDP (or on surges above the trend in cumulative capital inflows), so this criterion is used to identify the date of opening for several countries not included in the Tornell, Westermann, and Martinez database.

The final measure of financial openness (X_8) is that used in an IMF staff study (IMF 2007a), total capital inflows as a ratio of GDP. This measure is again the sum of inflows of direct investment, portfolio investment (equity and bonds), and other investment (mainly bank claims).

The next set of variables, V_1 through V_3, is for economic variables that interact with the financial-openness variables. Banking depth is measured by the ratio of banking institution assets to total assets of banks and the

---

12. Thus, an investment abroad by a resident is a capital outflow and has a positive sign for purposes of calculating gross flows. In contrast, repayment of debt held by a foreign lender, which has the same cash flow effect against reserves, enters the gross flows calculation with a negative sign, because it is counted as a negative inflow of foreign capital.

13. The function is $z = -3.092 + 1.158\ x1 + 0.472\ x2 + 0.666\ x3 + 2.527\ x6 + 0.336\ x7 + 0.192\ x8 + 20.44\ x9$, where capital controls are present on the following: x1 = capital-market securities; x2 = money market instruments; x3 = collective investment securities; x6 = financial credits; x7 = guarantees; x8 = direct investment; and x9 = liquidation of direct investment. The three other detailed categories do not enter the function (x4 = derivatives; x5 = commercial credits; x10 = real estate transactions). The critical value for the function is set at –0.3 to achieve the best balance between type 1 (false prediction of restriction) and type 2 (reverse) errors. Above this threshold the summary quasi-AREAER estimate is set at 1; below the threshold, it is set at 0. The quasi-AREAER, together with qualitative discussion of each country's practices in the yearly AREAER reports, form the basis for extending the Quinn-Toyoda measure from 1999 through 2004.

central bank.[14] Data on per capita income in 1980 dollars are from the IMF's *World Economic Outlook* database (IMF 2008a) for dollar value of GDP, and the IMF's *International Financial Statistics* database (IMF 2009a) for population, US producer price index to convert to 1980 prices, and local currency GDP and exchange rates for estimates prior to 1980. The variable V_3 for financial stability based on the black-market premium equals $(100 - \text{BMP})/100$, where BMP is the percent by which the black-market exchange rate exceeds the official rate (and the minimum value is constrained to zero). Black-market premium data are from Reinhart and Rogoff (2002).

The variables used in the models relating growth to direct investment are as follows: FX_1 is the ratio of direct investment inflows to GDP;[15] FX_2 is the natural logarithm of this same ratio expressed as a percent of GDP; and FX_3 is the ratio of the stock of direct investment liabilities to GDP.[16] For the interacting economic variables used in the direct investment impact models (FV_1 through FV_3), data are from the following sources: average years of male secondary schooling is from a dataset compiled by Barro and Lee (2000); and credit to the private sector as a fraction of GDP is from IMF (2009a), expressed either as a ratio (FV_2) or as the logarithm of private credit as a percent of GDP (FV_3).[17]

Table 3.3 summarizes the normalized coefficients developed in appendix 3A for the 11 general financial-openness models considered, in application to the standardized specification of the variables as just described. Table 3.4 reports the corresponding set of normalized coefficients set forth in the same appendix for the eight FDI models. The parameters for both tables pertain to only the subset of statistically significant model results reported in tables 2.1 and 2.2 of chapter 2. The first set of country-specific estimates developed in the present chapter applies these significant-only parameters. As discussed below, a second set of estimates then applies instead the meta-statistical parameter estimates based on inverse-variance weighting of both significant and nonsignificant results.

Results for General Financial Openness

Table 3.5 reports the results of applying the synthesis analysis to the 11 models of general financial openness listed in table 3.2. For the de facto

---

14. The sum of IMF (2009a) lines 22a–22f divided by this sum plus the sum of lines 12a–12f.

15. From IMF (2009a, line 78bed).

16. From IMF (2009a, line 79lbd). Note that "logarithm" refers to natural logarithm throughout.

17. The private credit variable uses IMF (2009a) data (lines 22d and 42d). Following Beck, Levine, and Loayza (2000), the average of beginning-of-year and end-of-year credit levels (and price indexes) are compared with current-year GDP to address measurement distortions otherwise caused by high inflation.

Table 3.3 Normalized coefficients of general openness models: Impact of financial openness on annual growth (percent rate)

Study	Impact coefficients and variables[a]
1. Quinn (1997)	$0.0154\,X_1$
2. Kraay (1998)	$11\,X_2{}^b$
3. Bailliu (2000)[c]	$-27\,X_3 + 46\,X_3\,V_1$
4. Edwards (2001)	$-0.428\,X_1 + 0.04956\,X_1 V_2$
5. Edison et al. (2002)	$10.1\,X_4$
6. Edison et al. (2002)	$18.3\,X_5$
7. Arteta, Eichengreen, and Wyplosz (2003)	$-0.0384\,X_1 + 0.0504\,X_1 V_3$
8. Fratzscher and Bussiere (2004)	$1.611\,X_6$
9. Tornell, Westermann, and Martinez (2004)	$1.9\,X_7$
10. IMF (2007a)	$8.62\,X_8$
11. Quinn and Toyoda (2008)	$0.022\,X_1$

a. For definition of variables, see table 3.2. Significant model results only.
b. For industrial countries, the coefficient is 7.
c. Model applies only to developing countries.

Source: See appendix 3A.

models, a ceiling is set at the 90th percentile of the openness variable as the representation of complete openness. For each of the past three decades and for the period 2000–04, the simple average of the 11 models' estimated contribution of financial openness to annual growth is shown in the first four columns. The second four columns report the corresponding "trimmed average," after omitting the highest and the lowest among the 11 underlying estimates for the period in question. The trimmed averages would appear to be more meaningful for several developing countries, especially those with lower income. Thus, for eight developing countries in the 1990s, the simple average growth contribution is –0.1 percent per year, where the trimmed average is +0.5 percent per year.[18] The principal reason for the divergence is the sizable negative estimate in the Edwards (2001) model from the interaction between financial openness and low per capita income.

In contrast, for the developed countries there are a few cases in which the simple average appears exaggerated compared with the trimmed average. Thus, the contribution of financial openness to growth is about 0.4 percent per year higher in the raw average than in the trimmed average in 2000–04 for already-high Belgium, Ireland, and the United States. The discussion that follows thus uses the trimmed averages rather than simple averages to identify the main patterns in the results.

Among the industrial countries, the United States shows a relatively steady and modestly rising annual growth contribution from financial

---

18. China, Colombia, Egypt, India, Indonesia, Pakistan, Peru, and Thailand.

Table 3.4   Normalized coefficients for impact of foreign direct investment on growth (contribution to average annual growth, percent)

Model	Coefficients and variables[a]
Borensztein, De Gregorio, and Lee (1998)[b]	$-85\ FX_1 + 162\ FX_1FV_1{}^c$
Haveman, Lei, and Netz (2001)	$74.1\ FX_1\ -178.4\ (FX_1)^2$
Reisen and Soto (2001)[b]	$10\ FX_1$
Carkovic and Levine (2005)	$119.2\ FX_1 + 93.6\ FX_1FV_2{}^d$
Hermes and Lensink (2003)[b]	$-1.587\ FX_2 + 0.621\ FX_2FV_3$
Blonigan and Wang (2005)[b]	$-215.2\ FX_1 + 283.6\ FV_1{}^e$
Lensink and Morrissey (2006)	$83\ FX_1$
IMF (2007a)	$3\ FX_3$

a. For definition of variables, see table 3.2. Significant model results only.
b. Applies to developing countries only.
c. Subject to maximum of 3.3.
d. Subject to maximum of 6.7.
e. Subject to maximum of 4.0.

Source: See appendix 3A.

openness of a bit more than one percentage point per year for the past 35 years. The level and trend is similar for Germany. For France, the growth contribution is somewhat smaller in the 1980s but somewhat larger by 2000–04. Australia and New Zealand also have growth contributions averaging a bit over 1 percent per year. For Japan, there is a steady growth contribution of about 0.9 percentage point per year for the past quarter-century. The highest growth impacts are for Belgium and the United Kingdom, reaching 1.7 percent per year over the 1990s through 2004.[19] The unweighted average for industrial countries rises from 0.9 percent per year in the 1980s to about 1.4 percent in the 1990s through 2004.

The Latin American economies show more moderate growth contributions from financial openness than the industrial countries, largely reflecting the fact that their financial integration is more limited. Growth impacts averaging about 0.4 to 0.6 percentage point per year in the 1990s and 2000s are found for Brazil, Colombia, and Venezuela. The growth contributions are somewhat higher for Chile, Mexico, and Peru, in a range of 0.6 to 0.9 percent per year.[20] There is a strong pattern of minimal growth contribution in the 1980s, when several of these economies were closing capital markets (de jure measure) and experiencing low inflows or net

---

19. The two countries' estimates would have been even higher in the absence of the 90th percentile ceiling imposed on the de facto openness variables.

20. As noted, however, with their relatively lower income levels Colombia and Peru show substantially lower growth contributions using the simple average of models, which includes the Edwards (2001) negative results, whereas the trimmed average tends to omit the model.

Table 3.5 Growth impact of financial openness by country, 1970–2004: 11 statistically significant model average (percent per year)

Country	Average				Trimmed average			
	1970–79	1980–89	1990–99	2000–04	1970–79	1980–89	1990–99	2000–04
Algeria		0.0				-0.0		
Argentina		0.0	0.9	0.1		0.0	0.9	0.3
Australia	0.6	1.1	1.3	1.4	0.5	1.0	1.2	1.3
Austria	0.7	1.0	1.6	1.9	0.7	0.9	1.3	1.6
Belgium		1.4	2.0	2.0		1.4	1.7	1.7
Brazil		-0.1	0.3	0.4		0.0	0.4	0.6
Canada	1.2	1.3	1.6	1.7	1.2	1.2	1.4	1.5
Chile		0.1	0.6	0.8		0.2	0.7	0.9
China			0.0	0.2			0.4	0.5
Colombia	-0.1	0.0	0.2	0.1	0.2	0.3	0.6	0.7
Denmark		1.1	1.8	2.0		1.0	1.4	1.5
Egypt		0.0	-0.1	0.0		0.2	0.4	0.7
Finland		0.8	1.7	2.0		0.7	1.4	1.7
France		0.9	1.6	1.9		0.8	1.3	1.7
Germany	1.1	1.2	1.8	1.8	1.1	1.2	1.4	1.6
Greece		0.5	0.9	1.5		0.5	0.9	1.4
Hong Kong				1.5				1.5
Hungary		0.0	0.5	1.0		0.1	0.6	1.1

India		−0.6	−0.6			0.2	0.3	
Indonesia		0.1	0.1	−0.2		0.3	0.4	0.2
Ireland	0.7	0.9	1.6	2.2		0.9	1.4	1.7
Israel	0.5	0.3	0.8	1.2	0.8	0.3	0.7	1.1
Italy	0.6	0.8	1.6	1.6	0.5	0.7	1.4	1.4
Japan		1.0	1.3	1.4	0.6	0.9	0.9	1.1
Korea		0.2	0.7	0.8		0.3	0.6	0.7
Malaysia	0.5	0.6	0.6	0.4	0.9	0.9	0.8	0.5
Mexico		0.1	0.5	0.6		0.2	0.7	0.6
Netherlands	1.1	1.4	1.8	2.1	1.0	1.3	1.5	1.7
New Zealand	0.3	0.8	1.3	1.4	0.3	0.8	1.3	1.4
Norway		0.9	1.7	2.2		0.8	1.2	1.7
Pakistan		−0.2	−0.1	−0.2		0.2	0.3	0.1
Peru		−0.1	0.2	0.3		0.0	0.8	0.9
Philippines		0.0	0.1	−0.2		0.2	0.7	0.5
Poland			0.1	0.6			0.2	0.7
Portugal		0.3	1.2	1.6		0.4	1.2	1.6

(continued on next page)

Table 3.5   Growth impact of financial openness by country, 1970–2004: 11 statistically significant model average (percent per year) (continued)

Country	Average				Trimmed average			
	1970–79	1980–89	1990–99	2000–04	1970–79	1980–89	1990–99	2000–04
Singapore	1.1	1.5	1.6	1.5	1.3	1.5	1.7	1.6
South Africa	0.0	–0.1	0.4	0.3	0.0	0.0	0.5	0.5
Spain		0.6	1.2	1.5		0.5	1.2	1.6
Sweden	0.6	1.0	1.7	1.8	0.4	0.8	1.4	1.5
Switzerland			2.1	2.1			1.6	1.6
Thailand		0.1	0.3	0.1		0.4	0.6	0.3
Turkey	1.9	0.2	0.3	0.3	0.4	0.2	0.5	0.5
United Kingdom	0.7	1.5	1.8	2.0	0.6	1.5	1.6	1.7
United States	1.2	1.4	1.7	1.9	1.1	1.2	1.3	1.4
Venezuela	0.4	0.0	0.3	0.4	0.6	0.1	0.5	0.5
Averages								
Industrial	...	1.0	1.6	1.8	...	0.9	1.3	1.5
Developing Asia	...	0.2	0.3	0.4	...	0.5	0.6	0.7
Latin America	...	0.0	0.4	0.4	...	0.1	0.7	0.7
Middle East and South Africa	...	0.1	0.4	0.5	...	0.1	0.5	0.8
Developing Europe	...	0.1	0.3	0.6	...	0.1	0.4	0.8

Blank cells = data unavailable

Source: Author's calculations.

outflows (debt crisis). The growth contribution in the 1980s is typically only 0 to 0.2 percentage point per year. For its part, Argentina conforms to the regional pattern in the 1980s, considerably exceeds it in the 1990s (0.9 percent per year contribution), but then falls below the regional average in the 2000s in association with its debt default (0.3 percent per year). The unweighted average for the region rises from 0.1 percent in the 1980s to 0.7 percent in the 1990s through 2004.

In Asia, China shows a moderate (and perhaps to some, surprisingly high) growth contribution from financial openness of 0.4 to 0.5 percent per year in the 1990s and 2000–04. India obtains a more modest growth contribution of 0.2 to 0.3 percent per year in the 1970s and 1980s (data are incomplete for 2000–04). In China and especially India, these trimmed model averages are more favorable than the simple averages, because of the exclusion of the severely negative estimates of the Edwards (2001) model with its interaction term yielding a negative impact on low-income economies. The (trimmed average) impacts are comparable for Indonesia, in a range of 0.2 to 0.4 percent per year for the 1980s through 2004. Korea similarly shows a 0.3 percent impact in the 1980s, but a strong (for the region) 0.6 to 0.7 percent per year impact by the 1990s and 2000–04 when openness was higher.[21] Malaysia consistently shows the highest gains from financial integration in the region in the 1970s through the 1990s (about 0.9 percent per year), but by 2000–04 the impact declines (to 0.5 percent), reflecting a reduction in de jure openness in the late 1990s and after. Thailand shows gains rising from 0.4 percent per year in the 1980s to 0.6 percent in the 1990s but then easing to 0.3 percent per year in 2000–04.[22] The unweighted average for the region rises from 0.5 percent per year in the 1980s to 0.6 percent in the 1990s and 0.7 percent in 2000–04.

For Eastern Europe, the Middle East, and South Africa, the pattern is similar to that for Latin America, with the annual growth contribution from financial openness amounting to only about 0.1 percent per year in the 1980s, rising to about 0.5 percent in the 1980s and 0.8 percent by 2000–04.

The pattern of similarities and divergences among models can be examined by considering model-specific growth-impact estimates averaged across all countries in a particular grouping. This set of results is shown in table 3.6 for three country groupings: industrial, Latin America, and developing Asia.

The first pattern to examine is whether some models run persistently

---

21. The Quinn de jure measure rose from about 48 in the 1980s to about 58 in the early 1990s and 68 by the late 1990s and after. De facto flows showed increases but also large swings, with gross flows peaking at 13 percent of GDP in 1996, plunging to –2 percent in 1998, and rebounding to about 7 percent by 2003–04.

22. Thailand is virtually unique in swinging from large positive gross flows through 1996 to persistent negative gross flows from 1997–2004, reflecting repayments after the 1997 crisis. In contrast, Korea had negative gross flows in just one year, 1998.

Table 3.6 Growth impact of financial openness by country groupings, 1970–2004: Average results for statistically significant model (percent per year)

Study	1970–74	1975–79	1980–84	1985–89	1990–94	1995–99	2000–04
Industrial countries							
Quinn (1997)	0.9	1.0	1.0	1.2	1.3	1.4	1.4
Kraay (1998)	0.5	0.6	0.6	0.7	0.7	1.2	1.5
Edwards (2001)	1.1	2.1	1.3	2.4	3.9	4.5	4.6
Edison et al. (2002)[a]	0.3	0.2	0.2	0.6	0.6	1.0	1.3
Edison et al. (2002)[b]	0.3	0.3	0.2	0.6	0.6	0.9	1.2
Arteta, Eichengreen, and Wyplosz (2002)	0.7	0.7	0.7	0.9	1.0	1.0	1.0
Fratzscher and Bussiere (2004)	0.3	0.4	0.5	0.7	1.1	1.4	1.4
Tornell, Westermann, and Martinez (2004)	1.4	1.4	1.6	1.8	1.9	1.9	1.9
IMF (2007a)	0.4	0.5	0.5	0.5	0.5	0.8	0.9
Quinn (2008)	1.3	1.4	1.5	1.7	1.9	2.0	2.0
Average	0.7	0.8	0.8	1.1	1.4	1.6	1.7
Trimmed average	0.7	0.8	0.8	1.0	1.2	1.4	1.5
Developing Latin America							
Quinn (1997)	0.7	0.7	0.6	0.6	0.9	1.1	1.2
Kraay (1998)	0.3	0.4	0.4	-0.1	0.6	0.9	0.6
Bailliu (2000)	0.2	0.2	0.1	-0.1	0.3	0.5	0.1
Edwards (2001)	-2.7	-2.3	-2.0	-2.2	-3.0	-2.8	-3.6
Edison et al. (2002)[a]	0.0	0.1	0.1	0.1	0.5	0.6	0.5
Edison et al. (2002)[b]	0.0	0.1	0.2	0.2	0.7	0.9	0.6
Arteta, Eichengreen, and Wyplosz (2002)	-0.1	0.3	0.0	-0.5	0.4	0.7	0.7

Fratzscher and Bussiere (2004)	0.5	0.6	0.5	0.0	0.2	0.6	0.6
Tornell, Westermann, and Martinez (2004)	0.3	0.3	0.3	0.3	1.3	1.6	1.9
IMF (2007a)	0.2	0.3	0.2	-0.1	0.3	0.5	0.2
Quinn (2008)	1.1	1.0	0.9	0.9	1.4	1.6	1.7
Average	0.0	0.1	0.1	-0.1	0.3	0.6	0.4
Trimmed average	0.2	0.3	0.3	0.0	0.6	0.8	0.7
Developing Asia							
Quinn (1997)	0.7	0.7	0.8	0.8	1.0	1.0	1.0
Kraay (1998)	2.4	1.0	0.9	0.6	0.9	0.4	0.8
Bailliu (2000)	1.2	0.6	0.6	0.2	0.5	-0.1	-0.5
Edwards (2001)	-4.3	-3.4	-3.4	-3.4	-3.1	-2.8	-2.9
Edison et al. (2002)[a]	0.9	0.2	0.3	0.3	0.4	0.5	0.6
Edison et al. (2002)[b]	1.4	0.4	0.4	0.4	0.6	0.7	0.6
Arteta, Eichengreen, and Wyplosz (2002)	0.3	0.4	0.4	0.4	0.5	0.7	0.7
Fratzscher and Bussiere (2004)	0.4	0.6	0.6	0.6	0.6	0.3	0.2
Tornell, Westermann, and Martinez (2004)	0.6	0.6	0.6	0.9	1.4	1.7	1.9
IMF (2007a)	1.2	0.6	0.5	0.3	0.5	0.2	0.3
Quinn (2008)	1.0	1.0	1.1	1.2	1.4	1.4	1.4
Average	0.5	0.2	0.2	0.2	0.4	0.4	0.4
Trimmed average	0.9	0.6	0.6	0.5	0.7	0.6	0.6

a. See table 3.3, study 5.
b. See table 3.3, study 6.

Source: Author's calculations.

"hot" (high growth-impact estimate) while others run "cold" (low estimate). Based on the simple average across all seven of the five-year time periods and for the three country groupings, two models are consistently hot: Tornell, Westermann, and Martinez (2004) and Quinn-Toyoda (2008). No models are consistently cold in the sense of always showing the lowest growth impacts. The most conspicuous model-specific pattern is for Edwards (2001), which runs very hot for industrial countries (almost +3 percent annual growth contribution) and very cold for developing countries (about –3 percent average growth contribution). The idiosyncrasy of the Edwards model reflects its strong influence of per capita income interacting with openness. The trimmed averages systematically omit the high Edwards estimates for 1985–2004, on the high side, and those from the IMF staff model (IMF 2007a), on the low side.

For the developing countries, the Edwards model once again gets trimmed out, but this time because of its large negative estimates. This time, however, the highest-impact model (usually Quinn-Toyoda) is much closer to the rest of the field, so that the effect of trimming the high and low estimates yields a trimmed average that is consistently about 0.2 percentage point higher than the simple average for Latin America, and about 0.3 percentage point higher for Asia.

Another question is whether de jure models tend to give different results from de facto models. As can be seen by combining the information from tables 3.2 and 3.3, the de jure models include Quinn (1997), Edwards (2001), Arteta, Eichengreen, and Wyplosz (2003), Fratzscher and Bussiere (2004), and Quinn and Toyoda (2008). The de facto variable models include Kraay (1998), Bailliu (2000), both of the Edison et al. (2002) models, Tornell, Westermann, and Martinez (2004), and IMF (2007a) staff model. One de jure model (Edwards 2001) gives both the highest (industrial country) and lowest (developing country) estimates. If the Edwards model is excluded, the de jure models give modestly larger growth-impact estimates than the de facto models (a difference of about one-fourth of a percent per year for the industrial countries and Latin America, and one-tenth of a percent for Asian developing countries).[23]

Weighting Nonsignificant Model Estimates

As discussed in chapter 2, a key issue in interpreting the statistical literature on financial globalization is how to treat nonsignificant results. It is suggested in chapter 2 that there is a case for ignoring nonsignificant re-

---

23. Thus, averaging over all seven five-year periods, the average annual growth contribution in the de jure models (excluding Edwards) is 1.13 percent for industrial countries, 0.66 percent for Latin America, and 0.76 percent for developing Asia. The corresponding averages for the de facto models are 0.87 percent for industrial countries, 0.39 percent for Latin America, and 0.67 percent for developing Asia.

sults if they are not persuasive results showing nonrobustness of alternative significant results. The estimates in tables 3.5 and 3.6 are based on that premise. However, an alternative approach is to take the nonsignificant results into account as well, using the approach of "meta-statistics," which has been applied more widely in the fields of education and psychology than in economics. This approach weighs alternative results by the inverse of the variance of the parameter estimates.

As shown in appendix 2A, this is equivalent to weighting by the ratio of the square of the t-statistic to the square of the parameter estimate. Nonsignificant results will tend to receive less weight because their t-statistics will be low. However, when the nonsignificant parameter estimate is close to zero, its weight tends to rise (because the square of the parameter estimate is in the denominator of the weight). The second set of estimates of this chapter, set forth below, applies meta-statistical parameter estimates (rather than just the statistically significant estimates) to arrive at alternative calculations of the extent of growth gains realized from past financial openness. The expectation is that these estimates will be lower than those from the significant-only models and will thus tend to set a conservative bound for the estimated growth impacts.

The authors of some of the studies included in the synthesis estimates of this chapter consider the main thrust of their findings to represent "little" or "a mixed" impact of financial globalization on growth because a number of their tests yield results that are not statistically significant. Nevertheless, from the studies by those authors the estimates of tables 3.5 and 3.6 have applied the subset of their findings that *are* statistically significant.

An alternative set of estimates can be constructed that attempts instead to incorporate the insignificant results of the set of studies questioning the impact of financial globalization. For convenience, all of the studies can be divided into two groups. In Group A are the studies that find statistically significant impacts of financial openness on growth and consider these results the most meaningful. This group includes Quinn (1997), Bailliu (2000), Edwards (2001), Arteta, Eichengreen, and Wyplosz (2002), Tornell, Westermann, and Martinez (2004), and Quinn and Toyoda (2008). In Group B are studies that instead consider the significant model results they do obtain to be superseded by robustness tests that turn the influence of financial openness insignificant. This set includes Kraay (1998), Edison et al. (2002), Fratzscher and Bussiere (2004), and IMF (2007a). Instead of applying the statistically significant model obtained in each study (as done in tables 3.5 and 3.6), the alternative set of estimates uses a meta-statistical (inverse-variance) weighted average of the significant and insignificant models in each of the Group B studies.[24] These are

---

24. This process involves applying several different models from within each of the Group B studies, and they are too numerous to report in the model descriptions of appendix 3A. Note further that for the Kraay (1998) study, because the parameter values of the nonsignificant

combined with the significant results already used for the Group A studies.

Another approach to the alternative estimates would be to apply meta-statistical weighting to the various model results within the Group A studies as well. Experimentation with this approach yields the overall effect of boosting rather than reducing the estimated growth impacts, in comparison with the significant-only results. The reason is that within some of the studies (Edwards 2001; Arteta, Eichengreen, and Wyplosz 2002), there are model variants that do not include interaction variables, and weighting by inverse variance tends to give these models much more weight than those with interaction terms, even though the authors consider the interactive models to be more meaningful. It is the interaction term (especially in the Edwards 2001 model) that is responsible for substantially negative results for developing economies, and reducing the weight of the interactive models raises the average positive impact estimates. Because the principal concern is that the use of significant-only results will overstate the growth impacts, it does not make sense to suppress the weight of significant interactive models as a consequence of inverse-variance weighting. The simpler solution is to stick with the significant models considered best among their results by the Group A authors but to apply the meta-statistical averages for Group B studies to allow their nonsignificant results to be taken into account.

Tables 3.7 and 3.8 report this alternative set of estimates. Using the trimmed averages, figure 3.5 presents summary growth contributions of financial openness by period for the three country groupings.[25] Because even these estimates do not capture the considerably lower estimates obtained using both intra- and inter-study levels for the meta-statistical analysis (see chapter 2, table 2.1), the estimates of tables 3.7, 3.8, and figure 3.5 are best seen as the principal "high-variant" findings of this study. The results shown in tables 3.5 and 3.6 then serve mainly to support these high-end results by showing that the estimates would be even higher if only significant estimates were considered.

The broad results in figure 3.5 show first that there has been a substantial growth contribution from financial openness for all three groupings (with the notable exception of Latin America in the late 1980s). Second, the contribution has systematically been higher for industrial than for developing countries. Third, there has been a relatively steady upward trend for the industrial countries, but greater fluctuations for the emerging-market economies (with a collapse of the growth contribution in Latin America in

---

results are not reported, it is necessary to impute them at zero in order to arrive at the alternative estimate. With two of three models in that study insignificant, the effect is to reduce the estimates to one-third of the magnitudes shown for the Kraay study in tables 3.5 and 3.6.

25. The figure omits 1970–75 for developing countries because lack of data makes the estimates for that period less representative.

Table 3.7 Growth impact of financial openness by country, 1970–2004: Statistically significant (group A) and weighted all–model (group B) results

Country	Average				Trimmed average			
	1970–79	1980–89	1990–99	2000–04	1970–79	1980–89	1990–99	2000–04
Algeria		-0.1				0.0		
Argentina		0.0	0.6	0.3		0.0	0.6	0.5
Australia	0.6	0.9	1.1	1.1	0.5	0.8	0.9	1.0
Austria	0.7	0.9	1.4	1.4	0.6	0.8	1.0	1.1
Belgium		1.0	1.5	1.4		0.9	1.2	1.1
Brazil		-0.2	0.2	0.3		0.0	0.3	0.4
Canada	1.0	1.1	1.4	1.4	0.9	1.0	1.1	1.1
Chile		0.1	0.4	0.4		0.2	0.4	0.6
China			-0.2	0.1			0.2	0.4
Colombia	-0.1	0.0	0.1	-0.0	0.2	0.2	0.5	0.5
Denmark		1.0	1.6	1.6		0.8	1.1	1.1
Egypt		-0.1	-0.1	-0.2		0.1	0.4	0.5
Finland		0.8	1.4	1.5		0.7	1.1	1.2
France		0.9	1.3	1.4		0.8	1.0	1.1
Germany	1.0	1.1	1.5	1.5	0.9	1.0	1.1	1.2
Greece		0.5	0.8	1.1		0.4	0.8	1.0
Hong Kong				1.1				1.0
Hungary		-0.1	0.2	0.6		0.0	0.3	0.7

(continued on next page)

Table 3.7   Growth impact of financial openness by country, 1970–2004: Statistically significant (group A) and weighted all–model (group B) results *(continued)*

Country	Average 1970–79	Average 1980–89	Average 1990–99	Average 2000–04	Trimmed average 1970–79	Trimmed average 1980–89	Trimmed average 1990–99	Trimmed average 2000–04
India		-0.7	-0.7			0.2	0.2	0.3
Indonesia		-0.1	0.0	-0.1		0.2	0.3	0.3
Ireland	0.6	0.7	1.3	1.7	0.6	0.7	1.1	1.2
Israel	0.3	0.3	0.7	1.0	0.2	0.2	0.6	0.9
Italy	0.6	0.8	1.3	1.4	0.6	0.8	1.1	1.1
Japan		0.8	1.2	1.2		0.7	0.8	0.9
Korea		0.1	0.6	0.7		0.3	0.5	0.6
Malaysia	0.2	0.3	0.4	0.3	0.6	0.5	0.5	0.3
Mexico		0.0	0.4	0.5		0.1	0.5	0.5
Netherlands	0.9	1.1	1.5	1.5	0.8	1.0	1.1	1.1
New Zealand	0.3	0.7	1.1	1.1	0.2	0.7	1.0	1.0
Norway		0.9	1.6	1.8		0.8	1.1	1.2
Pakistan		-0.3	-0.2	-0.2		0.1	0.2	0.2
Peru		-0.2	0.0	0.1		0.0	0.6	0.7
Philippines		-0.1	-0.1	-0.2		0.1	0.5	0.5
Poland			0.0	0.4			0.2	0.5
Portugal		0.2	0.9	1.0		0.3	0.9	1.0
Singapore	0.8	1.0	1.2	1.1	0.9	1.0	1.1	1.1
South Africa	0.0	0.0	0.2	0.2	0.0	0.1	0.3	0.3

Spain	0.6	0.6	1.0	1.1		0.5	0.9	1.0
Sweden		1.0	1.4	1.4	0.4	0.8	1.0	1.1
Switzerland			1.8	1.7			1.2	1.1
Thailand		-0.1	0.2	0.0		0.3	0.5	0.3
Turkey	2.1	0.2	0.3	0.3	0.4	0.2	0.4	0.5
United Kingdom	0.6	1.1	1.4	1.6	0.5	1.1	1.2	1.2
United States	1.2	1.3	1.5	1.7	1.0	1.0	1.1	1.1
Venezuela	0.2	-0.1	0.1	0.2	0.4	0.0	0.3	0.3
Averages								
Industrial	0.7	0.9	1.3	1.4	0.7	0.8	1.0	1.1
Developing Asia	0.5	0.0	0.1	0.3	0.7	0.3	0.5	0.5
Latin America	0.0	-0.1	0.3	0.2	0.3	0.1	0.5	0.5
Middle East and South Africa	0.1	0.0	0.3	0.3	0.1	0.1	0.5	0.6
Developing Europe	2.1	0.1	0.2	0.5	0.4	0.1	0.3	0.5

Blank cells = data unavailable

Source: Author's calculations.

Table 3.8 Growth impact of financial openness by study and region: Statistically significant (group A) and weighted all-model (group B) results (percent per year)

Study	Type[a]	1970–74	1975–79	1980–84	1985–89	1990–94	1995–99	2000–04
Industrial countries								
Quinn (1997)	A	0.96	1.01	1.10	1.24	1.39	1.44	1.44
Kraay (1998)	B	0.15	0.19	0.21	0.27	0.26	0.44	0.52
Edwards (2001)	A	0.62	1.51	1.53	2.66	4.27	4.88	5.00
Edison et al. (2002)	B	0.09	0.13	0.14	0.30	0.34	0.44	0.50
Arteta, Eichengreen, and Wyplosz (2002)	A	0.71	0.73	0.78	0.92	1.03	1.05	1.01
Fratzscher and Bussiere (2004)	B	0.05	0.03	0.04	0.06	0.10	0.13	0.13
Tornell, Westermann, and Martinez (2004)	A	1.45	1.45	1.68	1.88	1.90	1.90	1.90
IMF (2007a)	B	0.04	0.07	0.08	0.11	0.10	0.16	0.21
Quinn (2008)	A	1.37	1.44	1.57	1.77	1.99	2.06	2.06
Average		0.60	0.73	0.79	1.02	1.26	1.39	1.42
Trimmed average		0.56	0.72	0.77	0.93	1.00	1.07	1.09
Latin America								
Quinn (1997)	A	0.74	0.68	0.64	0.62	0.95	1.14	1.16
Kraay (1998)	B	0.11	0.14	0.12	-0.05	0.19	0.31	0.19
Bailliu (2000)	A	0.17	0.23	0.08	-0.13	0.31	0.53	0.08
Edwards (2001)	A	-2.66	-2.34	-2.01	-2.25	-3.03	-2.79	-3.57
Edison et al. (2002)	B	-0.00	-0.02	-0.03	-0.05	0.12	0.29	0.23
Arteta, Eichengreen, and Wyplosz (2002)	A	-0.12	0.27	-0.01	-0.49	0.39	0.71	0.67

Fratzscher and Bussiere (2004)	B	0.12	0.12	0.03	-0.01	0.03	0.06	0.05
Tornell, Westermann, and Martinez (2004)	A	0.27	0.27	0.27	0.33	1.30	1.63	1.90
IMF (2007a)	B	0.01	0.03	0.03	0.01	0.06	0.08	0.07
Quinn (2008)	A	1.05	0.97	0.91	0.88	1.35	1.63	1.66
Average		-0.03	0.03	0.00	-0.11	0.17	0.36	0.24
Trimmed average		0.16	0.21	0.14	0.03	0.42	0.59	0.51
Developing Asia								
Quinn (1997)	A	0.71	0.72	0.79	0.83	0.95	0.99	0.99
Kraay (1998)	B	0.79	0.33	0.29	0.20	0.29	0.14	0.25
Bailliu (2000)	A	1.19	0.59	0.59	0.21	0.48	-0.14	-0.47
Edwards (2001)	A	-4.26	-3.44	-3.40	-3.36	-3.15	-2.77	-2.90
Edison et al. (2002)	B	0.07	0.11	0.13	0.15	0.20	0.26	0.25
Arteta, Eichengreen, and Wyplosz (2002)	A	0.27	0.43	0.40	0.44	0.50	0.65	0.67
Fratzscher and Bussiere (2004)	B	0.10	0.14	0.13	0.11	0.12	0.07	0.02
Tornell, Westermann, and Martinez (2004)	A	0.57	0.57	0.57	0.91	1.44	1.71	1.90
IMF (2007a)	B	0.02	0.06	0.07	0.06	0.08	0.07	0.09
Quinn (2008)	A	1.02	1.03	1.12	1.18	1.36	1.41	1.41
Average		0.05	0.05	0.07	0.07	0.23	0.24	0.22
Trimmed average		0.44	0.37	0.37	0.36	0.50	0.43	0.40

a. A = significant only (table 3.6); B = meta-statistical average (see text).

Source: Author's calculations.

Figure 3.5 Summary growth-impact estimates for general financial openness, 1970–2004

percent per year

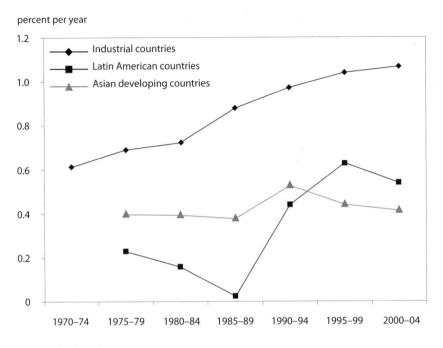

Source: Author's calculations.

the late 1980s before a surge by the 1990s, and a more moderate decline in Asia in the late 1990s from the early 1990s peak).

Finally, a lower-bound alternative can be obtained by considering the meta-statistical estimates of chapter 2. It was found there that for the general growth-impact studies, and considering only models without interactive variables, the simple average of significant-only results for complete openness versus complete closedness was a growth contribution of 1.99 percent per year. The corresponding average of the meta-statistical within-study averages was 1.57 percent per year. It is this estimate that corresponds to the principal high-variant estimates of tables 3.7 and 3.8. When the meta-statistical average was taken across all studies jointly, the growth impact parameter dropped to 0.56 percent per year. So the ratio of across-study meta-statistical to the high-variant counterpart was 0.36 to 1. If this ratio is applied to the trimmed averages of table 3.8, then for 1990–2004 the resulting growth contribution from realized openness amounts to 0.38 percent per year for industrial countries, 0.18 percent per year for Latin America, and 0.16 percent per year for emerging-market Asia. The corresponding averages for the principal high-variant results (table 3.8) are 1.1 percent, 0.51 percent, and 0.44 percent, respectively.

Results for Direct Investment Openness

For direct investment, there are eight models available for the synthesis analysis. Of these, four apply to all countries, and the other four apply only to developing countries. In seven of the eight studies the authors regard their principal significant-parameter result to be the most meaningful, and these are applied here. For the eighth study (Carkovic and Levine 2005), the authors judge that their significant-parameter results fail subsequent robustness tests, so the estimates here apply a meta-statistical average of all of the model results in that study. In the estimates here, the 90th percentile of the de facto openness variable is once again applied as a ceiling representing complete openness. Table 3.9 reports the results of the FDI synthesis analysis at the level of individual countries. The table again reports both the average, including all applicable models, and the trimmed average, excluding the highest and lowest model results. For industrial countries the trimmed average is thus narrowed to the two intermediate models, whereas for developing economies the trimmed average reflects the results of six of the eight models.

The discussion of patterns in the FDI results is once again based on the trimmed averages. For industrial countries, the growth-impact estimates are centered at a fairly high level, about 0.9 percent per year for the full period 1980–2004. Japan is a clear outlier, averaging only 0.04 percent annual growth contribution. This finding is consistent with the stylized fact that FDI has made minimal inroads into Japan. The next three lowest industrial countries are Italy, Germany, and Austria, averaging (trimmed) FDI growth contributions of 0.3 to 0.5 percent per year.

The next three industrial countries average about 0.6 percent per year growth contribution from FDI: the United States, Greece, and Denmark. Norway, Finland, France, and Greece average about 0.8 percent per year. Several industrial countries average from 1 to 1.5 percent per year FDI contribution to growth: in ascending order, Switzerland, Sweden, Australia, Ireland, Portugal, Spain, and the United Kingdom. The Netherlands and New Zealand average 1.7 percent. Belgium is in a class by itself, at 2.1 percent trimmed average annual growth contribution from FDI.

Among the developing countries, based on the average of trimmed averages for 1980–2004, there emerges a considerable similarity for a large number of economies centered around 1 percent per year growth contribution, ranging from 0.7 to 1.3 percent. These include (from lowest in this cluster to highest): Brazil, Israel, South Africa, Venezuela, the Philippines, Poland, Argentina, Egypt, Peru, Colombia, Thailand, and Mexico. A lower-impact cluster including Algeria, Turkey, Pakistan, India, Korea, and Indonesia centers around 0.4 percent per year growth contribution.

At the opposite end of the spectrum is a group of six economies with

Table 3.9 Growth impact of foreign direct investment openness by country, 1970–2004: Eight-model average (percent per year)

Country	Average				Trimmed average			
	1970–79	1980–89	1990–99	2000–04	1970–79	1980–89	1990–99	2000–04
Algeria	0.2	0.0	0.1	0.3		0.0		
Argentina	0.1	0.3	1.5	1.6		0.4	1.4	1.5
Australia	0.7	1.0	1.1	1.8	0.7	1.0	1.1	1.8
Austria	0.2	0.2	0.5	1.2	0.2	0.2	0.5	1.1
Belgium	0.4	1.0	2.5	2.9		1.0	2.6	3.4
Brazil	0.3	0.3	0.7	1.6		0.3	0.7	1.6
Canada	1.2	0.6	1.0	1.4	1.1	0.6	1.0	1.4
Chile	0.5	1.4	2.2	2.6		1.3	2.3	2.7
China		0.3	2.2	2.2			2.2	2.2
Colombia	0.2	0.7	1.3	1.9	0.2	0.7	1.3	1.8
Denmark	0.2	0.2	0.9	1.1		0.2	0.9	0.9
Egypt	0.3	1.2	1.1	1.0		1.1	0.9	0.8
Finland	0.1	0.2	0.7	1.6		0.2	0.8	1.6
France	0.1	0.3	1.0	1.7		0.3	1.0	1.6
Germany	0.2	0.1	0.3	1.0	0.2	0.1	0.3	1.0
Greece	0.3	0.6	0.5	0.5		0.7	0.5	0.4
Hong Kong		1.0	1.5	2.9				3.0

Hungary		0.0	2.2	2.5			2.5	2.5
India	0.0	0.0	0.3	0.7			0.3	0.6
Indonesia	0.1	0.1	0.7	-0.8		0.1	1.0	
Ireland	0.8	0.6	1.9	1.7	1.3	0.5	2.0	1.7
Israel	0.5	0.2	0.7	1.7	0.5	0.3	0.8	1.9
Italy	0.2	0.2	0.2	0.7	0.2	0.2	0.2	0.7
Japan	0.0	0.0	0.0	0.1		0.0	0.0	0.1
Korea	0.1	0.5	0.9	1.2		0.3	0.6	0.9
Malaysia	1.2	2.0	2.9	2.1	1.4	2.0	2.9	2.1
Mexico	0.2	1.0	1.6	1.9		0.8	1.4	1.9
Netherlands	0.8	1.0	1.8	2.3	0.8	1.0	2.0	2.5
New Zealand	0.7	1.5	1.9	1.5	0.9	1.7	1.8	1.4
Norway	0.3	0.3	0.9	1.0		0.3	0.9	1.0
Pakistan	0.1	0.2	0.6	0.7		0.2	0.5	0.6
Peru	0.2	0.1	1.5	1.7		0.1	1.8	1.6
Philippines	0.2	0.4	1.5	1.1		0.5	1.3	1.0
Poland		0.0	1.4	2.0		0.0	1.3	2.0

(continued on next page)

Table 3.9 Growth impact of foreign direct investment openness by country, 1970–2004: Eight-model average (percent per year) (continued)

Country	Average				Trimmed average			
	1970–79	1980–89	1990–99	2000–04	1970–79	1980–89	1990–99	2000–04
Portugal	0.2	0.7	1.2	2.2		0.8	1.4	2.5
Singapore	2.4	3.2	3.0	3.1	2.7	2.9	2.9	2.9
South Africa	0.1	0.0	0.7	1.4			0.6	1.2
Spain	0.3	0.8	1.2	2.3		0.9	1.3	2.4
Sweden	0.1	0.3	1.4	1.9	0.1	0.3	1.4	1.8
Switzerland	0.2	0.5	1.1	1.8		0.6	1.1	1.7
Thailand	0.1	0.4	1.4	2.3		0.4	1.4	2.4
Turkey	0.0	0.1	0.2	0.5	0.1	0.1	0.3	0.6
United Kingdom	0.9	1.0	1.5	1.9	1.0	1.1	1.7	2.0
United States	0.1	0.4	0.6	0.8	0.1	0.4	0.6	0.9
Venezuela	–0.1	0.1	1.4	1.5		0.1	1.4	1.5
Averages								
Industrial	...	0.5	1.1	1.5	...	0.6	1.1	1.5
Developing Asia	...	0.8	1.5	1.6	...	0.9	1.5	1.8
Latin America	...	0.6	1.4	1.8	...	0.5	1.5	1.8
Middle East and South Africa	...	0.3	0.7	1.1	...	0.5	0.8	1.3
Developing Europe	...	0.0	1.3	1.7	...	0.1	1.3	1.7

Blank cells = data unavailable

Source: Author's calculations.

especially high growth impacts of FDI. This impact turns out to be 2 to 2.5 percent per year for Chile, China, Malaysia, and Hungary. The high estimate for China is consistent with the stylized fact of China's gargantuan presence in direct investment inflows. Thus, in 2005–07, total net direct investment inflows to the emerging-market economies averaged about $200 billion annually, and inflows to China alone averaged about $80 billion (IMF 2009a, IIF 2008). Finally, two city-state financial centers, Singapore and Hong Kong SAR, show the highest growth contributions from FDI, at about 3 percent annually.[26]

The FDI synthesis analysis results are shown by model in table 3.10. Among the models, the Blonigan and Wang (2005) and Borensztein, De Gregorio, and Lee (1998) models run "warm," averaging around 2 percent for 1980–2004 for Latin America and 1.7 percent for developing Asia. The meta-statistical averages for the Carkovic-Levine model place it about in the middle for industrial and Latin American economies but "warm" for Asia (where it shows an average of 2 percent for 1980–2004).

On the cool side are the models of Reisen and Soto (2001), Hermes and Lensink (2003), and IMF staff (IMF 2007a), which show 1980–2004 ranges of annual growth contribution of 0.2 to 0.5 percent annually for Latin America and 0.1 to 0.5 percent for Asian developing countries. In the middle are the Haveman, Lei, and Netz (2001) and Lensink and Morrissey (2006) models, which for 1980–2004 indicate annual growth contributions in the range of 1.3 to 1.6 percent for Latin America and 1 to 1.2 percent for Asian developing economies. The Haveman, Lei, and Netz model also places the industrial-country growth impact at 1 percent annually, leaving the IMF staff model (IMF 2007a) as the lowest (at 0.4 percent) for industrial countries.

Figure 3.6 shows summary time trends in the growth contribution of FDI for the industrial, Latin American, and Asian developing economies, using the trimmed averages of the model average results in table 3.8. There is a striking upward trend over time for all three areas. For FDI, moreover, growth impacts for developing countries are comparable to or higher than those for industrial countries, the reverse of the findings in figure 3.5 for general financial openness. In addition, for at least the developing countries the impacts tend to be higher for FDI openness than for general financial openness. For example, in the period 1990–99, general openness contributes about 0.5 percentage point to annual growth in developing countries but FDI openness contributes 1.4 percentage points (figure 3.5 versus figure 3.6). For industrial countries the contribution is the same from both sources, at 1 percent per year the 1990s. The conclusion of this chapter considers the implications of the apparent finding that growth contributions from FDI openness equal or exceed those from total financial openness.

---

26. These high-end estimates would have been even higher without the 90th percentile ceiling on the FDI variables.

Table 3.10 Growth impact of foreign direct investment openness by country groupings, 1970–2004: Average results by model (percent per year)

Model	Type[a]	1970–74	1975–79	1980–84	1985–89	1990–94	1995–99	2000–04
Industrial countries								
Haveman, Lei, and Netz (2001)	A	0.7	0.4	0.4	0.8	0.9	1.4	1.6
Carkovic and Levine (2005)	B	0.5	0.4	0.3	0.5	0.6	0.9	1.2
Lensink and Morrissey (2006)	A	0.8	0.5	0.5	0.9	1.0	1.7	2.0
IMF (2007a)	A	0.2	0.2	0.2	0.3	0.4	0.6	0.8
Average		0.6	0.4	0.4	0.6	0.7	1.1	1.4
Trimmed average		0.6	0.4	0.4	0.6	0.8	1.2	1.4
Developing Latin America								
Haveman, Lei, and Netz (2001)	A		0.3	0.5	0.7	1.0	2.3	2.1
Carkovic and Levine (2005)	B		0.4	0.5	0.8	1.1	2.3	2.1
Lensink and Morrissey (2006)	A		0.4	0.6	0.8	1.2	2.8	2.5
IMF (2007a)	A	0.2	0.2	0.2	0.3	0.4	0.6	0.8
Borensztein, De Gregorio, and Lee (1998)	A		0.3	0.8	1.2	1.8	2.9	2.9
Reisen and Soto (2001)	A		0.0	0.1	0.1	0.1	0.3	0.3
Blonigan and Wang (2005)	A		0.3	1.0	1.4	2.3	3.4	3.4
Hermes and Lensink (2000)	A		0.0	0.0	0.2	0.2	0.5	0.5
Average		0.2	0.2	0.5	0.7	1.0	1.9	1.8
Trimmed average			0.3	0.4	0.6	0.9	1.9	1.8

Developing Asia

Study	Type							
Haveman, Lei, and Netz (2001)	A		0.6	0.5	0.6	1.1	1.5	1.1
Carkovic and Levine (2005)	B		1.8	1.6	1.5	2.1	2.6	2.3
Lensink and Morrissey (2006)	A		0.7	0.6	0.7	1.3	1.8	1.3
IMF (2007a)	A	0.2	0.2	0.2	0.3	0.4	0.6	0.8
Borensztein, De Gregorio, and Lee (1998)	A		0.5	0.5	1.0	1.7	2.3	2.0
Reisen and Soto (2001)	A		0.1	0.1	0.1	0.2	0.2	0.2
Blonigan and Wang (2005)	A		0.2	0.5	1.2	2.1	2.9	2.4
Hermes and Lensink (2000)	A		0.2	0.2	0.2	0.5	0.9	0.7
Average			0.5	0.5	0.7	1.2	1.6	1.3
Trimmed average			0.4	0.4	0.6	1.2	1.6	1.3

a. A = principal significant-parameter model from study in question; B = meta-statistical average of all models from study in question.

Source: Author's calculations.

Figure 3.6   Impact of foreign direct investment openness on growth, 1970–2004

percent per year

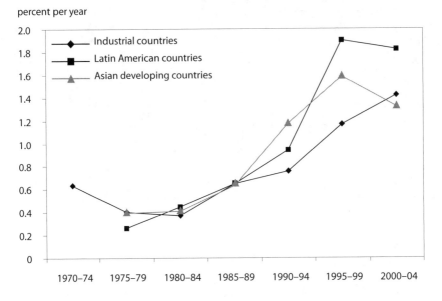

Source: Author's calculations.

Comparison with Theoretical Expectations

It is important to consider whether these synthesis estimates are in plausible ranges given what would be expected on theoretical grounds. There are two fundamental theoretical bases for expecting financial globalization to contribute to growth. First, capital inflows should boost the capital stock and the rate of investment. It can be shown with the standard neoclassical model that the result should be a higher growth rate. Second, financial openness should increase the rate of TFP growth in the economy. Direct investment should be expected to improve efficiency, for example, because of transfer of technology.

Standard production function analysis provides a basis for setting the broad range of growth impact to be expected from a boost to the capital stock, or capital deepening. In the Cobb-Douglas production function, output (Q) is a function of capital (K) and labor (N). Specifically:

$$Q = \Gamma K^{\alpha} N^{(1-\alpha)},$$

(3.2)

where α is the elasticity of output with respect to capital, $(1 - \alpha)$ is the elasticity of output with respect to labor, and Γ is a constant that not only permits translation of the right-hand side units (billions of dollars and million workers, for the full economy) into the left-hand side units (billions of dollars), but also incorporates an efficiency multiplier (yielding higher GDP for a more efficient economy with the same capital and labor).

The change in output, or at the national level, real GDP, for a given change in capital will equal the marginal product of capital multiplied by the amount of the capital increase. If net foreign capital inflows amount to the fraction ϕ_F of GDP, and if the fraction Ω_I of foreign capital inflow is invested (rather than consumed), then the change in the amount of capital available as a consequence of financial openness will be $\Delta K = \Omega_I \phi_F Q$.

For its part, the marginal product of capital is obtained by taking the derivative of the production function with respect to capital, or:

$$\partial Q/\partial K = \alpha \Gamma K^{(\alpha-1)} N^{(1-\alpha)} = \alpha \frac{Q}{K}. \tag{3.3}$$

The total change in output will then be:

$$\Delta Q = \partial Q/\partial K \times \Delta K = \alpha \frac{Q}{K} \times \Phi_F \Omega_I Q = (\alpha \Phi_F \Omega_I) \frac{Q}{B}, \tag{3.4}$$

where B is the capital/output ratio. Dividing both sides by output yields the proportionate growth rate contribution of the foreign capital from the standpoint of capital deepening:

$$g_k \equiv \frac{\Delta Q}{Q} = \frac{\alpha \Phi_F \Omega_I}{B}. \tag{3.5}$$

Using this relationship, it is possible to apply stylized facts about the relevant parameters to arrive at a plausible benchmark for the contribution of financial openness to growth. In the dataset used in this chapter, during the 1990s the 90th percentile in the distribution of net capital inflows was 9 percent of GDP in Latin America and 12 percent of GDP in developing Asia. (The calculations here would not apply to industrial countries, because in the neoclassical model they should be supplying capital to the developing countries rather than receiving net capital inflows.) One interpretation might then be that complete financial openness would be associated with net inflows on the order of 10 percent of GDP. That level would probably be excessive, however, from the standpoint of long-term sustainability. If net external liabilities are to be held at a ceiling of 50 percent of GDP, for example, annual net inflows as a percent of GDP should not exceed one-half of the growth rate in dollar terms.[27] A moderately-rapidly growing developing country with real growth of 6 percent,

---

27. Essentially, the long-term ratio of net liabilities to GDP will converge to the marginal rate. The marginal rate is a ratio that has net capital inflows as the numerator and the change of dollar GDP in the denominator. Dividing both the numerator and denominator by GDP gives net capital inflows as a percent of GDP in the numerator and the growth rate of dollar GDP (percent) in the denominator, the proposition in the text.

combined with global dollar price inflation of 3 percent, would place dollar GDP growth at 9 percent. So an alternative benchmark for net capital inflows under complete financial openness might be half of this level, or 4.5 percent of GDP ($\phi_F = 0.045$).

The share of capital income in national accounts is the elasticity of output with respect to capital in the neoclassical model (α), and in developing countries the capital share is typically around 40 percent ($\alpha = 0.4$). In the analysis of the Gourinchas-Jeanne model in appendix 2B in chapter 2, the capital/output ratio (B) for developing countries is placed at 1.4. This ratio is probably somewhat higher in at least the emerging-market economies, perhaps in the range of 2.

Finally, the fraction of capital inflows that goes into investment rather than consumption could be in the range of $\Omega_I = 0.8$.[28] With these stylized parameters in hand, the annual growth contribution from complete financial openness might be expected to be on the order of $g^* = [\alpha \times \phi_F \times \Omega_I] / B = [0.4 \times 0.045 \times 0.8] / 2 = 0.0072$, or 0.7 percent per year. If instead the 90th percentile net capital inflow were applied ($\phi_F = 0.10$), the annual growth contribution would be $g^* = 0.016$, or 1.6 percent per year. This benchmarking exercise suggests that on the basis of standard neoclassical theory, it would be reasonable to expect complete financial openness to contribute somewhere on the order of 1 percent per year to growth solely from the standpoint of capital deepening in a developing economy. Most economies will only be partially open, so the actual observed growth contribution would be somewhat less.

The second component of growth enhancement from financial globalization comes from the stimulus to TFP growth, g_{tfp}. In terms of the aggregate production function in equation 3.2, this influence can be seen as the contribution of financial globalization to the annual rise in the efficiency parameter Γ, or $g_{tfp} = \dot{\Gamma}_f$.

Sizing the plausible contribution of financial globalization to TFP growth can usefully begin with considering the overall magnitude of TFP growth. Using data for 84 countries for 1960–2000, Bosworth and Collins (2003) estimated that TFP contributed 1 percent per year to growth in each of three major groupings: industrial countries, East Asia less China, and South Asia.[29] In China the contribution was 2.6 percent per year, but in

---

28. Borensztein, De Gregorio, and Lee (1998) find that FDI in particular has a high investment fraction of unity or even more as a consequence of induced domestic supplier investment. However, debt capital is more likely to be devoted in at least some proportion to financing consumption rather than investment.

29. Output growth rates vary considerably more across the regions than the contribution from TFP, reflecting higher rates of growth of capital and the labor force in developing countries. Expressed as a fraction of output growth per worker not attributable to capital accumulation or increased educational stock, TFP accounted for about half in the industrial countries, China, and South Asia, and about one-fifth to one-quarter in Latin America and East Asia excluding China.

Latin America it was only 0.2 percent (and was negative in the 1980s). IMF (2006, 4, chapter 3) estimates that from 1970 to 2005, TFP contributed 0.75 to 2 percentage points to annual growth in India, Japan, the newly industrialized economies, and Thailand. A reasonable stylized-fact number for TFP growth, then, would be 1 percent per year.

The fraction of this total amount that might be attributable to financial globalization, and more specifically the size of the change in TFP growth that could be expected from moving from complete financial closedness to openness, is highly uncertain. Kose, Prasad, and Terrones (2008) conduct statistical tests explaining TFP with alternatively de jure and de facto measures of financial openness. For the de jure tests, they find that economies with capital account openness achieve 0.11 to 0.15 percentage point higher annual TFP growth than economies with extensive capital controls. For the de facto tests, they find that for each 10 percent of GDP increase in the ratio of FDI stock to GDP, TFP growth is 0.4 percentage point per year higher; but surprisingly, for each 10 percent of GDP increase in the ratio of external debt to GDP, TFP growth is 0.2 percentage point lower.

The 90th percentile in the distributions of international equity and debt liabilities to GDP can serve as a marker for "complete" financial openness. This benchmark for the countries examined in this chapter, and for the 1990s, turns out to be at the following levels. For FDI together with portfolio equity, 76 percent of GDP for industrial countries, 118 percent for developing Asia, and 34 percent for Latin America. The corresponding 90th percentile levels for bonds and other debt are 149 percent of GDP for industrial countries, 165 percent for developing Asia, and 63 percent for Latin America. A notional level for complete financial integration might thus be on the order of 100 percent of GDP for equity liabilities and 150 percent of GDP for debt liabilities (approximately the average for the 90th percentiles of the industrial and Asian developing countries). The somewhat peculiar opposite-signed estimates in Kose, Prasad, and Terrones (2008) would thus imply annual contribution to TFP growth amounting to +4 percent from equity ([100/10] x 0.4) but −3 percent from debt ([150/10] x [−0.2]), for a net of 1 percent per year. The study's range of potential contribution to TFP growth from full financial openness thus ranges from about 0.12 percent per year under the de jure test to about 1 percent per year under the de facto test. A conservative average would be about one-third of 1 percent. This would mean that one-third of typical TFP growth would be attributable to financial globalization.[30]

With capital deepening providing a potential of about 1 percent per year growth and TFP another one-third percent, the benchmark for potential growth contribution from complete financial openness for developing countries would be $g = g_k + g_{tfp} = 1\frac{1}{3}$ percent per year. For industrial coun-

---

30. Although this share could overstate, because the total TFP benchmark is actual observed outcome, whereas the contribution from financial openness is for complete openness.

tries, in principle the capital-deepening component would be absent, but the TFP component would still be present, suggesting an expected growth contribution on the order of one-third of a percent per year.

Against these levels that might be expected on grounds of theory combined with stylized-fact parameters, the results of this chapter appear reasonable for the developing countries for general financial openness, but on the high side for industrial countries for general financial openness and on the high side for both industrial and developing economies when the estimates are for direct investment. Thus, figure 3.5 places the growth contribution of general financial openness at about 0.5 percent per year for both Latin America and developing Asia from 1990–99. This estimate is consistent with a benchmark of 1⅓ percent per year for complete financial openness. The figure also shows a higher growth contribution for industrial countries, however, averaging about 1 percent per year for this same period. But with no expectation of capital deepening for these economies, the expected rate might be only about one-third of a percent. The implication would seem to be that the model estimates may overstate for industrial countries, or that capital deepening does play a role for several of them, or that TFP gains from financial openness are higher than the stylized-fact estimate, or some combination of all three of these. As discussed above, the estimates of tables 3.7 and 3.8, and figure 3.5, are thus best seen as the high-variant findings; low-variant results are then based on the ratio of the intra- and inter-study meta-statistical averages to the high-variant averages.

For FDI, figure 3.6 indicates an average realized growth contribution of about 1 percent per year for industrial countries and 1.4 percent for emerging-market economies in the 1990s. This rate would be consistent with the benchmark 1⅓ percent contribution from complete financial openness for emerging-market economies, *if* most of them were completely open to FDI *and* FDI were the principal source of growth benefits (in contrast to other forms of capital: portfolio equity, bonds, and bank loans). In fact, on the basis of a main de facto measure of FDI openness—FX_1 (FDI inflows as a percent of GDP)—most emerging-market economies in the 1990s were relatively open. Their average ratio stood at 2.7 percent of GDP, in comparison with the benchmark 4.7 percent of GDP designating complete openness.[31]

Nonetheless, the underlying source of the relatively high estimates is that the models tend to imply a larger growth contribution from complete FDI openness than suggested by the back-of-the-envelope calculation of the theoretical expectation. Thus, the simple average of the coefficients reported in the literature survey of chapter 2 (table 2.3) shows an annual growth impact of 0.57 percent of GDP for each 1 percent of GDP in FDI

---

31. This is the 90th percentile across both industrial and emerging-market economies for the full period 1970–2004.

inflow.[32] This coefficient would generate 2.7 percent annual growth contribution from FDI at complete openness as gauged at the benchmark 4.7 percent of GDP FDI inflow, or about twice the contribution suggested from the simple theoretical expectation estimate of this section.

The broad implication of the high level of the FDI impact estimates from the model synthesis is that there is substantial support for the notion that FDI is particularly powerful in contributing to growth. Even so, a further appropriate inference may be that application of the model-based estimates tends to err somewhat on the upside for the estimates of growth contribution from FDI alone, even after taking special account of a major study in which many of the estimates are insignificant.

Conclusion

This chapter has provided a synthesis analysis of two broad sets of statistical studies relating growth to financial openness. The first set is for general financial openness; the second is for openness to direct investment. The results show relatively strong realized growth contributions from financial openness, especially by the 1990s and after. On the basis of application of 11 models, the degree of financial openness attained by the 1990s provided a boost to growth rates on the order of 1 percent annually for industrial countries and about one-half of a percent for emerging-market economies (figure 3.5). Correspondingly, based on eight models for FDI, the degree of openness to FDI attained by the same period was contributing about 1 percent per year to growth in the industrial countries and about 1.4 percent in emerging-market economies (figure 3.6).

These estimates apply the principal statistically significant result from each of the studies in question when the study's authors consider it their main finding. For those studies in which the authors judge that their alternative tests remove the robustness of the initial significant result, the estimates here adopt the approach of meta-statistics, which weights alternative findings by the inverse of the variance of the parameter estimate. The effect is to reduce the magnitude of the central estimates to somewhat below those that would be obtained using solely statistically significant results. Even so, the results are considerably higher than would be found when applying meta-statistical averaging both within and across studies. The results of tables 3.7 and 3.8, and figure 3.5, should therefore be seen as the high-end variant of the findings of this study.

The discussion of theoretical expectations tends to place the potential gains from financial opening at this high-variant range for emerging-mar-

---

32. Applying the meta-statistical variant for Carkovic-Levine, the 58th percentile education for Blonigan and Wang, and including the Balasubramanyam, Salisu, and Sapsford (1996) estimate.

ket economies. However, the theoretical expectation is lower for industrial countries, where the capital-deepening effect should generally not be present.

For the emerging-market economies (but not industrial countries), it turns out that the estimates of realized growth contributions from FDI openness (about 1.4 percent annually in the 1990s) exceed those from general financial openness (about 0.5 percent). Some analysts might conclude from these results that open capital accounts *reduce* economic growth for all types of capital except FDI. This interpretation would be a mistake. There is no extensive body of empirical work demonstrating that non-FDI capital openness has a negative effect on growth. On the contrary, the principal set of empirical studies on subsets of capital other than FDI—that on portfolio equity—typically finds large positive growth effects. Out of the scores of empirical studies on growth effects of financial openness, only two suggest that openness to bank flows may have a negative impact. Both qualify the result by suggesting that sufficient domestic financial development reverses (Reisen and Soto 2001) or attenuates (Kose, Prasad, and Terrones 2008) the negative effect.

Instead of proving that financial openness outside of FDI is bad for growth, the divergence between the higher growth-impact estimates for FDI (figure 3.6) than for general financial openness (figure 3.5, for emerging-market economies in both cases) should be read more simply as providing additional evidence from the specific case of FDI in support of the general proposition that financial openness is beneficial to growth. The main estimates of growth gains from financial openness, in this approach, would be those from the general studies. The role of the higher FDI-based estimates would then primarily be to indicate that, if anything, the central estimates understate rather than overstate the gains from openness. Several other influences of financial globalization on growth that are discussed in chapter 2 are not included in the synthesis analyses of this chapter. The influence of financial globalization on domestic financial development, and thence to growth, is one important dimension not included in the calculations here. Nor are the parameters of the models measuring equity-market liberalization impacts included here, although these typically tend to be high. Nor do the calculations of this chapter synthesize the welfare gains from consumption smoothing and risk diversification discussed in chapter 2. At the same time, the synthesis analysis of this chapter does not specifically incorporate models of financial-crisis impact, although again these are reviewed in chapter 2. The broad effect of incorporating all of these additional dimensions would seem to be to bolster the conclusion that financial globalization has made an important contribution to growth and welfare, even though typically such additional estimates would appropriately be seen as parallel rather than additive to the estimates of this chapter.

The synthesis estimates show generally rising trends over time in the growth contribution from realized financial opening. There is, in particular, a large increase from relatively modest contributions in the 1970s to a large growth impact by the 1990s in the FDI estimates. A rising trend after the 1980s is also found for both the industrial and Latin American countries using the more general financial-openness models (although these models show a sizable but relatively flat growth contribution over time for Asian emerging-market economies). The general trend toward greater growth contributions associated with general increases in financial openness (figures 3.1, 3.3, and 3.4) suggest that it is important to global growth to preserve the degree of financial globalization that has been achieved, despite likely new fears and doubts raised by the financial crisis of 2007–09. The final chapter of this volume turns to that issue.

Appendix 3A
Normalizing Model Coefficients for Synthesis Analysis

This appendix clarifies the way in which the coefficients from some of the models are normalized to correspond to the standardized units applied.

General Financial-Openness Models

The first general model is that of Quinn (1997). That study used a capital-openness variable ranging from 0 for complete closedness to 4 for complete openness. The same measure is applied in Quinn and Toyoda (2008) but converted into a scale of 0 to 100. In Quinn (1997), the coefficient of per capita growth on financial openness, after controlling for other variables explaining growth, ranges from 0.3 to 0.47. The calculations here apply the average, or 0.385. This coefficient must be divided by 25 to take account of the fact that the range of the openness variable is 25 times larger in the form applied here than in the Quinn (1997) results. The normalized coefficient for application to openness variable X_1 (table 3.3) is thus $0.385/25 = 0.0154$.

The next general model is that of Kraay (1998). The coefficient of growth on gross capital inflows and outflows as a fraction of GDP is 0.07 for the full sample and 0.11 for non-OECD countries. The dependent variable is growth in pure numbers, so conversion to growth in percentage terms must multiply by 100. So the coefficients to be applied to openness variable X_2 are 7 for industrial countries and 11 for developing countries.

The third general financial-openness model is that of Bailliu (2000). Her key equation is $g = -0.27 F + 0.056 B + 0.46 F \times B$, where F is the ratio of net capital flows to GDP (or X_3, table 3.3), and B is the banking-depth variable (V_1). Her dependent variable is per capita growth in pure numbers, so her coefficients need to be multiplied by 100 for normalization. For purposes of analyzing the impact of financial openness, only the terms X_1 and $X_1 \times V_1$ are relevant.[33]

The fourth general model is that of Edwards (2001). His growth equation is $g = -0.107q_4 + 0.01239 \ln y_{80} \times q_4$, where q_4 is the Quinn (1997) openness variable with a scale of 0 to 4 and y_{80} is per capita income at market exchange rates in dollars of 1980. His growth rate is expressed as a pure number. So whereas the coefficients must be multiplied by 100 to convert to percent growth, they must be divided by 25 to convert from q_4 to the corresponding X_1 here (with scale 0 to 100). The result is to normalize the coefficients to $-0.428 X_1 + 0.04956 X_1 V_2$.

Edison et al. (2002) provide the fifth and sixth general models. Here

---

33. In effect the term involving B (or V_1) by itself is part of the set of other control variables, not directly examined in the meta-analysis of the impact of financial openness.

the normalization is simply to convert the dependent growth variable from pure numbers to percentage rates, so the only change in their coefficients it to multiply them by 100.[34]

The seventh general model, by Arteta, Eichengreen, and Wyplosz (2003), once again applies the Quinn (1997) openness measure. So once again its coefficient must be divided by 25 to convert from the 0–4 scale to the 0–100 scale in the Quinn (2008) version used here.[35]

In the eighth general model, Fratzscher and Bussiere (2004) apply the IMF's binary AREAER measure of capital-market restrictions (but subtract it from unity, so openness is 1 and closedness is 0). Their coefficient of 1.611 can thus be applied directly to the present study's AREAER-based variable (X_6). Their growth variable is already in percentage rate terms.

Similarly, the ninth general model (Tornell, Westermann, and Martinez 2004) translates directly without normalization, as the openness variable is the same as theirs. Thus, the coefficient from their table 3 for the contribution of financial openness to growth in percentage terms is $1.9 \times X_7$.

The 10th general model is from the IMF staff study (IMF 2007a). From its table 8, the coefficient for the impact of total capital inflows relative to GDP on growth (as a percent) is 8.62. This coefficient translates directly without normalization for application to X_8.

The final general model included in the meta-analysis is that of Quinn and Toyoda (2008). It is of the same form as Quinn (1997) but with the openness variable scaled to a 0–100 range. With the revised scaling, the 2008 coefficient on openness (0.022) applies without normalization to this variable as used here, X_1.

Direct Investment Openness Models

For the eight models amenable to meta-analysis of the impact of FDI on growth, there are several considerations that require special attention in deriving normalized coefficients. First, caution must be used in limiting application of the model only to developing countries, in the case of the four models that are estimated excluding industrial countries. As discussed in chapter 2, this distinction is emphasized by Blonigan and Wang (2005), who argue that estimates pooling data from both categories of countries will yield misleading results. Second, one of the models applies logarithmic formulations on variables that have fractional values,

---

34. Their coefficient of 0.101 on the ratio of FDI and portfolio inflows and outflows to GDP becomes 10.1 to be applied to X_4; and their coefficient of 0.183 on the ratio of FDI and portfolio inflows to GDP becomes 18.1, applied to X_5.

35. Their equation: $-0.96 \ q4 + 1.26 \ q4 \ V_3$, referring to the black-market premium variable in table 3.3, becomes: $-0.0384 \ X_1 + 0.0504 \ X_1 V_3$.

such that the direct calculation of coefficient times variable will yield a negative result. These negative results only make sense in the context of the constant term and contribution of other variables, on average, to the outcome. In particular, an increase in a fraction will cause the logarithm to be less negative, raising the growth rate but against an unknown base constant. Third, one of the models was estimated in a period and with a dataset with much smaller maximum values for the direct investment inflows than experienced in more recent years, so some form of constrained application becomes necessary to avoid exorbitantly large impact estimates when applied to the more recent data.

The first FDI study is that by Borensztein, De Gregorio, and Lee (1998) and applies only to developing countries. The only normalization needed for this study is conversion from expression of the growth variable in pure numbers to percentage rates, but it turns out that it is also necessary to impose a maximum constraint on the estimate. For the former, multiplying the original coefficients by 100, the growth contribution of FDI becomes $g = -85\, FX_1 + 162.3\, FX_1\, FV_1$ (see table 3.4).[36] Because the model is linear and was estimated on a sample set ending in 1989, when educational levels were considerably lower than by the end of the period considered here, the unconstrained model generates some extreme results.[37] This problem is addressed by setting a ceiling on the estimated growth contribution based on application of the model to a benchmark "extreme high" for education in the period of the model estimation and the average of direct investment relative to GDP. In the dataset developed here, for developing countries in the period 1970–89 the 95th percentile level of average male secondary schooling was 2.37 years, and average direct investment relative to GDP was 0.011. Applying these values yields a growth contribution of 3.3 percent per year. This value is adopted as the ceiling constraint in applying the Borensztein, De Gregorio, and Lee (1998) model here.

The second FDI study, by Haveman, Lei, and Netz (2001), applies to all countries. It uses the logarithm of FDI inflows as a fraction of GDP and thereby poses the negativity problem noted above. The resolution of this problem here is to transform the logarithmic function into a quadratic function, under the assumption that the dependent variable (growth contribution from FDI) falls to zero when the level of direct investment inflows relative to GDP is 0.01.[38] In the Haveman, Lei, and Netz function,

---

36. Borensztein, De Gregorio, and Lee (1998, table 1, regression 1.3).

37. For example, Korea's ratio of direct investment inflows to GDP rose from 0.0048 in 1989 to 0.021 in 1999, and average male secondary schooling rose from 3.5 to 4.6 years, so the unconstrained function yields a growth contribution of 2.3 percent per year in 1989 but an outsized 13.8 percent in 1999.

38. With a stylized 2 percent per capita growth and FDI inflows of 2 percent of GDP, an implied constant term would be 0.1146. That is, $0.02 = \alpha + 0.025\ \ln(0.02)$; $\alpha = 0.1146$. When this benchmark is applied to inflows of 1 percent of GDP (0.01 in pure number form), the

the coefficient of per capita growth (pure number) on the ratio of FDI to GDP (FX_1 here) is 0.025.[39] In the dataset here, a representative high value of inflows is 25 percent of GDP ($FX_1 = 0.25$), the broad maximum range for such economies as Chile, Ireland, and Hong Kong (well below the 92 percent sample maximum found in Belgium; see table 3.2). Applying the logarithmic coefficient, the growth contribution from FDI rises from zero at 1 percent of GDP to about 8 percent at 25 percent of GDP (and about 2.5 percent at inflows of 3 percent of GDP). A quadratic approximation of this curve, with a forced zero intercept, is $g_\# = 0.741\ FX_1 - 1.784\ (FX_2)^2$, where the subscript # refers to pure number form for growth. Converting for growth in percentage rate terms, the normalized coefficients for the Haveman, Lei, and Netz (2001) study become $g = 74.1\ FX_1 - 178.4\ (FX_1)^2$.

The third model estimate for FDI effects is that by Reisen and Soto (2001). They find that a rise in FDI inflows by 10 percent of GDP would increase the growth rate by 1 percent of GDP. So in terms of the normalization here, their coefficient translates into $g = 10\ FX_1$ for growth expressed as a percentage rate (that is, $10 \times 0.10 = 1.0$). Their model applies only to developing countries.

The fourth FDI model is from Carkovic and Levine (2005), which applies to all countries. As discussed in chapter 2, of their OLS results with significant effects, they distrust the one involving interaction with educational level because it has what they consider to be the wrong sign on education. The other result uses private credit as a share of GDP as the term to interact with the direct investment term. Their dependent variable is already growth contribution expressed as a percent rate. So their coefficients are applied directly to obtain $g = 119.2\ FX_1 + 93.6\ FX_1\ FV_2$.[40] However, this equation results in absurdly high growth contributions in a few cases (such as 30 percent growth contribution for Germany in 2000 when FDI inflows reach 11 percent of GDP). The dataset considered here has considerably higher maximum values of FDI relative to GDP than the dataset used in the Carkovic and Levine study. Their maximum ratio was $FX_1 = 0.043$. Applying this maximum together with their average for private credit at $FV_2 = 0.4$ yields a plausible maximum of $g = 6.7$ percent growth contribution implied by their study. This is the ceiling that is imposed on the equation as applied here.

The fifth FDI model is that of Hermes and Lensink (2003), estimated for developing countries. The coefficients are from their table 3, equation 4. The dependent variable is in percentage rate terms, and needs no units conversion. The logarithmic versions of the independent variables are applied to those variables expressed as percentages of GDP, and so do not

---

result is growth contribution of approximately zero.

39. Haveman, Lei, and Netz (2001, table 2, equation 10).

40. Carkovic and Levine (2005, table 8.5, equation 6, OLS).

raise the problem of negativity of the logarithm of a fraction. The resulting specification is $g = -1.587\ FX_2 + 0.621\ FX_2\ FV_2$, where FX_2 is the logarithm of FDI inflows as a percent of GDP and FV_2 is the logarithm of private credit as a percent of GDP.

The sixth FDI model, also for developing countries only, is that of Blonigan and Wang (2005). Its growth variable is a pure number, so the study's coefficients must be multiplied by 100 for normalization. The model has the same format as that of Borensztein, De Gregorio, and Lee (1998), with a negative coefficient on the ratio of FDI to GDP alone but a positive coefficient on the product of this variable with the variable for education. The contribution of direct investment to growth is thus $g = -215.2\ FX_1 + 283.6\ FX_1\ FV_1$. The model has the same structure as that of Borensztein, De Gregorio, and Lee (1998), but the ratio of its coefficient on the interaction term to the coefficient on direct investment alone is smaller. This difference removes the problem of implausibly high estimates for more recent periods with higher educational levels.[41] However, it introduces another upward bias from the standpoint that both FDI ratios and educational levels reached much higher levels in the 1990s and early 2000s than observed in the estimation period, 1970–89. Unconstrained application of the function thus yields extreme values in some cases.[42] Once again the problem is addressed by imposing a limit based on high value extremes in the observation period. This turns out to be a ceiling of 4 percent per year growth impact, the level identified at the 97th percentile of the distribution when the model parameters are applied to the developing countries considered in the period 1970–89.

The seventh FDI model is that of Lensink and Morrissey (2006). It applies to both industrial and developing economies. The model relates growth to direct investment inflows as a percent of GDP and to the volatility of FDI as a percent of GDP. The coefficients are 1.46 on the FDI/GDP percent and −1.67 on volatility.[43] In their sample, for both the medians and the means, the volatility measure is 0.43 times the FDI-as-a-percent-of-GDP variable. So the formulation can be seen as shrinking the growth benefits of FDI by this proportion when considering the contribution from FDI. On this basis, an adjusted coefficient on the FDI-as-a-percent-of-GDP variable (and omitting a separate variable for volatility) is 0.83 (= 1.46 x [1 − 0.42]). Normalizing to adjust for the fact that the FDI variable is in percentage rather than pure number form in the study, the growth impact from the model becomes $g = 83\ FX_1$.

The eighth and final model considered for the impact of FDI on growth

---

41. This ratio is 1.9 in Borensztein, De Gregorio, and Lee (1998) and 1.3 in Blonigan and Wang (2005).

42. For example, 25 percent growth contribution in Chile in 2004.

43. Lensink and Morrissey (2006, 485, equation 3.3).

is that estimated in the IMF staff report (IMF 2007a). That study finds that an increase in the stock of FDI by 10 percent of GDP boosts the growth rate by 0.3 percentage point annually. (This is the only model in the group considered here that works with the stock rather than flow of FDI.) The stock variable used here is in ratio (pure number) rather than percent form, so normalization of the coefficient yields $g = 3\ FX_3$.

Appendix 3B
Temporary versus Permanent Growth Acceleration in the Henry Model

The main text of this chapter considers the theoretical expectation of financial openness on growth, identifying two components: capital deepening and increased TFP growth. The benchmarks suggested are based on stylized-fact levels for robust capital/inflow and capital/output ratios, as well as specific estimates of a recent study for TFP growth effects. They place the potential capital-deepening contribution from financial openness at around 1 percent per year and the TFP growth contribution at about one-third of a percent. There is no time limit to these rates, which by implication are permanent increments.

In contrast, Henry (2007) argues that financial opening should generate a temporary burst of increased growth but that after the first five years or so, the increment in the growth rate should have largely died out. His analysis is based on a steady-state formulation of the capital-deepening effect, and explicitly omits any ongoing TFP growth effect. The framework of steady-state growth inherently leads to the notion of a temporary boost to the growth rate from financial opening, followed by a gradual convergence back to the steady-state growth rate (Mankiw, Romer, and Weil 1992). This appendix reviews the Henry formulation of this question and considers its relationship to that in the main text.

Henry also uses the Cobb-Douglas production function (as in equation 3.2) but includes labor-augmenting technical progress by multiplying raw labor, L, by a technical change efficiency coefficient A, to obtain:

$$Y = K^{\alpha}(AL)^{1-\alpha},$$ (3C.1)

where Y is output. Defining $k = K/(AL)$ as the amount of capital per unit of "effective" labor and $y = Y/(AL)$ as the amount of output per unit of effective labor yields:

$$y = f(k) = k^{\alpha}.$$ (3C.2)

In the steady-state growth literature, a country's capital per effective worker rises until it reaches a constant level. At this level, capital per (raw) worker, and production per (raw) worker, continues to grow but only at the rate at which the technical efficiency parameter A grows. Capital per unit of effective labor rises as a consequence of saving (at rate s) but erodes at the pace of depreciation (at rate δ), the rate of raw labor force growth (n), and the rate of labor-augmenting technical change ($\dot{A}/A$, or g in Henry's notation, again with the overdot indicating change). Capital per unit of effective labor at time t thus rises at:

$$\dot{k} = sf(k_t) - (n + g + \delta)k_t,$$ (3C.3)

where the overdot indicates (absolute) change.

At the steady state, the marginal product of capital equals the interest rate plus the depreciation rate:

$$f'(k_{ss}) = r + \delta, \tag{3C.4}$$

where subscript ss indicates the steady state. Equation 3C.4 applies to the developing economy in autarky. Financial liberalization allows the economy to obtain capital at a cheaper international interest rate, r^*, so it will proceed to deepen its ratio of capital to effective labor until it reaches the higher international steady-state ratio,

$$f'(k_{ss}^*) = r^* + \delta. \tag{3C.5}$$

The steady-state growth literature in principle implies an immediate surge in capital per worker to the international level. In practice, there is some period of transition from the autarkic steady state to the financially integrated steady state. Once this transition is accomplished, growth of output per raw labor will return to its original autarkic pace, g, the rate of labor-augmenting technical change. In the interim, however, the growth rate will rise because of the transition to a higher capital/labor ratio. This is why Henry emphasizes that the theoretical expectation should be that observed increases in growth rates from financial opening should be temporary, over a few years, rather than permanent, over several decades.

Henry specifies the rate of growth of output per unit of raw labor during the transition as follows:

$$\gamma_{\frac{Y}{L}} = \alpha \frac{\dot{k}_t}{k_t} + \frac{\dot{A}}{A}. \tag{3C.6}$$

This formulation follows from the fact that the proportionate change in output in the Cobb-Douglas production function equals the proportionate change in capital multiplied by the elasticity of output with respect to capital, which is the exponent α. Equation 3C.6 in fact nicely reveals the approach of the main text by separating the growth contribution into a capital-deepening effect (the first term) and an effect capturing the boost to TFP growth—which would be an *increment* to the final right-hand side of Henry's equation if he considered this effect. Instead, the final term $(\dot{A}/A)$ is the unchanged rate of labor-augmenting technical change, assumed in Henry's formulation to be the same under autarky and financial integration.

Henry then uses an exponential decay function to describe how rapidly the buildup in capital per unit of effective labor occurs; in other words, how soon the change in this ratio reaches zero because the ratio itself has reached the international steady-state level. Thus:

$$k_t = k_{ss}^* + (k_{ss} - k_{ss}^*)e^{-\lambda t}, \qquad (3C.7)$$

where, λ, the parameter for the "speed of convergence," or the term in the exponential decay function for the difference between autarkic and international steady-state capital per effective worker, turns out to be:

$$\lambda = (1-\alpha)(n+g+\delta). \qquad (3C.8)$$

Mankiw, Romer, and Weil (1992, 422) give the same formulation of λ. They use a central estimate of $n + g + \delta = 0.06$, based on labor-augmenting technical change at about 2 percent, depreciation at 3 percent, and population growth at 1 percent (pp. 413–14). They note that in the simple two-factor Cobb-Douglas production function, with capital share at $\alpha = \frac{1}{3}$, the result is that $\lambda = 0.04$. This value means that the difference between the initial and steady-state income per effective unit of labor falls by 4 percent per year and thus declines by half over 17 years. But they prefer a production function in which human capital is a separate factor, and the first right-hand side of equation 3C.8 becomes $(1 - \alpha - \beta)$, where β is the elasticity of output with respect to human capital. Using $\alpha = \beta = \frac{1}{3}$, their resulting preferred value is $\lambda = 0.02$, which means that "the economy moves halfway to steady state in about 35 years" (p. 423).

Henry (2007) notes that this early work placing the convergence rate at about 2 percent was challenged on methodological grounds by Caselli, Esquivel, and Lefort (1996), who found instead that the rate was about 10 percent. However, the crux of Henry's (2007, 899) argument is that using either end of this range, growth will surge early in the horizon, but "there is no statistically detectable impact of liberalization on growth over long horizons." Returning to his model, he suggests that the world interest rate is 8 percent ($r^* = 0.08$) and the autarkic interest rate is twice as high ($r = 0.16$). He assumes the depreciation rate is $\delta = 0.04$. From equations 3C.4 and 3C.5, it can be derived that the steady-state ratio of capital to unit of effective labor is $k_{ss}^* = 4.63$ internationally and $k_{ss} = 2.15$ in autarky.[44]

Henry then argues that with these parameters, and using equation 3C.7, the average growth rate of k_t will be 3.8 percent per year in the first five years. He then multiplies this growth rate by the elasticity of output with respect to capital, $\alpha = \frac{1}{3}$, to get the resulting "average deviation of the growth rate of output per worker from its long-run steady-state value" in the first five years, or 1.27 percent per year (p. 899). But because of the

---

44. From equation 3C.4, the marginal product of capital per effective unit of labor is $f'(k_{ss}) = \alpha k_{ss}^{(\alpha-1)} = (r + \delta)$. Solving: $k_{ss} = [(r + \delta)/\alpha]^{1/(\alpha-1)}$. With $\alpha = \frac{1}{3}$, and $\delta = 0.04$, this equation yields $k_{ss} = 2.15$ for $r = 0.16$, and $k_{ss}^* = 4.63$ for $r^* = 0.08$.

slowdown in incremental growth as the economy converges to the international steady state, average growth in capital per effective worker in years 6 through 30 is only 1.5 percent per year. Applying the elasticity of output with respect to capital, this means the increment in growth associated with capital deepening from convergence slows down to 0.51 percent per year. At this point, Henry invokes typical standard errors encountered in regressions of growth on a variable for the share of years with open capital markets. He argues that these standard errors are relatively large compared with an increment of 0.51 percent per year, so that statistical tests would fail to identify the increment as significant, even though the increment was truly present.

What is the right way to think about the Henry proposition that it is a short-term rather than long-term increase in growth that should be expected from theory? First, the proposition is somewhat misleading because in the end Henry rests his case on the view that the amount of the noise in the data will make it impossible to distinguish the growth increment in the long term. This argument is quite different from the idea that theory says there is no difference at all in the long term. That would be true but of questionable relevance; the steady state never really arrives and is an infinite horizon.

Second, comparison of the first five years against the rate for the subsequent 25 years is somewhat of a straw man. Using Henry's parameters, the average growth rate increment for the first five years is 1.27 percent. The rate remains relatively high at successive horizons when stated from the initial year: 1.1 percent for the first decade, 0.9 percent for the first 15 years, 0.8 percent for the first 20 years, and 0.7 percent for the first 30 years. Most empirical estimates span one to three decades and do not tend to consider short initial periods (such as the first five years) after a liberalization separately from the full horizon.

Third, the Mankiw, Romer, and Weil (1992) convergence rate of 2 instead of 4 percent would reduce the force of Henry's deceleration argument. Thus, the average growth rate falls from 0.7 percent in the first five years to 0.6 percent in the first 10 years and 0.5 percent in the first 20 years, less deceleration than with the higher convergence rate. Henry cites the Caselli, Esquivel, and Lefort (1996) estimate of a much higher convergence rate and calls 4 percent convergence intermediate. But the Caselli, Esquivel, and Lefort estimate is based on a particular econometric estimate instead of parameters calibrated from theoretical benchmark levels, so it may not warrant the same weight as the Mankiw, Romer, and Weil rate.

Fourth, the Henry model rules out an increase in growth from a permanent increase in the rate of TFP growth.

Overall, it seems reasonable to treat the Henry critique as a useful reminder that there may be some upward bias if incremental growth from financial opening is measured based on experience in just the first few years. However, the critique is not a convincing refutation of the idea that growth increments on the order of 1 percent from full financial opening could persist for horizons of two or three decades, as just illustrated using Henry's own parameters. Yet this is the range found in chapter 2 and in this chapter.

Essentially, Henry starts with a stylized fact that the statistical literature does not find growth gains from financial openness and seeks to counter that fact by appealing to a theoretical expectation that the growth effects should be strongly front-end loaded and hence will be missed in tests on long-term data where the impact is modest relative to data noise. In contrast, the present study argues that many of the econometric findings of "no impact" should be ignored because their coefficients are not significant and that when attention is focused on the statistically significant results, the empirical literature does indeed identify a sizable positive growth impact. This appendix shows that the results of the subset of studies with meaningful results are consistent with the theoretical expectations that Henry proposes, especially if increased TFP growth is added to expected effects.

Appendix 3C
Degree of Correlation among Alternative Measures of Financial Openness

The eight alternative measures of general financial openness and the three measures of openness to FDI presented in table 3.2 do not necessarily present the same diagnoses of the extent of openness. In particular, countries identified as relatively closed by de jure measures may in practice have relatively high degrees of financial integration and hence high de facto measures of openness. This appendix considers patterns of similarities and differences among the alternative measures.

Among the eight general openness variables in table 3.2, two are de jure: the Quinn openness variable (X_1) and the IMF's indicator of capital account openness (X_6). Of the nine de facto measures, there are two that are for gross inflows and outflows: gross capital flows of all types relative to GDP (X_2), and gross flows of direct and portfolio investment relative to GDP (X_4). The other six variables are all for capital inflows: net capital flows relative to GDP (X_3); FDI and portfolio inflows relative to GDP (X_5); total capital inflows relative to GDP $(X_8$, which includes bank flows); direct investment inflows relative to GDP (FX_1); the logarithm of direct investment inflows as a percent of GDP (FX_2); and the stock of direct investment liabilities relative to GDP (FX_3). Finally, one de facto measure, X_7, is a binary variable set at zero before liberalization and unity after, with the liberalization year identified by cumulative inflows above a given threshold or by a surge from trend.

Table 3C.1 reports the rankings of the 24 developing economies considered in this chapter, from 1 for the most financially closed to 24 for the most open, for the final decade considered. Where a number of countries are tied, they are all given the midpoint ranking of their group (e.g., Peru, Hong Kong, and Argentina are tied at most open under X_1, Quinn openness, and are all given a rank of 23). The countries are shown in order of most to least open based on the average across all 11 measures. On this basis, Hungary, Singapore, Hong Kong, Chile, and Peru turn out to be the most open; Algeria, Pakistan, Indonesia, India, and Turkey are the most closed. Chile is a good example of a country ranking highly on de facto openness but poorly on de jure (again consider X_1, Quinn openness, on which it ranks 10th from the bottom). China is a notable surprise because it emerges in the middle of the upper quintile on openness, despite its extremely low ranking on de jure openness (X_1). This outcome reflects its higher ranking on actual flows, especially inflows of FDI (the FX series). China also illustrates another pattern: It has relatively high openness based on inward FDI (ranking 20th) but a more intermediate ranking on the basis of gross inflows and outflows (from 16th to 13th on X_2 and X_4). This difference reflects openness to FDI inflows in particular but closedness with respect to the general ability of residents to send capital abroad.

Table 3C.2 reports the correlation coefficients between the various pairs of openness measures for 24 developing countries in 1995–2004. Those combinations that are statistically significant at the 5 percent level or better, as measured by the Spearman rank correlation coefficient, are indicated with asterisks.

The two de jure indicators are relatively closely correlated with each other but not with the other measures: the Quinn measure (X_1) and the IMF measure (X_6). Their correlation coefficient is 0.5, significant at the 5 percent level. This similarity is no surprise, as the Quinn estimate is based on the IMF capital account surveys. Among the de facto variables, there is relatively high and, usually, significant correlation among pairs of seven measures: $X_2, X_4, X_5, X_8, FX_1, FX_2$, and FX_3. The Tornell, Westermann, and Martinez measure (X_7) is unique in that it shows little correlation with any of the other indicators. This difference reflects the fact that it is always either "on" (after liberalization) or "off" (before), so that it does not capture variations in capital flow levels across years in which liberalization has already occurred.

Table 3C.2 also reports the rank correlation coefficients between each of the openness variables and the ranking of countries by the overall average of these variables. Once again it is variables $X_2, X_4, X_5, X_8, FX_1, FX_2$, and FX_3 that show high and significant correlation with the overall average, and X_7 that shows the lowest overall correlation with the average ranking. It is reassuring that of the seven closely correlated de facto variables, two of them $(X_2$ and $X_4)$ are for gross flows, suggesting that the other five based on inflows (two general, X_5 and X_8, and three FDI—FX_1, FX_2, and $FX_3)$ tend to be associated with general openness and not solely one-way and one-type flows (inward direct investment).

The measure least correlated with the other alternative openness indicators is X_3, the ratio of net capital flows to GDP. The most extreme divergence for this measure occurs for the cases of Singapore and Hong Kong. Both economies rank toward the extreme high end for financial openness on the other measures, but by the net capital flow measure they are located toward the extreme low end. This divergence stems from the fact that this is the only variable measured on a net basis. Because these two economies have sustained high current account surpluses, they have large negative net capital flows. Their situation illustrates the inherent problem with this measure. The only model that uses X_3 is that of Bailliu (2000), and this model applies only to developing countries. So the distortion from treating net inflows as a measure of financial openness only arises for those developing economies that were in the position of exporting capital "uphill" (i.e., to some industrial countries). Although current account surpluses were more frequent among emerging-market economies in 2000–04, for most of the rest of the three-decade period examined in this study there were few emerging-market economies other than Singapore and Hong Kong that had persistent surpluses.

Figure 3C.1   Financial openness rankings on de jure versus de facto measures for 24 developing countries, 1995–2004

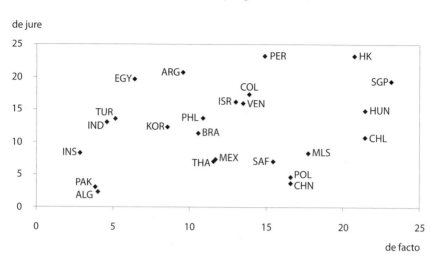

Note: Rankings are from 1 for most closed to 24 for most open. For country abbreviations, see figure 1C.1.

Source: Author's calculations.

Figure 3C.1 shows the results of ranking the 24 developing countries by financial openness under two broad criteria: de jure and de facto. For de jure, the Quinn measure (X_1) is given a weight of two-thirds, and the ARE-AER measure (X_6), a weight of one-third. For de facto, the seven leading variables just mentioned are all weighted equally. It is clear from the broadly upward sloping pattern in the scatter diagram that there is some correlation between the two approaches. It is also clear, however, that there are important cases of relative closedness on one criterion in contrast to relative openness on the other. Again China serves as an important example, with a rank of only 3.7 on de jure openness but a rank of 17 on de facto openness.

Overall, the correlations of the openness variables as a group are moderate, and in particular there is a tendency toward a different perspective depending on whether the measure is de jure or de facto.

Finally, table 3C.3 reports the correlation coefficients for the financial-openness variables for the 21 industrial countries examined in this chapter. There is no entry for X_7, because by this period all of the industrial countries had liberalized capital flows and all showed a value of 1 on the Tornell, Westermann, and Martinez measure, providing no basis for differentiation to establish a ranking. The patterns in the table are broadly similar to those in table 3C.2 for developing counties, with an important exception. The variable that is specified on the basis of net flows, X_3, systematically shows negative correlation with the other variables. This result reflects the fact that for industrial countries, it is to be expected that net capital flows are negative, as capital flows from richer to poorer countries.

Table 3C.1 Rankings of 24 developing economies on alternative measures of financial openness, 1995–2004

Country	X_1	X_2	X_3	X_4	X_5	X_6	X_7	X_8	FX_1	FX_2	FX_3	Average
HUN	13	22	24	21	20	18.5	14.5	23	22	22	20	20
SGP	21	24	2	23	21	16	14.5	24	23	24	23	19.6
HK	23	21	3	24	22	23.5	14.5	7	24	23	24	19
CHL	10	23	18	22	19	12	14.5	22	21	21	22	18.6
PER	23	11	22	15	13	23.5	14.5	16	16	16	17	17
MLS	6.5	20	10	16	12	12	14.5	18	19	18	21	15.2
COL	20	15	19	18	15	12	14.5	15	11	13	10	14.8
CHN	3	16	17	13	14	5	14.5	14	20	20	19	14.1
SAF	4.5	19	14	20	18	12	14.5	21	8	8	14	13.9
POL	4.5	14	23	17	17	5	3	20	18	19	11	13.8
ISR	15	18	11	19	8	18.5	14.5	19	10	10	7	13.6
PHL	18	12	21	12	9	5	14.5	17	9	9	8	12.2
VEN	14	17	4	10		20	3	8	14	14	18	12.2
MEX	8.5	8	20	8	10	5	14.5	12	15	17	12	11.8
BRA	9	9	15	9	11	16	14.5	11	13	12	9	11.7
ARG	23	10	6	7	5	16	14.5	6	12	11	16	11.5
THA	8	4	7	11	16	5	14.5	3	17	15	15	10.5
KOR	16	13	13	14	7	5	14.5	13	6	5	2	9.9
EGY	19	5	5	5	3	21	14.5	5	7	7	13	9.5
TUR	8.5	7	12	6	6	23.5	14.5	9	3	2	3	8.6
IND	17	6	16	4	4	5	3	10	4	3	1	6.6
INS	6.5	2	8	2	1	12	14.5	2	2	6	5	5.5
PAK	2	3	9	3	2	5	14.5	4	5	4	6	5.2
ALG	1					5	1				4	2.8

Note: Rankings are from 1 for most closed to 24 for most open. For variables, see table 3.2. For country abbreviations, see figure 1C.1.

Source: Author's calculations.

Table 3C.2 Rank correlation coefficients for alternative measures of financial openness for 24 developing economies, 1995–2004

	X_1	X_2	X_3	X_4	X_5	X_6	X_7	X_8	FX_1	FX_2	FX_3
X_1	1										
X_2	0.2	1									
X_3	−0.15	0.16	1								
X_4	0.24	0.94*	0.15	1							
X_5	0.1	0.79*	0.21	0.89*	1						
X_6	0.52*	0.24	−0.26	0.27	0.14	1					
X_7	0.11	0.12	−0.30	0.12	0.05	0.36	1				
X_8	0.05	0.84*	0.48*	0.77*	0.64*	0.06	−0.07	1			
FX_1	0.16	0.72*	0.1	0.74*	0.85*	0.16	0.1	0.50*	1		
FX_2	0.14	0.71*	0.14	0.73*	0.84*	0.14	0.1	0.53*	0.98*	1	
FX_3	0.2	0.66*	−0.12	0.65*	0.75*	0.32	0.3	0.39	0.89*	0.87*	1
Average	0.28	0.90*	0.27	0.91*	0.88*	0.32	0.17	0.76*	0.86*	0.87*	0.81*

Note: Asterisk indicates significance at the 5 percent level or more.

Source: Author's calculations.

Table 3C.3 Rank correlation coefficients for alternative measures of financial openness for 21 developed economies, 1995–2004

	X₁	X₂	X₃	X₄	X₅	X₆	X₇	X₈	FX₁	FX₂	FX₃	Average
X₁	1											
X₂	0.23	1										
X₃	−0.38	−0.44*	1									
X₄	0.28	.94*	−0.53*	1								
X₅	−0.04	0.59*	−0.05	.63*	1							
X₆	.46*	0.37	−0.20	0.37	0.19	1						
X₇							1					
X₈	0.12	.95*	−0.26	.91*	.68*	0.27		1				
FX₁	0.23	0.75*	−0.38	.79*	.51*	0.36		.74*	1			
FX₂	0.15	.68*	−0.29	.72*	.50*	0.38		.69*	.97*	1		
FX₃	0.06	.59*	−0.20	.60*	.49*	0.25		.61*	.85*	.90*	1	
Average	0.22	.86*	−0.31	.88*	.67*	.46*		.89*	.93*	.90*	.78*	1

Note: Asterisk indicates significance at the 5 percent level or more.

Source: Author's calculations.

4

The Financial Crisis of 2007–09 and Financial Globalization

The literature survey in chapter 2 and the synthesis estimates of chapter 3 suggest that over recent decades, rising financial openness in most countries has been beneficial for global economic growth. As this study was being completed, however, the most severe international financial crisis since the Great Depression struck first the United States and then Europe, with adverse spillover effects in emerging-market economies and Japan. The principal objective of this chapter is to consider whether policy guidelines on the merits of, and approaches to, financial globalization should have changed in light of this experience. The chapter begins with a summary overview of the evolution of the crisis and the outlook as of late 2009.[1] The discussion briefly considers the main alternative hypotheses on the origins of the crisis. (More detailed descriptions and diagnoses are presented in appendix 4A on crisis events and policy responses and in appendix 4B on the origins of the crisis.)

The discussion then turns to the initial evidence on whether more financially open emerging-market economies have fared worse in the international crisis than those that are more closed, followed by an examination of the policy implications that should be drawn. Appendix 4C reproduces several of the author's contemporaneous website postings analyzing key aspects of the crisis during its most intense phase. Appendix 4D examines the Private-Public Investment Program for providing market liquidity for troubled assets held by the banks. Appendix 4E presents calculations ex-

---

1. The analysis draws in part on William R. Cline, "The Global Financial Crisis and Development Strategy for Emerging-Market Economies," speech to the Annual Bank Conference on Development Economics, World Bank, Seoul, South Korea, June 23, 2009, available at www.piie.com (accessed on January 4, 2010).

amining the World Bank's mid-2009 estimates of the financing gap facing emerging-market economies.

The crisis of 2007–09 has already spawned several important analyses, including Barth (2009), Brunnermeier (2009), Caprio, Demirgüç-Kunt, and Kane (2008), Fox (2009), Gorton (2008), Wessel (2009), and Zandi (2009). Proposals for policy change to avert future crises, especially in the regulatory area, have also been advanced (e.g., Goldstein 2008, US Treasury 2009) and in some regards are already being implemented (e.g., in US Federal Reserve guidelines on prudential incentive structures in the compensation practices of large financial firms). As of late 2009, legislative proposals were under consideration on such key issues as "resolution authority" to deal expeditiously with near-bankruptcy situations at large financial firms, increasing capital requirements, and reforming supervisory structures. Even potentially radical steps such as breaking up institutions deemed "too large to fail" and/or reversing the 1999 legislation (Gramm-Leach-Bliley) that repealed Depression-era rules separating commercial and investment banking (Glass-Steagall) were being endorsed by leading authorities such as Bank of England Governor Mervyn King and former US Federal Reserve Chairmen Paul Volcker and Alan Greenspan.[2]

This chapter does not address these important questions concerning future reforms but instead seeks to provide a succinct review of the evolution and causes of the crisis and its principal implications for financial globalization. A key issue is whether the emerging-market economies should retreat from financial openness in order to protect themselves from possible future international financial crises. Ironically, one of the first such responses was Brazil's decision in October 2009 to reinstate a modest tax on capital inflows, which had begun to resume as international risk aversion had eased, causing the currency to appreciate. Rather than the feared "financing gap" predicted by many (including official entities), the problem facing many emerging-market economies was once again a possible embarrassment of riches.[3]

Evolution

The downturn in the US housing market, the seizing up of the market for subprime mortgages and mortgage-backed securities (MBS), and an ensuing credit crunch by mid-2007 set the stage for the ensuing global

---

2. Jill Treanor, "King Calls for Banks to be Cut Down to Size," *Guardian*, June 17, 2009; *Wall Street Journal*, "Too Big to Ignore," September 26, 2009; Michael McKee and Scott Lanman, "Greenspan Says U.S. Should Consider Breaking Up Large Banks," Bloomberg.com, October 15, 2009.

3. "What India Can Learn from Brazil about Controlling Capital Flows," *Economist*, October 29, 2009.

financial crisis that reached an acute phase in October 2008 and remained severe through March 2009. In the second quarter of 2009 some degree of stability began to return, as increased confidence in banks following the Federal Reserve's "stress test" set the stage for a rally in US and global equity markets. In the real economy, however, the most widespread global recession since the 1930s was in progress.

The early landmarks of the evolving crisis included deep cuts in the US federal funds interest rate; introduction of the Term Auction Facility at the Federal Reserve in late 2007; nationalization of UK bank Northern Rock in early 2008; the forced takeover of investment bank Bear Stearns in March 2008; and creation of the Primary Dealers' Credit Facility at the Federal Reserve in March. After an interlude of relative calm, in September 2008 the acute phase of the crisis began with the placement of Fannie Mae and Freddie Mac in government conservatorship and, within a week, the bankruptcy of Lehman Brothers and effective government takeover of insurance giant AIG. Immediate fallout included the takeover of investment firm Merrill Lynch by Bank of America, conversion of investment banks Goldman Sachs and Morgan Stanley to bank holding company status for purposes of access to Federal Reserve support, and takeover of failing banks Washington Mutual by JP Morgan Chase and Wachovia by Wells Fargo.

At this point the US-led crisis spread aggressively to Europe and then the emerging-market economies. The Federal Reserve sharply expanded swap lines to European central banks at the end of September, as emergency programs were mobilized for European banks Dexia, Fortis, and Hypo Real Estate, and as the banking system of Iceland went into virtual collapse. At the beginning of October, Congress first rejected and then (after severe market turmoil) passed the US Treasury's $700 billion Troubled Asset Relief Program (TARP). The US Federal Deposit Insurance Corporation (FDIC) raised deposit insurance coverage from $100,000 to $250,000 per account, and the G-7 and the IMF called for international coordination in fighting the financial crisis.

The UK government then led the way to bank recapitalization with large purchases of preferred shares and suspension of dividends. Within a week other European governments followed suit, and the United States earmarked $250 billion of the TARP for similar bank recapitalization but on a voluntary basis. The Federal Reserve also announced it would guarantee new debt incurred by banks. Equity markets served as a sensitive barometer of the growing financial panic, as well as of the increasing likelihood of severe recession. In the United States, stock prices had fallen about 20 percent from the beginning of 2008 to late September but then plunged an additional 25 percent by late October. Declines in equity markets abroad were even greater. From end-2007 to end-2008, US equities fell 38.5 percent (measured by the S&P 500). They then fell another 25.1 percent by March 9, 2009, before approximately returning to their end-2008 level by mid-year and rising about 15 percent by end-October, 2009.[4]

Causes

Appendix 4B considers in detail several alternative, or complementary, possible causes of the crisis. They include the housing bubble, the special role of residential mortgage-backed securities (RMBS), excessive leverage in major financial institutions, the effects of financial innovation, regulatory laxity, "agency" problems (perverse incentives of intermediaries) and underpricing of risk, misleading risk models, excessive monetary ease in 2002–05, and a global saving glut.

The most important cause of the crisis was surely the decline in housing prices following a long period of increases that had become an asset bubble. From the beginning of 2000 to their peaks in the second quarter of 2007 (US Federal Housing Finance Agency, FHFA, index) or in July 2006 (Case-Shiller index), housing prices rose by a range of 70 to 106 percent, respectively. From the peaks to 2009 levels, they then fell by a range of 14 percent (FHFA for May) to 33 percent (Case-Shiller for April, followed by a rebound of 5 percent by August). The resulting swing from a positive to negative wealth effect, along with the effect on the construction sector, would inevitably have a severe impact on the US economy and financial institutions holding mortgage claims. The collapse in prices came as a shock because most economists had read the postwar record of housing prices to mean that serious price corrections were confined to geographical regions. For the nation as a whole, the market was generally interpreted to adjust by following a period of sustained increases with a prolonged period of flat, but not declining, prices.

However, it was the combination of the housing market trends with a pervasive financial product—RMBS based on securitization of subprime mortgage loans—that turned a potentially severe recessionary pressure into a financial panic and threat to the banking system. The subprime loan itself was premised on rising housing prices; otherwise the marginally creditworthy borrowers would be unable to build equity validating the initially high leverage of the loan. Securitization bundled these mortgages into queued risk tranches in a financial alchemy that transformed 80 percent of the total into triple-A rated instruments. The agencies that provided these ratings have been criticized for conflict of interest, but their ratings were surely less bizarre seen from an ex ante perspective of ever-rising housing prices than they appear today with the benefit of hindsight.

---

4. The respective S&P 500 levels were as follows: end-2007, 1,468.36; end-2008, 903.25; March 9, 2009, 676.53; June 30, 2009, 919.32; and October 30, 2009, 1,036.19 (*Wall Street Journal*, online market data, available at http://online.wsj.com).

The systemic problem was that once the RMBS became suspect, as they did dramatically in early 2007 with the introduction of a widely followed (and widely traded) index (the ABX), investors faced uncertainty about which financial institutions were holding them and what the instruments were worth. This lack of information provoked what amounted to a classic bank panic (Gorton 2008, Brunnermeier 2009), in which banks (and the "shadow" banking sector) suddenly found themselves frozen out of normal short-term borrowing given investors' new doubts.

Financial engineering brought not only the RMBS but the credit default swap (CDS). This latter instrument turned out to have massive adverse consequences for the giant insurance firm AIG. The Financial Products Unit of AIG had accumulated large insurance obligations and was instrumental during 2004–05 in getting the RMBS market off the ground. Investment banks needed the asset insurance to reduce capital requirements, and AIG's status as an insurance company meant its corresponding capital requirements were less demanding. The forced intervention to support AIG likely helped prevent collapse of financial institutions around the world but has required US government exposure on the order of $200 billion.

Overall, one can think about the crisis as a key episode in the family of the "real business cycle." Usually a positive technological breakthrough stimulates investment and expansion, according to this school of thought (e.g., the steam engine, the internet). Much of the financial engineering of the early 2000s seems to have amounted to a major technological shock with negative rather than positive consequences for eventual growth.

Regulatory laxity also contributed to the crisis by permitting such distortions as the use of structured investment vehicles (SIVs) by banks to escape normal capital requirements, only to be forced to bring the assets of these entities back onto bank books for reputational purposes when the alternative was collapse of the entities. Regulation on subprime mortgage practices was, with the benefit of hindsight, also too lax, and overoptimistic that the new instruments were bringing home ownership to more marginal households rather than creating systemically dangerous assets. Gaps in regulation facilitated the emergence of what amounted to a huge hedge fund within insurance company AIG.

Monetary policy was probably too lax during 2003–05. The extremely low policy interest rate (federal funds rate) would certainly be the simplest overall explanation for the stoking of the housing bubble (as well as the run-up in commodity prices). In contrast, blaming the "global saving glut" ignores the fact that the 10-year treasury bond stood at about the same relationship to the federal funds rate in early 2007 as it had in early 2002. Market forces determine the 10-year rate, whereas the Federal Reserve controls the short-term federal funds rate. If an avalanche of foreign money were truly causing low long-term interest rates in the period 2004–07, then by 2007 the 10-year rate should have been much lower relative to the federal funds rate than it had been before the foreign surpluses ballooned. That being said, nonfinancial-sector net debt (i.e., that owed by households, corporations, and the federal and state and local governments) rose each year by about 17 percent of GDP during the period from 2003–07, at a time when the average US current account deficit stood at 4.5 percent of GDP. It can thus be argued that about one-third of the build-up in US debt was being financed by the foreign saving glut and therefore that it played at least a supporting role, if not the leading one, in the financial tragedy.

In short, the solution to the mystery of the financial crisis of 2007–09 is similar to that of the murder on the Orient Express: All of the suspects did it. Their collaboration had sufficient synergy to cause the worst financial crisis and global recession since the Great Depression.

Status by Late 2009

Financial-Sector Risk

By the second quarter of 2009 the acute phase of jeopardy to the financial system seemed largely to be over. The state of banking fragility is typically gauged by the size of the risk premium banks charge to lend to each other. This spread between the interbanking lending rate (LIBOR) and the risk-free overnight interest swap (OIS) rate peaked at 350 basis points in October 2008.[5] By early July the spread was back close to precrisis levels for one-month swaps, and only about one-tenth of the peak level for three-month swaps (figure 4.1). By the fourth quarter of 2009 both spreads were approximately back to their precrisis levels.

The aggressive action of the US Federal Reserve, Bank of England, and European Central Bank, as well as forceful intervention measures such as the US Treasury's purchase of preferred bank shares through the TARP, averted collapse of the banking system. In the United States, the stress test and subsequent repayment of TARP monies by several major banks marked a major step toward normalization.

The rebuilding of confidence in the major banking systems helped ease the increase in global risk aversion. For the emerging-market economies, the result was a substantial reduction in sovereign risk spreads, which had surged in the final quarter of 2008 (figure 4.2). The JP Morgan Emerging Markets Bond Index (global composite) showed sovereign spreads rising from about 200 basis points at the end of 2007 to a peak of 780 basis points in October 2008 and then declining to about 300 basis points by October

---

5. The OIS is a vehicle that enables one financial institution to swap an obligation at floating overnight rates with another institution holding a short-term fixed-rate obligation. In the United States, the federal funds rate is used in calculating the spread. A similar measure, the TED spread, instead shows the spread between LIBOR and the short-term treasury bill rate.

Figure 4.1 LIBOR–overnight index swap spread

basis points

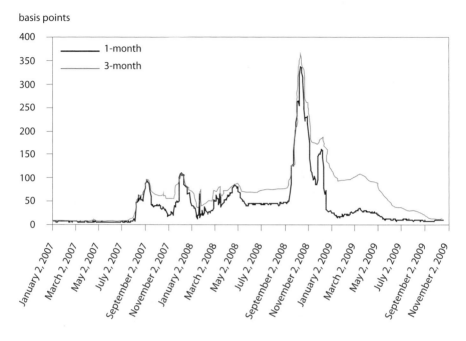

LIBOR = London Interbank Offered Rate

Sources: Reuters; BBA; Datastream.

2009. Even at their peak, the spreads did not reach the heights experienced in financial crises in the late 1990s (the East Asian and Russian crises) and in 2001–02 (in Argentina and pre-election Brazil).

Banking-Sector Recovery

In its *Global Financial Stability Report* of October 2009, the IMF estimated that total credit losses for banks in 2007–10 would amount to $1.02 trillion in the United States, $814 billion in the euro area, and $604 billion in the United Kingdom (IMF 2009d, 10).[6] Relative to total bank assets outstanding at the end of 2007, these losses amounted to 9.1 percent for the United States, 2.3 percent for the euro zone, and 5.2 percent for the United Kingdom.[7] By this measure, it might be said that the banking crisis had been about four times as severe in the United States as in the euro area and nearly twice as severe as in the United Kingdom. Even though banks con-

---

6. Excludes government-sponsored entities in the United States.

7. The IMF (2009d, 177) reported end-2007 total bank assets at $11.2 trillion in the United States, $35.1 trillion in the euro area, and $11.7 trillion in the United Kingdom.

**Figure 4.2   Emerging Markets Bond Index spreads, December 1997–
September 2009**

basis points

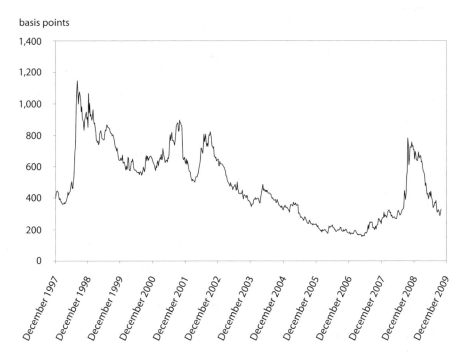

Sources: JP Morgan; Datastream.

stitute a smaller portion of total credit in the United States than in Europe,
these comparisons suggest that European growth performance in the
global recession was surprisingly negative relative to that of the United
States. Thus, as indicated in table 4.1, economic growth for 2009 is estimated to have amounted to –3.9 percent in the euro area and –4.6 percent
in the United Kingdom, in contrast to –2.5 percent in the United States.

The IMF (2009f, 15) estimated that at the end of the second quarter
of 2009, the amounts already written down by banks stood at $610 bil-
lion in the United States, $350 billion in the euro zone, and $260 billion in
the United Kingdom; the corresponding amounts of new capital raised to
confront the crisis amounted to $500 billion, $220 billion, and $160 billion,
respectively (IMF 2009f, 15). On this basis, US banks had already written
down about 60 percent of prospective credit losses, compared with about
43 percent in both UK and eurozone banks.[8] The IMF estimated that for

---

8. The IMF's mid-2009 diagnosis of relatively greater progress toward cleaning the balance
sheets in US banks than in euro area and UK banks is the reverse of the earlier view set forth
in Posen and Véron (2009).

Table 4.1   Real GDP growth in 34 major economies, 2007–10f

Country	GDP, 2008 (trillions of dollars)	Growth (percent) 2007	2008	2009e	2010f
Industrial	39.7	2.5	0.5	−3.4	1.8
Australia	1.01	4.0	2.4	0.7	2.6
Canada	1.51	2.7	0.4	−2.5	2.6
Euro area	13.6	2.7	0.8	−3.9	1.1
Japan	4.92	2.4	−0.7	−5.5	1.3
Norway	0.46	3.1	2.1	−1.2	1.3
Sweden	0.49	2.6	−0.2	−4.5	1.1
Switzerland	0.49	3.3	1.8	−2.5	0.4
United Kingdom	2.67	3.0	0.7	−4.6	1.3
United States	14.3	2.0	0.4	−2.5	2.7
Developing Asia	8.53	10.0	6.7	4.9	7.5
China	4.40	13.0	9.0	8.5	9.4
Hong Kong	0.22	6.4	2.4	−3.0	4.4
India	1.21	9.3	7.3	6.0	7.5
Indonesia	0.51	6.3	6.1	4.3	5.1
Korea	0.95	5.1	2.2	−0.5	5.0
Malaysia	0.22	6.3	4.6	−2.3	4.8
Philippines	0.17	7.2	3.8	1.5	3.4
Singapore	0.18	7.8	1.1	−3.3	5.4
Taiwan	0.39	5.7	0.1	−4.4	2.9
Thailand	0.27	4.9	2.6	−2.9	4.5
Latin America	3.72	5.6	3.9	−2.5	3.6
Argentina	0.33	8.7	6.8	−2.6	1.9
Brazil	1.57	5.7	5.1	0.0	4.5
Chile	0.17	4.7	3.2	−1.8	4.4
Colombia	0.24	7.5	2.5	0.1	2.6
Mexico	1.09	3.3	1.3	−6.9	3.6
Venezuela	0.32	8.4	4.8	−2.2	1.5
Developing Europe	3.31	6.6	4.0	−5.7	2.9
Czech Republic	0.22	6.0	2.7	−4.2	1.6
Hungary	0.16	1.1	0.6	−6.0	0.0
Poland	0.53	6.7	4.9	1.6	2.2
Russia	1.68	8.1	5.6	−8.1	3.2
Turkey	0.73	4.7	0.9	−5.8	3.6

(continued on next page)

Table 4.1   Real GDP growth in 34 major economies, 2007–10f *(continued)*

Country	GDP, 2008 (trillions of dollars)	Growth (percent)			
		2007	2008	2009e	2010f
Middle East, South Africa	0.96	4.4	4.0	−0.7	3.0
Israel	0.20	5.4	4.0	0.5	3.5
Saudi Arabia	0.48	3.5	4.4	−0.5	3.0
South Africa	0.28	5.1	3.1	−1.8	2.6
34 economies	56.1	4.1	2.0	−2.2	2.9
Rest of world	4.60	—	—	—	—

e = estimate; f = forecast

Sources: IMF (2010); World Bank (2010); Blue Chip (2010); Deutsche Bank (2010); Consensus (2010).

the second half of 2009 and the full year 2010, expected retained earnings would not fully cover expected writedowns (at $310 billion versus $420 billion, respectively, in the United States; $360 billion versus $470 billion in euro area banks; and $110 billion versus $140 billion in UK banks). It correspondingly estimated that in order to meet a relatively demanding capital criterion of 4 percent tangible common equity relative to total assets, US banks would need to raise an additional $130 billion in capital; euro area banks, $310 billion; and UK banks, $120 billion.[9]

The US banks seemed to be recovering by the second quarter of 2009, at least as gauged by the Federal Reserve's "stress test" of 19 large banks with assets of $100 billion or more each. In late February 2009, the Federal Reserve began its Supervisory Capital Assessment Program (SCAP) examining these banks (US Federal Reserve 2009a). The test examined likely losses under macroeconomic conditions considered considerably more pessimistic than baseline forecasts. Real economic growth was set at −3.3 percent in 2009 and 0.5 percent in 2010, versus the then-consensus baseline of −2 and + 2.1 percent, respectively. Unemployment was set at 8.9 percent in 2009 and 10.3 percent in 2010, versus the baseline of 8.4 and 8.8 percent, respectively. Housing prices were premised to decline 22 percent in 2009 and 7 percent in 2010, versus the baseline declines of 14 and 4 percent, respectively. By January 2010 the prospective baseline was somewhat worse on growth for 2009 (−2.5 percent) but better for 2010 (+2.7 percent; see table 4.1). The baseline was worse on unemployment (which stood at 10 percent in the fourth quarter of 2009 and 9.7 percent in January 2010; see Bureau of Labor Statistics 2010). Nonetheless, the test arguably remained meaningfully stressful.

---

9. Tangible capital equity excludes preferred shares. Whereas regulators in the past have primarily judged capital adequacy based on Tier 1 capital, which includes preferred shares, by early 2009 financial markets were focusing instead on tangible capital equity as the concept most indicative of value that would be left in the event of dissolution, thereby treating preferred shares as more similar to debt.

The exercise found that in the stress conditions, losses at the 19 large banks in 2009 and 2010 could reach $600 billion (US Federal Reserve 2009b). About three-fourths would come from "accrual loan portfolios," mainly residential mortgages and other consumer-related loans. Cumulative two-year losses would amount to 9.1 percent of total loans, which the Federal Reserve report emphasized would be "higher than during the historical peak loss years of the 1930s" (p. 3).[10] Prospective losses on securities amounted to $35 billion, of which half would be on MBS. This category of losses was surprisingly small in view of the MBS origins of the crisis, but the report noted that the banks held only $200 billion in nonagency MBS. In addition, losses of $100 billion were estimated (under stress) for trading-related exposures, including derivatives.

The losses would be in addition to the $350 billion in losses already recognized by the firms from mid-2007 through the end of 2008. The Federal Reserve noted that because end-2008 Tier 1 capital stood at $835 billion for the 19 firms, they already had sufficient capital to cover these adverse-case losses.[11] Nonetheless, the SCAP concluded that the banks needed an additional $185 billion in capital, primarily to reach 4 percent of assets in "Tier 1 common capital" (tangible capital equity). Because these banks had already taken some "capital actions" in the first four months of 2009, and after taking account of first-quarter profits, the remaining capital gap amounted to only $75 billion.[12]

The results of the SCAP indicated additional capital needs of $34 billion for Bank of America, $5.5 billion for Citigroup, $11.5 billion for GMAC, and $13.7 billion for Wells Fargo, in addition to smaller needs at six other institutions. In contrast, nine banks were found to need no additional capital, including the important cases of Goldman Sachs and JP Morgan.[13] By early June 2009, 10 large banks were cleared to exit from the

---

10. The average stress-case loss rates for the 19 banks were first lien mortgages, 8.8 percent; other lien mortgages, 13.8 percent; commercial and industrial loans, 6.1 percent; commercial real estate loans, 8.5 percent; and credit card loans, 22.5 percent. Losses on securities were placed at $35 billion, surprisingly low considering that this category included the infamous MBS.

11. Note that their Tier 1 common capital was $412 billion and their risk-weighted assets $7.8 trillion.

12. The SCAP identified additional losses under stress at $600 billion. It identified "resources other than capital" available at $363 billion, from "net revenue" over 2009–10. The difference of $237 billion was somewhat larger than the target it set for additional capital ($185 billion), apparently because the additional capital target was driven by a 4 percent goal for tangible capital equity rather than a concept of the gap between prospective losses and prospective earnings. Nonetheless, the two amounts (tangible capital equity gap and loss versus earnings gap) were broadly comparable.

13. The relatively small capital need for Citigroup reflected credit for equity capital already planned in the conversion of $25 billion of preferred shares held by the Treasury under TARP support, along with a comparable amount of privately held preferred shares to be converted.

TARP, repaying TARP funds and thereby graduating from the restrictions on executive salaries and other restraints of the program.[14] By late May, major US banks had already raised about $60 billion in additional capital following the release of the stress-test results.[15]

Global Recession

Despite signs of improved confidence and a seeming turnaround in the banking crisis, by the second quarter of 2009 the global financial crisis had precipitated a severe global recession. Weighting by market (rather than purchasing power parity) exchange rates for 34 major economies accounting for 92 percent of world output in 2008, real economic growth fell from 4.1 percent in 2007 to 2.0 percent in 2008 and an estimated –2.2 percent in 2009, but was expected to revive to 2.9 percent in 2010 (table 4.1).[16]

The closest analogue to the global recession of 2009 is that of 1982, when world output growth fell from 2.2 percent in 1981 to 0.9 percent before returning to 2.8 percent in 1983 and 4.6 percent in 1984 (IMF 2009b).[17] The 2009 recession is marked by a much more synchronous and widespread pattern of output reductions and is also considerably more severe for industrial countries as a group, but milder (if the projections prove accurate) for Latin America (figure 4.3, panels A and C). The present recession is also milder for the East Asian economies than was the regional crisis of 1998 (figure 4.3, panel B).[18] A crucial difference from 1982 is that high interest rates from the "Volcker shock" to confront high inflation were the cause of that recession, and the natural policy for prompting recovery was reducing interest rates to more moderate levels. In the present global recession, in contrast, financial crisis has precipitated the downturn, and short-term interest rates are already effectively zero. These circumstances approximate the classic Keynesian "liquidity trap," and it is perhaps no surprise under these conditions that aggressive fiscal stimulus has regained a prominent role after languishing for decades as an instrument

---

14. Eric Dash, "10 Large Banks Allowed to Exit U.S. Aid Program," *New York Times*, June 10, 2009.

15. See statement by Treasury Secretary Timothy F. Geithner to the US Senate Banking Committee, May 20, 2009.

16. The estimates are a simple average of two sets of official projections (IMF and World Bank) and two private-sector projections (Blue Chip and Deutsche Bank). For industrial countries not covered by Blue Chip, estimates are from Consensus Forecasts.

17. The IMF estimates use purchasing power parity GDP and hence give a greater weight to developing countries. Even so, for just the advanced economies the downturn was less concentrated in 1982 than in 2009, as growth fell from 1.8 percent in 1981 to a still (barely) positive 0.1 percent, before rebounding to 2.9 percent in 1983 (IMF 2009b).

18. The East Asian economies are Indonesia, Korea, Malaysia, Philippines, and Thailand.

Figure 4.3 Real economic growth in current and past recessions: Industrial countries, East Asia, and Latin America

a. Industrial countries

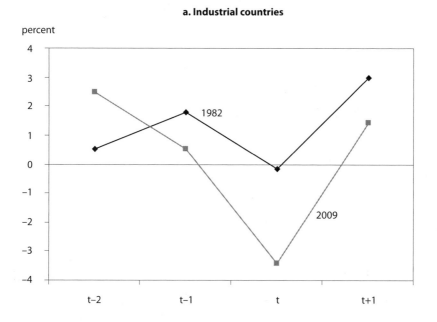

b. East Asia

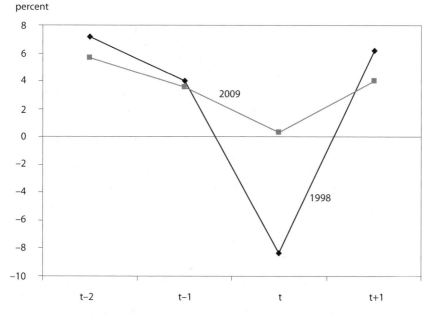

(continued on next page)

Figure 4.3   Real economic growth in current and past recessions: Industrial countries and Latin America, and East Asia *(continued)*

c. Latin America

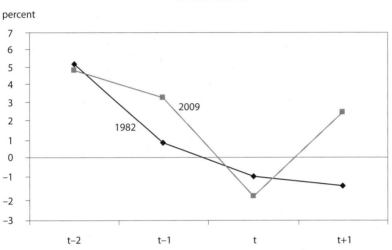

percent

Sources: IMF (2009g); World Bank (2010); Blue Chip (2010); Consensus (2010); Deutsche Bank (2010).

considered too slow and politically fraught to serve as an effective countercyclical tool, other than through automatic stabilizers.[19]

For the United States, the Great Recession is shaping up to be considerably more severe than the recession of 1982. Using real per capita GDP as the gauge, and based on consensus private forecasts, the comparison for four years after the prior peak is zero increase from 2007 to 2011 in contrast to 10.1 percent increase for 1981–85. The only episodes more severe were in the demobilization after World War II (a per capita output decline of 14.3 percent from 1944 to 1948) and the Great Depression (28.9 percent decline from 1929 to 1933).[20]

The global recession was marked by extreme declines in industrial production and trade. As shown in figure 4.4, for the export-oriented economies of Germany, Japan, Korea, and Singapore, exports (dollar values) fell by about 30 percent from the first quarter of 2008 to the first quarter of 2009. These economies all held large external reserves, so the explanation

---

19. Taylor (2009) argues that this judgment should remain intact because the temporary tax rebates of 2001 and 2008 had little detectable influence on consumption. In contrast, Krugman (2009) argues that the global economy is in the liquidity trap and that the US fiscal stimulus adopted in early 2009 was too small.

20. Calculated from BEA (2009), IMF (2008b), US Census Bureau (2000), and Blue Chip (2010).

Figure 4.4   Change in industrial production and exports, 2009Q1 from a year earlier, selected countries

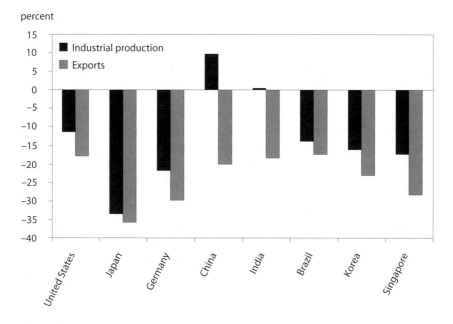

percent

Sources: The Economist, various issues; IMF (2009a).

is likely to lie in severe contraction of foreign demand rather than in a cut-off in trade finance. The severe declines in industrial production, coupled with the prominent role of international production chains, help explain the sharp reductions in exports.[21]

Fiscal Consequences

A major adverse effect of the financial crisis is the prospect of relatively large increases in public-sector debt in the United States, the United Kingdom, and some other industrial countries. Following the historical pattern identified by Reinhart and Rogoff (2008), the bulk of the increase is likely

---

21. The export reductions are more severe than would be expected from the usual trade elasticities. For example, if the general income elasticity of exports is 1.5 and there is also another 2.0 additive component for cyclical swings (see Cline 2005, 74), then a 1 percent decline in the foreign growth rate would reduce exports by 3.5 percent. Industrial-country growth fell from 0.5 percent in 2008 to –3.4 percent in 2009, or by 3.9 percentage points. Applying the usual elasticities would imply a reduction of other countries' exports to these countries by about 14 percent, considerably less than observed, even though the nonindustrial-country markets have not experienced growth reductions as large as those of industrial countries.

to be attributable to fiscal losses associated with deep recession, rather than to direct fiscal losses from bank bailouts.

For the United States, in the fiscal year ending September 2009 the federal deficit reached 9.9 percent of GDP, according to the Congressional Budget Office (CBO 2009b). Under the Obama administration's 2010 budget proposals released in early 2009, the CBO (2009a) projected that the federal deficit would remain high at 9.6 percent of GDP in 2010 and 6.4 percent in 2011, before settling at a plateau of about 4.2 percent over 2012–15. Federal debt held by the public would rise from 37 percent of GDP in 2007 and 40.8 percent in 2008 to 57 percent in 2009, 65 percent in 2010, and 69 percent in 2011. It would then rise steadily to 82 percent of GDP by 2019. Of the 24 percent of GDP surge in debt from 2008 to 2010, only about 5 percent of GDP was attributed to narrow bailouts.[22] About 5.5 percent of GDP stemmed from the fiscal stimulus program of 2009 ($787 billion). The rest was associated with sluggish revenue until the economy returns to potential growth. In the administration's 2011 budget released in early 2010, the projected deficit was at 10.6 percent of GDP for 2010 and 8.3 percent for 2011, reaching a plateau of about 4 percent in 2013–20 (OMB 2010). Debt held by the public was projected to reach 61.6 percent of GDP in 2011 and 69.3 percent by 2020.

For the advanced economies in the G-20, the IMF (2009c) has estimated "headline support" for the financial sector at a GDP-weighted average of 43 percent of GDP, with the highest levels in the United States (74 percent), Sweden (70 percent), United Kingdom (48 percent), and the Netherlands (40 percent).[23] Most of this support is against offsetting assets, and the upfront financing costs amount to about 5 percent of GDP. The eventual fiscal costs of the support will depend on whether assets acquired can be subsequently sold off without loss. In contrast, total public debt will have risen by 14 percent of GDP over 2008–09, of which only about one-fifth would be offset by assets acquired. The rest is from fiscal stimulus (including from automatic stabilizers) and revenue losses induced by recession. By 2014, the IMF expects the public-debt-to-GDP ratios for the advanced G-20 countries to average 25 percentage points of GDP higher than at the end of 2007.

The overall implication is that the financial crisis and global recession are expected to boost medium-term public debt burdens by about 20 percentage points of GDP for the main industrial countries. This increase

---

22. The CBO placed expected losses from Fannie Mae and Freddie Mac and the TARP at 2.9 percent of GDP, and the budget proposal provided for another 1.8 percent of GDP for additional rescue contingencies. See William R. Cline, "The Global Financial Crisis" (at footnote 1). Largely because the contingent resources were not drawn upon, the fiscal deficit for 2009 was about 3 percent of GDP smaller than initially projected (CBO 2009a, b).

23. Headline support is lower in France (19 percent), Germany (22 percent), and Japan (13 percent).

aggravates already unfavorable long-term trends in fiscal accounts associated with rising social spending and demographic trends. An important early effect is to narrow the space for additional fiscal stimulus if the initial round fails to revive economies. Longer-term effects are likely to include higher interest rates and greater difficulty of mobilizing official development assistance.

Capital Flows

There has been great concern about a severe downswing in private capital flows to emerging-market economies as one of the consequences of the global financial crisis. After reaching a peak of about $1.2 trillion in 2007, net private capital flows to 30 major emerging-market economies fell to about $670 billion in 2008 and $440 billion in 2009, but they are projected by the Institute of International Finance (IIF 2009, 2010) to rebound to $720 billion in 2010 (figure 4.5). As happened in the East Asian crisis, FDI has held up remarkably well. The greatest collapse was in net flows from banks, from $430 billion in 2007 to –$60 billion in 2009. Portfolio equity also swung to major outflows in 2008 but rebounded fully in 2009.

What is seldom recognized, however, is that, at least in the aggregate, the large capital flows prior to the crisis were not really crucial for growth, because the emerging-market economies have been running large surpluses in their current accounts, at about $560 billion annually in 2007–08 and still about $380 billion annually in 2009–10. So the huge inflows of capital, plus the earnings from current account surpluses, were going to finance massive buildups in reserves and private capital outflows from emerging-market economies. The corollary is that the sharp drop-off in capital flows in 2008–09 mainly served to curb further increases in reserves rather than choke off imports needed for development. Thus, for the 30 major emerging-market economies, increases in reserves reached $1 trillion in 2007 but fell to an average of about $520 billion annually in 2008-09. In that light, the promises of several hundred billion dollars for the IMF have served mainly as a confidence booster rather than a true source of extra capital likely to be needed. Indeed, the IIF projections show a still-puny $62 billion annual average in net official capital flows to emerging-market economies in 2009-10.

Financing Gaps

In April 2009, the summit meeting of the G-20 leaders in London committed $1 trillion in additional international official lending capacity to confront the financial crisis. Lending to the IMF from the United States, European Union, Japan, China, and other G-20 members was to amount to $500 billion; new SDR issues amounting to $250 billion were endorsed; and another $250 billion was pledged for trade finance (appendix 4A;

Figure 4.5   Net private capital flows to 30 emerging-market economies, 2007–10

billions of US dollars

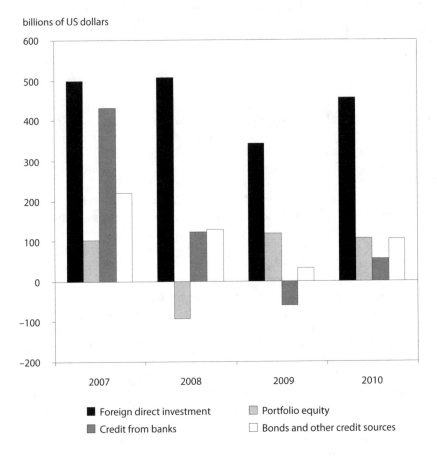

Foreign direct investment   Portfolio equity

Credit from banks   Bonds and other credit sources

Source: IIF (2009, 2010).

see also G-20 2009). In June, the World Bank (2009a) reported that the downswing in capital flows in 2009 could cause a "financing gap" of $350 billion to $635 billion for the developing countries. These large numbers seemed to vindicate the earlier push for a larger emergency financing capability.

Appendix 4E recalculates the financing gaps for 2009 using the World Bank methodology but showing estimates at the country level and comparing the "gaps" with the amount of "usable reserves" that should be readily available to finance them. If 25 percent of reserves is considered a safe benchmark for use, which would seem reasonable in the worst year of global financial crisis in decades, then the "net" financing gap after using this portion of reserves falls to only $88 billion (instead of $350 billion) in the base case and $273 billion in the World Bank's "low" capital flow case rather than $635 billion.[24] If a minimum cushion of reserves is applied at six months' imports of goods and services, reducing the estimate of usable reserves for several countries, then the net gap is somewhat larger but still only about two-thirds the World Bank estimates.

The calculations indicate that in the base case and allowing use of 25 percent of reserves, a long list of major debtor countries should not face a net financing gap because of ample reserve coverage. These countries include Argentina, Brazil, Chile, India, Latvia, Peru, Russia, Thailand, Tunisia, Ukraine, and Venezuela. Moreover, by early in the third quarter of 2009, it was becoming evident that new bond issues by emerging-market economies could be much more robust than had been feared.[25]

Overall, the G-20 decision to triple IMF lending capacity, increase SDRs, and seek to ensure trade finance seems likely to have contributed to an important boost in confidence at a vulnerable moment. The subsequent strengthening in emerging bond markets likely reflected in part a perception of reduced risk in view of the greater official support capacity. In practice, however, it seems likely that only a modest amount of the additional emergency funding will actually be used, in view of reserve levels and some recovery in private financing prospects. Indeed, as of the end of September 2009, total IMF lending commitments to its borrowing members amounted to only SDR 109 billion ($172 billion; see IMF 2009e). Moreover, of this amount almost half was in contingent Flexible Credit Line obligations to just the three economies that had enlisted for this facility (Colombia, Mexico, and Poland), none of which seemed likely to draw upon it. So the IMF seemed likely to actually use only about one-eighth of the $750 billion war chest it had built up as a consequence of the international policy response to the crisis.

Importance and Adequacy of Reserves

The global financial crisis does make the strategy of building reserves appear more vindicated than might have been anticipated. The buildup in reserves was of course the most dramatic in China, where they rose from $300 billion in 2003 to more than $2 trillion by mid-2009 (IMF 2009a). But the buildup of reserves has been a much more widespread pattern in the main emerging-market economies. India, Brazil, Korea, and Russia all now hold more than $200 billion in reserves. For 12 major emerging-market economies, on average the holdings of reserves rose more than threefold over the past six years. The popular lore has it that this was

---

24. The calculations are for the 50 largest developing-country debtors, which account for 98 percent of total private external debt of developing countries.

25. David Oakley, "Emerging Markets Rush to Issue Debt," *Financial Times*, July 26, 2009.

a reaction to the dangers revealed by the East Asian financial crisis. But that explanation is dubious. If it were accurate, the acute phase of reserve buildup would have been from 1999 to 2003. In that period, reserves of the same countries rose less than 10 percent per year.[26] A simpler explanation for the explosion of reserves in 2003–07 is on the supply side rather than the demand side. The Federal Reserve's low interest rate policy and the reduction of risk spreads brought a wall of money into emerging-market economies, and they sensibly set most of it aside in reserves rather than spending it on an import binge.

Indeed, the stylized fact is that this became the period of a new mercantilist growth model that has emphasized increasing exports rather than importing capital equipment. China has been the prototype, but the pervasive buildup in reserves has given the impression that the mercantilist model is much more widespread. In fact it is only a handful of mainly Asian economies that have pursued the model. If one sets as the criteria for mercantilist growth an end-period current account surplus of 2 percent of GDP or more, and a rising surplus trend, and if oil exporters are excluded, then from 1999–2007 only eight large emerging-market economies are in this group: Singapore, Malaysia, Hong Kong, China, Taiwan, and the Philippines in Asia, and only Chile and Israel elsewhere. In contrast, 13 other major emerging-market economies did not meet these criteria of mercantilist growth. India, for example, was far from qualifying (it kept a steady 1 percent of GDP current account deficit), despite its massive buildup in reserves. So rising reserves have probably contributed to an optical illusion that most emerging-market economies are pursuing mercantilist growth.

It would be the wrong lesson for emerging-market economies to draw from the financial crisis that they should join the mercantilist growth bandwagon in order to build up enough reserves to be safe. First of all, most of these economies had such large reserves already that they were able to weather the crisis from 2008 to early 2009 with only a modest loss of reserves. The largest loss was by Russia, yet its reserves remain massive. More fundamentally, for the next decade it will be increasingly problematic for emerging-market economies to count on ever-widening surpluses and resulting larger international imbalances. The United States will need to hold its current account deficits to the range of 3 to 4 percent of GDP, despite rebounding oil prices, instead of the much higher 6 percent reached in 2006. Even China and the rest of the East Asian mercantilist group will need to curb their surpluses. The mercantilist model will not support a piling on by a long list of additional emerging-market economies without putting renewed pressure on external imbalances with the United States and some other (mainly Anglo-Saxon) developed economies that have had large deficits but now need to adjust.

---

26. Excluding Russia, where the 1999 level was abnormally low.

Implications for Financial Openness in Emerging-Market Economies

Through 2007 and much of 2008 a dominant view was that the emerging-market economies had achieved decoupling from the industrial countries, and could continue to grow rapidly and provide a source of global demand despite the credit crunch and worsening economic conditions in the United States and subsequently Europe and Japan. However, by October 2008 it was clear that the crisis was spreading to the emerging-market economies as well. Ukraine and Hungary were forced to seek large financial support from the IMF and the European Union. In Korea the government stepped in to guarantee $100 billion in the Korean banks' external debt and provide additional support to the banks. In the face of this contagion to emerging-market economies, the Federal Reserve extended currency swap lines of $30 billion each to the central banks of Brazil, Mexico, Korea, and Singapore, after having announced unlimited swap lines to major European central banks.

There was a widespread sell-off in emerging-market currencies and stock markets in September and October 2008, in part associated with a broad collapse in prices for commodities and oil. The euro also fell sharply against the dollar, however, and for most major emerging-market economies the currency decline was no greater than that of the euro.[27] Even the commodity price decline was a rollback from exceptionally high earlier levels rather than a plunge to multiyear lows.

Most emerging-market currencies reached their low points in March 2009 and then staged a substantial recovery against the dollar. Figure 4.6 shows the path of regional indexes of real bilateral exchange rates against the dollar for major emerging-market economies with flexible exchange rates from end-2007 through June 2009.[28] The figure confirms this pattern of currency shock in the fourth quarter of 2008 followed by recovery in the second quarter of 2009. By mid-2009, real exchange rates against the dollar were essentially back to the same level as in mid-2007, after having risen substantially in early 2008 during the period of supposed decoupling (except in Asia) and then plunging by late 2008 as the crisis entered its most severe phase. As for stock prices, the emerging-market indices broadly followed those in the United States, Europe, and Japan, again showing a collapse in late 2008 through March 2009 followed by some recovery by mid-2009.

---

27. From end-August to end-October, the euro fell 13.5 percent against the dollar. Emerging-market currency declines were substantially larger than this benchmark for only a few major emerging-market economies: Brazil, –24 percent; Colombia, –23 percent; Mexico, –21 percent; and Turkey, –22 percent.

28. The countries are Argentina, Brazil, Chile, Colombia, Mexico, and Peru in Latin America; India, Indonesia, Korea, the Philippines, and Thailand in Asia; Hungary, Poland, Russia, and Turkey, in Europe; and South Africa.

Figure 4.6   Real exchange rates against the dollar: Emerging-market regional indexes for flexible currencies, July 2007– September 2009

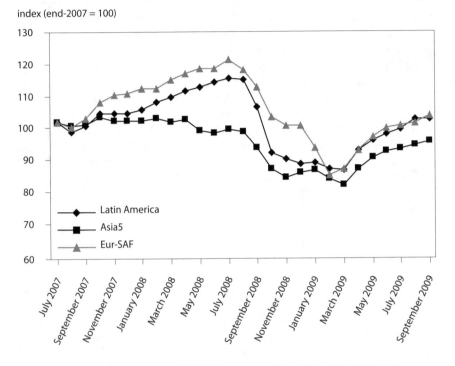

index (end-2007 = 100)

Note: Latin America = Argentina, Brazil, Chile, Colombia, Mexico, and Peru; Asia5 = India, Indonesia, Korea, the Philippines, and Thailand; Eur-SAF = Hungary, Poland, Russia, Turkey, and South Africa.

Source: Author's calculations.

A natural question that arises from recent experience is whether countries would be well advised to reduce the openness of their capital markets in light of new evidence on the potential costs of spillover from international financial crises. So far the evidence does not support the notion that countries with less-open financial markets have enjoyed insulation from the crisis of 2007–09. For the 24 emerging-market economies examined in chapter 3, figure 4.7 shows on the vertical axis changes in growth from the three-year average in 2005–07 to the expected average for 2008–10 (from table 4.1). The horizontal axis reports the Quinn index of financial openness (for 2000–04). Except for Algeria, there is little if any correlation between the growth decline experienced by the economy and its financial openness. Moreover, some of the most financially open economies have the largest shares of trade in GDP and so were especially sensitive to the collapse in world trade.

A simple regression of the change in three-year average growth as the

Figure 4.7 Change in average real growth from 2005–07 to 2008–10 and financial openness (Quinn index)

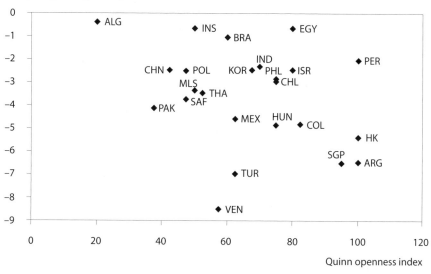

Note: For country abbreviations, see figure 1C.1.

Source: Calculated from table 4.1, IMF (2009g), and Quinn and Toyoda (2008) databases.

dependent variable against Quinn openness and the ratio of exports to GDP in 2007 yields the following results, with openness Q, export/GDP ratio X, and t-statistic in parentheses:

$$dg = -2.6 - 0.01\ Q - 1.33\ X;\ R^2adj = 0.02 \tag{4.1}$$
$$(-1.6)\,(-0.41)\quad(-1.3).$$

The regression indicates that there was no significant relationship between the change in growth in the period of the global financial crisis and the degree of financial openness of the economy in question.[29] As expected, there was a negative relationship between change in growth and the initial ratio of exports to GDP, although the coefficient was not significant.

Figure 4.8 correspondingly shows the percent change in real stock prices (vertical axis) from end-2007 to March 9, 2009, the low point for international equity prices, on the vertical axis; and again Quinn financial openness on the horizontal axis. It is evident that there is no relationship between the two. Somewhat counterintuitively, then, the financial crisis did not impose greater stock market collapses on more financially open emerging-market economies than on more closed ones.

---

29. See chapter 1, footnote 25, for a critique of the opposite result in Ostry et al. (2010).

Figure 4.8   Real change in stock prices and financial openness (Quinn index), end-2007 to March 2009

change in stock (percent)

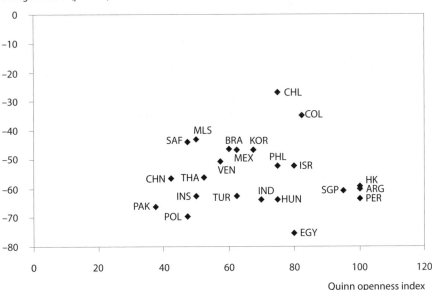

Quinn openness index

Note: For country abbreviations, see figure 1C.1.

Source: Author's calculations.

Similarly, if the 23 economies are grouped into three categories as more closed, intermediate, and more open on the Quinn variable, and the average stock index is obtained for each group (with end-2007 = 100), the resulting time series do not show superior insulation from international equity shocks for the more-closed ones (figure 4.9).[30] The time path of stock indexes for the more-closed economies is almost identical to that for the more open ones through the trough in March 2009. Thereafter there was somewhat greater recovery of stock prices in the more-open than in the more-closed economies. The countries in the intermediate group showed a lesser decline, and by October 2009 their average index stood somewhat higher than that of the more-open group and, especially, the more-closed group.

The principal case of economic collapse in emerging markets associated with the crisis of 2007–09 was that of the Baltic states. In Estonia, Lithuania, and Latvia average growth plunged from 9.3 percent in 2005–07 to –7.4 per-

---

30. More-closed economies: China, Indonesia, Malaysia, Pakistan, Poland, South Africa, Thailand, and Venezuela. Intermediate: Brazil, Chile, Hungary, India, Korea, Mexico, the Philippines, and Turkey. More open: Argentina, Colombia, Egypt, Hong Kong, Israel, Peru, and Singapore.

Figure 4.9   Real stock price index by financial-openness grouping, end 2007–October 2009

index (end 2007 = 100)

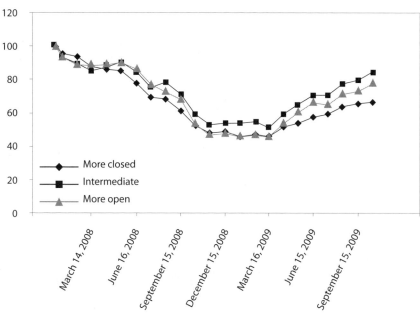

Source: Author's calculations.

cent annually in 2008–10 (IMF 2009g). Some have argued that this experience demonstrates severe vulnerability of financially open economies. It is true that the economies were highly open financially; indeed, their banks are owned by Nordic banks (Rosenberg 2008). However, the fundamental blame for their collapse surely stems from the risky approach their policymakers took toward external imbalances. The current account deficits of the three economies stood at an average of 14.9 percent of GDP in 2005–07. Only the misperception of the special political relationship with the European Union as a guarantor could have made the failure to adjust fixed exchange rates and fiscal policies to curb the outsized external deficits seem sustainable. In the event the imbalances were not sustainable, and the severe recessions cut them to average current account deficits of 1.9 percent of GDP in 2008–10 (IMF 2009g). The Baltic lesson is not that financial openness should be avoided; it is that sound macroeconomic and regulatory policies, including sustainable strategies on external imbalances, are essential complements of openness. Moreover, the unique historical-political situation of these economies in transition and their extremely small size make their experience of little relevance for the larger emerging-market economies.

Elsewhere in Eastern Europe, it is true that Hungary both experienced a more severe crisis and had somewhat greater financial openness than Poland (figure 4.7). Hungary was forced to resort to IMF support under a Stand-by Arrangement in late 2008, whereas Poland avoided doing so. However, lack of policy caution again appears to have played a role in the different outcomes. Hungary's average fiscal deficit in 2004–07 was considerably higher (at 7.1 percent of GDP) than Poland's (4.0 percent), and its average current account deficit in the period was also much higher (7.5 percent of GDP versus 3.2 percent; EBRD 2009 and IMF 2009g). More broadly, a recent empirical study by the European Bank for Reconstruction and Development (EBRD 2009, iv) finds that despite the vulnerabilities revealed by the crisis of 2007–09, "Macroeconomic and sector-level analysis shows that financial integration did in fact boost long-term growth in the transition region" but that "its risks must be better managed."

Overall, for most emerging-market economies the evidence to date on the financial crisis of 2007–09, from both the equity markets and growth trends, supports the view that greater financial openness does not lead to more adverse spillover effects from international crises.

Conclusion

At first glance it might seem that the global financial crisis of 2007–09 serves as a stern warning that a country is taking major risks by allowing its capital markets to be open to international finance. A deeper lesson, however, is what might be called the "100-year storm effect." This crisis is the financial counterpart of the 100-year storm. If in such a storm the edifices remain largely intact, the event can be seen as a confirmation of their strength and of the strategy that led them to be put in place. Despite the severe global recession, the prospects are for emerging-market economies to return to reasonable growth relatively soon (figure 4.3). There is no evidence that, after taking account of exposure to international trade, greater financial openness caused more severe spillover to domestic economies in this international crisis (equation 4.1 and figure 4.8). There are no general grounds for emerging-market economies that have adopted some degree of financial openness to reverse course; on the contrary, having withstood the 100-year storm test, they might equally as well conclude that more openness may not be as risky as some had warned. As for industrial countries, most already have open financial markets, and despite the severity of the crisis, none have called for an international "Bretton Woods II" agreement designed to return to capital controls of the nature that were endorsed by Bretton Woods I.

The principal implication of this chapter is that the severity of the global financial crisis of 2007–09 does not constitute grounds for reversing the overall finding of this study that financial openness is broadly favorable for growth (chapter 2) and has already contributed significantly to growth in those economies that have pursued it (chapter 3).

Appendix 4A
Key Events and Policy Responses

The initial driving force behind the US financial crisis was the downturn in the housing market and the consequential turmoil in subprime mortgage loans and, especially, MBS. Housing prices peaked in July 2006. By March 2007, the first manifestations of the financial crisis were evident in falling prices of these securities (see figure 4B.2 in appendix 4B), and by July 2007 these price declines were severe.

Four phases can be identified for the financial crisis, with the first three successively more severe but the fourth marking a substantial easing of the crisis. The first began in July 2007. The second began in March 2008 with the collapse of Bear Stearns and its takeover by JP Morgan. The third began in mid-September 2008 when large financial institutions entered a round of takeovers, rescues, and in one case (Lehman Brothers), bankruptcy. The fourth phase began in the second quarter of 2009, when the results of the "stress test" for US banks, and forceful international action supporting the IMF, helped revive confidence.

Phase One: July 2007 to February 2008

Two events marked the onset of the crisis (table 4.1). In July 2007, the investment bank Bear Stearns closed two MBS funds, and in August, the French bank BNP Paribas temporarily suspended withdrawals from three investment funds on grounds that the seizing up in the MBS market in the United States made it impossible to determine a fair valuation for withdrawals. There was a temporary rebound in market confidence in the autumn of 2007 that brought equity markets to their peak in October. By December 2007, however, financial market conditions were sufficiently stressed to cause the Federal Reserve to create a Term Auction Facility, initially set at $40 billion but subsequently enlarged, for purchase on an auction basis of one- to three-month term assets from banks. It did so recognizing that:

> ...the resurgence of stresses in financial markets in November...reflected evidence that the performance of mortgage-related assets was deteriorating further, potentially increasing the losses that were being borne in part by a number of major financial firms, including money-center banks, housing-related government-sponsored enterprises, investment banks, and financial guarantors.... Among other factors, banks were experiencing unanticipated growth in loans as a result of continuing illiquidity in the market for leveraged loans, persisting problems in the commercial paper market that had sparked draws on back-up lines of credit, and more recently, consolidation of assets of off-balance-sheet affiliates onto banks' balance sheets.... Heightened worries about counterparty credit risk, balance sheet constraints, and liquidity pressures affected interbank funding markets and commercial paper markets, where spreads over risk-free rates rose to levels that were, in some case, higher than those seen in August. (US Federal Reserve 2007, 5–6).

Thus began the extraordinary sequence of central bank lending facility interventions (as opposed to interest rate cuts) that have marked the crisis.

Phase Two: March 2008 to August 2008

A new phase of greater intensity of the crisis began in March 2008 with the collapse of the investment bank Bear Stearns and its takeover by JP Morgan. This collapse reflected the vulnerability of the investment-bank model in which high leverage, on the order of $30 in assets to $1 of capital (in contrast to leverage of about $10 to $1 in regular banks), was combined with reliance on short-term funding. Bear Stearns faced the additional vulnerability of having been especially active in MBS. Its demise also represented another key challenge to the structure of US financial institutions: By more than a century of practice, the lender-of-last-resort function of the Federal Reserve had been confined to depository banks, yet the structure of lending in the US economy had shifted from being primarily through banks to being primarily through nonbanks.

JP Morgan took over Bear Stearns, but only with the support of a $29 billion loan from the Federal Reserve collateralized by Bear Stearns assets. This extraordinary action reflected the judgment that Bear Stearns could not be allowed to go into bankruptcy without provoking massive chain-reaction effects in the financial system.[31] At the same time the Federal Reserve moved to create a quasi-lender-of–last-resort function for an important class of nonbanks: the "primary dealer" large investment banks, establishing the Term Securities Lending Facility to provide one-month credit to such banks, against high-grade collateral.

In April 2008, Treasury staff reportedly conducted work on a "break the glass" emergency plan that included as options a request to Congress for a $500 billion fund to buy MBS from banks and securities firms; Federal Reserve purchases of these securities (as from Bear Stearns); government guarantees of such securities; and a request to Congress for permission "to purchase equity stakes in financial institutions" (Wessel 2009, 177). As tensions eased in financial markets, however, the plan was set aside, in part because the crisis was not yet severe enough to force congressional action. When the crisis did become acute enough in late September, Treasury in effect revived the "break the glass" plan, initially depicting the TARP as

---

31. Wessel (2009, 159) reports that the Bear Stearns rescue was eventually interpreted by some as a case of "too interconnected to fail," rather than too big to fail. It had open trades with 5,000 other firms and was a party to 750,000 derivatives contracts. He quotes Federal Reserve Vice Chairman Donald L. Kohn as having stated in an interview that without the Federal Reserve's loan to enable the absorption of Bear Stearns, "...lots of other folks [firms] would be brought down with consequences I couldn't imagine...destroying lots of financial intermediaries."

an asset purchase program but almost immediately transforming it into an equity injection plan.

By the second quarter of 2008 there seemed to be a temporary reprieve for the financial crisis, as financial markets were relieved that the Federal Reserve had not allowed a bankruptcy by a large investment bank. The Federal Reserve had already cut the key policy interest rate (federal funds rate for overnight lending among banks) by 125 basis points, from 4.25 percent at the end of 2007 to 3 percent by February. It cut the rate by another 100 basis points by May. A fiscal stimulus package passed by Congress in February was to provide $170 billion in tax rebates of $600 to low- and middle-income families. However, by July a new intensification of the crisis loomed because of the precarious position of Fannie Mae and Freddie Mac, the two government-sponsored entities (GSEs) that together accounted for about $4.5 trillion in mortgage loans (about one-third) and guarantees (two-thirds). The Treasury announced a plan to invest in the two entities, but this commitment proved insufficient.

Phase 3: September 2008 to March 2009

Unfortunately, the confidence-building gambit for the GSEs did not work. The price of Fannie Mae stock, which had stood at $40 per share at the end of 2007, had fallen to $10 by July 11, 2008 before the Treasury announcement of support. After a brief rebound it fell to $7 on September 5. After Treasury announced that the two housing GSEs were being placed in conservatorship, the price fell to 73 cents per share on September 8. The terms of the conservatorship granted Treasury warrants to purchase shares at one one-thousandth of a cent, essentially wiping out shareholders but guaranteeing the debt of Fannie Mae.

Foreign central banks were important holders of these obligations. Foreign official institutions had made net purchases of agency bonds (mainly Fannie and Freddie obligations) totaling $119 billion in 2007 and $48 billion in the first half of 2008 (US Treasury 2008).[32] The US government had little alternative to assuring the debt of the two GSEs. It is possible that the manner in which the bailout was managed, in particular the punitive treatment of shareholders, was unavoidable politically at the time. A bailout that instead retained more shareholder value could have been seen as unacceptable. However, the precedent of shareholder liquidation seems likely to have contributed to an environment of severe market stress on financial institutions in the subsequent weeks. The Fannie-Freddie conservatorship was arguably the beginning of a perverse dynamic in which stock prices of large financial firms deemed vulnerable fell as the risk of a

---

32. Their appetite decreased after the intervention, as foreign official purchases swung to net sales averaging $13 billion per month in July through October.

too-big-to-fail bailout increased—because in such a bailout the shareholders would be wiped out. But as vulnerable companies' stock prices fell, they sent a signal of increased likelihood of default, making counterparties even more loath to fund them and providing a self-fulfilling prophecy.[33] (There is a substantial literature on how stock prices serve as a proxy for probability of default; see Byström 2003).

The crest of the wave of financial crisis in 2008 occurred on the weekend of September 15. The large investment bank Lehman Brothers could not secure funding, and this time the Federal Reserve and Treasury decided to let a large financial firm go bankrupt. Perhaps they sought to send a signal that financial "moral hazard" would not be allowed to build without end. Perhaps they believed that, as in the example of emerging markets at end-2001 when Argentina defaulted, the long period of market awareness of the danger prior to the collapse meant that in Lehman's case contagion would be limited because market participants had known for months that the firm was under pressure and would have had ample time to position themselves defensively. The Federal Reserve later stated that technically it could not have supported Lehman because the firm lacked sufficient collateral. However, Lehman executives had sought to convert to bank holding company status to obtain greater support, and the Federal Reserve denied that request—but subsequently welcomed such conversion for Goldman Sachs and Morgan Stanley.

The decision not to support Lehman after having supported Bear Stearns came as a shock to the financial sector, and to some it represented "a series of flip-flops that have exacerbated the uncertainty gripping the marketplace" (Barth 2009, 219). As Wessel (2009, 274) puts it:

[Federal Reserve Chairman Ben] Bernanke and [US Treasury Secretary Henry] Paulson convinced themselves the system could withstand [the Lehman bankruptcy] because the warning signs had been so many and so visible. They were wrong about that. They didn't realize the lesson many people had drawn from Bear Stearns: the Fed would somehow find a way to keep Lehman going. They didn't appreciate the tidal wave that a Lehman bankruptcy would cause.

For another large investment bank, Merrill Lynch, the remarkable weekend of September 15, 2008 included its takeover by Bank of America, thereby obviating any need for a bailout. There was a far less fortunate outcome that same weekend for the large US insurance company, AIG, which was similarly under severe pressure. As Federal Reserve and Treasury authorities reviewed AIG's massive exposure on CDSs, they came to the conclusion that AIG could not be allowed to default because the

---

33. In an article on September 13, 2008 (p. 17), the *Economist* approved the bailout as necessary to restore confidence, in part because "a debtor nation could not afford to antagonize its lenders," but it noted that "the stock market rally lasted just one day, before investors switched their worries to Lehman Brothers, a struggling investment bank."

consequences for the financial system would be too severe.[34] Instead they applied the Fannie Mae model, and placed the firm under conservatorship that secured its debt but largely wiped out the shareholders. They announced $85 billion in support to the firm (subsequently to be expanded sharply) but charged a high 10 percent interest rate for it and in addition received new shares amounting to 80 percent of equity. The shareholder dilution cut AIG's share price, which had already fallen from $23 on September 8 to $12 on September 12 to only $2 on September 17 after the bailout. As in the case of shareholders of Fannie Mae and Freddie Mac, those in AIG found that too-big-to-fail status translated into the kiss of death.

There ensued an eerie calm for a week or so, as no great disorder seemed to follow the announcement of Lehman's bankruptcy. At first the Argentina noncontagion model seemed to be working. The main sign of trouble was that a large money market mutual fund (the Reserve Fund) "broke the buck," informing holders that accounts were worth less than 100 cents on the dollar as a consequence of losses from the collapse of Lehman. Such funds were central to the commercial paper market, which was increasingly under pressure. The Federal Reserve sought to shore up that market by creating the Asset-Backed Commercial Paper Money Market Mutual Fund Liquidity Facility. The Treasury moved to reassure holders of money-market mutual fund assets by launching a year-long temporary guarantee of money market funds that signed up, in exchange for a minimal insurance premium.[35]

More generally, Federal Reserve and Treasury authorities concluded that the case-by-case (or finger-in-the-dike) approach to fighting the financial crisis was no longer sufficient. Despite the successive interventions involving major individual firms (Bear Stearns, the two GSEs, Lehman Brothers, indirectly Merrill Lynch, and AIG), the crisis was not yet under control. They gravitated toward addressing the initial source of the problem: opaque and by-now highly illiquid assets, especially MBS, that resided on the balance sheets of major financial institutions and represented a source of great uncertainty about the solvency of these institutions. The result was that interbank lending in particular and credit markets more generally were seizing up, as firms could not be confident in counterpar-

---

34. Wessel (2009, 192) states that "nearly every major financial institution in the world had bought financial insurance of some sort or placed huge bets with AIG." As examples he cites amounts of $4.1 billion at stake for Société Générale and nearly $6 billion for Goldman Sachs. Wessel notes that "in the wake of the messy Lehman bankruptcy, [then New York Federal Reserve Chairman Timothy] Geithner added, the system couldn't withstand another disorderly disintegration of a major financial institution."

35. By November 24, 2008, when Treasury announced the extension of the program through April 30, 2009, the amount of assets covered by it had reached $3 trillion (US Treasury 2008). The Treasury pledged its $50 billion Exchange Stabilization Fund, which had been used in the Mexican peso crisis in 1994, as backing for the money market guarantee program, arguably thereby tying its hands in the event of a similar foreign crisis in the near future.

ties. One attempt at a more general approach was to place a temporary ban on "naked" short-selling of shares of financial firms, an initiative by the Securities and Exchange Commission in late September that had little lasting impact. The principal new initiative, however, was the TARP.

In late September, Treasury Secretary Henry Paulson called on Congress to pass a $700 billion program to purchase troubled assets from financial institutions as a more systemic means to fight the financial crisis, instead of a case-by-case approach. The central idea was to make the opaque instruments on financial firms' balance sheets more transparent by a process of price discovery through prices set in "reverse auctions," whereby the TARP would announce purchases of MBS and other illiquid assets. However, the apocalyptic terms in which Paulson painted the financial stability threat in the effort to convince Congress seemed to have had a counterproductive effect. When Congress failed to pass the proposal on Monday, September 29, the US stock market fell sharply (by 8.8 percent in a single day, for the S&P 500 index). Sobered, the legislators passed the measure at the end of that week.

By then, however, it was evident that the severity of the financial crisis was increasing in an important dimension: It was spreading to Europe. The central banks of Belgium, the Netherlands, Luxembourg, and France had been forced to stage coordinated rescue operations for large banks with operations sizably exceeding the scope of their home-country central bank (Belgium for Fortis, and Belgium and France for Dexia). Central bank interventions or rescues were also necessary in the United Kingdom (Bradford & Bingley) and Germany (Hypo Real). The entire country of Iceland was entering into currency collapse, and bank suspensions were handled in a manner that enraged UK residents with deposits. All of these disruptions reflected the further seizing up of credit markets. Within a week of the passage of the TARP, US equity markets had fallen 19 percent from their previous low point on the day of the initial defeat of the TARP.

It was at this point that the UK Treasury launched a new strategy that soon became the dominant framework for the next phase of action in the crisis. It announced that it would inject £50 billion capitalization into UK banks through the purchase of preferred shares. At the same time many economists and financial observers were criticizing the proposal to use TARP funds for the purpose of purchasing troubled assets and called instead for the resources to be used for bank recapitalization, and/or for Treasury to require that banks suspend dividends and issue new stock.[36] Some were concerned that asymmetric information would result in the government purchasing only the lemons from the banks; others, that shareholders would reap unfair benefits. However, in the aftermath of the decimation of shareholders in the rescues of Fannie Mae, Freddie Mac,

---

36. Zingales (2008) and Sebastian Mallaby, "A Bad Bank Rescue," *Washington Post*, September 21, 2008.

and AIG, a serious risk was that the specter of public-sector capitalization of the banks would cause a plunge in bank stocks precisely from the kiss-of-death effect discussed above. Severe stock dilution could be expected to depress prices, sending a death-throes signal of near bankruptcy.

Nonetheless, the Treasury faced events moving faster than its capacity to implement meaningful asset purchases. MBS are complex, and it was becoming clear that a responsible program of purchases would require the mounting of a sophisticated operation implemented with considerable help from financial market experts outside the Treasury. In this atmosphere, the Treasury shifted gears and moved forcefully to a bank recapitalization mode.[37]

In mid-October the Treasury successfully pressured the nine largest US banks to accept $125 billion in TARP purchases of preferred shares on terms designed to be relatively market-friendly. Some of the large banks were reportedly not interested in participating but were induced to do so to avoid undermining market confidence in others that did so.[38] Interest on the preferred shares was set at 5 percent, rising to 9 percent in the fifth year. Warrants to purchase common stock amounting to 15 percent of the capital injected were to be priced at market on the day of issue of the warrants (rather than a de minimus price as in the case of Fannie Mae). Another $125 billion in similar preferred share purchases was to be extended to all other banks interested in applying.

It was at this point that the center of the US financial system was essentially shored up (see appendix 4C, section on "Bank Nationalization? Not Quite," p. 309). The government had not nationalized the large banks; the deal did not even require that they suspend dividends. However, the capitalization marked a line of demarcation that strongly implied that the next step for these systemic banks, if need be, would indeed be outright nationalization. They would not be allowed to fail. Indeed, by this time the decision to allow Lehman to fail was increasingly regarded in the United States and especially abroad as a major policy mistake.

Although the battle to secure the core of the US banking system was thus greatly advanced if not won by mid-October 2008, a significant aftershock occurred within the space of a few weeks. It was triggered by the Treasury's announcement on November 12 that it had abandoned its

---

37. Wessel (2009, 227) reports that Federal Reserve Chairman Ben Bernanke had expected all along that government purchases of equity would be needed, based on past international experiences in banking crises, and concluded "it became clear…we needed something quick, and capital injection was quicker than asset purchases." He states that in the crisis week of September 29, 2008, which began with rejection by the US House of Representatives of the TARP proposal, Paulson also reached the conclusion that purchases of preferred shares would be needed but judged he could not say so openly until the TARP passed on the second attempt.

38. Goldman Sachs and JP Morgan did not need the capital, according to Wessel (2009, 237). Later they were among the first to exit from the TARP and its restrictions on executive pay.

initial plan to use the TARP to purchase troubled assets.[39] Within days of this announcement, the share prices of Citigroup and some other relatively more-exposed banks plummeted.[40] US authorities stepped in with a potentially massive rescue for Citigroup. The Treasury, FDIC, and Federal Reserve undertook a guarantee of "$306 billion of largely residential and commercial real estate loans and certain other assets, which will remain on the bank's balance sheet."[41] Citigroup would bear the first $29 billion in losses on this portfolio. Thereafter it would absorb 10 percent and the official sector 90 percent of losses. The first $5 billion in losses would come from Treasury's TARP; the next $10 billion from the FDIC; and the remainder would come from the Federal Reserve. The official sector thus stood to lose as much as $249 billion in support of this single bank, an amount equal to the entire bank capital injection of the TARP in its first phase. In return, Citigroup gave $7 billion in preferred shares to the Federal Reserve and FDIC, in what might be viewed as the payment of an insurance premium for the guarantee. In addition, Treasury bought $20 billion in preferred shares paying 8 percent, using TARP funds and thus bringing the total for Citigroup to $45 billion.[42] The Citigroup arrangement was further dramatic evidence that the center core of large banks had indeed been ring-fenced and would be supported against collapse at all costs.

The final conspicuous episode of public-sector bailout in 2008 was not for the financial sector but for the three major US automobile producers. After initial resistance, the Treasury granted short-term support from the TARP amounting to $17 billion to enable General Motors and Chrysler to avert bankruptcy. This decision illustrated the transition of the crisis from the financial sector to the real sector of the economy, as well as the close interconnections in view of the special troubles of the auto financing companies (GMAC).

By January 2009, it became clear that larger-than-expected losses by Merrill Lynch placed Bank of America in a more precarious position from the takeover than previously anticipated. On January 15, US authorities provided an additional $20 billion in recapitalization from the TARP to Bank of America, in addition to a $118 billion guarantee of asset-backed securities and derivatives. The bank was to be responsible for the first $10 billion in losses and 10 percent of losses beyond that amount. Of the 90 percent official-sector responsibility thereafter, Treasury and the FDIC

---

39. Krishna Gutha, "US Abandons Toxic Asset Buy-Out," *Financial Times*, November 13, 2008.

40. Citigroup shares fell from $9.64 on November 12 to $3.77 on November 21.

41. Eric Dash, "Citigroup to Halt Dividend and Curb Pay," *New York Times*, November 24, 2008.

42. Citigroup, Bank of America, and JP Morgan had each received $25 billion in preferred share investments in the plan announced on October 13.

incurred the first $10 billion and the Federal Reserve the rest in the form of nonrecourse loans at 300 basis points above the OIS rate on drawn amounts.

Although much of the public and policy debate on management of the crisis in the last quarter of 2008 concentrated on the TARP, in important ways much larger intervention was occurring through the Federal Reserve, the FDIC, and a huge Treasury guarantee of money-market mutual funds adopted without congressional action. Some critics suggested that Treasury had discovered it could outsource the TARP to the Federal Reserve. Moreover, by end-2008 Treasury had used only the first half of its $700 billion in potential TARP funds; it had not yet gone back to Congress for authorization to use the second half.

For its part, the FDIC in October 2008 increased the amount of deposits eligible for insurance from $100,000 per account to $250,000. The CBO estimates that this action raised the total amount of deposits covered by FDIC insurance by $700 billion from a previous level of $4.5 trillion.[43]

The FDIC undertook an even larger guarantee program on October 14, 2008, when it launched its Temporary Liquidity Guarantee initiative, which provides a guarantee for senior unsecured debt of banks issued between October 14 and June 30, 2009. The eligible pool of debt is estimated at $1.4 trillion.[44] In addition, another $500 billion is eligible to be guaranteed in business transaction accounts bearing no interest. The initiative provides this guarantee at an insurance premium amounting to 75 basis points.[45]

The Federal Reserve undertook a massive increase in its balance sheet in an effort to provide liquidity to banks and other financial institutions. From end-2007 to end-2008, the total assets of the Federal Reserve rose from $873 billion to $2.2 trillion (US Federal Reserve 2008a). The Fed's holdings of Treasury obligations fell from $755 billion to $475 billion. So there was a crisis-related increase of about $1.6 trillion in its claims. Of this amount, about $500 billion was in swap lines to other central banks, and the rest in various facilities designed to shore up the banks and other financial institutions.

In particular, at end-2008 Federal Reserve holdings of bank assets under the Term Auction Facility had reached $400 billion. The Commercial

---

43. Eric Dash, "Deposit Plan Will Cost Banks More," *New York Times*, October 2, 2008. In comparison, the capital of the FDIC stands at $45 billion, making it perhaps the most leveraged financial institution of all. Of course, the guarantee of the US government stands behind it, at least in principle.

44. General Electric alone has guaranteed $139 billion under the program. Rachel Layne and Rebecca Christie, "GE Wins FDIC Insurance for Up to $139 Billion in Debt," Bloomberg.com, November 12, 2008.

45. Karey Wutkowski, "Debt Guarantee Program for U.S. Banks Is Altered," Reuters, November 21, 2008.

Paper Funding Facility accounted for another $330 billion; primary loans to banks, $88 billion; primary dealer credit, $36 billion; and the asset-backed commercial paper money market, $23 billion. Further claims arising from specific rescues amounted to $74 billion from Bear Stearns and $39 billion from AIG. In addition, the Federal Reserve had committed to provide up to another $600 billion in purchases of assets from Fannie Mae and Freddie Mac and $540 billion in the Money Market Investor Funding Facility (not yet off the ground), and to lend $230 billion if needed to Citigroup. These three commitments alone meant the balance sheet of the Federal Reserve could expand from $2.2 trillion to $3.5 trillion.

By January 2009 the combined total of official-sector guarantees, crisis-related loans and purchases, and contingent commitments amounted to about $9 trillion, or about 62 percent of GDP.[46] If the $4.5 trillion obligations of the GSEs are included, because they have been effectively nationalized, the total rises to about $13.5 trillion, or 95 percent of GDP.

Two final features of these interventions are important to recognize. First, those actions that guarantee assets held by banks, such as the $306 billion guarantee for Citigroup and the $118 billion guarantee for Bank of America, have the effect of sharply reducing capital required to be held against the assets (in both cases, to 20 percent of face value) because of risk-weighting. This effect frees up capital and brings institutions closer to, or further above, capital required for regulatory purposes. Second, the economic cost of the loans and guarantees should generally be modest or even minimal relative to face value. For example, the expected loss on the $3 trillion in guarantees offered to the money market funds was so small that Treasury felt justified in backing the guarantee with only the $50 billion available in its Exchange Stabilization Fund. Similarly, the assets held as collateral by the Federal Reserve tend to be high-grade and in addition are given some accounting "haircut" up front for purposes of the amount of the guarantee.

The principal expected losses so far have been in the TARP and the takeover of the GSEs. In its January 2009 report on the budget outlook, the CBO (2009a) used a 25 percent expected loss rate against the expected $700 billion total for the TARP as the basis for arriving at budgetary implications, causing a budgetary loss of $180 billion. For Fannie Mae and Freddie Mac, the CBO calculated that the present value of mortgage loans and guaranteed assets falls short of liabilities by $200 billion (4.4 percent of principal). In addition, it estimates $40 billion in subsidy costs for the two GSEs in 2009 for present-value losses on new business undertaken after the takeover. The total TARP and GSE losses in the budget amount to $420 billion for 2009, or about 3 percent of GDP. This impact is similar

---

46. Federal Reserve, $1.4 trillion crisis-related increase in balance sheet plus another $1.37 trillion contingent; FDIC, $2.6 trillion; and Treasury, $3.7 trillion just for money market fund guarantees and the TARP.

to the public losses from the savings and loan crisis of the early 1990s. It is a modest loss considering that the total loans, guarantees, and quasi-nationalized assets amount to nearly 100 percent of GDP. However, the costs of socializing the losses from the financial crisis of 2007–09 could rise well above these levels if the crisis proves to be longer lasting and more severe than suggested by the financial stabilization in the second quarter of 2009 and the beginnings of economic recovery in the third (when real GDP returned to positive growth at an annualized rate of 2.2 percent (BEA 2010).

Phase 4: April 2009 and After

As indicated in table 4A.1, by the second quarter of 2009 there were two events that helped strengthen confidence. The first was the decision at the London summit conference of the G-20 in early April to triple the funds available to the IMF, from $250 billion to $750 billion, and in addition to issue $250 billion in new SDRs. The increase in IMF resources by $500 billion was to come in increased borrowing through the New Arrangements to Borrow. Of the increase, $100 billion had already been pledged by Japan and another $100 billion by the European Union. Additional lending was expected from the United States ($100 billion), China ($40 billion), Canada ($10 billion), Norway ($4.5 billion), and Saudi Arabia and some other emerging-market economies.[47] The meeting participants also announced commitment to an additional $100 billion for the multilateral development banks, as well as a more amorphous undertaking to boost trade finance by $250 billion.[48]

The second major boost to confidence came from the results of the stress test for US banks (described in the main text above), released in early May. The improving environment was evident in the rebound of international equity markets. In the United States, the S&P 500 index rebounded by 36 percent from its trough on March 9 to the end of June.

By mid-2009 the worst of the financial crisis seemed to be over, from the standpoint of financial institution fragility. However, the legacy of the financial crisis was the worst postwar global recession, severe erosion in public debt positions in major economies, and a challenge for the Federal Reserve and other central banks to eventually unwind their massive intervention in a fashion that avoided either severe inflation or prolonged recession.

Another legacy of the crisis was an even more concentrated financial system than before, as a consequence of the mergers and rescues (see ap-

---

47. "Mission Possible," *Economist*, April 11, 2009, 69–70.

48. Some reports indicated that the trade finance was an annual figure for about $80 billion that would turn over three times during the course of the year.

pendix 4C), and a corresponding increase in the problem of "too big to fail." Whether that problem could better be addressed by breaking up the largest firms or instead by imposing additional capital requirements on them in the areas of risky activities emerged as a policy debate by late 2009. The too-big-to-fail syndrome was in some sense codified internationally at the G-7 meeting of finance ministers in October 2008. Federal Reserve Chairman Ben Bernanke's draft language for its communiqué had included the principles of making "all efforts to prevent the failure of any systemically important financial institutions," and if failures occurred, protecting "all creditors and counterparties, both secured and unsecured" (thereby committing not to repeat the Lehman bankruptcy and WaMu wipeout of creditors). The final communiqué omitted the latter qualification and simply committed G-7 authorities to "prevent their failure" (Wessel 2009, 234, 236).

Table 4A.1   Key financial-sector events in the global crisis of 2007–09

Date	Event	Support (billions of specified currency)	Comment
2007			
July 17	Bear Stearns closes two mortgage-backed securities (MBS) funds	—	"Effectively no value left..."
August 9	BNP Paribas suspends withdrawals from three investment funds	—	Cites "evaporation of liquidity" in US MBS market
December 12	US Federal Reserve (Fed) begins Term Auction Facility (TAF) for banks	$40 to $400	Auctions of one-month loans against broad range of collateral
2008			
February 17	UK nationalizes Northern Rock bank	—	£113 billion in assets
March 11	Fed begins Term Securities Lending Facility (TSLF) for nonbank primary dealers	$200	Lends primary dealers treasury securities for one month against investment-grade collateral
March 13	Takeover of Bear Stearns by JP Morgan	$29	Fed lends JP Morgan $29 billion against acquired Bear Stearns assets
March 16	Fed begins Primary Dealer Credit Facility	—	Lends overnight to primary dealers against triparty repos
July 13	Treasury plans to invest in Fannie Mae and Freddie Mac	—	Fed to lend to the two government-sponsored enterprises in interim
September 7	Fannie and Freddie placed in conservatorship	Up to $200	Fed states unable to support because of inadequate collateral
September 14	Lehman Brothers declares bankruptcy	—	
September 15	Bank of America takeover of Merrill Lynch	—	
September 16	AIG rescue loan by Fed	$85	Government takes 80 percent of stock; interest rate 10 percent

(continued on next page)

Table 4A.1 Key financial-sector events in the global crisis of 2007–09 *(continued)*

Date	Event	Support (billions of specified currency)	Comment
2008 *(continued)*			
September 16	Reserve Primary Fund "breaks the buck" (accounts worth less than 100 cents on the dollar)	—	Consequence of $700 million loss on Lehman bankruptcy
September 19	US, UK temporary ban on short-selling of financial stocks	—	
September 19	Fed begins Asset Backed Commercial Paper Money Market Mutual Fund Liquidity Facility (ABCP MMMF)	—	Lending to purchase ABCP from MMMFs. Commercial paper < 120 days, banks; <270 days, nonbanks
September 19; November 24	Treasury begins/extends guarantee program for money market funds	$3,000	Insurance premium of 2.2 basis points
September 22	Goldman Sachs, Morgan Stanley convert to bank holding companies	—	Provides greater access to Fed support
September 26	Washington Mutual bank seized by Federal Deposit Insurance Corporation (FDIC), sold to JP Morgan	—	Purchased for $1.9 billion
September 29	Congress rejects first Troubled Assets Relief Program (TARP)	—	S&P 500 falls 8.8 percent
September 29–30	Fortis, Dexia banks rescued by Belgium, Netherlands, Luxembourg, France	€11.2; €6.4	First large contagion to Europe; demonstrates management of multicountry bank crisis
September 29	Wachovia in forced takeover by Citigroup with contingent Fed support	—	Subsequently preempted by Wells Fargo without support after favorable tax interpretation
October 3	Congress passes revised TARP	$700	Increased oversight, references added to housing support
October 3	Fed announces Commercial Paper Funding Facility	—	Creates special-purpose vehicle (SPV) to purchase three-month unsecured and asset-backed commercial paper; up to $1.3 trillion eligible
October 3	FDIC insurance raised to $250,000 per account	—	

Date	Amount	Event	Notes
October 5–7	€50	Hypo Real Estate rescue	Bundesbank 40 percent, banks 60 percent
	—	Iceland nationalizes Landsbanki	Iceland financial crisis ensues
October 8; 10–11	$65	Two additional tranches of support to AIG ($38 billion; $27 billion)	
October 8	£50	UK Treasury announces bank recapitalization initiative through purchase of preferred shares	Shifts strategy from troubled asset purchase (original TARP) to bank recapitalization
October 13	—	Main central banks announce unlimited swap arrangement	Fed, Bank of England, European Central Bank, Swiss National Bank
October 13	€120 recapitalized; €1,020 guaranteed	European governments recapitalize banks, guarantee bank loans	France (40/320); Germany (80/400); Italy (–); Netherlands (0/200); Spain (0/100)
October 13	$250	US induces nine largest banks to accept $125 billion preferred share capitalization; another $125 billion pending for other banks	Shift from troubled-asset purchase to recapitalization as main TARP strategy
October 13	—	FDIC temporarily guarantees new bank debt	Newly issued senior unsecured
October 16	$60	Swiss National Bank supports UBS	Purchases illiquid securities
October 21	$540	Fed announces Money Market Investor Funding Facility (MMIFF)	Fed lends 90 percent to SPVs against short-term, high-quality assets
October 30	$120	Fed opens swap lines for Brazil, Korea, Mexico, Singapore	$30 billion each
November 12	—	US Treasury secretary backs away from asset purchases through TARP	Notes needs in consumer credit, housing

(continued on next page)

Table 4A.1   Key financial-sector events in the global crisis of 2007–09 *(continued)*

Date	Event	Support (billions of specified currency)	Comment
2008 *(continued)*			
November 23	Citigroup receives special support by Fed, Treasury. First large guarantee of troubled assets, following plunge in share prices	$20 recapitalization; $306 guaranteed	Extra $20 billion from TARP. Special Fed guarantee of $306 billion asset-backed securities (ABS) in return for $7 billion preferred shares transfer. Citigroup bears first $29 billion loss, 10 percent thereafter
November 25	Fed announces Term Asset-Backed Securities Loan Facility (TALF) for consumer, small business credit	$200	$20 billion from TARP used as credit protection for TALF
November 28	Royal Bank of Scotland nationalized	$31	UK government buys 60 percent stake
December 12	Senate fails to pass auto bailout	—	$14 billion requested
December 19	Administration grants short-term lending to big-three auto companies	$17	Reverses opposition to use of TARP for autos
2009			
January 15	Bank of America receives additional $20 billion from TARP and guarantees on $37 billion ABS and $81 billion derivatives	$20 recapitalization; $118 guaranteed	BOA absorbs first $10 billion loss and 10 percent of additional losses; pays $4 billion in preferred shares at 8 percent plus warrants for guarantee
February 10	Treasury announces stress tests for major banks, plans for further purchases of preferred shares, the Private-Public Investment Program (PPIP), expansion of the TALF, and a comprehensive housing program	—	PPIP to start at $500 billion, TALF expanded to up to $1 trillion, housing plan to be announced later
February 14	American Recovery and Reinvestment Act of 2009 signed into law	$787	$288 billion on tax relief
February 18	Homeowner Affordability and Stability Plan announced with $100 billion expansion in preferred holdings in Fannie Mae and Freddie Mac	—	Refinancing of conforming mortgages, $75 billion to modify eligible home loans

Date	Event	Amount ($ billions)	Notes
February 25	Stress test to include all banks with $100 billion in assets	—	Will examine range of future losses and resources to absorb losses over two-year time span
February 27	Citigroup preferred stock to be converted to common equity	$25	
March 2	AIG government assistance restructured	$30	Additional $30 billion from TARP, $40 billion preferred shares converted into preferred shares resembling common equity
March 3	Fed announces Term Asset-Backed Securities Loan Facility	Up to $200	$200 billion available for ABS backed by newly created loans
March 23	Details of PPIP announced. Plan will contain Legacy Loan Program and Legacy Securities Program	$500	$75 billion to $100 billion of TARP leveraged by FDIC and Fed split between the programs
April 2	G-20 announces large expansion of the International Monetary Fund and the multilateral development banks (MDBs)	$850	$500 billion increase to New Arrangements to Borrow, $250 billion new Special Drawing Rights, $100 billion increase for MDBs
May 7	Stress test of 19 largest banks released. Nine firms found to have enough capital	—	Total loses could be $600 billion. Ten banks need to raise combined $75 billion ($185 billion with 2009 revenues)
May 20	Helping Families Save their Home Act of 2009 signed	—	FDIC raises deposit insurance to $250,000 until October 3, 2014
June 1	GM files for Chapter 11 bankruptcy	—	
June 9	10 large US financial institutions are eligible to repay TARP money	—	

Appendix 4B
Causes of the Crisis

Important sources of the financial crisis include the housing market bubble, opaque securitization, asymmetric information, excessive leverage of both financial institutions and households, and policy miscalculations. There is also a debate on whether a global saving glut was a prime factor. This appendix examines these sources of the crisis.

The Housing Bubble

The proximate cause of the crisis was the decline in housing prices after their long climb in what became a housing bubble. Figure 4B.1 shows the S&P/Case-Shiller index of housing prices for 20 major US cities (Standard and Poor's 2009), as well as the FHFA (2009) national housing price index. The Case-Shiller index tends to overstate the price increase and subsequent declines because it focuses on major metropolitan areas in which the housing bubble was more pronounced. The FHFA index is preferable in terms of coverage, which is nationwide. However, it tends to understate the price increase and subsequent decline for three reasons. First, it pertains only to "conforming" loans (those that meet GSE standards) and thus does not include homes with subprime mortgages, where price declines probably have been more severe. Second, it uses unit weighting rather than value weighting, and hence tends to understate the loss of value in the high-priced regions. Third, it uses appraisal values, which tend to be overstated and lag behind transactions (Hatzius and Marschoun 2009, Office of Federal Housing Enterprise Oversight 2008).

Prices in the Case-Shiller cities doubled over six years, an annual increase of almost 12 percent. In the first part of this period US equity markets were imploding after the bursting of the dot-com bubble, and it seems likely that investors shifted the locus of their interest from stocks to real estate (just as they later shifted from real estate to oil and commodities, which enjoyed a much briefer bubble in 2006–07 before they collapsed by late 2008).[49] The index shows a peak in July 2006. From that peak until the trough in April 2009, the index shows a decline of 32.6 percent. By August 2009 the index showed a slight recovery, with an increase of 4.8 percent above the April low point. The FHFA price index shows a similar but somewhat more moderate increase (about 70 percent from the first quarter of 2000 to the peak in the second quarter of 2007), followed by a much smaller decline (by 13.6 percent from May 2007 to May 2009).

---

49. The commodity price index of the *Economist*, which excludes oil and precious metals, more than doubled from January 2005 to February 2008. After remaining at a high plateau through July, the index fell 45 percent by early December (*Economist*, October 25, 2008, 117; December 6, 2008, 121).

Figure 4B.1 US housing price indexes, January 2000–July 2009

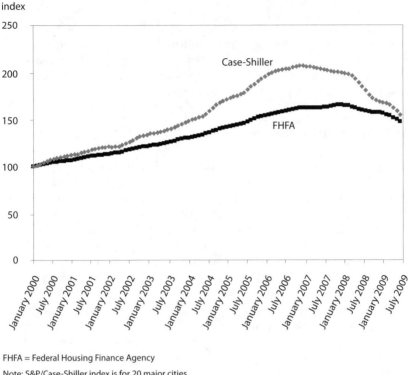

FHFA = Federal Housing Finance Agency
Note: S&P/Case-Shiller index is for 20 major cities.
Sources: FHFA (2009); Standard and Poor's (2009).

At the end of 2007, households held $20 trillion in real estate assets (US Federal Reserve 2009c). If one places the house price decline at 23 percent (the average between Case-Shiller and FHFA), the loss of wealth amounts to $4.6 trillion. Applying the normal rule of thumb for consumption out of wealth, the reduction in annual consumption that could be anticipated would be 4 percent of this amount (Mehra 2001), or $184 billion. This decline in consumption would amount to 1.25 percent of GDP. In comparison, real personal consumption fell by 0.2 percent in 2008 and by 0.6 percent in 2009, in contrast to growth of 2.6 percent in 2007 (BEA 2010).

Sources of the Bubble

Zandi (2009) provides an excellent analysis of the US housing boom and bust. Both demand and supply factors contributed. On the demand side, the policy of extraordinarily low interest rates pursued by the Federal Reserve after the dot-com stock market bubble burst in 2000 and after 9/11 drove a reduction in mortgage rates from their 6 to 8 percent average from 1994–2000 to a 4 to 6 percent range from 2001–06 (Zandi 2009, 65).[50] Low rates meant continued affordability even as home prices rose. Mortgage lenders pushed increasingly questionable practices, such as "stated income" and "negative amortization," in part spurred by increased Internet-based competition (p. 97). Adjustable-rate mortgages (ARMs) artificially reduced initial-period payments in the expectation that ever-rising home prices would make subsequent refinancing easy. The shift in lending toward the "originate to distribute" model through securitization removed perceived lender risk (p. 126). After the dot-com bust, investors shifted toward the housing market. "Flippers" came to account for more than one-fifth of home purchases in such markets as Miami, Phoenix, and Las Vegas (p. 61).

On the supply side, homebuilding shifted structurally toward large, publicly-owned companies. These had accounted for only about one-tenth of homes being built in the early 1990s, but their share reached about one-fifth by 1999 and nearly one-third at the peak in 2006 (Zandi 2009, 135). The companies concentrated on the more popular metropolitan markets, and their efforts to secure developable land in these markets pushed up land prices, which nationally account for 60 percent of home value (p. 251). Home construction was rising, but not fast enough to keep up with demand.

The number of housing starts rose from an annual average of about 1.8 million in 2001–03 to 2.1 million in 2004–05 and 2.3 million in 2006, but then collapsed to 1.5 million in 2007 and a rate of 1.1 million in the first quarter of 2008 (Zandi 2009, 140). Subsequently housing starts fell much further, to a trough of 498,000 in April 2009 before rebounding moderately to 563,000 in June (US Census Bureau 2009a). Zandi estimates "fundamental demand" at a nearly flat 1.8 million homes per year over the past decade, of which about two-thirds is for new households, one-tenth for second or vacation homes, and one-fifth for homes torn down (Zandi 2009, 139–40, 251). When the bubble burst, the inventory of vacant homes had risen from a normal level of about 1.25 million to 2.2 million in 2007 and early 2008 (p. 142), placing the vacancy rate at 2.9 percent instead of its normal 1.7 percent and leaving an excess inventory of about 1 million homes.

Home prices rose at average annual rates of about 4 percent in 1995–98 but then increased at 8 percent annually in 1999–2002 and 12 percent annually in 2003–05 (Zandi 2009, 161).[51] The ratio of home prices to rents, analogous to the price-earnings ratio for stocks, was flat at about 14 for

---

50. The lower rates are for adjustable mortgages; the higher ones for fixed-rate mortgages.

51. Zandi cites a private data source as well as the Bureau of Labor Statistics for housing prices.

1987–98 but then rose at an accelerating pace to 20 by 2003 and 25 by 2005 (p. 165). Yet the dominant policy view was that there could be no housing market bubble, because high transaction costs ruled out speculation and because by definition all real estate was local rather than national.

Once the bubble burst, it triggered a powerful adverse feedback loop from home prices to mortgage values to the securitized mortgage market and thence to availability of mortgage finance, causing still more downward pressure on prices. The onset of the 2007–09 financial crisis was arguably the end-July 2007 closure of two Bear Stearns funds exposed to RMBS. There was an almost immediate seizing up in the RMBS market, which in turn cut off a key source of finance for home purchases (Zandi 2008, 167). Default rates on first mortgages surged from an average of about 1.25 million from 2002–06 to 1.5 million in the third quarter of 2007 and 2.25 million by the first quarter of 2008 (p. 166).

Scope of the Housing Market Problem

How large can losses on US residential mortgages become, and how important would such losses be relative to bank capital? Total home mortgages amounted to $12 trillion at the end of 2007 (US Federal Reserve 2009c, table L.2).[52] So if losses amounted to 10 percent, there would be $1.2 trillion in writedowns needed. US banks would absorb about half of losses on US residential mortgages (Hatzius and Marschoun 2009, 14), with pension funds, foreign financial institutions, and other investors accounting for the other half. The capital base of the US banking sector broadly defined is on the order of $1 trillion. Thus, if there were a 10 percent loss on mortgages, implying a $600 billion loss in capital for US banks, the result would be to eliminate 60 percent of their capital, not counting losses in other categories associated with severe recession.

There are approximately 118 million households in the United States.[53] Of these, 66.2 percent are homeowners. Of the 78 million homeowners, approximately 50 million, or 64 percent, have mortgages outstanding. Of the 50 million, approximately 10 million have mortgages that are "under water," with unpaid principal equal to or greater than the present value of the home. The amount of these mortgages stands at $2.75 trillion (Zandi 2008, 44), or 23 percent of the value of mortgages outstanding. Nonetheless, Foote, Gerardi, and Willen (2008) have found that fewer than 10 percent of underwater mortgages result in foreclosures.[54]

---

52. Of the total, $11.2 trillion was for individual homes and about $800 billion for multifamily homes. In comparison, household residential wealth was $20 trillion, indicating that households held about $8 trillion in home equity.

53. US population was 305 million at mid-2008. Average household size was 2.59 persons in 2000 (US Census Bureau 2008).

54. Based on data for over 100,000 homeowners in Massachusetts who had negative home

Analysts at Goldman Sachs have developed mortgage loss estimates based on econometric equations relating housing prices to fundamentals (such as the ratio of principal and interest to rent, and the ratio of mortgage payments to family income), technical factors (such as the extent of over-supply of homes for sale), and the relationship of mortgage losses to housing price declines. Their estimates are based on data for regional housing cycles in the past in the United States. Their central scenario assumes that house prices decline another 10 percent from third-quarter 2008 levels, a decline that occurred by the first quarter of 2009 using the average of the Case-Shiller and FHFA indexes. US residential mortgage losses would amount to $1.1 trillion (with one-half accruing to US banks, as noted). In their more adverse scenario with a 25 percent price decline from the third quarter of 2008, the total losses would amount to $1.8 trillion.

The IMF (2009d, 35) places 2007–10 worldwide losses on residential mortgages originated in the United States at $1.4 trillion, intermediate between the central and high Goldman-Sachs estimates.[55] These losses would account for more than half of the $2.7 trillion total worldwide credit losses in this period estimated by the IMF for assets originated in the United States.[56] For its part, the Federal Reserve's stress test for the 19 large banks placed forward-looking mortgage-related losses at only $202 billion under the stress scenario (US Federal Reserve 2009b, 6).[57] This amount does not include losses already incurred in 2007–08, or losses of intermediate and smaller banks.[58]

Broadly, then, the credit losses associated with the US housing crisis account for about half of the total, whether the focus is global credit losses or losses for US banks. The housing sector thus triggered the financial crisis and is its largest source of losses, but induced losses on other credits affected by the recession (commercial, consumer, corporate, and municipal loans and securities) will approximately double the damage stemming from the sector.

---

equity in the early 1990s. They argue that economic theory would predict a low foreclosure rate even for underwater mortgages. Borrowers consider the probability that their home's price will rebound again in the future, as well as the cost of paying rent if they leave their home, both factors that weigh against default (to which may be added the stigma of not honoring the loan).

55. $431 billion for direct mortgages, and $990 billion for RMBS.

56. Expected losses on other loans amounted to $637 billion and losses on other securities, $654 billion.

57. The amounts were $102 billion on first-lien mortgages, $83 billion on junior mortgages, and $17 billion on RMBS.

58. The mortgage claims of the large banks amounted to about $2 trillion, based on the 9 percent loss rate and the $185 billion loss on direct mortgages (US Federal Reserve 2009b, 9).

Role of Mortgage-Backed Securities

The crisis-impact role of the housing correction has been amplified by a seizing up in the market for MBS. Sizable amounts of these assets are held by financial institutions rather than being spread widely across investors. For example, in the third quarter of 2008, Merrill Lynch sold $30.6 billion in face-value MBS for only $6.7 billion.[59] This transaction alone represented a loss on the order of one-half of capital.[60] Hatzius and Marschoun (2009) estimate that one-fourth of the RMBS are held by banks, whose total mortgage-related losses, including direct mortgage loans, thus reach $505 billion in their central case. Yet their estimate of the MBS losses is only about 20 cents on the dollar, much less than the 78 cents on the dollar loss in the Merrill Lynch transaction. The implication is that either this sale of distressed assets was at prices well below what would have been expected based on past relationships of mortgage losses to housing price declines, or that the Merrill Lynch portfolio was concentrated in the lower-rated tranches, or some combination of the two.

Severe losses and illiquidity for RMBS, and fire-sale prices far below what might be expected if held to maturity, were a principal reason for the original concept of the TARP as a vehicle to purchase distressed assets. A major reason for the severe discounts on MBS was that their original ratings had lost credibility, in part out of concern that the rating agencies had conflicts of interest in both rating the instruments and giving advice to underwriters about how best to package aggregations of mortgages to obtain the best ratings. The guide to valuation of these assets became the ABX.HE indices, created in 2006 by Markit and traded over the counter. Gorton (2008) attributes great importance to the sharp decline in these "ABX prices" in 2007. These prices, "together with the lack of information about location of the risks led to a loss of confidence on the part of banks in the ability of their counterparties to honor contractual obligations" (p. 3).

Figure 4B.2 shows the ABX indices for four cohorts of subprime MBS, with ratings classes for each cohort. It is evident that in July 2007 there was a collapse across the board in the ABX CDS prices.[61] It is also evident that the categories that have held up the best have been the AAA-rated issues from the first half of 2006, which had returned to about 80 cents on the dollar by October 2009 after reaching a low point of 60 in March at approximately the same time as the trough in equity markets. The three lowest rating classes have lost most of their value in all of the cohorts. For

---

59. Bradley Keoun, "Merrill Sells $8.55 billion of Stock, Unloads CDOs," Bloomberg.com, July 29, 2008.

60. The total assets of Merrill Lynch at end-2007 amounted to $876 billion; total capital stood at $43 billion (quarterly report filed with the Securities and Exchange Commission for the quarter ending September 26, 2008).

61. The ABX CDS are used to insure against default of subprime mortgages.

Figure 4B.2   Prices of ABX derivatives for subprime mortgage-backed securities, 2006 and 2007

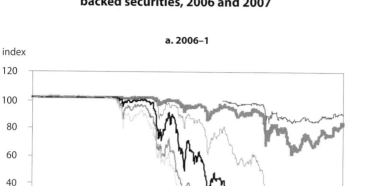

a. 2006–1

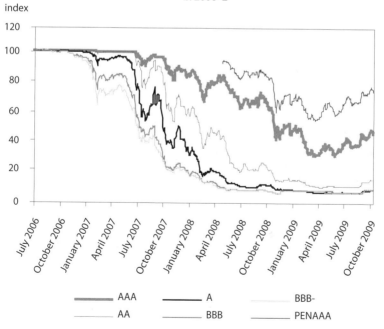

b. 2006–2

▬▬ AAA	▬▬ A	⋯⋯ BBB-
▬ AA	▬▬ BBB	▬▬ PENAAA

(continued on next page)

Figure 4B.2 Prices of ABX derivatives for subprime mortgage-backed securities, 2006 and 2007 *(continued)*

c. 2007–1

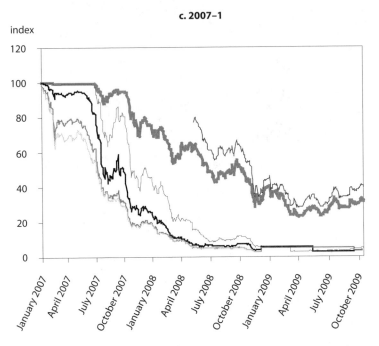

d. 2007–2

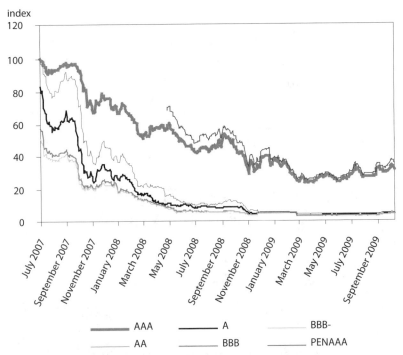

| AAA | A | BBB- |
| AA | BBB | PENAAA |

Sources: Markit; Datastream.

example, the AA-rated class from the first half of 2007 stood at only about 5 cents on the dollar by early December 2008, and even less thereafter. The 2007 cohorts have performed the worst more generally, with their AAA prices at a plateau of only about 30 cents on the dollar by November 2008 and after.[62]

Another pattern is also present in figure 4B.2. The acute phase of the financial crisis began in mid-September 2008 with the bankruptcy of Lehman Brothers and government takeover of Fannie Mae and Freddie Mac. There is a marked further decline in the stronger ABX indices after, but not in the months immediately prior to, this date. This pattern suggests that the acute phase of the crisis was not triggered by further declines in subprime and Alt-A mortgage-backed assets but contributed to an additional decline in their values.

Gorton (2008, 1–3) emphasizes the opacity of RMBS and the collapse in counterparty confidence that occurred when the ABX market seemed to provide information on their prices. He argues:

> [T]he problem at root is a lack of information.…[T]he interlinked or nested unique security designs that were necessary to make the subprime market function resulted in a loss of information to investors as the chain of structures—securities and special purpose vehicles—stretched longer and longer.…[Losses revealed by] the ABX [derivatives market] information [introduced in 2006] together with the lack of information about the location of the risks led to a loss of confidence on the part of banks in the ability of their counterparties to honor contractual obligations.…Like the classic panics of the 19th and early 20th centuries in the U.S., holders of short-term liabilities…refused to fund 'banks' [including the shadow banking system] due to rational fears of loss.…

Gorton also argues that it was the uniquely high sensitivity of the value of subprime mortgages and securitizations to housing prices that drove the crisis, and that other securitizations are less sensitive to underlying asset prices and thus to bubbles. The subprime loan is designed for riskier borrowers (insufficient funds for down payment, poor credit record, undocumented income). It is premised on a rising home price that builds equity, and the step-up interest rate after two or three years is intended to force refinancing when equity has risen and the borrower is on more solid ground. There is a relatively high probability of default, however, if housing prices do not rise or, especially, fall. Gorton also notes that with the advent of the ABX, "the ability to short subprime risk may have burst the housing bubble and, in any case, resulted in the market crowding on the short side to hedge, driving ABX prices very low" (p. 76).

Markowitz (2008) has also emphasized the inherent sensitivity of the RMBS to housing prices, making them much more vulnerable than their 80 percent triple A ratings suggested. For his part, Calomiris (2008) has

---

62. The premium "penultimate" class, PENAAA, was begun in May 2008 but has differed little from the AAA (except for the 2006-2 series).

argued that the securitizers had a perverse incentive to sell questionable securities because they did not retain the risk themselves (the "principal-agent" problem).

Leverage

Banking is based on borrowing at short maturities and low interest rates and lending at longer maturities and higher interest rates. Depositors provide a relatively stable base for bank borrowing, in part thanks to deposit insurance. Banks have had asset-to-capital leverage on the order of 10 to 1. Investment banks have tended to have higher leverage ratios, on the order of 20 or 30 to 1. They also have not had depositors but instead have relied on commercial paper and other forms of short-term funding. They were thus more vulnerable to a seizing up in financial markets. It is no coincidence that the two most prominent casualties of the crisis (aside from the GSEs and insurance company AIG) were both investment banks (Bear Stearns and Lehman Brothers). Nor is it a coincidence that the other large investment banks have become bank holding companies (Goldman Sachs, Morgan Stanley) or been taken over by a bank (Merrill Lynch by Bank of America), essentially eliminating a major category of the US financial sector. As discussed below, by early 2009 the question had become whether even the flagship banks had been so highly leveraged that their prospective losses meant their problems were more ones of insolvency rather than illiquidity.

The use of off–balance sheet vehicles to avoid regulatory capital meant that in practice the core banks were more leveraged than they appeared. SIVs set up by banks to pool loans into asset-backed securities borrowed short-term commercial paper and conduits for constructing MBS, in effect enabling banks to develop asset bases off balance sheet. When the crisis hit, both reputational factors and credit-line obligations to the entities turned out to force the assets back onto the balance sheets, straining capital adequacy. By late 2008 the SIVs were defunct, as Citigroup and other major banks had taken assets back onto their balance sheets.

Financial Innovation

At the annual Jackson Hole, Wyoming meeting of central bankers in 2005, Rajan (2005, i) argued that although financial-sector innovation had "made the world much better off," it had increased systemic risk. He noted:

> A number of financial transactions have moved from being embedded in a long-term relationship between a client and a financial institution to being conducted at arm's length in a market....The standardization of contractual terms allows a loan to be packaged with other contracts and sold as a diversified bundle....This process of 'securitization' allows for specialization...[T]hose who have specific

capabilities in originating financial transactions can be different from those who ultimately hold the risk (pp. 6–7)....The changes have allowed [banks] to focus on their core business of customization and financial innovation...[and their] risks have not become any lower. New risks are, however, now spread more widely in the economy (p. 16)....[The new instruments of] credit derivatives...have the appearance of producing very high alphas (high returns for low risk).... Every once in a while, however, they will blow up (p. 20).... Not only can [the new] intermediaries accentuate real fluctuations, they can also leave themselves exposed to certain small probability risks that their own collective behavior makes more likely. As a result, under some conditions, economies may be more exposed to financial sector-induced turmoil than in the past. (p. i)

At the time, Rajan's concern was viewed as what one observer described as that of an "antimarket Luddite, wistful for the old days of regulation."[63] With the benefit of hindsight, it seems clear that financial innovation and financial engineering played a key role in the crisis. Perhaps the most important instance was in its effect in the market for subprime lending, where the creation of RMBS resulted in opaque assets that turned the financial sector into a minefield once the housing market turned and the value of the assets became highly questionable. The construction of MBS out of subprime mortgages might have been safer if it had stopped at simply creating pools of them and selling shares. Instead, securitization created risk tranches. All mortgages paid into the investment pool, but first priority in payments went to the senior tranches. The major credit rating agencies cooperated with the originators to rate the tranches. Remarkably, 80 percent of the typical RMBS was rated at the top, Aaa. In the middle "mezzanine" layers were most of the rest (11 percent Aa, 4 percent B, 3 percent Baa). Only 2 percent was left at the unrated bottom "equity" tranche (Zandi 2009, 115). Financial engineering was creating almost entirely silk purses out of almost entirely sows' ears. Foreign and domestic entities that needed to remain in investment-grade assets took comfort in the triple A rating of the top tranches, although some have argued that the investor community had long been aware that RMBS ratings were not as stringent as those for corporations.

RMBS were not the only financial innovation. There were also collateralized debt obligations (CDOs) that were securities based on pools of RMBS, often together with other underlying assets such as credit card debt. As the securitization market heated up and the raw material of subprime loans was not arriving fast enough to keep up with the demand for securities, securitizers created CDOs of CDOs (CDOs squared, and sometimes cubed).

Another financial innovation that figured prominently in the demise of AIG but has so far otherwise not wreaked damage comparable to that of RMBS was the credit default swap (CDS). The seller of this instrument

63. Justin Lahart, "Mr. Rajan Was Unpopular (But Prescient) at Greenspan Party," *Wall Street Journal*, January 2, 2009.

provides an insurance policy to the buyer that pays the principal of an obligation if the debtor defaults. The notional value of CDS reached a peak of $57.9 trillion at end-2007, still stood at $57.3 trillion in June 2008, but then fell to $41.9 trillion at the end of 2008 (BIS 2009, A103). This amount far exceeds the underlying debt.[64] Often the CDS is not even linked to a specific existing bond or debt, but instead is in effect a wager by the buyer against the credit of the name on which the CDS is written. Buying the CDS is a means of shorting the debt.

The placement of AIG under conservatorship, and a total of some $180 billion in US official-sector support so far to AIG, was forced by policymaker fears of the consequences to the financial system if the company were unable to deliver as the counterparty to an enormous amount of CDS.[65] In a recent article, Michael Lewis examines the AIG experience and emphasizes that the giant insurer was a key ingredient in the take-off of RMBS in 2004–05. He finds that AIG sharply expanded its CDS deals with Wall Street but that top officials were unaware that bundles of subprime loans, rather than general consumer debt, had mushroomed to be 95 percent of the CDS total. When top management became aware of this concentration, AIG stopped writing RMBS-based CDS, but by then Wall Street firms had moved toward taking the risk themselves. The collapse of the subprime market in mid-2007 caused collateral calls on AIG by Wall Street firms holding its CDS insurance. The public sector supported AIG out of fear about massive ramifications to the major financial firms if it could not meet its obligations. Lewis also suggests that it was the advent of the RMBS, combined initially with the willingness of AIG to insure them with CDS, that thwarted the Federal Reserve's move in 2004 toward higher interest rates.[66] Gillian Tett also reports that in the development of

---

64. Most of the CDS notional volume represents offsetting long and short positions. For the top 1,000 corporations and sovereigns, on July 10, 2009, gross notional value of CDS amounted to $15.2 trillion in 2 million contracts, but net notional value was $1.38 trillion. See DTTC (2009).

65. By early November 2008, federal support amounted to $40 billion in an equity stake and another $112.5 billion in loans and asset purchases (Mark Felsenthal and Lilla Zuill, "AIG Reworks Bailout; Fed Ups Support to $150B, Lowers Interest Rate," Insurance Journal, November 9, 2008). In early March 2009, the Treasury committed an additional $30 billion from the TARP in contingent assistance to AIG. Andrew Ross Sorkin and Mary Williams Walsh, "U.S. Is Said to Offer Another $30 Billion in Funds to A.I.G," New York Times, March 2, 2009.

66. Michael Lewis, "The Man Who Crashed the World," Vanity Fair, August 2009. Lewis continues: "In June 2004 the Fed began to contract the money supply, and interest rates rose.... [F]rom June 2004 to June 2005 prime-mortgage lending fell by half. But in that same period subprime lending doubled—and then doubled again. In 2003 there had been a few tens of billions of dollars in subprime-mortgage loans. From June 2004 until June 2007, Wall Street underwrote $1.6 trillion of new subprime-mortgage loans and another $1.2 trillion of so-called Alt-A loans....The subprime sector of the financial economy clearly was responding to different signals than the others—and the result was booming demand for housing and

derivative pools of loans by JP Morgan, insurance by AIG was a key to reducing regulatory capital required as backing, a factor that reflected less burdensome capital reserves for insurance companies than banks.[67]

Regulatory Laxity and Gaps?

There are grounds for concluding that insufficient, or at least inefficient, regulation contributed to the crisis. In the housing market in particular there were arguably regulatory mistakes.[68] It was not until late 2006, after most of the damage had been done, that regulators issued their first formal guidance on subprime lending (Zandi 2009, chapter 9). They warned against making loans without verifying income, and called for lenders to disclose prepayment penalties. In follow-up guidance in June 2007 they directed subprime lenders to evaluate borrowers' qualifications on the loan's full monthly cost rather than at the initially low "teaser" interest rate, and required that following a large increase in payments, at least 60 days be allowed to refinance before prepayment penalties could be charged.

Regulation of subprime lending was highly fragmented across different regulators: the Federal Reserve for bank holding companies, Office of the Comptroller of the Currency for nationally chartered banks, Office of Thrift Supervision for savings and loan associations, and state regulators for state-chartered banks and mortgage brokers (Zandi 2009, 146). About half of subprime mortgages in 2005 were originated by companies with no federal supervision. One board member of the Federal Reserve, Edward Gramlich, had unsuccessfully proposed to Chairman Alan Greenspan that the Federal Reserve send examiners to scrutinize predatory lending in consumer-finance firms that were units of bank holding companies regulated by the Federal Reserve.[69]

It seems likely that the politics of expanding home ownership contributed to what may be seen at least in hindsight as relatively lax regulation of subprime lending (Zandi 2009, chapter 9). In 1977, the Community Reinvestment Act made it illegal for banks to "redline" neighborhoods where they would not lend, and in the 1990s regulators began to require banks to target underserved neighborhoods. The Federal Reserve used statistical models to flag banks that practiced lending discrimination, and

a continued rise in house prices. Perhaps the biggest reason for this was that the Wall Street firms packaging the loans into bonds had found someone to insure against what turned out to be the rather high risk that they'd go bad...[AIG]."

67. Gillian Tett, "Genesis of the Debt Disaster," *Financial Times*, May 3, 2009.

68. Barth (2009, 292) states that "...it was quite obvious that a housing bubble was forming and that insufficient regulatory actions were taken to limit its growth and magnitude while there was still time to take preventive containment measures."

69. Greg Ip, "Did Greenspan Add to Subprime Woes?" *Wall Street Journal*, June 9, 2007.

could deny requests for mergers to those that did. In the early 2000s the Office of Federal Housing Enterprise Oversight set targets for lending to low-income groups by Fannie Mae and Freddie Mac, and the two GSEs responded by becoming major purchasers of the Aaa tranches of MBS.

The overall effect was that by 2006 most subprime borrowers were taking on adjustable rate mortgages with extremely low initial teaser rates that would reset in two years, and put down little or no money of their own. In many cases borrowers overstated their income on loan documents ("stated income" or "liars' loans") with the tacit approval of the lenders (Zandi 2009, 17). The premise was that rising housing prices would enable them to refinance before payments escalated sharply.

Inadequate regulation of CDS derivatives, and/or loopholes in official supervision of insurance company subsidiaries, turned out to be responsible for one of the most costly shocks of the crisis, the need to bail out AIG in order to prevent severe chain reaction effects on large financial firms that were counterparties to its CDS. Wessel (2009, 194) quotes Fed Chairman Bernanke as stating that:

> AIG exploited a huge gap in the regulatory system….[Its financial products division] was a hedge fund, basically, that was attached to a large and stable insurance company, made huge numbers of irresponsible bets, took huge losses. There was no regulatory oversight because there was a gap in the system….

A central regulatory question is whether the Gramm-Leach-Bliley Act in 1999 ending the Glass-Steagall separation of commercial banking from investment banking was responsible for increasing risk in the financial system. Former Federal Reserve Chairman Paul Volcker, for one, has advocated what one account summarized as a "proposal [that] would roll back the nation's commercial banks to an earlier era, when they were restricted to commercial banking and prohibited from engaging in risky Wall Street activities."[70] In contrast, Barth (2009, 238) argues that blaming Gramm-Leach-Bliley for the financial crisis is "totally wrong." He notes that the three large investment banks that got into the most trouble (Merrill Lynch, Lehman Brothers, and Bear Stearns) were all unaffiliated with commercial banks. Moreover, it was large banks that helped solve the problem they posed, as JP Morgan absorbed Bear Stearns and Bank of America absorbed Merrill Lynch. However, this view would seem to give too little recognition to the problem of toxic assets that some of the large banks themselves had acquired even before those two takeovers, and to the major problem that had arisen in the off–balance sheet risks of the large banks in their SIV entities. Ironically, under the risk-weighting principle of capital requirements of Basel II, in principle there should be no problem of allowing banks to engage in risky business, so the Volcker critique implies skepticism that such requirements can be applied effectively.

---

70. Louis Uchitelle, "Volcker Fails to Sell a Bank Strategy," *New York Times*, October 21, 2009.

Agency Problems and Underpricing Risk

A central element in Rajan's (2005) warning was concern that perverse incentives characterized the new structure of financing. Intermediary managers had an incentive to seek immediate high returns with seemingly low risk but hidden "tail" risk of catastrophe. He suggested requiring fund managers to have some portion of their pay vested in the funds they manage. Testifying before Congress in October 2008, Alan Greenspan also emphasized the agency problem, noting that already in 2005 he had raised concerns about the underpricing of risk. A "surge in global demand for U.S. subprime securities by banks, hedge, and pension funds supported by unrealistically positive rating designations by credit agencies was, in my judgment, the core of the problem." Securitizers and lenders "never put their shareholders' capital at risk and hence did not have the incentive to evaluate the credit quality of what they were selling." Subprime underwriting standards collapsed from 2005 forward. Greenspan noted that in the future securitizers should be required to retain a meaningful part of the securities they issue. However, he also noted that for a long time these markets will be far more restrained than would be the effect of any new regulatory regime. Noting that "structured investment vehicles, Alt-A mortgages, and a myriad of other exotic financial instruments are not now, and are unlikely to ever find willing investors," he expressed regret that subprime mortgages are also on that list and called for ways to reestablish a more sustainable subprime mortgage market.[71]

Ironically, some of the worst losses have been concentrated in institutions that had not necessarily arranged to pass on all the risk. Michael Lewis notes that traders at AIG Financial Products were required (and happy) to "leave 50 percent of their bonuses in the company."[72] Moreover, the problem of toxic assets held on the books of such large banks as Citigroup suggests that they did not necessarily have an agency problem stemming from indifference to the fate of securities they created and marketed.[73]

Misleading Risk Models?

A particular aspect of financial engineering that may further have proved dangerous was the nature of the main risk measurement models, which

---

71. Alan Greenspan, testimony before the US House of Representatives Committee on Oversight and Government Reform, October 23, 2008.

72. Michael Lewis, "The Man Who Crashed the World," *Vanity Fair,* August 2009.

73. However, a considerable portion of these assets reverted to the institutions when for reputational purposes they found it necessary to stand behind the SIVs they had set up, and earlier perceptions may have been that the risk had indeed been shed.

probably conveyed a false sense of security. The value-at-risk (VaR) models developed at JP Morgan and based on modern portfolio theory (Markowitz 1952) sought to assure CEOs that their company had (for example) 99 percent assurance that their loss over the next week would not exceed a specified amount. The model was typically implemented with data on probability distributions and asset correlations from relatively recent years and thus did not reflect more adverse periods; in any event it was designed with the extreme short term in mind. In one roundtable of expert practitioners assessing VaR soon after the Asian financial crisis, critics emphasized the large standard error in the VaR calculated, the unreliability of correlation matrices, feedback effects that lead to contagion and hence prove diversification to have been illusory, and more fundamentally the conflation of measurable risk with what economist Frank Knight called unmeasurable uncertainty (Kolman et al. 1998). Nonetheless the VaR, which was often featured in annual reports, conveyed a sense of assurance that risk was being expertly managed.

Greenspan is a prominent critic of the mathematical models developed to evaluate risk. In the same congressional testimony mentioned above, he noted that they had been the underpinning of the derivatives market, but that this "whole intellectual edifice...collapsed in the summer of last year because the data inputted into the risk management models generally covered only the past two decades, a period of euphoria." When markets in August 2007 "trashed the credit agencies' rosy ratings," doubt was cast on pricing of securities with "any taint of subprime backing."[74]

Monetary Policy

Former US Treasury Under-Secretary John Taylor has argued that unduly lax monetary policy was the principal cause of the crisis.[75] He states:

> The classic explanation of financial crises is that they are caused by excesses— frequently monetary excesses—which lead to a boom and an inevitable bust. This crisis was no different: A housing boom followed by a bust led to defaults, the implosion of mortgages and mortgage-related securities at financial institutions, and the resulting financial turmoil. Monetary excesses were the main cause of the boom. The Fed held its target interest rate, especially in 2003–2005, well below known monetary guidelines that say what good policy should be based on historical experience....The effects of the boom and bust were amplified by several complicating factors including the use of subprime and adjustable-rate mortgages, which led to excessive risk taking. There is also evidence that excessive risk taking was encouraged by the excessively low interest rates.

---

74. Alan Greenspan, testimony before the US House of Representatives Committee on Oversight and Government Reform, October 23, 2008.

75. John B. Taylor, "How Government Created the Financial Crisis," *Wall Street Journal*, February 9, 2009.

Taylor also argues that the mishandling of the call for TARP legislation, and seeming inconsistency in ad hoc decisions to save some institutions and not others, caused unnecessary panic and aggravated market turmoil in the fourth quarter of 2008.

Responding to Taylor, Greenspan argued that it was long-term rates, not short-term rates controlled by the Federal Reserve, that had been abnormally low.[76] He attributed low long-term rates to the global phenomenon of excess global intended saving over intended capital investment (the global saving glut, examined below). He argued that the global downward pressure on long-term interest rates meant the "empirical relationships of earlier decades...no longer apply." With respect to the "Taylor Rule" for interest rates, Greenspan judged it had been "consistently unable to anticipate the onset of recessions or financial crises. Counterfactuals from such flawed structures cannot form the sole basis for successful policy analysis...."

The debate on whether excessive monetary ease was the main cause of the crisis will not be settled here. Suffice it to say that the historically low federal funds rates pursued by the Federal Reserve in the aftermath of the 2001 recession and arguably maintained too long thereafter almost certainly contributed to the housing bubble as well as the underpricing of risk. This strategy was in part associated with the view of the Federal Reserve under Greenspan that central banks should not attempt to pierce bubbles before they become dangerously large, because it is never possible to diagnose the correct asset price level, and the pieces can be picked up by corrective monetary policy if a bubble does burst.

Figure 4B.3 shows the unusually large and long gap between the federal funds rate, which the Federal Reserve controls directly, and the 10-year treasury bond rate, which it does not, from the fourth quarter of 2001 through about the second quarter of 2005. It also shows that the relationship between the 10-year rate and the federal funds rate by the end of 2006 was essentially the same as in the second half of 2000. There is no apparent epochal divergence to be explained by a historically unprecedented global saving glut.

Figure 4B.4 shows the volume of net household mortgage borrowing from 1998 through the first quarter of 2009. This borrowing peaked at about $1 trillion annually in 2005–06. Its period of large increase was from 2001 through 2005, precisely the period when the federal funds rate was abnormally low. It would seem that part of the paradox of limited response to rising policy interest rates beginning in June 2004 was simply that the pace of their increase was relatively slow. The figure also shows the collapse of new mortgage borrowing in 2008 with the arrival of the financial crisis and the drying up of securitized subprime loans.

---

76. Alan Greenspan, "The Fed Didn't Cause the Housing Bubble," *Wall Street Journal*, March 11, 2009.

Figure 4B.3   US interest rates: Federal funds and 10-year treasuries, 1991Q1–2009Q2

percent

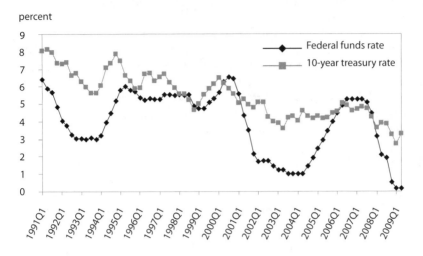

Sources: IMF (2009a); US Federal Reserve (2010).

Global Savings Glut

Finally, a popular explanation for the financial crisis is that a "global savings glut" caused an excess of investable funds seeking placement, driving down global interest rates and unduly reducing the price of risk as investors proceeded to "reach for yield."[77] Although there is undoubtedly some truth to this proposition, it suffers from several problems when elevated to the role of a prime causal force of the financial crisis.

A major problem is that long-term interest rates did not fall dramatically during the period of the upswing in the foreign current account surpluses, the crux of the so-called global saving glut. As shown in figure 4B.3, the US 10-year treasury bond rate was the same at the apex of the saving glut in mid-2007 as it had been at the beginning of this period in early 2001: 5 percent. The rate did dip to 4 percent in the period from the second quarter of 2002 to the second quarter of 2005. However, as is evident in the figure, it was being pulled down by the extraordinary reduction in the federal funds rate, controlled by the Federal Reserve. If the driving force had been a flood of foreign funds seeking investment in the United States, one would have expected to see a decline in the yield curve instead of a rise: Long-term interest rates would have fallen by more than the Federal Reserve allowed the federal funds rate to fall.

Moreover, if the "search for yield" argument is carried to the extreme,

---

77. See, for example, Wolf (2008).

Figure 4B.4   Net mortgage borrowing by households, 1998–2009Q2

billions of dollars; beginning 2007, quarterly at annual rate

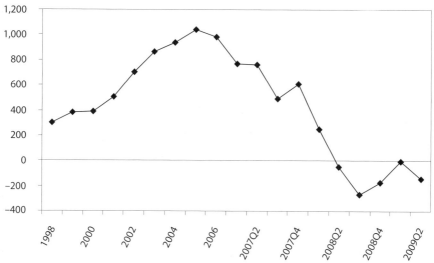

Source: US Federal Reserve (2009c).

that a global saving glut is considered to have "caused" the surge in such financial instruments as RMBS and CDS, the proposition becomes highly implausible. It requires an assumption that actors in financial markets do not maximize profits at all times but instead only respond with new instruments when forced to do so by a decline of interest rates below a "target return" level. This is not the standard assumption of economic actors, nor does it seem likely that new approaches in behavioral economics would lead to this conclusion.

It is certainly true that there has been a major rise in global current account imbalances over the past several years. As shown in figure 4B.5, the sum total of current account surpluses of about 70 countries in surplus each year rose from about $400 billion in 2001 to $1.7 trillion by 2007. China alone accounted for about one-third of the increase. Necessarily, the mirror image of the rising surpluses was a collective increase of current account deficits in about 120 countries in a typical year. The swing of the global discrepancy from deficit at the beginning of the period to surplus by the end meant that the increase of the combined deficits was somewhat smaller: from about $600 billion in 2001 to about $1.5 trillion in 2007.[78] The peak of the cumulative upswing in the US current account deficit, from 2001 to 2006 accounted for about $400 billion of the deficit-country total, or a bit more than one-half.

---

78. The data are from IMF (2009b).

Figure 4B.5 World sums of current account surpluses and deficits, surplus of China, and US deficit, 2000–07

billions of dollars

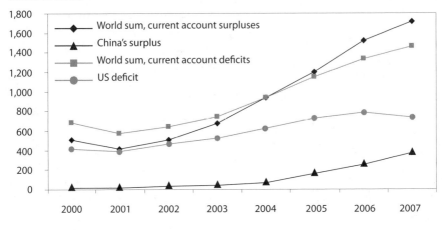

Source: IMF (2009b).

Figure 4B.6 US current account deficit and annual increase in net debt of the nonfinancial sector, 2001–08

percent of GDP

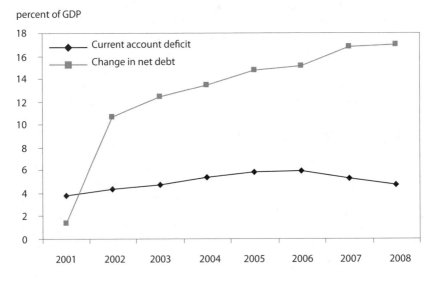

Source: IMF (2009b).

From end-2000 to end-2007, cumulative US current account deficits amounted to $4.2 trillion. In contrast, total credit debt of the US nonfinancial sector minus total credit assets of the sector rose from $15 trillion to $25.4 trillion.[79] So the external imbalance financed by foreign saving provided about 40 percent of the financing for the increase in nonfinancial-sector debt. Figure 4B.6 shows these relationships annually, as a percent of GDP. The annual increase in nonfinancial sector net debt amounted to an average of 14.5 percent of GDP during the period 2003–2007. (The pace continued to be high in 2008, at 17 percent of GDP, but the increase in net debt that year was concentrated in the federal government, whereas household debt remained almost unchanged.) In comparison, the current account deficit stood at an average of 4.5 percent of GDP. At the height of the run-up in the housing bubble, then, resources from abroad could be said to have been financing about one-third of the rise in net debt of US households, corporations, and the public sector. The level of this net nonfinancial-sector debt rose from 150 percent of GDP in 2001 to 184 percent in 2007 (US Federal Reserve 2009c).

On balance, the evidence suggests that external imbalances account for a substantial but nonetheless moderate portion of the rise in US debt. The "foreign saving glut" thus warrants characterization as at most having played a supplementary role rather than being the principal cause of the financial crisis.

---

79. US Federal Reserve (2009c, Z1 flow of funds accounts, table L.1).

Appendix 4C
Contemporary Policy Diagnoses from September 2008 to February 2009

In September 2008, as the financial crisis reached a new and acute phase, the Peterson Institute for International Economics launched a daily commentary on the crisis on its website entitled "RealTime Economic Issues Watch." This appendix reproduces five of the author's postings on this site, in part because of their at least partial continued relevance, and in part because they may help convey a sense of the financial policymaking atmosphere at the time.

Spending $700 Billion Wisely (September 22, 2008)

The Bernanke-Paulson proposal to spend $700 billion to shore up the financial system can be helpful if done wisely. That will require only purchasing assets at prices reflecting their medium-term value. Doing so would provide much needed liquidity while promising minimal costs to taxpayers.

Subprime mortgage-backed securities (MBS) outstanding have a face value somewhere on the order of $1 trillion (IMF 2008c). Their composition is approximately two-thirds AAA, one-fifth AA, and about 8 percent each for A and BBB/BBB– (Fender and Hordahl 2008). The current prices range respectively from about 90 cents to 15 cents on the dollar, for 2006 and earlier vintages, and about 60 to 8 cents on the dollar for 2007 vintages (Markit ABX index; figure 4C.1). (PENAAA is a special category above triple-A.) About three-fourths of the volume outstanding is AAA or better for 2006 vintages and about two-thirds for 2007 vintages. A rough estimate is that the overall weighted ratio of current market value to face value is about 70 percent for the 2006 and earlier vintages and about 50 percent for the 2007 vintages.

As the Brady Plan for Latin American debt in the 1980s demonstrated, crisis resolution based on security and liquidity in exchange for a haircut can restore market stability. The challenge is for the Federal Reserve and Treasury to develop internal reference prices applicable to each rating class and vintage of MBS that reflects reasonable medium-term values. These should be based on default probabilities and loss given default. The default probabilities should be based in part on prospective housing prices, for example, taking account of the Case-Shiller housing prices futures. Application of this type of approach will tend to generate medium-term (e.g., three-year-horizon) prices that exceed the fire-sale levels of today's prices on these securities.

The Treasury should then be prepared to purchase at auction substantial blocks of each class and cohort of this paper, but only at prices that are

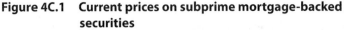

Figure 4C.1   Current prices on subprime mortgage-backed securities

index

2007-2
2007-1
2006-2
2006-1

PENAAAA   AAA   AA   A   BBB   BBB–

Source: Markit.

no higher than the internal reference price estimates. The result will be to restore liquidity and some upward price movement to a market currently frozen at crisis price levels. Moreover, when prices are established in such sales, financial institutions not actually selling should be permitted to mark-to-market over a phased period such as three years, for purposes of regulatory capital. Otherwise the cure could be worse than the disease for them, because they might be forced to mark down to prices that are below medium-term values even though they plan to hold the assets for appreciation.

Implemented in this way, the program would not bankrupt the US government. Gross US debt today is $9.6 trillion, but after taking account of claims held by one part of government on other parts, the debt held by the public is $5 trillion, or 36 percent of GDP. The government added somewhere between $1.5 trillion (direct) to $5 trillion (including guarantees) when it essentially nationalized Fannie and Freddie, but it gained an (almost) equal amount of assets, leaving the net debt little changed. Against a benchmark of some $11 trillion to $14 trillion total gross debt, another $700 billion is not enormous, and the rise in net debt would be minimal if the assets are purchased at prudent prices so they can be resold in the future at little loss or even a profit. The challenge is to keep any prospective losses to a minimum while restoring market liquidity and confidence. The approach outlined here would seem capable of achieving this objective.

Mark to What Market? (October 3, 2008)

On Tuesday the Securities and Exchange Commission (SEC) issued guidelines that gave banks greater leeway to avoid marking down their complex mortgage-backed assets to current fire-sale prices. That was the right decision and can help complement the $700 billion Troubled Asset Relief Program (TARP).

The new SEC guidance provides that "When an active market for a security does not exist...[expected] cash flows...[and] appropriate risk premiums" are an "acceptable" basis for valuation.[80] The new guidelines came after pressure from bankers and conservative Republicans in Congress. The American Bankers Association (ABA) argued that fair value rules under SFAS (Statement of Financial Standards) No. 157 are "flawed because they do not provide a framework...when markets become illiquid." The ABA called for the SEC to "provide immediate guidance that intrinsic value or economic value are appropriate proxies for fair value."[81] The bill passed by the Senate includes a provision clarifying that the SEC has the authority "to suspend...application of [SFAS 157]" if it is "necessary or appropriate in the public interest and is consistent with the protection of investors" (section 132).

The Financial Accounting Standards Board's (FASB) "fair value" accounting seeks "the price that would be received in an orderly transaction."[82] SFAS 157, which took force this year, provides the following framework for fair value. "Level 1" assets are to be valued at "quoted prices in active markets for identical assets or liabilities."[83] More opaque "Level 2" assets are valued at "mark to model" based on "observable" market prices and other variables. "Level 3" assets without a liquid market are based on unobservable inputs to their models. The key new SEC determination is that "distressed or forced liquidation sales are not orderly transactions," so the existence of a distress-market sale price does not require marking to that price.

The international debt crisis of the 1980s is a good example of when mark-to-market would have been seriously destabilizing. By the mid-1980s there had developed a secondary market, often characterized by sales of holdings by smaller banks that wanted to be able to say they held no Latin debt. Argentine debt, for example, fell as low as 20 cents on the dollar. Banks that planned to continue holding the claims in the expecta-

---

80. SEC Press Release 2008-234, September 30, 2008.

81. Letter from Edward L. Yingling, president of the ABA, to SEC chairman Christopher Cox, September 23, 2008.

82. Robert H. Herz and Linda A. MacDonald, "Some Facts about Fair Value," *Understand the Issues*, Financial Accounting Standards Board, May 2008 (accessed on January 4, 2010).

83. Ibid.

tion that the economy would recover did not need to mark them down immediately to this distressed level, although they did set aside reserves against possible losses. Eventually the claims rebounded to about 70 cents on the dollar, with the help of the Brady Plan, named after Treasury Secretary Nicholas F. Brady. If banks had been forced to write down drastically early in the crisis because of the presence of a limited number of secondary market transactions, a number of them would have been technically bankrupt, because their claims on Latin American governments exceeded their capital. Artificially forcing a collapse of the US banking system in the mid-1980s in the name of absolute belief that "the market" is always right at every moment, even if the only market transactions taking place involve a limited set of distressed sales, would have needlessly damaged the US and global economies.

Mortgage-backed securities, especially subprime and "Alt-A," are in a similar distressed market now. In late July, Merrill Lynch sold $31 billion in face value of mortgage-backed securities at 22 cents on the dollar. An overly ambitious accountant might then have demanded that all other holders of such assets mark them down to this price. In contrast, PIMCO's Bill Gross argues that on average the mortgage-backed securities are worth about 60 to 65 cents on the dollar. Every such asset has a CUSIP (Committee on Uniform Securities Identification Procedures) number. Each such asset has specified properties (e.g., whether it is at the front or the back of the repayment queue for the mortgages backing it). Probability distributions exist for the likelihood of default and the amount of recovery given default for these differing characteristics. The TARP is premised on holding government "reverse auctions" that purchase these assets at prices consistent with such medium-term valuation analysis. A similar valuation process should be considered fair for the accounting of banks that decide to hold such assets rather than sell them in a TARP auction.

Those who argue that investors will be cheated if mark-to-market is not imposed, despite a distressed market, miss the point that such valuation can in fact mislead the investor even more than the type of valuation just described. Especially the small investor who bails out at the bottom will be the one cheated by unnecessary mark-downs imposed by the mark-to-market straitjacket. Nonetheless, it would be extremely valuable for increased transparency if the banks were to include in notes to quarterly balance sheets a disclosure of the total mortgage-backed securities being held on their books, with a breakdown according to the principal classes and vintages.

A new problem could arise as the TARP is applied. Because of its restraints on compensation of top executives of banks seeking to sell assets, the program may wind up setting prices that are still below what many institutions believe comparable assets are worth. Technically the question would be whether the TARP auctions constitute an orderly market. Arguably the answer is no, because the sales occur under duress. In practice it seems likely that valuation by institutions not seeking TARP assistance will tend toward TARP auction prices if they are considerably closer to expected longer-term cash flow values than recent distressed prices, but that such institutions will instead continue Level 3 treatment if not. The SEC guidelines would appear to permit them to do so regardless of the TARP prices, although that too remains to be seen.

Bank Consolidation: More Stability Now for Oligopoly Later? (October 7, 2008)

The US financial sector has undergone a remarkable concentration as a consequence of the financial crisis. This consolidation potentially strengthens the resilience of the system by making its core institutions "really too big to fail" (no more Lehman Brothers). The longer-term price, however, may be greater oligopoly power of the super-banks.

Despite the consolidation, bank capital adequacy remains under pressure, and banks are reluctant to lend. At the same time, after a major money market fund "broke the buck," money market mutual funds holding commercial paper are losing funds to those holding treasury obligations. As a consequence, the threat is shifting from jeopardy to the financial system to a credit squeeze on manufacturing and nonfinancial services.

To help ease that credit crunch, the Federal Reserve and the US Treasury have stepped in with a new Commercial Paper Funding Facility (CPFF). Although unprecedented, the new CPFF follows logically from the present situation in which normal bank intermediation between depositors and borrowing real-economy firms is being squeezed, and there is a need for some entity to take on the intermediation role.

This note focuses on the question of bank consolidation. For purposes of scaling the issue, figure 4C.2 shows the size of each major block of the financial services sector as of June 2008 (and hence before the morphing of investment banking into bank holding companies). As a whole, the sector holds about $24 trillion in assets, or about 170 percent of GDP. Commercial banks accounted for 37 percent in June and are now 46 percent after the shift of Goldman Sachs and Morgan Stanley to bank holding company status.

The size of the forced transformations in the financial industry is huge against this benchmark. As shown in figure 4C.3, the entities that have been forced into mergers (Countrywide, Bear Stearns, Merrill Lynch, Washington Mutual), placed under conservatorship (Fannie and Freddie, AIG), or allowed to enter bankruptcy (Lehman) amount to over $6 trillion in assets.[84]

---

84. The amount here for Fannie and Freddie is their direct assets only and excludes guarantees.

Figure 4C.2 Composition of financial-sector assets, June 2008

trillions of dollars

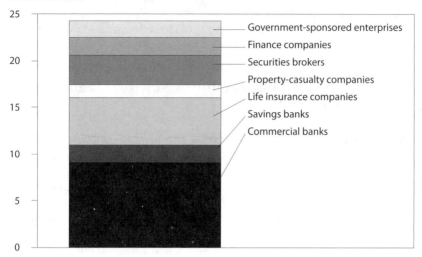

Sources: US Federal Reserve; and firms' annual reports.

One consequence of these transformations is that a large block of the financial services sector has effectively been socialized: The government-sponsored enterprises (Fannie and Freddie) and AIG together account for assets of $2.8 trillion. Another consequence is that a large block of assets has been shifted from weak institutions to larger and hopefully stronger ones. Figure 4C.4 shows five institutions that have become extinct, as well as the remaining largest banks. A total of $2.7 trillion in assets has been shifted in this manner to four large banks.[85] Another $690 billion has in effect evaporated from the US banking system with the bankruptcy of Lehman Brothers.

The consolidation has established only six banks as accounting for 67 percent of the assets of the banking system (figure 4C.5).[86] Bank of America, Citigroup, and JP Morgan Chase each account for about 15 percent of the total system. Goldman Sachs, Morgan Stanley, and Wells Fargo

---

85. To JP Morgan Chase, $395 billion from Bear Stearns and $310 billion from WAMU; to Bank of America, $212 billion from Countrywide and $966 billion from Merrill Lynch; to Citigroup and/or Wells Fargo, $812 billion from Wachovia.

86. Total banking system assets for this calculation are the $9.1 trillion held by commercial banks in June plus the $2.1 trillion in Goldman Sachs and Morgan Stanley assets shifted to bank holding company status.

Figure 4C.3 Forced transformations of major financial institutions in 2008

trillions of dollars

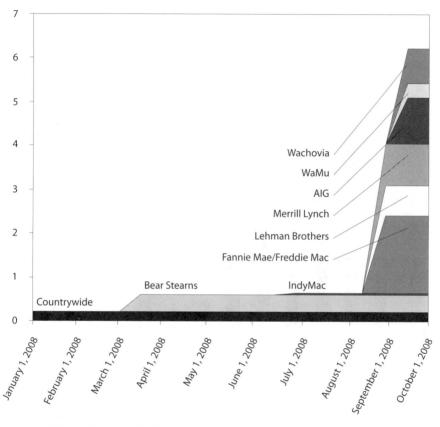

Sources: US Federal Reserve; and firms' quarterly reports.

each account for about 7 percent.[87] The US subsidiaries of Deutsche Bank and HSBC account for about 4 percent and 3 percent of system assets, respectively, and US Bancorp and Bank of New York, about 3 percent and 1 percent, respectively. Bank size drops off rapidly after that, with the combined assets of the next 10 largest banks amounting to only about 7 percent of the system's total.

For the longer term, the increased concentration in US banking is problematic, because it poses questions of oligopoly pricing on the one hand and moral hazard inherent in too-big-to-fail status on the other. For

---

87. The figure assumes that half of Wachovia goes to Citigroup and the other half to Wells Fargo.

Figure 4C.4   Assets of major disappearing and surviving banks, June 30, 2008

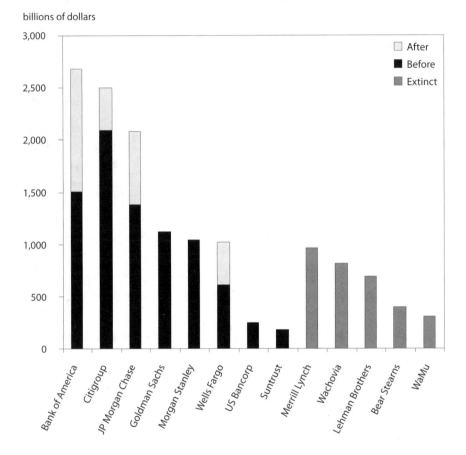

billions of dollars

Sources: US Federal Reserve; and firms' quarterly reports.

the present crisis phase, however, the consolidation is helpful. It means that if one of the remaining super-banks gets into extreme difficulty, it will almost certainly be saved through some variety of nationalization, while the other remaining banks are each too small to be system-threatening.

The expansion of FDIC coverage from $100,000 to $250,000 also should bolster confidence in the system. With an arguably stronger banking system, the focus of the crisis seems to have shifted from the financial sector toward the real economy.

Figure 4C.5 Assets of largest banks as percentage of US banking system total, June 30, 2008

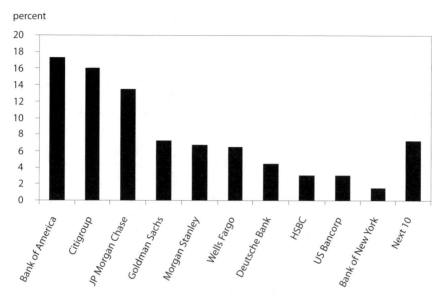

percent

Sources: US Federal Reserve (2008b); firms' quarterly reports.

Bank Nationalization? Not Quite (October 14, 2008)

The United States government has now announced its plan to inject capital into the nation's banking system, in parallel with similar recent actions in Europe. Although the press has reported the plan will "partly nationalize the nine major banks,"[88] there will not be much nationalization at all in a meaningful sense of the word. The early signs are that this action can restore confidence whereas the announcement of TARP's troubled asset purchase plan had failed to do so. Yesterday's stock price surge, the fifth largest on record, reflected anticipation of a government plan to recapitalize banks and announcement of forceful similar measures in Europe. However, fundamental constraints on the capacity of the financial sector to expand credit seem likely to remain for some time.

Although some of the nine large banks were reluctant to participate, Treasury Secretary Henry Paulson pressed them to do so for the good of the financial system, in order to avoid a stigma of weakness for any participating bank. The terms of the plan are as follows. First, $125 billion from the TARP will be used to purchase preferred shares in the nine largest banks,

---

88. David Cho, Neil Irwin, and Peter Whoriskey, "U.S. Forces Nine Major Banks to Accept Partial Nationalization," *Washington Post*, October 14, 2008.

up to a ceiling of $25 billion, or 3 percent of the amount of risk-weighted assets. JP Morgan and Citigroup both qualify for the $25 billion. Second, the shares will pay a coupon of 5 percent, which rises to 9 percent in the fifth year. Third, Treasury will receive warrants amounting to 15 percent of the capital injected in the bank, with the right to purchase the common stock in the future at the price on the day the warrants are issued. Fourth, participating banks cannot take tax deductions on more than $500,000 in salary paid to each top official, nor can they create new golden parachutes. Fifth, participating banks cannot raise dividends without government approval. Sixth, through a closing date of November 14, another $125 billion will be available for similar preferred equity purchases in the rest of the nation's some 8,000 banks, in amounts of 1 to 3 percent of risk-weighted assets. Seventh, in addition to the bank capitalization plan, the FDIC will extend its insurance coverage to newly issued bank debt (i.e., bonds, not just deposits) and to all noninterest-paying bank deposits (typically those of small businesses) regardless of the $250,000 limit.

Secretary Paulson opposed proposals for publicly-supported bank recapitalization just a few weeks ago, in favor of purchasing mortgage-backed securities and other troubled assets. However, last week's stock market collapse and seizing up of interbank lending have forced the shift to potentially faster-acting injection of capital. Many economists have preferred such recapitalization over troubled asset purchase all along. But by diluting existing shareholders' equity (even using preferred shares, if tied to warrants at low prices), public capital injection risks pushing bank stock prices down (as has just happened in Royal Bank of Scotland and Lloyds). Falling stock prices are a powerful signal of bank weakness. There is even an academic literature that measures default probability by stock price weakness. What has happened, however, is that the bank stocks already fell so sharply that any further negative confidence effects from the dilution effect were likely to be dominated by the positive effects from improved confidence of bank survival with higher capitalization.

The new plan would not inject capital in common shares, and the preferred shares would be nonvoting. So the fundamental feature of nationalization—government control—will be absent. That is all to the good, as the history of nationalized banking systems is one of "directed lending" disasters. Even the warrants represent minimal potential control of common shares. The 15 percent amounts to $18.75 billion (for the nine large banks), or 3 percent of their current stock market capitalization. More fundamentally, President Bush has emphasized that the program is temporary, so in the event of a successful outcome in which the warrants are exercised and make a profit for the taxpayer, the shares acquired will almost certainly be sold back to the private sector rather than being retained to establish a toehold for a nationalized banking system. All this being said, the influence of the government on these and other participating banks will rise to some extent (as illustrated by control over dividends).

The underlying objective of the TARP as originally envisioned and now as recast to emphasize capital injection was to get the banking system back into a position to extend new loans to households, factories, and farms. It seems likely, however, that bank credit expansion will remain far below the pace of recent years even with the new recapitalization plan. Some slow-down was desirable: bank credit growth rose from an average of 6.7 percent annually in the 1990s to an outsized 11.8 percent average in 2004–07. In contrast, this year the annual pace from March to September was only 2.5 percent. From the standpoint of individual bank prudence, shrinking the balance sheet in order to raise the ratio of capital to assets makes perfect sense under circumstances of far greater uncertainty and doubts about borrowing access. The more compelling immediate goal is to avoid further outright collapses at the heart of the financial sector, like that of Lehman Brothers. Policymakers would do well to concentrate on that systemic survival issue first and tread cautiously along the path of pressuring banks to expand lending—which could indeed become a form of "directed lending" and partial nationalization. In the meantime, firms seem likely to have to rely more on retained profits, and households more on saving, than in recent years, as part of a healthy process of deleveraging the US economy.

Sizing Up the Hole in the Banks: Nationalization Is Not Inevitable (February 6, 2009)

The time-honored principle of public-sector intervention to support banks is that of Walter Bagehot, who wrote in 1873 that the central bank should provide lender-of-last-resort lending to solvent banks in a panic but should not lend to insolvent banks. However, because of the too-big-to-fail effect, in which failures of large institutions cause systemic damage (as demonstrated by Lehman Brothers), public policy in the current crisis has tended to support the key financial institutions without making too fine a distinction between whether they are illiquid or insolvent.

Nouriel Roubini has estimated that credit losses for US institutions could reach $3.6 trillion, of which half would be in banks and broker dealers. He observed that if so, the US banking system would be "effectively insolvent."[89] Paul Krugman wrote a column coyly describing a "hypothetical" bank ("Gothamgroup") with $2 trillion in assets, $100 billion in capital, and $400 billion in troubled assets that might be worth only $200 billion, leaving it a "zombie bank" with negative net worth but still $20 billion in market capitalization only because of the expectation of a govern-

---

89. Henry Meyer and Ayesha Daya, "Roubini Predicts U.S. Losses May Reach $3.6 Trillion," Bloomberg.com, January 20, 2009 (accessed on January 4, 2010).

ment bailout.[90] The implication is that some large US banks may already be insolvent. If so, because they are too big to fail, the Bagehot principle would not apply and instead they might need to be nationalized.

The key question for the solvency of the major banks is whether their core capital exceeds their prospective losses. From mid-2007 through the end of the third quarter of 2008, large US banks had writedowns of $413 billion and raised new capital of $399 billion.[91] Through this period their new capital thus approximately offset their losses. More recently, however, the plunge in bank shares has ruled out the raising of new capital through stock issuance. Instead, new capital has had to come from the public sector.

Both the International Monetary Fund and Goldman Sachs have recently estimated cumulative prospective credit losses on US residential real estate, commercial real estate, credit cards, automobile loans, and commercial and industrial loans at about $2.1 trillion, of which about half is from residential real estate (IMF 2009g, Hatzius and Marschoun 2009). The Goldman Sachs authors calculate that the share of US banks in these losses will amount to almost $1 trillion. The implication is that the US banks have another $600 billion of losses that will need to be recognized, beyond amounts already declared by the end of the third quarter.

A bank's net worth can be broadly approximated by its Tier 1 capital.[92] This is mainly the sum of original purchases of stock issued plus cumulative retained earnings. For the 17 large US banks (including the large investment banks now converted to bank holding companies), which represent about 90 percent of US banking assets, at the end of the third quarter of 2008 total Tier 1 capital amounted to $588 billion.[93] They subsequently received approximately $180 billion in new Tier 1 capital from the Troubled Asset Relief Program (TARP) in the form of preferred shares, boosting their net worth to about $770 billion.

The further prospective losses would thus eliminate about 70 percent of the net worth of the large banks.[94] The implication is that the large US banks as a group are not yet insolvent, although they are skating on thin ice. The situation could be worse for individual, relatively more exposed banks, and it could be much worse for the large banks as a group if the Roubini estimate turns out to be right.

---

90. Paul Krugman, "Wall Street Voodoo," *New York Times*, January 19, 2009.

91. Rodney Yap and Dave Pierson, "Banks' Subprime Market-Related Losses Top $732 billion: Table," Bloomberg.com, December 15, 2008.

92. In contrast, so-called Tier 2 capital includes long-term subordinated debt, representing resources that may provide a handy war chest but ultimately must be repaid.

93. Calculated from quarterly reports for 17 large US banks.

94. Applying the 90 percent share of the total, additional losses would amount to $540 billion for the 17 largest banks, or 70 percent of the $770 billion in third-quarter net worth (after enhancement by TARP disbursements).

To the extent that public support is given to insolvent banks too big to fail, the result is to "socialize" the losses. Because there could be sizable efficiency losses from public rather than private operation of the banks, some amount of loss socialization may be warranted to avoid nationalization. The large banks have assets of about $10 trillion. Suppose they were all nationalized. Suppose that lesser efficiency of government management and diversion of lending toward lower-return politicized objectives were to cause a reduction of just 1 percent in annual return on assets. The consequence would be a social loss of $100 billion per year. If the nationalization lasted a decade, the total social cost would be on the order of $1 trillion.

This thought experiment suggests that it might be socially worth somewhere on the order of $1 trillion to keep the large US banks under private ownership and management. The Obama administration's effort to avoid nationalization seems to be premised on such a view. It is reportedly on the verge of launching either a "bad" (or "aggregator") bank that would buy up questionable assets (the original TARP idea); or guaranteeing additional large blocks of such assets (as it did for about $300 billion for Citigroup and $120 billion for Bank of America); or doing a combination of the two. In either case the contingent loss to the government would be undertaken because the alternative social loss from nationalization would be even larger.

The bottom line is that it will require some form of troubled asset alleviation, combined with further recapitalization, to consolidate the process of shoring up the systemically important banks. After recognition of pending losses, to restore Tier 1 capital to 4 percent of the $10 trillion in assets would require recapitalization on the order of $170 billion.[95] Providing additional public-sector capital injections on this scale through the TARP and/or its successor could be a bargain if the illustrative $1 trillion is in the right ballpark for the social inefficiency costs of major bank nationalization.

---

95. For the 17 largest banks, $770 billion Tier 1 capital at end-third quarter 2008, less $540 billion further losses to recognize, would leave $230 billion net worth. Topping them up to $400 billion would require recapitalization of $170 billion.

Appendix 4D
Economics of the Geithner Plan[96]

The Private-Public Investment Program (PPIP), or "Geithner Plan," would ironically use financial leverage to help resolve a financial crisis caused in considerable part by excessive leverage. As Robert Samuelson, citing Yale economist John Geanakoplos, has pointed out, a rationale for this paradox is that the process of deleveraging has gone too far in the opposite direction as loanable funds for leveraged investment have dried up.[97] The premise of the plan is that troubled assets on the books of the banks cannot be sold except at prices far below their long-term cash-flow value because of lack of liquidity in this distressed market. The PPIP seeks to jumpstart a return to liquidity for this asset market, thereby setting the stage for a normalization of the banking sector and financial conditions more generally. A key motive of this arrangement is to use private investors, rather than bureaucrats, for "price discovery," addressing a central problem that derailed the original TARP plan of Geithner's predecessor, Henry Paulson: difficulty in determining a price that will be fair to both the taxpayer and the bank. For this purpose, the government would in effect provide lending to enable the leverage needed to attract private-sector investors.

Problems with Critiques of the Private-Public Investment Program

Some prominent economists have decried the plan as a giveaway of public funds to the banks and private investors such as hedge funds, private equity firms, pension and endowment funds, and others. Jeffrey Sachs has attacked it as a "massive transfer of wealth."[98] Joseph Stiglitz has called it "robbery of the American people."[99] They as well as Paul Krugman[100] have provided numerical examples of large overpayment to private investors at the public's expense.

---

96. This appendix was coauthored with Thomas Emmons. It was posted April 1, 2009 on the Peterson Institute for International Economics website at www.piie.com (accessed on January 4, 2010).

97. Robert J. Samuelson, "Geithner's Hedge Fund," *Washington Post*, March 30, 2009.

98. Jeffrey Sachs, "Will Geithner and Summers Succeed in Raiding the FDIC and Fed?" VoxEU, March 25, 2009. For Sachs' calculations considered in this paper, see Jeffrey Sachs, "Obama's Plan Could Rob the Taxpayer," *Financial Times*, March 25, 2009.

99. Susan Fenton and Deborah Kan, "Geithner Plan Will Rob American Taxpayers: Stiglitz," Reuters, March 24, 2009. For a calculation similar to that presented by Sachs, see Joseph E. Stiglitz, "Obama's Ersatz Capitalism," *New York Times*, April 1, 2009.

100. Paul Krugman, "Geithner Plan Arithmetic," *New York Times* (blog entry), March 23, 2009 (accessed on January 4, 2009).

A fundamental problem with these attacks is that they omit on the benefit side of a cost-benefit analysis the potential gains to the public from an improvement in the economy that could flow from a normalization of the financial system. Even on the narrower analytics ignoring such social externalities, however, the analyses tend to make crucial assumptions that seriously bias them toward the conclusion that investors will pay far too much for the troubled assets and thus that the public will experience serious losses as a result while the banks and private investors enjoy any gains. This appendix will illustrate this bias using the Sachs results.

The essence of the critiques is that government loans for leveraged private investors on a nonrecourse basis create a "heads I win, tails you lose" situation for the investors. Nonrecourse borrowing means that if the assets purchased go sour, the investing firm walks away from both the assets and the loans it borrowed from the government using the assets as collateral. The defaulted assets become the property of the government, which seeks to recover what it can but is unlikely to recover much, and the government has no recourse to recover from the private investing firm itself.

However, a key feature of the PPIP will limit this asymmetric risk. The amount the government will lend will apply a variable "haircut" against the face value of the loans in arriving at what will be acceptable as collateral value. For the Legacy Loan Program, the FDIC will exercise oversight; for the Legacy Securities Program, the Federal Reserve will do so. Both are almost certain to require larger haircut discounts in determining the collateral value for more risky loans or securities.[101] With lower permissible collateral, the investor would not be able to make as large an offer. The critiques of Sachs, Krugman, and Stiglitz do not take this into account.[102]

In the case of the Sachs analysis, as set forth below, the conclusion of overpayment is exaggerated for four reasons. First, he assumes an unrealistically high probability of default. Second, he assumes an unrealistically low rate of recovery given default. Third, he applies a leverage ratio higher than that available in the PPIP. Fourth, he assumes perfect competition and therefore zero profits for the investing firm, instead of a more realistic target profit rate.

Moreover, two further considerations suggest that there is consider-

---

101. The Treasury documentation of the PPIP indicates that for the Legacy Loan Program, "the FDIC will conduct analyses to determine the amount of funding it is willing to guarantee. Leverage *will not exceed* a 6-to-1 debt-to-equity ratio" [emphasis added]. US Treasury, "Fact Sheet: Public-Private Investment Program," available at www.ustreas.gov (accessed on January 4, 2010).

102. The Sachs exercise is described below. It assumes the FDIC would approve $643 collateral value on a $1,000 loan with an 80 percent default probability and only 20 percent recovery rate. Instead, the FDIC would likely set the permissible collateral much lower on such a damaged loan.

able reason to fear that the private-public initiatives will underpay rather than overpay for the troubled assets. The economist who has been credited in part for the conceptual framework of the PPIP, Lucian Bebchuk of Harvard University, has emphasized that insufficient competition among prospective private-sector participants could cause the prices offered to be too low, because of what is technically "oligopsony power" used to extract a "rent" from the potential sellers.[103] For this reason he has emphasized the need for many participants competing against each other. The Legacy Loan half of the PPIP is structured with many investors in mind, but the Legacy Securities half only calls for five initial hedge funds—a number that may or may not be sufficient to overcome the oligopsony problem.

The other reason for concern about underpayment is the recent political climate, in which private-sector bonuses and profits at firms in some way involved in the credit crisis and, especially, the public-sector intervention to address it, have become the target of retroactive taxation. The shaky rule of law substantially increases the risk to private-sector partners in the PPIP.

Overall, these considerations suggest that the outcry of some economists against the PPIP as a giveaway to banks and private investors is at best useful as an alert to the need for close monitoring of the mechanism (especially in FDIC and Federal Reserve determination of the collateral haircut) but at worst constitutes an unhelpful undermining of public confidence in an approach that could play an important role in stabilizing the financial crisis.

The rest of this appendix provides a specific analysis of the Sachs diagnosis of overpayment in the PPIP.

Recalculating the Sachs Private-Public Investment Program Overpayment Estimate

Jeffrey Sachs has produced an arithmetic example indicating that investors in the PPIP (the "Geithner Plan") would be willing to pay as much as $714,000 for a toxic asset with face value of $1 million but a true value of only $360,000, based on a probability of default of 80 percent and a recovery ratio of 20 percent.[104] The amount offered would be almost twice the true value, calculated as the sum of 20 percent probability times face value for the good outcome ($200,000) and the recovery rate times face value times 80 percent probability ($200,000 x 0.8) for the bad outcome.

The Sachs model, reverse-engineered from his example, is as follows. Let E = equity of the investing firm, X = the price it will offer, L = the size of

103. Lucian Bebchuk, "Jump-Starting the Market for Troubled Assets," *Forbes*, March 3, 2009.

104. Jeffrey Sachs, "Obama's Plan Could Rob the Taxpayer," *Financial Times*, March 25, 2009.

the loan from the government, λ = the leverage ratio (defined as the ratio of total purchase price to investor equity), π_G = profit in the good outcome, π_B = profit in the bad outcome, P_d = probability of default on the asset, and F = face value of the assets. Let V = the probability-weighted value of the asset, R = the recovery value if the asset defaults, and $r = R/F$ the recovery rate on the defaulted assets. The question is then how much will the investor be willing to pay (X) for the asset. The Sachs (and Krugman) proposition is that X is much greater than V.

Following Sachs, the problem is simplified by ignoring government equity and treating the investment solely as one by a private investor obtaining nonrecourse borrowing.

The amount of equity the investor will need is:

$$E = X / \lambda. \tag{4D.1}$$

The size of the loan from the government is:

$$L = X \, \frac{\lambda-1}{\lambda}. \tag{4D.2}$$

Profit in the good outcome will be the full face value of the asset minus the amount of the loan the investor needs to repay and minus the investor's original equity, or:

$$\pi_G = F - L - E. \tag{4D.3}$$

In the bad outcome the investor walks away from the asset, which becomes the property of the government, but loses his initial equity, so profit is minus the original equity:

$$\pi_B = -E. \tag{4D.4}$$

This equation changes if the recovery ratio is high enough to keep the investor loss to a lesser amount than the entire equity investment. In this case,

$$\pi_B = Max[rF - L - E; -E]. \tag{4D.4'}$$

At this point, Sachs (and Krugman and Stiglitz) assume perfect competition and zero expected profit. As a result, the probability-weighted good-outcome and bad-outcome profits sum to zero.

$$(1 - P_d)\pi_G + P_d \, \pi_B = 0. \tag{4D.5}$$

However, zero profit is unlikely to be acceptable to private investors. If instead they demand a hurdle profit rate of θ (defined as the equivalent of a capital gain after a moderate holding period such as three to five years), then the profit equation becomes:

$$(1-P_d)\pi_G + P_d\pi_B = \theta E. \tag{4D.5'}$$

In the Sachs formulations of low recovery (equation 4D.4 rather than 4D.4') and zero profit (equation 4D.5 rather than 4D.5'), substituting and solving for X leads to:

$$X = \frac{\lambda(1-P_d)F}{(1-P_d)\lambda + P_d}. \tag{4D.6}$$

In the more general case, taking account of higher recovery (equation 4D.4') and profit motive (equation 4D.5'), the offer price becomes:

$$X = MAX\{\frac{\lambda(1-P_d)F}{(1-P_d)\lambda + P_d + \theta}; (\frac{\lambda}{\lambda + \theta})[(1 - P_d)F + P_d rF]\}. \tag{4D.6'}$$

In contrast, the underlying value of the asset is its probability-weighted value under the two alternative outcomes, good and bad. Thus:

$$V = P_d R + (1 - P_d)F = F\{1 - P_d(1 - r)\}. \tag{4D.7}$$

In the Sachs case with zero profit and low recovery, the ratio of the price offered to the underlying value of the asset is then the ratio of equation 4D.6 to equation 4D.7, or:

$$X/V = \frac{\lambda(1-P_d)}{\{(1-P_d)\lambda + P_d\} \times \{1 - P_d(1 - r)\}}. \tag{4D.8}$$

In the more general case the corresponding ratio of offer price to underlying value is the ratio of equation 4D.6' to equation 4D.7.

In Sachs' example (in thousands), with $F = 1{,}000$, $P_d = 0.8$, and $\lambda = 10$, it turns out that the price the investor is willing to offer is 714, or 98 percent above the true value based on default probability and recovery ratio.[105] Ironically, under these circumstances the recovery ratio does not enter at all into what the investing firm is willing to pay, because it is not the firm's concern—the government gets the recovery of collateral because the investor walks away from the loan.

This estimate of overpayment appears to be seriously overstated, however. For the probability of default, Sachs uses 80 percent, and for recovery, 20 percent. In contrast, recent estimates by Goldman Sachs suggest that nonprime bank mortgage claims have a weighted average default

---

105. In equation 4D.8, $X/V = [10 \times 0.2]/\{(0.2) \times 10 + 0.8\} \times \{1 - 0.8(1 - 0.2)\} = 2/(2.8 \times 0.36) = 1.984$.

Table 4D.1 Private-Public Investment Program price offer relative to underlying value (X/V): Sachs versus this study

Concept	Symbol	Sachs	This study
Probability of default	P_d	0.8	0.32
Recovery ratio	r	0.2	0.5
Leverage ratio	λ	10	7
Profit hurdle rate	θ	0	0.25
Offer price/underlying value	X/V	1.98	1.07

probability of 32 percent and recovery rate of 50 percent.[106] Overstatement of default probability and understatement of recovery leads to understatement of loan value and overstatement of the ratio of the offer price to loan value.

Similarly, Sachs overstates the leverage ratio. In the description of the Legacy Loan Program of the PPIP, US Treasury documentation illustrates with the example of a loan portfolio purchased at $84 for a $100 face-value loan, with $6 in equity from the private investor, $6 from the Treasury, and $72 in loans guaranteed by the FDIC.[107] The loan is of sufficient quality that the collateral haircut is only 16 cents on the dollar, and the leverage ratio is 7 to 1 (purchase price to equity, or equivalently, 6 to 1 for loan to equity). As for the Legacy Securities Program, the leverage ratio is even lower, ranging from 3 to 4. Sachs instead uses a leverage ratio of 10.

Table 4D.1 compares the parameters and results of the Sachs calculation, discussed above, with those that would be more appropriate on the basis of the discussion above. For "this study" (referred to in the title of the table) the estimates calculated from the Goldman Sachs study are applied (32 percent default probability and 50 percent recovery rate). A leverage ratio of 7 is used, consistent with the maximum allowable under the Legacy Loan Program description and well above that in the Legacy Securities Program. The calculation here assumes a profit hurdle (capital gains target) of 0.25, which is probably on the modest side.

The result is that the offer price exceeds the underlying value by only 7 percent, a radically different conclusion from Sachs' 98 percent.

Figure 4D.1 shows alternative fields of PPIP investor offer prices for an asset with face value of $1,000 under differing assumptions about the leverage ratio, default probability, and recovery rate. Panel A is for the Sachs zero-profit case; Panel B sets the capital gains target at 25 percent

---

106. These include Alt-A, subprime, option ARM, closed-end second mortgages, and home equity lines of credit. Calculated from Hatzius and Marschoun (2009).

107. US Treasury, "Fact Sheet: Public-Private Investment Program," available at www.ustreas. gov (accessed on January 4, 2010).

Figure 4D.1   Private-Public Investment Program investor offer price for an asset with $1,000 face value under alternative default probability, recovery rate, leverage, and profit target assumptions

a. Zero profit

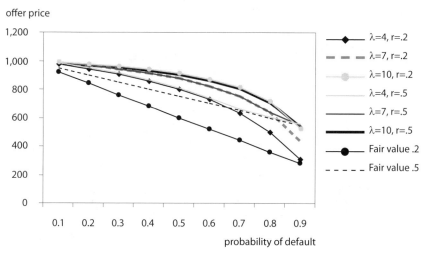

b. 25 percent capital gains (θ = 0.25)

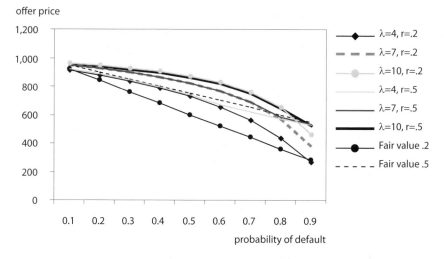

(continued on next page)

Figure 4D.1 **Private-Public Investment Program investor offer price for an asset with $1,000 face value under alternative default probability, recovery rate, leverage, and profit target assumptions** *(continued)*

c. 50 percent capital gains (θ = 0.5)

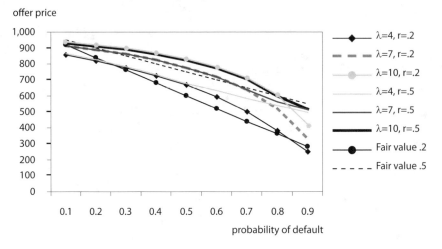

Note: λ = leverage ratio; r = recovery rate. Fair value is the underlying value at \recovery rate of 0.2 or 0.5.

Source: Author's calculations.

($\theta = 0.25$) and Panel C sets it at 50 percent ($\theta = 0.5$). Because the recovery rate enters into the calculation only at high probabilities of default, over most of the range the lines for a given leverage ratio overlie each other, but they diverge for the highest default probabilities.

Table 4D.2 simplifies the field of results by focusing on three alternative default probabilities (0.3, 0.5, and 0.7) and two alternative recovery rates (0.5 and 0.2), using only the intermediate profit target ($\theta = 0.25$) and only one leverage ratio ($\lambda = 0.7$). The table reports the ratio of offer price to underlying value for each of these six cases. It is clear that if the recovery rate is as high as the relatively standard 50 percent, the range of overpayment is quite limited, remaining in a range of 6 to 10 percent. In contrast, if the recovery rate is the low 20 percent assumed by Sachs, the overpayment is moderate (18 percent) only when the default rate is at the lower end of this central range (30 percent); at the higher end (70 percent) overpayment is large, at 56 percent. However, it is precisely for assets with such high default probabilities and low recovery rates that the FDIC (or the Federal Reserve) would be likely to insist on larger haircuts for permissible collateral, meaning that the leverage ratio allowed would be considerably smaller than the 7 to 1 ratio for higher quality assets.

Table 4D.2 Ratio of offer price to underlying value for illustrative default probabilities and recovery rates

Recovery rate	Default probability		
	0.30	0.50	0.70
0.5	1.06	1.10	1.06
0.2	1.18	1.37	1.56

Note: For leverage $\lambda = 7$ and profit target $\theta = 0.25$.

Overview

In short, the Sachs conclusion that PPIP will cause investors to pay twice as much for distressed assets as they are worth is likely to be a considerable exaggeration. His leverage ratio of 10 is much higher than those in the PPIP (7 for legacy loans, and as low as 3 for legacy securities). His probability of default of 80 percent is much higher than usually attributed to these assets. More appropriate leverage ratios, default probabilities, recovery rates, and assumptions about profit hurdle rates lead to lower excess-price results. If one considers the top row of table 4D.2 and only the first entry of the bottom row as illustrative (because at higher default rates and low recovery the allowable leverage would be lower than used in the table), an appropriate range for the estimation of overpayment in the PPIP would be on the order of 10 to 20 percent, not 100 percent.

If the PPIP does lead to prices of, say, even 25 percent above long-term value being paid for distressed assets, it is not obvious that the taxpayer will have lost. This arithmetical model does not take account of the macroeconomic benefits to be expected from normalization in the banking system. Introducing greater liquidity to distressed assets held by banks could make an important contribution to that normalization, making it possible to avoid much more disruptive outcomes such as the nationalization of some of the largest banks. Similarly, if the "illiquidity discount" is about 25 percent, then the "overpayment" becomes "discovery of the appropriate price" from the standpoint of longer-term value under more liquid conditions. On balance, the taxpayer could gain from a moderate price boost to these assets from the PPIP by being pound wise rather than penny wise.

Appendix 4E
Financing Gaps, Reserves, and Official Finance in the Global Financial Crisis

The World Bank (2009a, 82) has estimated that in 2009 the developing countries face an "external financing gap" amounting to $352 billion in the "base case" and $635 billion in an adverse "low case." It reports that of 98 countries with "financing needs," there are 59 with a financing gap in the base case, and 69 in the low case. The broad policy implication seems to be an acute need for several hundred billion dollars in additional official finance. A closer examination of the estimates, however, suggests that the bulk of the headline number stems from major emerging-market economies that have accumulated massive reserves and can prudently draw upon them to cover financing gaps without needing to resort to official finance.

The World Bank defines the external financing gap (EFG) as the amount of the external financing needs (EFN) that cannot be covered by private capital flows (PKF). Financing needs are the sum of the current account deficit (CAD) and principal repayments on private debt (PRP). Principal repayments on private debt are the sum of short-term debt (STD) and amortization coming due on private medium- and long-term debt, whether guaranteed by the government (APG) or nonguaranteed (APN). Private capital flows are the sum of new private loans (NLP), expected net equity flows of direct and portfolio investment (EF), less unidentified capital outflows, or what may be summarized as resident outflows (RO)—what used to be called "capital flight." The financing gap concept does not directly address the use of reserves but implicitly asks whether reserves are large enough to cover the gap without additional international official support.

The relationships, then, are:

$$FN = CAD + PRP \qquad (4E.1)$$
$$PRP = STD + APG + APN \qquad (4E.2)$$

$$PKF = NLP + EF - RO \qquad (4E.3)$$
$$EFG = FN - PKF. \qquad (4E.4)$$

Table 4E.1 reports the aggregate World Bank estimates for these concepts.[108] The World Bank presents its financing gap estimates by region but not by country. The largest gap is in Europe and Central Asia: $100 billion in the base case and $250 billion in the low case. Next is Latin America

---

108. The concepts here treat the financing needs, financing gap, and current account deficit in algebraic terms and hence as positive numbers rather than the World Bank's use of negative numbers.

Table 4E.1   World Bank estimates of financing gaps in 2009
(billions of dollars)

Financing gap		Base case	Low case
Number of countries with financing gaps		59	69
External private debt		2,760	n.a.
Short-term		535	n.a.
Medium- and long-term		2,226	n.a.
External financing needs	A	959	1,005
Current account deficit		217	7
Principal repayments on private debt		742	n.a.
Short-term		535	n.a.
Medium- and long-term (APG + APN)		207	n.a.
Private capital flows	B	607	371
Equity flows		90	70
Disbursements of private debt		691	520
Short-term		492	380
Long-term		199	141
Unidentified outflows		−173	−219
External financing gap	= A − B	352	635

APG = amortization on private guaranteed long-term debt; APN = amortization on private
nonguaranteed long-term debt
n.a. = not available

Source: World Bank (2009a); author's calculations.

and the Caribbean ($110 billion or $180 billion). Sub-Saharan Africa is next
($50 billion or $60 billion). Both Eastern Asia and the Pacific and Southern
Asia have similar gaps (about $25 billion or $50 billion each). The Middle
East and North Africa has the lowest gap (about $10 billion or $12 billion)
(World Bank 2009a, 84).

To determine whether the "gap" is a serious problem that cannot be
covered by reserves, however, it is necessary to examine projections for
individual countries. The World Bank (2009a) does not report its estimates
by country. It states that "reserves are unlikely to be sufficient to meet financing gaps," although it notes that "some countries will be able to rely
on reserves built up over the past few years" (p. 84).

To examine this question, it is possible to replicate the World Bank
estimates as closely as possible using country-level data. Table 4E.2
presents estimates of each of the components of the financing gap for the
42 countries found to have financing gaps out of the 50 largest debtor
emerging-market economies.

In table 4E.2, the data sources and assumptions are as follows. The
current account deficit is the World Bank (2009a) estimate as a percent

Table 4E.2   Financing gap components for the 42 largest emerging-market debtor countries (billions of dollars)

Country	Debt[a]	GDP	Current account deficit	Short-term debt	APG	APN	Financing needs	Private capital flows		External financing gap	
								Base	Low	Base	Low
Argentina	107	310	-3.1	38.1	1.8	6.3	43.1	42.8	28.0	0.3	15.1
Brazil	211	1,269	24.1	39.2	7.9	17.7	89.0	46.7	24.6	42.3	64.4
Bulgaria	30	51	7.2	14.0	0.1	2.4	23.8	16.2	11.0	7.6	12.8
Chile	57	136	4.3	13.3	0.9	11.3	29.8	23.7	15.2	6.2	14.6
Colombia	33	198	8.3	5.3	1.6	3.0	18.3	7.2	3.7	11.1	14.5
Croatia	45	59	4.5	5.1	1.3	5.2	16.0	11.2	7.2	4.9	8.9
Egypt	6	188	11.5	1.5	0.3	0.4	13.7	-1.0	-1.8	14.7	15.4
India	169	1,186	16.6	43.7	3.9	14.8	79.0	44.1	23.7	34.9	55.3
Indonesia	111	468	11.7	34.9	1.1	5.8	53.6	35.1	21.9	18.4	31.7
Kazakhstan	94	102	8.6	11.7	0.2	14.6	35.2	24.9	16.1	10.2	19.1
Latvia	43	27	1.8	20.9	0.0	4.1	26.7	25.2	17.4	1.6	9.4
Mexico	167	827	22.3	9.0	13.9	17.2	62.4	31.5	15.8	31.0	46.7
Nigeria	5	168	14.7	4.9	0.1	0.0	19.7	2.3	0.7	17.4	19.0
Pakistan	17	163	8.5	2.2	0.1	0.1	10.8	-0.4	-1.2	11.3	12.0
Peru	21	123	4.4	5.8	1.6	0.4	12.2	6.5	3.8	5.7	8.4
Poland	129	403	17.3	60.4	0.0	8.8	86.5	64.1	42.6	22.4	43.9

(continued on next page)

a. Private external debt, end–2007.

Table 4E.2 Financing gap components for the 42 largest emerging-market debtor countries (billions of dollars) (continued)

Country	Debt[a]	GDP	Current account deficit	Short-term debt	APG	APN	Financing needs	Private capital flows		External financing gap	
								Base	Low	Base	Low
Romania	71	166	14.0	30.5	0.8	5.9	51.1	35.6	23.8	15.6	27.3
Russia	360	1,164	-27.9	79.1	6.8	27.6	85.5	97.9	60.8	-12.4	24.7
South Africa	43	243	14.8	16.6	3.1	2.1	36.6	19.4	12.1	17.2	24.5
Sudan	13	52	3.9	6.3	0.0	0.0	10.2	5.6	3.7	4.6	6.5
Thailand	59	269	-10.2	21.6	0.5	7.9	19.9	26.1	16.5	-6.2	3.4
Tunisia	19	40	1.9	14.5	0.7	0.0	17.2	15.5	10.7	1.7	6.5
Turkey	229	552	10.5	41.8	3.7	33.3	89.3	71.2	45.0	18.0	44.3
Ukraine	69	115	-0.1	22.9	0.7	9.1	32.7	31.7	21.1	1.0	11.5
Venezuela	40	294	2.4	11.7	1.4	1.2	16.7	10.1	5.4	6.6	11.3
Vietnam	5	89	13.3	4.7	0.1	0.0	18.1	3.5	2.0	14.6	16.1
16 other countries[b]	278	691	23.1	32.7	5.6	10.0	71.4	39.5	23.2	32.0	48.2
Total[c]	2,431	9,353	208.3	592.6	58.2	209.3	1,068.4	735.9	452.9	351.1	615.5

APG = amortization on private guaranteed long-term debt; APN = amortization on private nonguaranteed long-term debt

a. Private external debt, end-2007.

b. Angola, Belarus, Bosnia and Herzegovina, Republic of Congo, Costa Rica, Côte d'Ivoire, Dominican Republic, Ecuador, El Salvador, Jamaica, Lebanon, Morocco, Panama, Philippines, Serbia, and Uruguay.

c. For financing gap: positive entries only.

Source: World Bank (2009a); author's calculations.

of GDP, applied to 2009 GDP projections by the IMF (2009b). Short-term debt is the amount outstanding at the end of 2007, the latest date available (World Bank 2009a). Amortization coming due on long-term private debt is for 2008 and is prorated between guaranteed and nonguaranteed in the same proportions as in 2007.[109] For private capital flows in 2009, the World Bank's assumptions on rollover rates are applied. In the base case, these are 92 percent for short-term debt, 129 percent for publicly-guaranteed private long-term debt, and 86 percent for nonguaranteed long-term debt. For the low case (i.e., "high" financing gap), the corresponding rates are 65 percent, 85 percent, and 55 percent (World Bank 2009a, 83). For equity flows, on the basis of the aggregates reported by the World Bank, country estimates are set at 13 percent of the total private flows for short- and long-term debt. For "other" capital flows, mainly resident outflows, the aggregate reported by the World Bank ($173 billion outflows) is apportioned in proportion to GDP, which works out to –1.8 percent of GDP. The resulting estimates for private capital flows, financing needs, and financing gaps follow equations 4E.1 through 4E.4.

Table 4E.2 successfully replicates the World Bank's aggregate estimates. Among the 50 countries accounting for 98 percent of total private external debt are 42 that have combined 2009 financing gaps of $350 billion in the base case and $615 billion in the low case.[110] These estimates are approximately the same as obtained by the World Bank (2009a, 82): $352 billion and $635 billion, respectively.

The next question is whether these gaps can reasonably be financed by existing reserves. Table 4E.3 reports the amount of reserves at the end of 2008, along with imports of goods and services in 2008 (IMF 2009a). The table then posits two alternative benchmarks for reserves available to finance external gaps. The first is the excess of reserves above six months' imports of goods and services. The second is simply 25 percent of existing reserves. The table reports the difference between these "available" reserves and the external financing gap as the "net financing gap," under each of the two concepts.

It turns out that if the base case is considered and 25 percent of reserves can be devoted to covering financing needs, the "net" external financing gap declines to only $88 billion, or about one-fourth of the $350 billion aggregate indicated by the World Bank. However, if a larger reserve cushion of at least six months' imports is kept untouched, the net financing gap

---

109. Although the World Bank (2009a) includes projections of amortization due in 2009, these figures typically understate amounts coming due because they pertain to amortization schedules on long-term debt already contracted by end-2007 and omit debt incurred in 2008.

110. At end-2006, total private external debt of developing and emerging-market economies stood at $2.31 trillion, including short-term debt, private debt publicly guaranteed, and private nonguaranteed debt. See World Bank (2008).

Table 4E.3   External financing gaps: Total and net after consideration of usable reserves

| Country | Financing gap | | Reserves | Imports[a] | Net financing gap[b] | | | | | |
| | Base | Low | | | Base | | Low | | | |
					Mbasis	Rbasis	Mbasis	Rbasis		
Argentina	0.3	15.1	44.9	53.4	0.0	0.0	0.0	3.8
Brazil	42.3	64.4	192.8	157.8	0.0	0.0	0.0	16.2
Bulgaria	7.6	12.8	16.8	34.0	7.6	3.4	12.8	8.6
Chile	6.2	14.6	23.1	54.0	6.2	0.4	14.6	8.9
Colombia	11.1	14.5	23.5	37.4	6.3	5.2	9.8	8.7
Croatia	4.9	8.9	13.0	29.5	4.9	1.6	8.9	5.6
Egypt	14.7	15.4	32.2	53.7	9.3	6.6	10.1	7.4
India	34.9	55.3	247.4	127.1	0.0	0.0	0.0	0.0
Indonesia	18.4	31.7	49.6	109.6	18.4	6.0	31.7	19.3
Kazakhstan	10.2	19.1	17.9	44.9	10.2	5.8	19.1	14.6
Latvia	1.6	9.4	5.0	17.8	1.6	0.3	9.4	8.1
Mexico	31.0	46.7	95.1	306.0	31.0	7.2	46.7	22.9
Nigeria	17.4	19.0	51.3	46.1	0.0	4.6	0.0	6.2
Pakistan	11.3	12.0	7.2	37.5	11.3	9.5	12.0	10.2
Peru	5.7	8.4	30.3	23.9	0.0	0.0	0.0	0.8
Poland	22.4	43.9	59.3	184.2	22.4	7.6	43.9	29.1
Romania	15.6	27.3	36.9	74.0	15.6	6.4	27.3	18.1

Russia[a]	0.0	24.7	412.5	282.5	0.0	0.0	0.0	0.0
South Africa	17.2	24.5	30.6	98.2	17.2	9.6	24.5	16.9
Sudan	4.6	6.5	1.4	10.7	4.6	4.3	6.5	6.2
Thailand[a]	0.0	3.4	108.7	162.9	0.0	0.0	0.0	0.0
Tunisia	1.7	6.5	8.8	20.8	1.7	0.0	6.5	4.3
Turkey	18.0	44.3	70.4	177.0	18.0	0.4	44.3	26.7
Ukraine	1.0	11.5	30.8	72.2	1.0	0.0	11.5	3.8
Venezuela	6.6	11.3	33.1	53.0	0.0	0.0	4.7	3.0
Vietnam	14.6	16.1	23.9	65.8	14.6	8.7	16.1	10.2
16 others[b]	32.0	48.2	139.7	310.0	32.0	0.0	48.2	13.3
Total	351.1	615.5	1,806.2	2,644.0	233.8	87.5	408.5	272.7

a. Financing gap set to zero if negative.
b. Financing gap minus usable reserves (excess over six months' imports, Mbasis; 25 percent of reserves, Rbasis).

Source: Table 4E.2; IMF (2009a); author's calculations.

rises to $234 billion, about two-thirds of the World Bank estimate. In the low case, the two alternative concepts give estimates of net financing gaps of 43 and 64 percent, respectively, of the World Bank estimates.

Public reports of the World Bank estimates did not take account of reserve availability to cover the gaps.[111] It is evident in table 4E.3, however, that many of the major emerging-market economies have built up large enough reserves to cover the financing gap comfortably. Indeed, it would be curious if the large war chests of reserves were not used for this purpose in the worst international financial crisis in decades. Thus, the following countries do not have net financing gaps (or have nearly zero amounts in this concept) under the base projections and using the 25 percent of reserves criterion: Argentina, Brazil, Chile, India, Latvia, Peru, Russia, Thailand, Tunisia, Ukraine, and Venezuela. Moreover, 16 other smaller countries do not have a net financing gap under this concept in the aggregate.

---

111. Annys Shin, "World Bank Predicts Deeper Economic Contraction," *Washington Post*, June 12, 2009. The World Bank's press release did not mention reserve coverage either. See World Bank (2009b).

References

Abiad, Abdul, and Ashoka Mody. 2005. Financial Reform: What Shakes It? What Shapes It? *American Economic Review* 95, no. 1 (March): 66–88.

Aghion, Philippe, Peter Howitt, and David Mayer-Foulkes. 2005. The Effect of Financial Development on Convergence: Theory and Evidence. *Quarterly Journal of Economics* 120, no. 1: 173–222.

Alesina, Alberto, Vittorio Grilli, and Gian Maria Milesi-Ferretti. 1993. *The Political Economy of Capital Controls.* NBER Working Paper 4353. Cambridge, MA: National Bureau of Economic Research.

Alfaro, Laura, Areendam Chanda, Sebnem Kalemli-Ozcan, and Selin Sayek. 2004. FDI and Economic Growth: The Role of Local Financial Markets. *Journal of International Economics* 64, no. 1 (October): 89–112.

Alfaro, Laura, and Andrew Charlton. 2007. Growth and the Quality of Foreign Direct Investment: Is All FDI Equal? Paper presented at Conference on New Perspectives on Financial Globalization, International Monetary Fund, Washington, April 26–27.

Alper, C. Emre, Oya Pinar Ardic, and Salih Fendoglu. 2007. *The Economics of Uncovered Interest Parity Condition for Emerging Markets: A Survey.* MPRA Paper 4079. Munich: Munich Personal RePEc Archive. Available at http://mpra.ub.uni-muenchen.de/4079.

Arteta, Carlos, Barry Eichengreen, and Charles Wyplosz. 2003. When Does Capital Account Liberalization Help More than It Hurts? In *Economic Policy in the International Economy: Essays in Honor of Assaf Razin,* ed. Elhanan Helpman and Efraim Sadka. Cambridge: Cambridge University Press.

Backus, David, Finn Kydland, and Patrick Kehoe. 1994. Dynamics of the Trade Balance and the Terms of Trade: The J-Curve? *American Economic Review* 84, no. 1 (March): 84–103.

Bailliu, Jeannine N. 2000. *Private Capital Flows, Financial Development, and Economic Growth in Developing Countries.* Bank of Canada Working Paper 2000-15 (July). Ontario, Canada.

Balasubramanyam, V. N., M. Salisu, and David Sapsford. 1996. Foreign Direct Investment and Growth in EP and IS Countries. *Economic Journal* 106, no. 434 (January): 92–105.

Baltagi, Badi, Panicos Demitriades, and Siong Hook Law. 2007. Financial Development, Openness and Institutions: Evidence from Panel Data. Paper presented at Conference on New Perspectives on Financial Globalization, International Monetary Fund, Washington, April 26–27.

Barth, James R. 2009. *The Rise and Fall of the U.S. Mortgage and Credit Markets*. New York: John Wiley & Sons.

Barro, Robert J., and Jong-Wha Lee. 2000. *International Data on Educational Attainment: Updates and Implications*. CID Working Paper 42 (April). Cambridge, MA: Center for International Development, Harvard University.

Barro, Robert J., and Xavier Sala-i-Martin. 1992. Convergence. *Journal of Political Economy* 100, no. 2 (April): 223–51.

Barro, Robert J., N. Gregory Mankiw, and Xavier Sala-i-Martin. 1995. Capital Mobility in Neoclassical Models of Growth. *American Economic Review* 85 (March): 103–115.

BEA (Bureau of Economic Analysis). 2010. National Income and Product Accounts Tables. Washington: US Department of Commerce. Available at www.bea.gov.

Beck, Thorsten, Ross Levine, and Norman Loayza. 2000. Finance and the Sources of Growth. *Journal of Financial Economics* 58, no. 1-2: 261–300.

Bekaert, Geert, Campbell R. Harvey, and Christian Lundblad. 2000. *Emerging Equity Markets and Economic Development*. NBER Working Paper 7763 (June). Cambridge, MA: National Bureau of Economic Research.

Bekaert, Geert and Campbell R. Harvey. 2005. Does Financial Liberalization Spur Growth? *Journal of Financial Economics* 77, no. 1 (July): 3–55.

Bhagwati, Jagdish. 1998. The Capital Myth: The Difference between Trade in Widgets and Dollars. *Foreign Affairs* (May/June): 7–12.

BIS (Bank for International Settlements). 2009. *BIS Quarterly Review* (June). Basel.

Blonigan, Bruce A., and Miao Wang. 2005. Inappropriate Pooling of Wealthy and Poor Countries in Empirical FDI Studies. In *Does Foreign Direct Investment Promote Development?* ed. Theodore H. Moran, Edward M. Graham, and Magnus Blomström. Washington: Institute for International Economics and Center for Global Development.

BLS (Bureau of Labor Statistics). 2010. *Labor Force Statistics from the Current Population Survey* (February). Washington. Available at http://data.bls.gov/cps.

Blue Chip. 2010. *Blue Chip Economic Indicators* (January 10). New York: Aspen.

Bonfiglioli, Alessandra, and Caterina Mendicino. 2004. *Financial Liberalization, Banking Crises, and Growth: Assessing the Links*. Working Paper Series in Economics and Finance 567. Stockholm, Sweden: Stockholm School of Economics.

Borensztein, Eduarod, José De Gregorio, and Jong-Wha Lee. 1998. How Does Foreign Direct Investment Affect Growth? *Journal of International Economics* 45 (June): 115–35.

Bosworth, Barry P., and Susan M. Collins. 1999. Capital Flows to Developing Economies: Implications for Saving and Investment. *Brookings Papers on Economic Activity*, no. 1: 143–80.

Bosworth, Barry P., and Susan M. Collins. 2003. The Empirics of Growth: An Update. Brookings Institution, Washington. Photocopy.

Bradford, Scott C., Paul L. E. Grieco, and Gary Clyde Hufbauer. 2005. The Payoff to America from Global Integration. In *The United States and the World Economy: Foreign Economic Policy in the Next Decade*, C. Fred Bergsten and Institute for International Economics. Washington: Institute for International Economics.

Brunnermeier, Markus K. 2009. Deciphering the Liquidity and Credit Crunch 2007–2008. *Journal of Economic Perspectives* 23, no. 1 (Winter): 77–100.

Byström, Hans N. E. 2003. *Estimating Default Probabilities Using Stock Prices: The Swedish Bank Sector During the 1990s Banking Crisis.* Research Paper 92. Sydney: Quantitative Finance Research Centre, University of Technology.

Calomiris, Charles W. 2008. The Subprime Turmoil: What's Old, What's New, and What's Next. Paper presented at a symposium of the Federal Reserve Bank of Kansas City, Jackson Hole, Wyoming, August 21–22.

Caprio, Gerard, and Daniela Klingebiel. 1996. *Bank Insolvencies: Cross-Country Experiences.* World Bank Policy Research Paper 1620. Washington: World Bank.

Caprio, Gerard, and Daniela Klingebiel. 2002. Episodes of Systemic and Borderline Financial Crises. In *Managing the Real and Fiscal Effects of Banking Crises*, ed Daniela Klingebiel and Luc Laeven. World Bank Discussion Paper 428. Washington: World Bank.

Caprio, Gerard, Asli Demirgüç-Kunt, and Edward J. Kane. 2008. The 2007 Meltdown in Structured Securitization: Searching for Lessons not Scapegoats. Williams College, Williamstown, MA. Photocopy (September).

Card, David, and Alan B. Krueger. 1995. Time-Series Minimum-Wage Studies: A Meta-analysis. *American Economic Review* 85, no. 2 (May): 238–43.

Carkovic, Maria, and Ross Levine. 2005. Does Foreign Direct Investment Accelerate Growth? In *Does Foreign Direct Investment Promote Development?* ed. Theodore H. Moran, Edward M. Graham, and Magnus Blomström. Washington: Institute for International Economics and Center for Global Development.

Caselli, Francesco, Gerardo Esquivel, and Fernando Lefort. 1996. Reopening the Convergence Debate: A New Look at Cross-Country Growth Empirics. *Journal of Economic Growth* 1, no. 3: 363–89.

CBO (Congressional Budget Office). 2009a. *The Budget and Economic Outlook: Fiscal Years 2009 to 2019.* Statement of Robert A. Sunshine, Acting Director, before the Committee on the Budget, United States Senate, January 8.

CBO (Congressional Budget Office). 2009b. *An Analysis of the President's Budgetary Proposals for Fiscal Year 2010* (June). Washington.

CBO (Congressional Budget Office). 2009c. *Monthly Budget Review* (October). Washington.

Chanda, Areendam. 2005. The Influence of Capital Controls on Long Run Growth: Where and How Much? *Journal of Development Economics* 77: 441–66.

Chari, Anusha, and Peter Blair Henry. 2004. Risk Sharing and Asset Prices: Evidence from a Natural Experiment. *Journal of Finance* 59, no. 3: 1295–324.

Chinn, Menzie D., and Guy Meredith. 2005. *Testing Uncovered Interest Parity at Short and Long Horizons During the Post-Bretton Woods Era.* NBER Working Paper 11077. Cambridge, MA: National Bureau of Economic Research.

Choe, Jong Il. 2003. Do Foreign Direct Investment and Gross Domestic Investment Promote Economic Growth? *Review of Development Economics* 7, no. 1: 44–57.

Cline, William R. 1984. *International Debt: Systemic Risk and Policy Response.* Washington: Institute for International Economics.

Cline, William R. 1992. *The Economics of Global Warming.* Washington: Institute for International Economics.

Cline, William R. 1995. *International Debt Reexamined.* Washington: Institute for International Economics.

Cline, William R. 1999. Comment on Sebastian Edwards, International Capital Flows and the Emerging Markets: Amending the Rules of the Game? In *Rethinking the International Monetary System*, ed. Jane Sneddon Little and Giovanni P. Olivei. Boston: Federal Reserve Bank of Boston.

Cline, William R. 2004. *Trade Policy and Global Poverty*. Washington: Center for Global Development and Institute for International Economics.

Cline, William R. 2005. *The United States as a Debtor Nation*. Washington: Institute for International Economics and Center for Global Development.

Cole, H., and M. Obstfeld. 1991. Commodity Trade and International Risk Sharing: How Much Do Financial Markets Matter? *Journal of Monetary Economics* 28: 3–24.

Consensus Economics. 2010. *Consensus Forecasts* (January). London.

De Mello, Luiz R. Jr. 1999. Foreign Direct Investment-Led Growth: Evidence from Time Series and Panel Data. *Oxford Economic Papers* 51: 133–51.

Demirgüç-Kunt, Asli, and Enrica Detragiache. 1998. The Determinants of Banking Crises in Developing and Developed Countries. *IMF Staff Papers* 45: 81–109. Washington: International Monetary Fund.

DTTC (Depository Trust & Clearing Corporation). 2009. *Trade Information Warehouse Data* (July 20). New York. Available at www.dtcc.com.

Desai, Mihir A., C. Fritz Foley, and James R. Hines, Jr. 2006. Capital Controls, Liberalizations, and Foreign Direct Investment. *Review of Financial Studies* 19, no. 4 (Winter): 1433–64.

Deutsche Bank Research. 2010. *Country InfoBase* (January). Frankfurt. Available at www.dbresearch.com.

EBRD (European Bank for Reconstruction and Development). 2009. *Transition Report 2009: Transition in Crisis?* (November). London.

Edison, Hali J., Ross Levine, Luca Ricci, and Torsten Slok. 2002. *International Financial Integration and Economic Growth*. NBER Working Paper 9164 (September). Cambridge, MA: National Bureau of Economic Research.

Edison, Hali J., Michael W. Klein, Luca Antonio Ricci, and Torsten Slok. 2004. Capital Account Liberalization and Economic Performance: Survey and Synthesis. *IMF Staff Papers* 51, no. 2: 220–56. Washington: International Monetary Fund.

Edwards, Sebastian. 1999. How Effective Are Capital Controls? *Journal of Economic Perspectives* 13, no. 4 (Autumn): 65–84.

Edwards, Sebastian. 2001. *Capital Mobility and Economic Performance: Are Emerging Economies Different?* NBER Working Paper 8076. Cambridge, MA: National Bureau of Economic Research.

Edwards, Sebastian. 2005. *Capital Controls, Sudden Stops, and Current Account Reversals*. NBER Working Paper 11170 (March). Cambridge, MA: National Bureau of Economic Research. Subsequently published in *Capital Controls and Capital Flows in Emerging Economies: Policies, Practice, and Consequences*, ed. Sebastian Edwards (Chicago: University of Chicago Press, 2007), 73–119.

Edwards, Sebastian. 2006. Financial Openness, Currency Crises and Output Losses. University of California, Los Angeles, CA. Photocopy (April).

Eichengreen, Barry J. 2001. Capital Account Liberalization: What Do Cross-Country Studies Tell Us? *World Bank Economic Review* 15, no. 3: 341–65.

Eichengreen, Barry J., Andrew K. Rose, and Charles Wyplosz. 1996. *Contagious Currency Crises*. NBER Working Paper 5681 (July). Cambridge, MA: National Bureau of Economic Research.

Eichengreen, Barry, Rachita Gullapalli, and Ugo Panizza. 2009. Capital Account Liberalization, Financial Development and Industry Growth: A Synthetic View. University of California, Berkeley. Photocopy (January). Available at www.econ.berkeley.edu.

FHFA (Federal Housing Finance Agency). 2009. Home Prices Fall in First Quarter; Pace of Decline Lessens Considerably. News Release, May 27. Washington. Available at www.fhfa.gov.

Fender, Ingo, and Peter Hordahl. 2008. Overview: A Cautious Return of Risk Tolerance. *BIS Quarterly Review* (June). Basel: Bank for International Settlements.

Fischer, Stanley. 1998. Capital Account Liberalization and the Role of the IMF. *Essays in International Finance* 207 (May): 1–10.

Fisher, Ronald A. 1925. *Statistical Methods for Research Workers.* Edinburgh: Oliver and Boyd.

Foote, Christopher L., Kristopher Gerardi, and Paul S. Willen. 2008. *Negative Equity and Foreclosure: Theory and Evidence.* Public Policy Discussion Papers 08-3. Boston: Federal Reserve Bank of Boston.

Forbes, Kristin J. 2003. *One Cost of the Chilean Capital Controls: Increased Financial Constraints for Smaller Traded Firms.* NBER Working Paper 9777. Cambridge, MA: National Bureau of Economic Research.

Fox, Justin. 2009. *The Myth of the Rational Market: A History of Risk, Reward, and Delusion on Wall Street.* New York: HarperCollins.

Frankel, Jeffrey A. 1992. Measuring International Capital Mobility: A Review. *American Economic Review* 82, no. 2 (May): 197–202.

Frankel, Jeffrey A., and Andrew K. Rose. 1996. Currency Crashes in Emerging Markets: An Empirical Treatment. *Journal of International Economics* 41, no. 3-4 (November): 351–66.

Fratscher, Marcel, and Matthieu Bussiere. 2004. *Financial Openness and Growth: Short-Run Gain, Long-Run Pain?* Working Paper 343 (April). Frankfurt: European Central Bank.

G-20 (Group of Twenty). 2009. *The Global Plan for Recovery and Reform* (April 2). London. Available at www. g20.org.

Glass, G. V. 1976. Primary, Secondary, and Meta-Analysis of Research. *Educational Researcher* 5: 3–8.

Glick, Reuven, and Michael Hutchison. 2005. Capital Controls and Exchange Rate Instability in Developing Economies. *Journal of International Money and Finance* 24, no. 3: 387–412.

Glick, Reuven, Xueyan Guo, and Michael Hutchison. 2006. Currency Crises, Capital Account Liberalization, and Selection Bias. *Review of Economics and Statistics* 88, no. 4: 698–714.

Goldsmith, Raymond W. 1969. *Financial Structure and Development.* New Haven, CT: Yale University Press.

Goldstein, Morris. 2008. A Ten Plank Program for Financial Regulatory Reform (December). Peterson Institute for International Economics, Washington.

Goldstein, Morris, Graciela L. Kaminsky, and Carmen M. Reinhart. 2000. *Assessing Financial Vulnerability: An Early Warning System for Emerging Markets.* Washington: Institute for International Economics.

Gorton, Gary B. 2008. *The Panic of 2007.* NBER Working Paper 14358 (September). Cambridge, MA: National Bureau of Economic Research.

Gourinchas, Pierre-Olivier, and Olivier Jeanne. 2006. The Elusive Gains from International Financial Integration. *Review of Economic Studies* 73: 715–41.

Grilli, Vittorio, and Gian Maria Milesi-Ferretti. 1995. *Economic Effects and Structural Determinants of Capital Controls.* IMF Working Paper WP/95/31 (March). Washington: International Monetary Fund.

Gupta, Nandini, and Kathy Yuan. 2006. On the Growth Effect of Stock Market Liberalizations. Kelley School of Business, Bloomington, IN. Photocopy (June).

Hatzius, Jan, and Michael A. Marschoun. 2009. *Home Prices and Credit Losses: Projections and Policy Options.* Global Economics Paper 177 (January 13). New York: Goldman Sachs.

Haveman, Jon D., Vivian Lei, and Janet S. Netz. 2001. International Integration and Growth: A Survey and Empirical Investigation. *Review of Development Economics* 5, no. 2: 289–311.

Hedges, Larry V., and Ingram Olkin. 1985. *Statistical Methods for Meta-Analysis*. New York: Academic Press.

Henry, Peter B. 2000. Stock Market Liberalization, Economic Reform, and Emerging Market Equity Prices. *Journal of Finance* 55, no. 2 (April): 529–64.

Henry, Peter Blair. 2003. *Capital Account Liberalization, the Cost of Capital, and Economic Growth*. NBER Working Paper 9488 (February). Cambridge, MA: National Bureau of Economic Research.

Henry, Peter Blair. 2007. Capital Account Liberalization: Theory, Evidence, and Speculation. *Journal of Economic Literature* 45 (December): 887–935.

Hermes, Niels, and Robert Lensink. 2003. Foreign Direct Investment, Financial Development and Economic Growth. *Journal of Development Studies* 40, no. 1: 142–63.

Hutchison, Michael M., and Ilan Noy. 2005. How Bad Are Twins? Output Costs of Currency and Banking Crises. *Journal of Money, Credit and Banking* 37, no. 4: 725–52.

IIF (Institute of International Finance). 1999. *Report of the Working Group on Financial Crises in Emerging Markets* (January). Washington.

IIF (Institute of International Finance). 2008. *Capital Flows to Emerging Market Economies* (March). Washington.

IIF (Institute of International Finance). 2009. *Capital Flows to Emerging Market Economies* (October). Washington.

IIF (Institute of International Finance). 2010. *Capital Flows to Emerging Market Economies* (January). Washington.

Imbs, Jean. 2006. The Real Effects of Financial Integration. *Journal of International Economics* 68, no. 2 (March): 296–324.

Imbs, Jean, and Paolo Mauro. 2007. *Pooling Risk Among Countries*. IMF Working Paper 07/132. Washington: International Monetary Fund.

IMF (International Monetary Fund). Various years. *Annual Report on Exchange Arrangements and Exchange Restrictions*. Washington.

IMF (International Monetary Fund). 2006. *World Economic Outlook: Financial Systems and Economic Cycles* (April). Washington.

IMF (International Monetary Fund). 2007a. *Reaping the Benefits of Financial Globalization* (June). Washington.

IMF (International Monetary Fund). 2007b. *World Economic Outlook Database: October 2007 Edition*. Washington. Available at www.imf.org.

IMF (International Monetary Fund). 2008a. *World Economic Outlook*. Washington.

IMF (International Monetary Fund). 2008b. *International Financial Statistics*. Washington.

IMF (International Monetary Fund). 2008c. *Global Financial Stability Report: Containing Systemic Risks and Restoring Financial Soundness* (April). Washington.

IMF (International Monetary Fund). 2009a. *International Financial Statistics* (CD-Rom). Washington.

IMF (International Monetary Fund). 2009b. *World Economic Outlook* (April). Washington.

IMF (International Monetary Fund). 2009c. *World Economic Outlook Update* (July). Washington.

IMF (International Monetary Fund). 2009d. *Global Financial Stability Report* (April). Washington.

IMF (International Monetary Fund). 2009e. *IMF Lending Arrangements as of September 30, 2009*. Washington.

IMF (International Monetary Fund). 2009f. *Global Financial Stability Report* (October). Washington.

IMF (International Monetary Fund). 2009g. *World Economic Outlook* (October). Washington.

IMF (International Monetary Fund). 2010. *World Economic Outlook Update* (January). Washington.

Kaminsky, Graciela Laura, and Sergio L. Schmukler. 2003. *Short-Run Pain, Long-Run Gain: The Effects of Financial Liberalization.* IMF Working Paper WP/03/34 (February). Washington: International Monetary Fund.

Kaminsky, Graciela Laura, and Carmen Reinhart. 1999. The Twin Crises: The Causes of Banking and Balance-of-Payments Problems. *American Economic Review* 89: 473–500.

King, Robert G., and Ross Levine. 1993. Finance and Growth: Schumpeter Might Be Right. *Quarterly Journal of Economics* 108, no. 3 (August): 717–37.

Klein, Michael. 2005. *Capital Account Liberalization, Institutional Quality and Economic Growth: Theory and Evidence.* NBER Working Paper 11112. Cambridge, MA: National Bureau of Economic Research.

Klein, Michael, and Giovanni Olivei. 1999 (revised 2006). *Capital Account Liberalization, Financial Depth, and Economic Growth.* Working Paper 99-6. Federal Reserve Bank of Boston.

Knack, Stephen, and Philip Keefer. 1995. Institutions and Economic Performance: Cross-Country Tests Using Alternative Institutional Measures. *Economics and Politics* 7, no. 3: 207–27.

Kolman, Joe, Michael Onak, Philippe Jorion, Nassim Taleb, Emanuel Derman, Blu Putnam, Richard Sandor, Stan Jonas, and Ron Dembo. 1998. *Roundtable on the Limits of VAR.* New York: Derivatives Strategy (April). Available at www.derivativesstrategy.com.

Kose, M. Ayhan, Eswar S. Prasad, and Marco E. Terrones. 2003. *Financial Integration and Macroeconomic Volatility.* IMF Working Paper no. WP/03/50 (March). Washington: International Monetary Fund.

Kose, Ayhan, Eswar Prasad, and Marco Terrones. 2007. How Does Financial Globalization Affect Risk Sharing? Patterns and Channels. Paper presented at Conference on New Perspectives on Financial Globalization, Washington, International Monetary Fund, April 26–27.

Kose, M. Ayhan, Eswar S. Prasad, and Marco E. Terrones. 2008. Does Openness to International Financial Flows Contribute to Productivity Growth? Cornell University, Ithaca, NY. Photocopy (August).

Kose, M. Ayhan, Eswar Prasad, Kenneth Rogoff, and Shang-Jin Wei. 2006. *Financial Globalization: A Reappraisal.* IMF Working Paper WP/06/189 (August). Washington: International Monetary Fund.

Kraay, Aart. 1998. In Search of the Macroeconomic Benefits of Capital Account Liberalization. World Bank, Washington. Photocopy (October).

Krugman, Paul. 1993. International Finance and Economic Development. In *Finance and Development: Issues and Experience*, ed. Alberto Giovannini. Cambridge, UK: Cambridge University Press.

Krugman, Paul. 2009. The Return of Depression Economics. Lionel Robbins Memorial Lectures 2009. London: London School of Economics. Available at http://cep.lse.ac.uk.

Lane, David M. 2010. *HyperState Online Statistics Textbook.* Houston: Rice University. Available at http://davidmlane.com.

Lane, Philip R., and Gian Maria Milesi-Ferretti. 2001. The External Wealth of Nations: Measures of Foreign Assets and Liabilities for Industrial and Developing Countries. *Journal of International Economics* 55: 263–94.

Lensink, Robert, and Oliver Morrissey. 2006. Foreign Direct Investment: Flows, Volatility, and the Impact on Growth. *Review of International Economics* 14, no. 3: 478–93.

Levchenko, Andrei, Romain Ranciere, and Mathias Thoenig. 2007. Growth and Risk at the Industry Level: The Real Effects of Financial Liberalization. Paper presented at Conference on New Perspectives on Financial Globalization, Washington, International Monetary Fund, April 26–27.

Levine, Ross. 2001. International Financial Liberalization and Economic Growth. *Review of International Economics* 9, no. 4: 688–702.

Levine, Ross, and David Renelt. 1992. A Sensitivity Analysis of Cross-Country Growth Regressions. *American Economic Review* 82, no. 4 (September): 942–63.

Levine, Ross, and Sara Zervos. 1998a. Stock Markets, Banks, and Economic Growth. *American Economic Review* 88, no. 3 (June): 537–58.

Levine, Ross, and Sara Zervos. 1998b. Capital Control Liberalization and Stock Market Development. *World Development* 26, no. 7 (July): 1169–83.

Lewis, Karen. 2000. Why Do Stocks and Consumption Imply Such Different Gains from International Risk Sharing? *Journal of International Economics* 52: 1–35.

Lipsey, Mark W., and David B. Wilson. 2001. Practical Meta-Analysis. *Applied Social Research Methods* 49. Thousand Oaks, CA: Sage Publications.

Mankiw, N. Gregory, David Romer, and David N. Weil. 1992. A Contribution to the Empirics of Economic Growth. *Quarterly Journal of Economics* 107, no. 2 (May): 407–37.

Markowitz, Harry M. 1952. Portfolio Selection. *Journal of Finance* 7, no. 1: 77–91.

Markowitz, Harry M. 2008. What to Do about the Financial Transparency Crisis. Index Fund Advisors, Irvine, CA. Photocopy (October).

McCloskey, Deirdre N., and Stephen T. Ziliak. 1996. The Standard Error of Regressions. *Journal of Economic Literature* 34, no. 1 (March): 97–114.

McKinnon, Ronald I. 1973. *Money and Capital in Economic Development*. Washington: Brookings Institution.

Mehra, Yash P. 2001. The Wealth Effect in Empirical Life-Cycle Aggregate Consumption Equations. *Economic Quarterly* (Spring): 45–67. Federal Reserve Bank of Richmond.

Mercereau, Benoît. 2006. *Financial Integration in Asia: Estimating the Risk-Sharing Gains for Australia and Other Nations*. IMF Working Paper WP/06/267 (December). Washington: International Monetary Fund.

Mitton, Todd. 2006. Stock Market Liberalization and Operating Performance at the Firm Level. *Journal of Financial Economics* 81, no. 3: 625–47.

Mody, Ashoka, and Antu Panini Murshid. 2005. Growing Up with Capital Flows. *Journal of International Economics* 65, no. 1 (January): 249–66. (Originally IMF Working Paper WP/02/75, April 2002, Washington: International Monetary Fund).

Montiel, Peter J. 1994. Capital Mobility in Developing Countries: Some Measurement Issues and Empirical Estimates. *World Bank Economic Review* 8, no. 3: 311–50.

Motulsky, Harvey. 1995. *Intuitive Biostatistics*. Oxford: Oxford University Press.

Mussa, Michael, and Morris Goldstein. 1993. Changing Capital Markets: Implications for Monetary Policy. Paper presented at a symposium sponsored by the Federal Reserve Bank of Kansas City, Jackson Hole, Wyoming, August 19–21.

Neyman, Jerzy, and Egon S. Pearson. 1933. On the Problem of the Most Efficient Tests of Statistical Hypotheses. *Philosophical Transactions of the Royal Society of London, Series A, Containing Papers of a Mathematical or Physical Character*, volume 231: 289–37.

Obstfeld, Maurice. 1994a. Evaluating Risky Consumption Paths: the Role of Intertemporal Substitutability. *European Economic Review* 38: 1471–86.

Obstfeld, Maurice. 1994b. Risk-Taking, Global Diversification, and Growth. *American Economic Review* 84, no. 5 (December): 1310–29.

Obstfeld, Maurice. 2009. International Finance and Growth in Developing Countries: What Have We Learned? *IMF Staff Papers* 56, no. 1: 63–111. Washington: International Monetary Fund.

OECD (Organization for Economic Cooperation and Development). 2002. Trends and Recent Developments in Foreign Direct Investment. *OECD International Investment Perspectives* (September). Paris.

Office of Federal Housing Enterprise Oversight. 2008. *Revisiting the Differences between the OFHEO and S&P/Case-Shiller House Price Indexes: New Explanations* (January). Washington.

OMB (Office of Management and Budget). 2010. *Budget of the United States Government, Fiscal Year 2011* (February). Washington. Available at www.whitehouse.gov.

Ostry, Jonathan D., Atish R. Ghosh, Karl Habermeier, Marcos Chamon, Mahvash S. Qureshi, and Dennis B. S. Reinhardt. 2010. *Capital Inflows: The Role of Controls*. IMF Staff Position Note SPN/10/24 (February). Washington: International Monetary Fund.

Pearson, Karl. 1904. Report on Certain Enteric Fever Inoculation Statistics. *British Medical Journal* 3: 1243–46.

Posen, Adam, and Nicolas Véron. 2009. *A Solution for Europe's Banking Problem*. Bruegel Policy Brief 2009/3. Brussels: Bruegel.

Prasad, Eswar, and Raghuram Rajan. 2008. A Pragmatic Approach to Capital Account Liberalization. *Journal of Economic Perspectives* 22, no. 3: 149–72.

Prasad, Eswar, Raghuram Rajan, and Arvind Subramanian. 2007a. *Foreign Capital and Economic Growth*. Washington: International Monetary Fund (April).

Prasad, Eswar, Raghuram Rajan, and Arvind Subramanian. 2007b. The Paradox of Capital. *Finance and Development* 44, no. 1 (March):16–19.

Prasad, Eswar, Kenneth Rogoff, Shang-Jin Wei, and M. Ayhan Kose. 2003. *Effects of Financial Globalization on Developing Countries: Some Empirical Evidence*. Washington: International Monetary Fund (March).

Quinn, Dennis. 1997. The Correlates of Change in International Financial Regulation. *American Political Science Review* 91, no. 3 (September): 531–51.

Quinn, Dennis, and A. Maria Toyoda. 2008. Does Capital Account Liberalization Lead to Growth? *Review of Financial Studies* 21, no. 3: 1403–49.

Rajan, Raghuram G., and Luigi Zingales. 1998. Financial Dependence and Growth. *American Economic Review* 88, no. 3 (June): 559–86.

Rajan, Raghuram G. 2005. *Has Financial Development Made the World Riskier?* NBER Working Paper 11728 (November). Cambridge, MA: National Bureau of Economic Research.

Ramsey, Frank P. 1928. A Mathematical Theory of Saving. *Economic Journal* 138, no. 152: 543–59.

Ranciere, Romain, Aaron Tornell, and Frank Westermann. 2005. *Systemic Crises and Growth*. NBER Working Paper 11076 (January). Cambridge, MA: National Bureau of Economic Research.

Reinhart, Carmen M., and Vincent R. Reinhart. 2008. *Capital Flow Bonanzas: An Encompassing View of the Past and Present*. NBER Working Paper 14321 (September). Cambridge, MA: National Bureau of Economic Research.

Reinhart, Carmen M., and Kenneth S. Rogoff. 2008. *Banking Crises: An Equal Opportunity Menace* (December). Cambridge, MA: National Bureau of Economic Research.

Reisen, Helmut, and Marcelo Soto. 2001. Which Types of Capital Inflows Foster Developing-Country Growth? *International Finance* 4, no. 1 (Spring): 1–14.

Rodrik, Dani. 1998. Who Needs Capital-Account Convertibility? *Essays in International Finance*, no. 207. Princeton, NJ: Princeton University.

Rodrik, Dani, and Arvind Subramanian. 2009. Why Did Financial Globalization Disappoint? *IMF Staff Papers* 56, no. 1: 112–38. Washington: International Monetary Fund.

Rodrik, Dani, and Andrés Velasco. 1999. *Short-Term Capital Flows*. NBER Working Paper 7364 (September). Cambridge, MA: National Bureau of Economic Research.

Rosenberg, Christoph B. 2008. The Baltic Party Need Not End in a Bust. *IMF Survey Magazine: Countries and Regions* (February). Washington: International Monetary Fund.

Sachs, Jeffrey, and Andrew Warner. 1995. Economic Reform and the Process of Global Integration. *Brookings Papers on Economic Activity* no. 1: 1–118. Washington: Brookings Institution.

Sala-i-Martin, Xavier X. 1997. I Just Ran Two Million Regressions. *American Economic Review* 87, no. 2: 178–83.

Schumpeter, Joseph A. 1911. *The Theory of Economic Development*. New York: Oxford University Press. Translation by Redvers Opie, 1934.

Shatz, Howard J. 2000.The Location of U.S. Multinational Affiliates. PhD dissertation, Harvard University.

Sørensen, Bent E., Yi-Tsung Wu, Oved Yosha, and Yu Zhu. 2007. Home Bias and International Risk Sharing: Twin Puzzles Separated at Birth. *Journal of International Money and Finance* 26, no. 4: 587–605.

Standard and Poor's. 2009. *S&P/Case-Shiller Home Price Indexes*. New York. Available at www2.standardandpoors.com.

Stanley, T. D. 2001. Wheat from Chaff: Meta-Analysis as Quantitative Literature Review. *Journal of Economic Perspectives* 15, no. 3 (Summer): 131–50.

Stiglitz, Joseph. 2002. *Globalization and Its Discontents*. New York: W. W. Norton.

Summers, Lawrence H. 2000. International Financial Crises: Causes, Prevention, and Cures. *American Economic Review* 90, no. 2 (May): 1–16.

Taylor, John B. 2009. The Lack of an Empirical Rationale for a Revival of Discretionary Fiscal Policy. *American Economic Review* 99, no. 2 (May): 550–55.

Tornell, Aaron, Frank Westermann, and Lorenza Martinez. 2004. *The Positive Link between Financial Liberalization, Growth and Crises*. NBER Working Paper 10293 (February). Cambridge, MA: National Bureau of Economic Research.

Tornell, Aaron, and Frank Westermann. 2005. *Boom-Bust Cycles and Financial Liberalization*. Cambridge, MA: MIT Press.

Tytell, Irina, and Shang-Jin Wei. 2004. *Does Financial Globalization Induce Better Macroeconomic Policies?* IMF Working Paper WP/04/84. Washington: International Monetary Fund.

US Census Bureau. 2000. Historical National Population Estimates: July 1, 1900 to July 1, 1999. Washington: US Census Bureau, Population Division. Available at www.census.gov (accessed on February 5, 2010).

US Census Bureau. 2008. *USA Quick Facts*. Washington.

US Census Bureau. 2009a. *New Residential Construction in June 2009*. News Release CB09-109, July 17, Washington.

US Census Bureau. 2009b. *Total Midyear Population for the World: 1950–2050*. International Data Base. Washington. Available at www.census.gov.

US Federal Reserve. 2007. *Minutes of the Federal Open Market Committee, December 11, 2007*. Washington.

US Federal Reserve. 2008a. *Factors Affecting Reserve Balances*. Statistical Release H.4.1 (December 29). Washington.

US Federal Reserve. 2008b. *Large Commercial Banks*. Statistical Release (June). Washington.

US Federal Reserve. 2009a. *The Supervisory Capital Assessment Program: Design and Implementation* (April 24). Washington.

US Federal Reserve. 2009b. *The Supervisory Capital Assessment Program: Overview of Results* (May 7). Washington.

US Federal Reserve. 2009c. *Flow of Funds Accounts of the United States: Flows and Outstandings, First Quarter 2009*. Statistical Release Z.1 (June). Washington.

US Federal Reserve. 2010. *Statistics and Historical Data*. Washington. Available at www.federalreserve.gov/econresdata/releases/statisticsdata.htm.

US Treasury Department. 2008. *Treasury International Capital Data for June* (August 15). Washington.

US Treasury Department. 2009. *Financial Regulatory Reform: A New Foundation* (June). Washington.

Van Wincoop, Eric. 1994. Welfare Gains from International Risksharing. *Journal of Monetary Economics* 34: 175–200.

Van Wincoop, Eric. 1999. How Big Are Potential Welfare Gains from International Risksharing? *Journal of International Economics* 47, no. 1: 109–35.

Vanassche, Ellen. 2004. The Impact of International Financial Integration on Industry Growth. Katholieke Universiteit Leuven, Belgium. Photocopy.

Vlachos, Jonas, and Daniel Waldenström. 2002. *International Financial Liberalization and Industry Growth*. IUI Working Paper 586. Stockholm, Sweden: Research Institute of Industrial Economics.

Wald, Abraham. 1939. Contributions to the Theory of Statistical Estimation and Testing Hypotheses. *Annals of Mathematical Statistics* 10, no. 4 (December): 299–326.

Wei, Shang-Jin. 1997. *Why is Corruption Much More Taxing than Taxes? Arbitrariness Kills.* NBER Working Paper 6255 (November). Cambridge, MA: National Bureau of Economic Research.

Wei, Shang-Jin. 2006. Connecting Two Views on Financial Globalization: Can We Make Further Progress? Paper prepared for the 18th Annual TRIO Conference, University of Tokyo, December 9–10.

Wessel, David. 2009. *In Fed We Trust: Ben Bernanke's War on the Great Panic.* New York: Crown.

Williamson, John. 2008. Crises, Consumption Smoothing, and Capital Mobility. Peterson Institute for International Economics, Washington. Unpublished paper (November).

Wolf, Martin. 2008. *Fixing Global Finance.* Baltimore: Johns Hopkins University Press.

World Bank. 1997. *World Development Report 1997: The State in a Changing World*. Washington.

World Bank. 2008. *Global Development Finance 2008: The Role of International Banking* (CD-Rom). Washington.

World Bank. 2009a. *Global Development Finance 2009: Charting a Global Recovery. Volume I: Review, Analysis, and Outlook. Volume II: Summary and Country Tables*. Washington.

World Bank. 2009b. As Global Sump Is Set to Continue, Poor Countries Need More Help. Press Release 2009/394/EXC, June 11. Washington.

World Bank. 2010. *Global Economic Prospects 2010: Crisis, Finance, and Growth* (January). Washington.

Zandi, Mark. 2009. *Financial Shock: A 360° Look at the Subprime Mortgage Implosion, and How to Avoid the Next Financial Crisis.* Upper Saddle River, NJ: FT Press.

Zingales, Luigi. 2008. Why Paulson Is Wrong. *Economists' Voice* 5, no. 5 (September). Available at www.bepress.com (accessed on February 2, 2010).

Index

Asset-Backed Commercial Paper Money
    Market Mutual Fund Liquidity
    Facility (Federal Reserve), 265
asset bubble, bursting of, 95
Australia
    banking-sector efficiency, 74
    diversification gains, 126
    foreign direct investment, 201
    growth-impact estimates, 185
Austria, 201
autarky
    model for, 155–58, 158f
    portfolio, 122
    risk sharing under, 162
automobile industry, 268

Bailliu, Jeannine N.
    capital-market openness study, 52–53,
        68n, 70
    country-specific estimates, 192, 193, 217
    financial development study, 72
bailout
    banking sector, 96, 96n, 263–71, 311–12
    public-sector, 268–69
bank accounts, foreign, ease of holding, 62
bank credits, threshold effect, 53–54
bank development measures, 72, 72n
banking crises, 17–18
    bailout costs, 96, 96n
    capital-market openness and, 60
    cumulative losses from, 97n, 100–101,
        101t
    currency crises with, 97, 141
    during global financial crisis, 29–30, 237,
        240
        government bailout, 263–71,
        311–12 (See also Troubled Asset Relief
        Program)
        loss estimates, 242, 245, 245n
        recovery from, 241–46
    impact studies, 95–97
    incidence of, 98, 98n, 100, 101t
    institutional and policy variables, 137n
    probability of, 98–100, 101t
    quantifying, 25–26, 26n, 34
    summary survey, 141
    time factors and degree of openness, 98,
        99f
banking depth, 14, 182–83
banking sector. See also specific bank
    assets of, 306, 308f, 309f
    capital adequacy, 244n, 245–46, 272, 292,
        305, 312

consolidation of, 305–8, 309f
efficiency of, 74
as FDI variable, 81–82
forced transformations in, 305–6, 307f
leverage ratios, 288
mortgage losses, 282–83, 295, 297f, 312
nationalization of, 267, 306, 309–13
net worth measures, 312
"stress test," 30, 237, 240, 244–45, 245n,
    261, 271
Bank of America
    bank consolidation and, 306
    capital needs, 245, 270, 313
    Merrill Lynch takeover, 237, 264, 268, 288
Bank of England, 240
Bank of New York, 307
Barro, Robert J., 52n, 117–18
Barth, James R., 292
Bear Stearns
    collapse of, 261, 262, 292
    forced takeover of, 237, 264, 265, 305
    leverage, 288
    rescue costs, 270
    RMBS exposure, 282
    as too-big-to-fail, 262n
Bekaert, Geert
    capital-market openness study, 59, 60
    direct investment study, 81
    financial development study, 74
    portfolio equity study, 86, 88, 89, 89n
    sectoral-level analyses, 109, 112
    summary survey, 131–32
Belgium, 185, 266
Bernanke, Ben, 264, 267n, 272, 292, 301
Bhagwati, Jagdish, 1, 35, 76, 91
bias
    endogeneity (See endogeneity)
    reviewer, 70–71
black-market variable, 56, 183
Blonigan, Bruce A.
    direct investment study, 82–83, 87t, 205,
        218, 221
    portfolio equity study, 90n
    threshold effect variables, 15
BNP Paribas, 261
Bonfiglioli, Alessandra, 60–61, 74–75
Borenzstein, Eduardo, 79, 82, 83, 87t, 205,
    210n, 219
Bosworth, Barry P.
    capital market-openness study, 51–52, 61
    country-specific estimates, 210–11
    direct investment study, 8n

total factor productivity study, 12
Brady Plan, 301, 304
Brazil
    capital-market openness, 54, 57n
    financing gap, 31–32, 32n, 253
    foreign direct investment, 201, 205
    global financial crisis effects, 255
    growth-impact estimates, 185
    reserve adequacy, 253, 332
    tax on capital flows, 236
"break the glass" emergency plan (US
    Treasury), 262–63
Bush administration, bank bailout, 310
business cycles
    capital-market openness and, 57
    consumption smoothing and, 128, 131
    foreign direct investment and, 84
    global financial crisis and, 239
Bussiere, Matthieu
    capital-market openness studies, 57–58,
        67t
    country-specific estimates, 192, 193, 218

calibrated theoretical models, 116–19
    consumption smoothing, 130
    country-specific estimates, 180–83
        versus synthesis approach, 208–13
    crisis effects, 25–26, 34, 143
    diversification gains, 120–21, 126, 161–64
    versus statistical models, 10
Calomiris, Charles W., 287–88
capital, marginal product of, 209, 209n
capital account liberalization, growth
    effects, 72, 94–95
capital adequacy, 244n, 245–46, 272, 292,
    305, 312
capital composition, 9–10, 35. *See also* debt
    capital; foreign direct investment;
    portfolio equity flows
    capital-market openness and, 53–54
    corruption and, 107–108, 134
    quantifying, 26–28, 41–44
    sequencing and, 11
capital deepening, 2, 92n
    steady-state formulation of, 223–27
    theoretical expectations, 12
capital flight risk, 140
capital flows
    banking crises and, 95
    disincentives to, 103–104, 140, 236
    global financial crisis effects, 251–52, 252f
    gross, 19, 177f, 177–82
    growth effects from, 52–53
    relative to GDP, 20n, 30–32, 230

    stock of, 55
    theoretical expectations, 11
    variables for, 229
    welfare gains from, 39, 40f
capital flow bonanza, 18, 98–100
capital income, share in national accounts,
    210
capital-market openness, 48–64
    degrees of intensity, 57
    to foreign bank entry, 74
    growth effects of, 74
    measures of, 55, 62
capital mobility
    crisis impact and, 93, 94n
    as dangerous influence, 45
    institutional and policy variables,
        104–108
    measures of, 5n, 5–6
capital productivity, 116–19
Carkovic, Maria
    country-specific estimates, 201
    direct investment study, 7n, 78–79, 82,
        87t, 205, 220
carry trade, 16
Case-Shiller index, 238, 279, 280f
CDOs (collateralized debt obligations), 289
CDS (credit default swaps), 29, 239, 289–90,
    290n, 292
Chile
    capital-market openness, 54
    crisis vulnerability, 17, 103–104
    encaje tax, 103, 104, 140
    financing gap, 253
    foreign direct investment, 205
    gross capital flow, 180n
    growth-impact estimates, 185
    reserve adequacy, 254, 332
China
    capital composition effects, 28, 44
    current account balance, 63, 168–69, 170,
        297, 298f
    foreign direct investment, 205
    growth-impact estimates, 189
    per capita growth, 176
    reserve adequacy, 253–54
    total factor productivity growth, 210–11
Chrysler, 268
CIP (covered interest parity), 5n, 5–6, 37f,
    37–38
Citigroup
    agency problems, 293
    bank consolidation and, 306
    capital needs, 245, 245n, 270, 310, 313
    leverage, 288

share price, 268
classic banking panic, 29, 239
Cobb-Douglas production function, 12n, 118, 155, 208, 223–25
collateral benefits, 135–36
collateralized debt obligations (CDOs), 289
Collins, Susan M.
  capital-market openness study, 51–52, 61
  country-specific estimates, 210–11
  direct investment study, 8n
  total factor productivity study, 12
Colombia, 185, 185n, 201, 205
Commercial Paper Funding Facility (CPFF), 269–70, 305
Committee on Uniform Securities Identification Procedures (CUSIP), 304
commodity price shocks, 127
Community Reinvestment Act, 291
complete versus zero openness, 14, 25, 27
  capital-market openness and, 50, 56, 66, 67t, 68–69, 69t
  financial development and, 74–75
  general growth-impact estimates, 200, 200f, 229
Congress, financial asset purchase, 266
conservatorship
  AIG, 237, 264–65, 290–91, 305
  Fannie Mae/Freddie Mac, 237, 263–65, 267, 287, 305–6
consumption smoothing, 10, 119–31, 142–43, 161–64, 163t
consumption volatility, 127n, 127–28, 134, 135n, 136n, 136–37, 143
contingent studies, 68–69, 69t
control variables, 47
  capital-market openness study, 54, 58
  country-specific estimates, 171, 175
  direct investment studies, 86n
  sectoral-level analyses, 110, 111n, 113n
  summary surveys, 137
convergence, 13, 22, 47, 55, 225
corporate taxation, 50
correlation coefficients, financial openness measures, 230–31, 233t, 234t
corruption, capital composition and, 107–108, 134
Côte d'Ivoire, 168
country groupings. *See also specific region*
  foreign direct investment, 201, 206t–207t
  growth-impact estimates, 189–92, 190t–191t, 194, 198t–199t
country-specific estimates, 171–234. *See also specific country*

calibrated models, 180–83
comparison of (*See* cross-country growth analysis)
direct investment openness, 201–207, 202t–204t, 213, 218–22
general financial openness, 183–92, 186t–188t, 194–200, 200f, 217–18, 229–34
  normalized coefficients, 183, 184t, 185t, 217–22
  synthesis approach, 172–73, 213–15
  versus theoretical expectations, 208–13
  variables used in, 180–83, 181t
trends in financial openness, 173–80, 175f, 214–15
weighting nonsignificant model estimates, 192–200, 195t–199t, 200f, 213
Countrywide, 305
covered interest parity (CIP), 5n, 5–6, 37f, 37–38
CPFF (Commercial Paper Funding Facility), 269–70, 305
credit, nontradable sector reliance on, 59–60
credit crunch, 236
credit default swaps (CDS), 29, 239, 289–90, 290n, 292
credit losses, associated with housing crisis, 283, 311–12
credit volatility, 17
crisis effects, 10–11, 16–18. *See also* global financial crisis; *specific crisis*
  capital-market openness, 58, 60, 98
  growth impact studies, 91–104, 101t
  quantifying, 25–26, 34
  summary surveys, 141, 141n, 143
  time factors, 98, 99f
  trade-off against growth gains, 101–103
critical range, 145–46
cross-country growth analysis, 3, 46–115
  capital composition, 27–28
  capital-market openness, 48–64
  crisis impact, 91
  diversification gains, 126–28
  financial openness measures, 5–6
  foreign direct investment, 76–81
  institutions and policy discipline, 104–105
  meta-statistical weighting, 145–54
  robustness, 65–66
  sample size, 65
  subcategories, 47
  summarizing, 64–71, 67t

summary surveys, 131–32, 137–38
currency crises, 18
  banking crisis with, 97, 141
  cumulative losses from, 100–101, 101*t*, 102*n*
  impact studies, 94–95, 96–97
  incidence of, 97–98, 100, 101*t*
  probability of, 97–100, 101*t*
  quantifying, 25–26, 26*n*, 34
  summary survey, 141
  time factors and degree of openness, 98, 99*f*
currency declines, 255, 255*n*, 256*f*
currency mismatches, 59
current account balance, 105–106. *See also specific country*
  global financial crisis and, 240, 249–51, 254, 297, 299
  growth impact studies, 167–70, 168*f*, 169*f*
  as proxy for financial openness, 62–63
  world total, 297, 298*f*
CUSIP (Committee on Uniform Securities Identification Procedures), 304
cyclical conditions. *See* business cycles

debt
  public (*See* public debt)
  short-term, 16–17, 91, 103–104, 329
  sovereign, crisis in, 95
debt capital openness, 9–10, 35
  quantifying, 26–28, 41–44
  sequencing of, 11
debt crises, 127
de facto measures, 4–5, 14, 19. *See also specific measure*
  capital-market openness, 51, 58, 63, 64*n*, 66, 67*t*
  country-specific estimates, 177–78, 192, 231, 231*f*
  current account deficit, 167
  versus de jure measures, 8
  normalization, 150
  sectoral-level analyses, 113–14
  total factor productivity, 211
default probability, Geithner Plan estimates, 320–22, 321*f*–323*f*
De Gregorio, José, 79, 82, 83, 87*t*, 205, 210*n*, 219
de jure measures, 4, 13–14, 19. *See also specific measure*
  capital-market openness, 51, 58, 63, 64*n*, 66, 67*t*
  capital mobility, 93

country-specific estimates, 173, 174*t*, 189*n*, 192, 230, 231, 231*f*
  crisis impact, 94
  current account deficit, 167
  versus de facto measures, 8
  institution and policy discipline, 106
  in meta-weighting example, 151
  sectoral-level analyses, 113–14, 114*n*
  summary surveys, 137
  TFP growth, 12*n*
  total factor productivity, 211
Denmark, 201
deposit insurance coverage, 237, 269, 288, 308, 320
Deutsche Bank, 307
developed countries. *See* industrial countries; *specific country*
developing countries. *See also specific country*
  capital composition effects, 43–44
  capital flows to, 251–52, 252*f*
  capital-market openness, 61–62
  capital productivity, 116–19
  consumption smoothing, 127, 129, 142–43
  contingent thresholds, 35, 133–34, 137
  crisis impact studies, 91, 95–98, 99*f*, 102–103
  cumulative growth effects, 22–25, 23*t*–24*t*, 34
  currency decline, 255, 255*n*, 256*f*
  current account deficits, 62–63, 167–70, 168*f*, 251
  debt liabilities, 211
  de facto measures, 178
  degrees of openness, 173, 174*t*, 231, 231*f*
  domestic financial development, 71, 214
  financial development, 72–73, 75
  financing gaps, 31–32, 236, 325–32, 326*t*–328*t*
  foreign direct investment, 76–82, 201, 205, 206*t*–207*t*, 208*f*, 219–22
    versus industrial countries, 212–14
  global financial crisis effects, 237, 240–41, 242*f*, 251, 255–60
  gross capital flows, 177*f*, 177–80
  growth gains, 20–22, 21*t*, 34, 256, 257*f*
  growth-impact estimates, 189–92, 190*t*–191*t*, 192*n*, 194, 199*t*, 200, 200*f*
    versus industrial countries, 212–14
  portfolio equity, 86, 89–90
  reserve adequacy, 253–54, 325–32, 330*t*–331*t*
  sectoral-level analyses, 111–12

short-term debt to reserve ratio, 103, 329
summary surveys, 133–34, 134–37
theoretical expectations, 12
trimmed averages
foreign direct investment, 201, 202t–207t, 205
growth-impact estimates, 184, 189, 192, 194, 200
Dexia, 237, 266
dichotomous vote-counting, 66, 70, 145–47, 153
direct endogeneity, 8
diversification gains, 10, 11, 119–31, 142
domestic financial sector development, 71–75, 214
dot-com stock market bubble, 280
dummy variables
capital-market openness, 48n, 48–49, 58
country-specific estimates, 175n
crisis impact studies, 91, 97
direct investment studies, 82
portfolio equity studies, 89

Eastern Europe. *See also specific country*
global financial crisis effects, 33, 33n, 258–60
growth-impact estimates, 189
economic growth. *See growth*
Edison, Hali J.
capital-market openness study, 53–55, 67t
country-specific estimates, 192, 193, 217–18
endogeneity, 8, 8n
institution and policy discipline study, 107, 165–66
summary survey, 131–32
Edwards, Sebastian
capital-market openness study, 54, 54n, 56, 67t, 69, 70
country-specific estimates, 184, 185n, 192, 193, 194, 217
crisis impact study, 93–94, 94n
interactive variables, 20n
portfolio equity study, 88
on short-term debt taxation, 17, 103
summary survey, 141, 141n
effective labor, 118, 155–57, 224
effect size, 65, 147–49, 151n, 154
efficiency
banking-sector, 74
financial openness and, 11
Egypt, 201, 205
Eichengreen, Barry
capital-market openness study, 55–56, 67t, 70

country-specific estimates, 192, 193, 218
crisis impact study, 93
macroeconomic thresholds, 11
sectoral-level analyses, 114n
summary survey, 131
emerging bond market, 31–32
emerging-market economies. *See developing countries; specific country*
encaje (Chile), 103–104
endogeneity, 7–9
capital-market openness and, 53–54
robustness and, 65
summary surveys, 141
endogenous growth theory, 116
endowment economy, 123, 130–31
Esquivel, Gerardo, 225
Estonia, 258–59
ethnic homogeneity, capital controls and, 62
Europe. *See also specific country*
banking crisis, 30, 266
consumption smoothing, 126
crisis vulnerability, 93, 95
foreign direct investment, 201
global financial crisis effects, 33, 33n, 237, 258–60, 266
growth-impact estimates, 189
European Bank for Reconstruction and Development, 58, 260
European Central Bank, 240
exchange rates
crisis impact and, 104, 255, 256f
trade-neutral effective, 76
Exchange Stabilization Fund (US Treasury), 265n, 270
exogenous investment rates, 8
exports, reduction in, during recession, 248–49, 249f
external dependence ratio, 109, 109n, 111, 114n
external financing gap, 325–32, 330t–331t

factor price equalization theorem, 129
factor reallocation models, 10
"fair value" accounting, 303
Fannie Mae
conservatorship, 237, 263–65, 267, 287, 305–6
fiscal losses from, 250n, 270
subprime lending and, 292
FASB (Financial Accounting Standards Board), 303
FDI. *See foreign direct investment*
Federal Deposit Insurance Corporation (FDIC), 237
expansion of coverage, 308

Legacy Loan Program, 316, 316n, 320
  public-sector bailout, 268–69
federal funds rate, 239–40, 254, 295–96, 296f
Federal Housing Finance Agency (FHFA)
  index, 238, 279
Federal Reserve
  Asset-Backed Commercial Paper Money
    Market Mutual Fund Liquidity
    Facility, 265
  Commercial Paper Funding Facility,
    269–70, 305
  currency swap lines, 255
  global financial crisis intervention, 240
    (See also specific action)
  interest rate policy, 31–32, 254, 263,
    295–96, 296f
  Legacy Securities Program, 316–17
  lender-of-last-resort function, 262, 311
  Primary Dealers' Credit Facility, 237
  public-sector bailout, 268–69
  "stress test," 30, 237, 240, 244–45, 245n,
    261, 271
  subprime lending regulation, 291
  Term Auction Facility, 237, 261, 269
  Term Securities Lending Facility, 262
  total assets of, 269–70
Feldstein-Horioka condition, 5
FHFA (Federal Housing Finance Agency)
  index, 238, 279
Financial Accounting Standards Board
  (FASB), 303
financial crises. See crisis effects; specific
  crisis
financial depth
  measures of, 72
  sectoral-level analyses, 109
financial development, 71–75
  sectoral-level analyses, 109
  summary surveys, 142
financial fragility, crisis impact and, 91–92
financial innovation, 28, 288–91, 293
financial opening, sequence for, 10–11
financial openness
  categories of, 3
  complete (See complete versus zero
    openness)
  degrees of intensity, 57, 173
  measures of, 4–6, 13–15, 20n, 171,
    173, 180, 211–12 (See also de facto
    measures; de jure measures; specific
    measure)
    degree of correlation among, 229–34
  trends in, 19, 173–80, 214–15
financial openness-growth impact

cross-country comparison (See cross-
  country growth analysis)
  debate over, 1–2
  empirical literature, 13–18
    critical survey of, 45–170
    summary surveys, 131–43
  evidence on, 32–33
  key analytical issues, 4–5
  negative effect case (See negative-impact
    case)
  positive effect case (See positive-impact
    case)
  quantification of, 3, 19–25
  range of, 14–15
  research context, 2–3
  synthesis estimates, 18–25, 34
  theoretical expectations, 11–13
  trade gains analogy, 1–2, 39, 40f, 140–41,
    178
financial regulation, lax, 29, 238–39, 291–92
financial-sector risk
  late 2009 status, 240–41, 241f
  measures of, 29
financial services sector. See also banking
  sector
  composition of, 305, 306f
  forced transformations in, 305–6, 307f
  foreign direct investment and, 80–81
financing gaps, 30–32, 236
  global financial crisis and, 251–53,
    325t–32, 326t–328t
Finland, 201
firm-level analyses, 112–14, 115t
fiscal costs
  crisis impact, 96, 104
  global financial crisis, 249–51, 270–71
Fischer, Stanley, 1, 35
Foley, C. Fritz, 112–13, 115t
foreign bank accounts, ease of holding, 62
foreign bank entry, ease of, 74
foreign direct investment (FDI), 9, 15–16,
  35, 205
  capital-market openness and, 52–55,
    59–62
  corruption and, 107–108, 134
  country-specific estimates, 178–79, 179f,
    182–83, 201–207, 202t–204t, 213
    industrial versus developing
      countries, 212, 214
    models, 218–22
  domestic preconditions for, 80–81
  effect on domestic investment, 61–62,
    82–83, 214
  flow relative to GDP, 20n

GDP ratio to, 76f, 76–77, 84
growth effect studies, 75–86, 87t
opening of, sequencing of, 11
openness to, measures of, 173
quantifying, 26–28, 41–44
summary surveys, 138–40, 141, 142
theoretical expectations, 11
tradable sector finance from, 59
trends in, 19
volatility of, 83–85
foreign direct investment (FDI)-interactive
coefficient, 79n, 79–81
foreign portfolio diversification, 10, 11,
119–31, 142
Fortis, 237, 266
France, 126, 185, 201, 266
Fratzscher, Marcel
capital-market openness studies, 57–58,
67t
country-specific estimates, 192, 193, 218
Freddie Mac
conservatorship, 237, 263–65, 287, 305–6
fiscal losses from, 250n, 270
subprime lending and, 292

GDP
annual real growth, 180
attributable to financial openness, 22–25,
23t–24t
capital flows ratio, 20n
currency crisis and, 100
current account balance ratio, 299
debt liabilities ratio, 211
foreign direct investment ratio, 76f,
76–77, 84, 178–79, 179f
gross capital flows ratio, 19, 177f, 177–82
portfolio equity flow ratio, 86
public debt ratio, 250–51
Geithner, Timothy, 265n
Geithner Plan, 28n, 315–23
Gemini model, 120, 128n, 130, 161–64
General Electric, 269n
generalized method of moments
techniques. See GMM techniques
General Motors, 268
Germany, 126, 185, 201, 266
Glass-Steagall Act, 236, 292
Glick, Reuven, 17, 94–95
Global Competitiveness Report (World
Economic Forum), 108
global financial crisis (2007-09), 235–332
analyses of, 35, 236
causes of, 28n, 28–29, 95, 238–40, 261,
279–99

contemporary policy diagnoses, 301–13
economic growth during, 30, 242,
243t–244t, 246–49, 256, 257f
evidence on, 32–33
evolution of, 236–38, 261–77
financing gaps, 251–53, 325–32, 326t–328t
fiscal consequences of, 249–51, 270–71
implications of, 28–33, 255–60
key events in, 273t–277t
late 2009 status, 29–30, 240–54
phase 1 (July 2007 to February 2008),
261–62
phase 2 (March 2008 to August 2008),
262–63
phase 3 (September 2008 to March 2009),
263–71
phase 4 (April 2009 and after), 236,
271–72
reserve adequacy, 253–54, 325–32,
330t–331t
role of mortgage-backed securities in (See
mortgage-backed securities)
Global Financial Stability Report (IMF), 241
global recession, 246–49, 247f–248f
global saving glut, 29, 238, 239, 296–99
GMAC, 245, 268
GMM (generalized method of moments)
techniques, 8
capital-market openness study, 52–55,
58, 60
crisis impact studies, 96–97
foreign direct investment study, 78–79,
79n
portfolio equity study, 87
Goldman Sachs
bank consolidation and, 306
bank holding company status, 237, 264,
288, 305
capital needs, 245, 265n, 267n
mortgage loss estimates, 283, 312
Gourinchas, Pierre-Olivier, 118–19, 155–59,
158f, 210
government reputation. See institutional
variables
government-sponsored entities (GSEs), 263,
265, 270–71, 288, 292
Gramlich, Edward, 291
Gramm-Leach-Bliley Act, 236, 292
Granger causality tests, 59
Greece, 201
Greenspan, Alan, 3, 236, 291, 293, 294, 295
Grilli, Vittorio, 48–49, 131
gross capital flows, 19, 20n, 177f, 177–80
Group of 7 (G-7), 13, 272

Group of 20 (G-20), 31, 251, 253, 271
growth
    effect of financial openness on (*See*
        financial openness-growth impact)
    during global financial crisis, 30, 242,
        243t–244t, 256, 257f
    as percentage rate, 180
    during recessions, 246–49, 247f–248f
    trade openness and, 1–2
growth per capita, as dependent variable,
    51, 51n, 59–60
GSEs (government-sponsored entities), 263,
    265, 270–71, 288, 292

Harvey, Campbell R.
    capital-market openness study, 59, 60
    direct investment study, 81
    financial development study, 74
    portfolio equity study, 86, 88, 89, 89n
    sectoral-level analyses, 109, 112
    summary survey, 131–32
Haveman, Jon D., 78, 87t, 205, 219–20
Henry, Peter Blair
    portfolio equity study, 16, 89–90, 90n
    summary survey, 139
    temporary *versus* permanent growth
        acceleration model, 223–27
Hermes, Niels, 15, 80–81, 87t, 205, 220–21
high leverage, 29
high-variant results, 20–22, 21t, 71
Hines, James R., 112–13, 115t
historical patterns
    crisis events, 17, 34
    growth gains, 19–20
Hong Kong
    capital composition effects, 28, 43–44
    current account balance, 63
    diversification gains, 126
    foreign direct investment, 205
    GDP-capital flow ratio, 230
    gross capital flow, 180n
    reserve adequacy, 254
"hot" models, 189–92
housing bubble, 28, 238. *See also* mortgage-
    backed securities
    regulatory mistakes, 291–92
    scope of problem, 282–83
    sources of, 280–82
housing starts, 281
HSBC, 307
human capital, 15, 77, 117–18, 225
Hungary, 33, 205, 255, 259–60
Hutchison, Michael M.

crisis impact study, 17–18, 25, 94–95,
    96–97, 97–98, 100
    summary survey, 141
Hypo Real Estate, 237, 266

Iceland, 237
IFC (International Finance Corporation),
    89, 112
IFI (international financial integration),
    54–55
IIF (Institute of International Finance), 16,
    251
Imbs, Jean, 128–29, 136
IMF. *See* International Monetary Fund
import-substitution orientation, 76
income inequality, 50
income level, 14
India
    capital composition effects, 28, 44
    capital flow bonanza, 18, 98
    crisis vulnerability, 92
    current account balance, 63
    financing gap, 253
    foreign direct investment, 201, 205
    growth-impact estimates, 189
    reserve adequacy, 253, 254, 332
indirect endogeneity, 8
Indonesia, 189, 201, 205
industrial countries. *See also specific country*
    capital-market openness, 50
    capital productivity, 116–19
    consumption smoothing, 125–26, 129
    crisis vulnerability, 93, 95–96
    cumulative growth effects, 22–25,
        23t–24t, 34
    current account balance, 169, 169f
    debt liabilities, 211
    de facto measures, 178
    degrees of openness, 173, 174t, 231, 234t
    diversification gains, 124–26
    financial development, 72–73, 75
    foreign direct investment, 77, 79, 82, 85,
        201, 206t, 208f
        versus developing countries, 212–14
    global financial crisis effects, 30
    gross capital flows, 177f, 177–80, 179
    growth gains, 20–22, 21t
    growth-impact estimates, 189–92, 190t,
        192n, 194, 198t, 200, 200f
        versus developing countries, 212, 214
    real economic growth, during recessions,
        246, 247f
    sectoral-level analyses, 111

summary surveys, 133–34
theoretical expectations, 12–13
total factor productivity growth, 210–11
trimmed averages
  foreign direct investment, 201, 202t–206t, 205
  growth-impact estimates, 184–85, 192, 194, 200
industrial production, during global recession, 248–49, 249f
inflation, 105–106
insignificant results
  averaging with statistically significant results, 14
  exclusion of, 147
  imputed at zero, 48, 146–47
  meaning of, 47–48, 65
  weighting, 192–200, 213
Institute of International Finance (IIF), 16, 251
institutional variables, 104–108
  capital-market openness study, 58
  potential circularity in, 165–66
  in summary surveys, 131–32, 137
instrumental variables
  capital-market openness study, 51–52, 55
  crisis impact studies, 96–97
  dubious, 6
  sectoral-level analyses, 110n
interactive variables, 14, 15, 20n
  country-specific estimates, 172, 194
interbanking lending rate (LIBOR), 29, 240, 241f
interest rates
  domestic *versus* foreign, 5
  global financial crisis and, 239–40, 254, 263, 295
  risk-free, 124–25
International Country Risk Guide database, 58, 106, 165–66
international debt crisis (1980s), 303–4
International Finance Corporation (IFC), 89, 112
international financial integration (IFI), 54–55
international interaction, alternative measures of, 78
International Monetary Fund (IMF)
  banking loss estimates, 242, 242f
  capital composition effects, 26–27
  capital control indicator, 103–104, 113n, 182
  capital-market openness data, 63
  capital mobility articles, 45

country-specific estimates, 175, 182, 192, 193, 218, 222, 229, 230
direct investment study, 85–86, 205
financial openness measures, 4, 13–14, 114n, 173 (*See also* AREAER measure)
global financial crisis estimates, 30, 250, 283, 312
Global Financial Stability Report, 241
International Financial Statistics, 52n, 183
lending capacity, 31, 251–52, 253, 271
meta-weighting example, 151–53, 152t, 154t
portfolio equity study, 88
summary surveys, 132–33, 136–37, 138, 140–43
World Economic Outlook database, 183
international risk sharing, 119–31, 161–64, 163t
International Standard Industrial Classification (ISIC) manufacturing sectors, 111, 113n
inverse-variance weighting, 14, 48, 66, 147–48
  country-specific estimates, 193, 194, 213
  example of, 151–54, 152t, 154t
  foreign direct investment studies, 79
  summary surveys, 138, 142
investment portfolios, diversification of, 10, 11, 119–31, 142
investment rates. *See also* foreign direct investment
  domestic, effect of FDI on, 61–62, 82–83, 214
  exogenous, 8
investment variable, capital-market openness, 50
Ireland, 4, 177f, 178, 201
ISIC (International Standard Industrial Classification) manufacturing sectors, 111, 113n
Israel, 201, 205, 254
Italy, 201

Japan
  consumption smoothing, 125–26
  crisis vulnerability, 95
  diversification gains, 126
  foreign direct investment, 201
  growth-impact estimates, 185
  international portfolio diversification, 121–22
JP Morgan
  Bear Stearns takeover, 261, 262
  capital needs, 267n, 291, 310

value-at-risk models, 294
JP Morgan Chase, 237, 245, 306
JP Morgan Emerging Markets Bond Index, 29–30, 240–41, 242f

Kaminsky, Graciela L., 26n, 56–58, 59, 96
King, Mervyn, 236
Klein, Michael W.
  country-specific estimates, 192, 193, 217–18
  financial development study, 72–73, 75
  institution and policy discipline study, 106–107, 107n, 165–66
  summary survey, 131–32
Korea
  banking-sector efficiency, 74
  crisis vulnerability, 16
  foreign direct investment, 201, 205, 219n
  global financial crisis effects, 255
  growth-impact estimates, 189, 189n
  reserve adequacy, 253
Kose, M. Ayhan
  capital-market openness study, 64, 67t
  consumption smoothing study, 129–30
  on crisis effects, 17
  direct investment study, 27, 87t
  diversification gains study, 126–28
  summary survey, 133, 134–36
  total factor productivity study, 12n, 27, 211
Kraay, Aart
  capital-market openness study, 51, 51n, 55, 67t, 68n
  country-specific estimates, 192, 193, 193n, 217
Krugman, Paul
  on bank nationalization, 311
  on capital mobility gains, 116, 119
  Geithner Plan critique, 315–16

labor, effective, 118, 155–57, 224
Latin America. See also specific country
  Brady Plan, 301, 304
  capital-market openness, 49n, 49–50, 61
  consumption volatility, 136n
  crisis vulnerability, 93, 95
  currency decline, 255, 256f
  debt crisis (1980s), 2, 86
  debt liabilities, 211
  financial development, 72–73, 75
  financing gap, 253
  foreign direct investment, 205, 206t, 208f
  global financial crisis effects, 30
  growth gains, 20–22, 21t, 34

growth-impact estimates, 185–92, 190t–191t, 192n, 194, 198t–199t, 200, 200f
  real economic growth, during recessions, 246, 248f
Latvia, 253, 258–59, 332
Lee, Jong-Wha, 79, 82, 83, 87t, 205, 210n, 219
Legacy Loan Program (FDIC), 316, 316n, 320
Legacy Securities Program (Federal Reserve), 316–17
legal origin, 108, 108n
Lehman Brothers
  bank consolidation and, 306
  bankruptcy of, 237, 261, 264n, 264–65, 287
  government inaction, 267, 305
  leverage, 288, 292
  as too-big-to-fail, 311
Lei, Vivian, 78, 87t, 205, 219–20
lender-of-last-resort function (Federal Reserve), 262, 311
lending
  IMF, 31, 251–52, 253, 271
  subprime (See subprime lending)
Lensink, Robert, 15, 80–81, 83, 84, 87t, 205, 220–21
less financially integrated economies (LFIE). See also developing countries
  consumption smoothing, 127
  summary survey, 133–34
leverage ratios, 288
Levine, Ross
  capital-market openness study, 49–50, 52, 52n, 53–55, 67t
  on capital productivity, 119
  country-specific estimates, 175, 201
  direct investment study, 7n, 78–79, 82, 87t, 205, 220
  endogeneity, 8, 8n
  financial development study, 71–75
  portfolio equity study, 90n
  summary survey, 139
Lewis, Karen, 120, 120n, 125–26, 130
Lewis, Michael, 290, 290n, 293
LIBOR (London Interbank offered Rate), 29, 240, 241f
liquidity trap, 246, 248n
Lithuania, 258–59
London Interbank offered Rate (LIBOR), 29, 240, 241f
long run, defining, 57
low-variant results, 22–25, 23t–24t, 71
Lundblad, Christian
  capital-market openness study, 59, 60
  direct investment study, 81

Quinn, Dennis

SDRs (Special Drawing Rights), 31
"search for yield" argument, 296–97
sectoral-level analyses, 108–14, 115t
Securities and Exchange Commission
    (SEC), 266, 303
sequencing, 10–11
settler mortality, 108, 108n
short run, defining, 57
short-term debt, 16–17, 91, 103–104, 329
Singapore
    capital-market openness, 70
    current account balance, 63, 167–68, 170
    diversification gains, 126
    financial openness, 4
    foreign direct investment, 205
    GDP-capital flow ratio, 230
    global financial crisis effects, 255
    reserve adequacy, 254
SIVs (structured investment vehicles), 239
size effect, 7, 148, 153
skewness, 17, 91–93, 92n
Slok, Torsten
    capital-market openness study, 53–55, 67t
    country-specific estimates, 192, 193,
        217–18
    endogeneity, 8, 8n
    institution and policy discipline study,
        107, 165–66
    summary survey, 131–32
Société Générale, 265n
Solow-type residuals, 116
Soto, Marcelo
    capital-market openness study, 53–54
    crisis impact study, 103
    direct investment study, 15, 26, 86n, 87t,
        205, 220
South Africa, 201, 205
sovereign debt crisis, 95
Spain, 201
Special Drawing Rights (SDRs), 31
S&P index of housing prices, 279, 280f
Stanley, T. D., 70
statistical models, versus calibrated
    theoretical models, 10
steady-state growth model, 117n, 117–18,
    155–59, 158f, 210
    of capital deepening, 223–27
Stiglitz, Joseph, 1, 35, 91
stock market measures
    as damage metric, 32–33
    diversification gains and, 120–21, 126
    FDI spillover effects, 81–82
    during global financial crisis, 237–38,
        238n, 255, 257–58, 258f

liquidity, 74
    portfolio equity and, 89
    sectoral-level analyses, 111n
    volatility, 56–57
"stratification" matching technique, 94n
"stress test" (banking), 30, 237, 240, 244–45,
    245n, 261, 271
structured investment vehicles (SIVs), 239
subprime lending
    face value of, 301, 302f, 304
    regulatory laxity, 291–93
    role in global financial crisis, 28, 95, 236,
        238–39, 261, 281, 284–87, 289
substitution parameter, 122, 122n
Summers, Lawrence H., 1, 35
Supervisory Capital Assessment Program
    (SCAP), 244, 245, 245n
Sweden, 49n, 201
Switzerland, 177f, 178, 201

Taiwan, 254
TARP. See Troubled Asset Relief Program
taxation
    corporate, 50
    short-term capital flows, 103–104, 140,
        236
Taylor, John, 294–95
TED spread, 240n
Temporary Liquidity Guarantee (FDIC), 269
Term Auction Facility (Federal Reserve),
    237, 261, 269
Term Securities Lending Facility (Federal
    Reserve), 262
Terrones, Marco E.
    capital-market openness study, 64, 67t
    consumption smoothing study, 129–30
    direct investment study, 27, 87t
    diversification gains study, 126–28
    summary survey, 133, 134, 136
    total factor productivity study, 12n, 27,
        211
TFP. See total factor productivity growth
Thailand
    crisis vulnerability, 16, 92
    financing gap, 253
    foreign direct investment, 201, 205
    growth-impact estimates, 189, 189n
    reserve adequacy, 332
theoretical studies. See calibrated theoretical
    models
Thoenig, Mathias, 113–14, 115t
thresholds, 10–11, 35
    bank credits and, 53–54
    capital flow bonanza, 98

cross-country growth regressions, 47, 64–65
current account surplus, 104
direct investment impacts, 77, 81–82
interactive variables creating, 14, 15, 20n
macroeconomic stability, 11, 14, 35, 133–34, 137
too-big-to-fail status, 236, 263–65, 264n, 272, 313
Tornell, Aaron
capital-market openness study, 20n, 58n, 58–60, 67t, 70
country-specific estimates, 182, 192, 193, 218
crisis impact study, 17, 91–93
summary survey, 141, 143
total factor productivity (TFP) growth
capital-market openness and, 54, 64, 223
country-specific estimates, 208–11
financial development and, 73–74
quantifying, 27
summary surveys, 138–40
theoretical expectations, 11–12, 12n
Toyoda, A. Maria, 64, 67t, 70. See also Quinn-Toyoda openness index
tradable sector, 59–60
trade, during global recession, 248–49, 249f
trade credit, short-term debt and, 91
trade openness
analogy to, 1–2, 39, 40f, 140–41, 178
in capital-market openness studies, 60
foreign direct investment and, 76
measures of, 3, 39
Treasury. See US Treasury
Troubled Asset Relief Program (TARP)
asset purchases, 267–69
congressional approval of, 237, 266
fiscal losses from, 250n, 312
government-sponsored entities, 270–71
mishandling of, 295
original concept of, 284, 304–5, 311
proposal for, 266, 267n
repayment of monies, 240, 246
SEC guidance, 303
Tunisia, 253, 332
Turkey, 74, 201, 205
"two-gap" models, 116

Ukraine, 253, 255, 332
uncovered interest parity (UIP), 5n, 5–6, 6n
underpricing risk, 293
United Kingdom
banking crisis, 237, 241–44, 266

capital flow-GDP ratio, 177f, 178
consumption smoothing, 126
financial openness, 4
foreign direct investment, 201
global financial crisis effects, 266
growth-impact estimates, 185
United Nations Industrial Development
Organization (UNIDO), Industrial
Statistics Database, 113n, 114n
United States
automobile industry, 268
banking crisis, 30, 95, 241–44, 305–8
bank recapitalization in, 237, 240, 310
capital flow-GDP ratio, 177f, 178
capital-market openness, 49n
consumption smoothing, 125–26
current account deficit, 29–30, 240, 250, 254, 297, 298f, 299, 302
diversification gains, 121–22, 125
economic growth rate, 244, 248
financial openness, 4
foreign direct investment, 201
global financial crisis effects (See global financial crisis)
growth-impact estimates, 24–25, 184–85
mortgage loss estimates, 282–83
US Bancorp, 307
US Department of Commerce, 112–13
US Treasury
bond rate, 296, 296f
"break the glass" emergency plan, 262–63
Commercial Paper Funding Facility, 269–70, 305
Exchange Stabilization Fund, 265n, 270
money market funds guarantee, 265, 269
public-sector bailout, 268–69
Uruguay, 95
utility function, 118, 118n, 130, 155, 161, 162

value-at-risk (VaR) models, 294
Vanassche, Ellen, 73, 75, 110–11, 115t
Van Wincoop, Eric, 119, 124–25, 130, 161
Venezuela
financing gap, 253
foreign direct investment, 201, 205
growth-impact estimates, 185
per capita growth, 176
reserve adequacy, 332
Volcker, Paul, 236, 292
Volcker shock, 246
vote-counting approach, 66, 70, 145–47, 153

Wachovia, 237

Wang, Miao
  direct investment study, 82–83, 87t, 205, 218, 221
  portfolio equity study, 90n
  threshold effect variables, 15
Washington Mutual, 237, 305
Wei, Shang-Jin, 17
  direct investment study, 134
  diversification gains study, 126
  institution and policy discipline study, 104–105, 107–108
  summary survey, 134–36
weighting, 6–7, 14, 48, 66. *See also specific method*
  nonsignificant model estimates, 192–200, 213
welfare gains, from risk diversification, 10, 11, 119–31, 142, 161–64, 163t
Wells Fargo, 237, 245, 306
Wessel, David, 262n, 265n, 267n, 292
Westermann, Frank

capital-market openness study, 20n, 58n, 58–60, 67t, 70
  country-specific estimates, 182, 192, 193, 218
  crisis impact study, 17, 91–93
  summary survey, 141, 143
World Bank
  financing gap calculations, 31, 252–53, 325–32, 326t
  trade regime classification, 76
Wyplosz, Charles
  capital-market openness study, 55–56, 67t, 70
  country-specific estimates, 192, 193, 218
  crisis impact study, 93
  macroeconomic thresholds, 11
  summary survey, 131

zero financial openness, versus complete openness. *See* complete versus zero openness

Other Publications from the Peterson Institute for International Economics

WORKING PAPERS

94-1 APEC and Regional Trading
Arrangements in the Pacific
Jeffrey A. Frankel with Shang-Jin Wei
and Ernesto Stein
94-2 Towards an Asia Pacific Investment
Code   Edward M. Graham
94-3 Merchandise Trade in the APEC
Region: Is There Scope for
Liberalization on an MFN Basis?
Paul Wonnacott
94-4 The Automotive Industry in Southeast
Asia: Can Protection Be Made Less
Costly?   Paul Wonnacott
94-5 Implications of Asian Economic
Growth   Marcus Noland
95-1 APEC: The Bogor Declaration and the
Path Ahead   C. Fred Bergsten
95-2 From Bogor to Miami . . . and Beyond:
Regionalism in the Asia Pacific and
the Western Hemisphere
Jeffrey J. Schott
95-3 Has Asian Export Performance Been
Unique?   Marcus Noland
95-4 Association of Southeast Asian
Nations and ASEAN Free Trade Area:
Chronology and Statistics
Gautam Jaggi
95-5 The North Korean Economy
Marcus Noland
95-6 China and the International Economic
System   Marcus Noland
96-1 APEC after Osaka: Toward Free Trade
by 2010/2020   C. Fred Bergsten
96-2 Public Policy, Private Preferences, and
the Japanese Trade Pattern
Marcus Noland
96-3 German Lessons for Korea: The
Economics of Unification
Marcus Noland
96-4 Research and Development Activities
and Trade Specialization in Japan
Marcus Noland
96-5 China's Economic Reforms:
Chronology and Statistics
Gautam Jaggi, Mary Rundle, Daniel
Rosen, and Yuichi Takahashi
96-6 US-China Economic Relations
Marcus Noland
96-7 The Market Structure Benefits of
Trade and Investment Liberalization
Raymond Atje and Gary Hufbauer
96-8 The Future of US-Korea Economic
Relations   Marcus Noland

96-9 Competition Policies in the Dynamic
Industrializing Economies: The Case
of China, Korea, and Chinese Taipei
Edward M. Graham
96-10 Modeling Economic Reform in North
Korea   Marcus Noland,
Sherman Robinson, and Monica
Scatasta
96-11 Trade, Investment, and Economic
Conflict Between the United States
and Asia   Marcus Noland
96-12 APEC in 1996 and Beyond: The Subic
Summit   C. Fred Bergsten
96-13 Some Unpleasant Arithmetic
Concerning Unification
Marcus Noland
96-14 Restructuring Korea's Financial Sector
for Greater Competitiveness
Marcus Noland
96-15 Competitive Liberalization and Global
Free Trade: A Vision for the 21st
Century   C. Fred Bergsten
97-1 Chasing Phantoms: The Political
Economy of USTR   Marcus Noland
97-2 US-Japan Civil Aviation: Prospects for
Progress   Jacqueline McFadyen
97-3 Open Regionalism   C. Fred Bergsten
97-4 Lessons from the Bundesbank on the
Occasion of Its 40th (and Second to
Last?) Birthday   Adam S. Posen
97-5 The Economics of Korean Unification
Marcus Noland, Sherman Robinson,
and Li-Gang Liu
98-1 The Costs and Benefits of Korean
Unification   Marcus Noland,
Sherman Robinson, and Li-Gang Liu
98-2 Asian Competitive Devaluations
Li-Gang Liu, Marcus Noland, Sherman
Robinson, and Zhi Wang
98-3 Fifty Years of the GATT/WTO:
Lessons from the Past for Strategies or
the Future   C. Fred Bergsten
98-4 NAFTA Supplemental Agreements:
Four Year Review
Jacqueline McFadyen
98-5 Local Government Spending: Solving
the Mystery of Japanese Fiscal
Packages   Hiroko Ishii and Erika Wada
98-6 The Global Economic Effects of the
Japanese Crisis   Marcus Noland,
Sherman Robinson, and Zhi Wang
98-7 The Relationship Between Trade and
Foreign Investment: Empirical Results
for Taiwan and South Korea
Li-Gang Liu, The World Bank and
Edward M. Grahm
99-1 Rigorous Speculation: The Collapse
and Revival of the North Korean
Economy   Marcus Noland,
Sherman Robinson, and Tao Wang

2566

WORKS IN PROGRESS

Reassessing US Trade Policy: Priorities and Policy Recommendations for the Next Decade
Jeffrey J. Schott
China's Energy Evolution: The Consequences of Powering Growth at Home and Abroad
Daniel H. Rosen and Trevor Houser
Global Identity Theft: Economic and Policy Implications   Catherine L. Mann
Growth and Diversification of International Reserves   Edwin M. Truman
Globalized Venture Capital: Implications for US Entrepreneurship and Innovation
Catherine L. Mann
Forging a Grand Bargain: Expanding Trade and Raising Worker Prosperity   Lori Kletzer, J. David Richardson, and Howard Rosen
East Asian Regionalism and the World Economy   C. Fred Bergsten
The Strategic Implications of China-Taiwan Economic Relations   Nicholas R. Lardy
The Limits of Export-Led Growth: Germany and the Future of Capitalism   Adam S. Posen
Devaluing to Prosperity   Surjit Bhalla
Global Forces, American Faces: US Economic Globalization at the Grass Roots
J. David Richardson
Financial Crises and the Future of Emerging Markets   William R. Cline
Global Services Outsourcing: The Impact on American Firms and Workers
J. Bradford Jensen, Lori G. Kletzer, and Catherine L. Mann
Policy Reform in Rich Countries
John Williamson, editor
Banking System Fragility in Emerging Economies
Morris Goldstein and Philip Turner
Witness to Transformation: Refugee Insights into North Korea   Stephan Haggard and Marcus Noland
Sovereign Wealth Funds and the International Financial System   Edwin M. Truman
Russia after the Global Economic Crisis
Anders Åslund, Sergei Guriev, and Andrew Kuchins, eds.
Figuring Out the Doha Round   Gary Clyde Hufbauer, Jeffrey J. Schott, and Woan Foong Wong

DISTRIBUTORS OUTSIDE THE UNITED STATES

**Australia, New Zealand,
and Papua New Guinea**
D. A. Information Services
648 Whitehorse Road
Mitcham, Victoria 3132, Australia
Tel: 61-3-9210-7777
Fax: 61-3-9210-7788
Email: service@dadirect.com.au
www.dadirect.com.au

India, Bangladesh, Nepal, and Sri Lanka
Viva Books Private Limited
Mr. Vinod Vasishtha
4737/23 Ansari Road
Daryaganj, New Delhi 110002
India
Tel: 91-11-4224-2200
Fax: 91-11-4224-2240
Email: viva@vivagroupindia.net
www.vivagroupindia.com

**Mexico, Central America, South America,
and Puerto Rico**
US PubRep, Inc.
311 Dean Drive
Rockville, MD 20851
Tel: 301-838-9276
Fax: 301-838-9278
Email: c.falk@ieee.org

Asia (*Brunei, Burma, Cambodia, China,
Hong Kong, Indonesia, Korea, Laos, Malaysia,
Philippines, Singapore, Taiwan, Thailand,
and Vietnam*)
East-West Export Books (EWEB)
University of Hawaii Press
2840 Kolowalu Street
Honolulu, Hawaii 96822-1888
Tel: 808-956-8830
Fax: 808-988-6052
Email: eweb@hawaii.edu

Canada
Renouf Bookstore
5369 Canotek Road, Unit 1
Ottawa, Ontario KlJ 9J3, Canada
Tel: 613-745-2665
Fax: 613-745-7660
www.renoufbooks.com

Japan
United Publishers Services Ltd.
1-32-5, Higashi-shinagawa
Shinagawa-ku, Tokyo 140-0002
Japan
Tel: 81-3-5479-7251
Fax: 81-3-5479-7307
Email: purchasing@ups.co.jp
*For trade accounts only. Individuals will find
Institute books in leading Tokyo bookstores.*

Middle East
MERIC
2 Bahgat Ali Street, El Masry Towers
Tower D, Apt. 24
Zamalek, Cairo
Egypt
Tel. 20-2-7633824
Fax: 20-2-7369355
Email: mahmoud_fouda@mericonline.com
www.mericonline.com

United Kingdom, Europe
(*including Russia and Turkey*)**, Africa,
and Israel**
The Eurospan Group
c/o Turpin Distribution
Pegasus Drive
Stratton Business Park
Biggleswade, Bedfordshire
SG18 8TQ
United Kingdom
Tel: 44 (0) 1767-604972
Fax: 44 (0) 1767-601640
Email: eurospan@turpin-distribution.com
www.eurospangroup.com/bookstore

**Visit our website at:
www.piie.com
E-mail orders to:
petersonmail@presswarehouse.com**